THE CAMBRIDGE COMPANION TO
AUGUSTINE'S CITY OF GOD

Augustine of Hippo's *The City of God* is generally considered to be one of the key works of Late Antiquity. Written in response to allegations that Christianity had brought about the decline of Rome, Augustine here explores themes in history, political science, and Christian theology, and argues for the truth of Christianity over competing religions and philosophies. This *Companion* volume includes specially commissioned essays by an international team of scholars that provide new insights into *The City of God.* Offering commentary on each of this massive work's twenty-two books, they sequentially and systematically explore *The City of God* as a whole. Collectively, these essays demonstrate the development and coherence of Augustine's argument. The volume will be an invaluable resource for students and scholars of ancient and contemporary theology, philosophy, cultural studies, and political theory.

Fr. David Vincent Meconi, S.J., Liz. Theol., D.Phil. (Oxon.) is Professor of Theology and the Director of the Catholic Studies Centre at Saint Louis University. He has published widely on the early Church; his most recent works include *Peter Chrysologus* (2020); *The Cambridge Companion to St. Augustine* (2014); and *Augustine On Self-Harm, Narcissism, Atonement, and the Vulnerable Christ* (2019).

CAMBRIDGE COMPANIONS TO RELIGION

This is a series of companions to major topics and key figures in theology and religious studies. Each volume contains specially commissioned chapters by international scholars, which provide an accessible and stimulating introduction to the subject for new readers and nonspecialists.

Other Titles in the Series

AMERICAN CATHOLICISM Edited by Margaret M. McGuinness and Thomas F. Rzeznick

AMERICAN ISLAM Edited by Juliane Hammer and Omid Safi

AMERICAN JUDAISM Edited by Dana Evan Kaplan

AMERICAN METHODISM Edited by Jason E. Vickers

ANCIENT MEDITERRANEAN RELIGIONS Edited by Barbette Stanley Spaeth

APOCALYPTIC LITERATURE Edited by Colin McAllister

AUGUSTINE'S "CONFESSIONS" Edited by Tarmo Toom

KARL BARTH Edited by John Webster

THE BIBLE, 2ND EDITION Edited by Bruce Chilton

THE BIBLE AND LITERATURE Edited by Calum Carmichael

BIBLICAL INTERPRETATION Edited by John Barton

BLACK THEOLOGY Edited by Dwight N. Hopkins and Edward P. Antonio

DIETRICH BONHOEFFER Edited by John de Gruchy

JOHN CALVIN Edited by Donald K. McKim

CHRISTIAN DOCTRINE Edited by Colin Gunton

CHRISTIAN ETHICS Edited by Robin Gill

CHRISTIAN MYSTICISM Edited by Amy Hollywood and Patricia Z. Beckman

CHRISTIAN PHILOSOPHICAL THEOLOGY Edited by Charles Taliaferro and Chad V. Meister

CHRISTIAN POLITICAL THEOLOGY Edited by Craig Hovey and Elizabeth Phillips

THE CISTERIAN ORDER Edited by Mette Birkedal Bruun

CLASSICAL ISLAMIC THEOLOGY Edited by Tim Winter

JONATHAN EDWARDS Edited by Stephen J. Stein

EVANGELICAL THEOLOGY Edited by Timothy Larsen and Daniel J. Treier

FEMINIST THEOLOGY Edited by Susan Frank Parsons

FRANCIS OF ASSISI Edited by Michael J. P. Robson

THE GOSPELS Edited by Stephen C. Barton

THE HEBREW BIBLE/OLD TESTAMENT Edited by Stephen B. Chapman and Marvin A. Sweeney

HEBREW BIBLE AND ETHICS Edited by C. L. Crouch

THE JESUITS Edited by Thomas Worcester

JESUS Edited by Markus Bockmuehl

JUDAISM AND LAW Edited by Christine Hayes

C. S. LEWIS Edited by Robert MacSwain and Michael Ward

THE CAMBRIDGE COMPANION TO

AUGUSTINE'S CITY OF GOD

Edited by

Fr. David Vincent Meconi, S.J.

Saint Louis University

CAMBRIDGE
UNIVERSITY PRESS

CAMBRIDGE
UNIVERSITY PRESS

University Printing House, Cambridge CB2 8BS, United Kingdom

One Liberty Plaza, 20th Floor, New York, NY 10006, USA

477 Williamstown Road, Port Melbourne, VIC 3207, Australia

314–321, 3rd Floor, Plot 3, Splendor Forum, Jasola District Centre,
New Delhi – 110025, India

79 Anson Road, #06–04/06, Singapore 079906

Cambridge University Press is part of the University of Cambridge.

It furthers the University's mission by disseminating knowledge in the pursuit of education, learning, and research at the highest international levels of excellence.

www.cambridge.org
Information on this title: www.cambridge.org/9781108422512
DOI: 10.1017/9781108505307

First published 2021

A catalogue record for this publication is available from the British Library.

ISBN 978-1-108-42251-2 Hardback
ISBN 978-1-108-43544-4 Paperback

For Eleonore Stump, conciuis in ciuitate Dei

Contents

Notes on Contributors

John C. Cavadini is Professor of Theology at the University of Notre Dame, having served as Chair from 1997 to 2010. Since 2000, he has served as the Director of the McGrath Institute for Church Life at Notre Dame. He received a B.A. in 1975 from Wesleyan University; an M.A. in 1979 from Marquette University; M.A., 1981, M.Phil., 1983 and his Ph.D. in 1988 from Yale University, before coming to Notre Dame in 1990, where he has taught and published widely in patristic and early medieval theology, the theology of Augustine, and the history of biblical and patristic exegesis. Cavadini was appointed by Pope Emeritus Benedict XVI to serve on the International Theological Commission, and in 2018 he received the Monika K. Hellwig Award from the Association of Catholic Colleges and Universities for Outstanding Contributions to Catholic Intellectual Life.

Mark Edwards was appointed University Lecturer in Patristics in the Faculty of Theology at the University of Oxford, and Tutor in Theology at Christ Church Oxford in 1993; he is now Professor of Early Christian Studies in the Faculty of Theology and Religion. His publications relevant to Augustine include *Optatus: Against the Donatists* (1997); *Neoplatonic Saints* (2000); and contributions to A. Fitzgerald (ed.), *Augustine through the Ages* (1999); M. Vessey (ed.), *A Companion to Augustine* (2012); E. Bermon and G. O'Daly (eds.), *Le De Trinitate de Saint Augustin* (2012); K. Pollmann (ed.), *The Oxford Guide to the Reception of Augustine* (2013); A. Marmodoro and B. D. Prince (eds.), *Causation and Creation in Late Antiquity* (2015); and R. Miles (ed.), *The Donatist Schism* (2016).

Dean Hammer is the John W. Wetzel Professor of Classics and Professor of Government at Franklin and Marshall College. He holds a Ph.D. in Political Science from the University of California at Berkeley. He has published widely in many areas of political thought, and is the author of *Roman Political Thought: From Cicero to Augustine* (2014); *Roman Political Thought and the Modern Theoretical Imagination* (2008); *The* Iliad *as Politics: The Performance of Political Thought* (2002); and is editor of *A Companion to Greek Democracy and the Roman Republic* (2015).

Andrew Hofer, O.P. is Associate Professor of Patristics and Ancient Languages at the Pontifical Faculty of the Immaculate Conception, Dominican House of Studies, Washington, DC, where he also serves as Director of the Doctoral

Program and book review editor of *The Thomist*. He is the author of *Christ in the Life and Teaching of Gregory of Nazianzus* (2013) and co-editor of *Thomas Aquinas and the Greek Fathers* (2019). Funded by a Calvin Institute Teacher-Scholar grant, his present project of *Patristic Preaching: The Word of God Becoming Flesh* considers the incarnational preaching of seven early Christian preachers, including Augustine, within the ancient dichotomy of words and deeds.

David G. Hunter, Ph.D. holds the Margaret O'Brien Flatley Chair of Catholic Theology at Boston College. He has published several books and numerous articles on Greek and Latin writers of the early Church, among them Augustine, Ambrosiaster, Jerome, and John Chrysostom. His most recent books include *Marriage and Sexuality in Ancient Christianity* (2018) and *Marriage, Celibacy, and Heresy in Early Christianity: The Jovinianist Controversy* (2007). He is also co-editor of the *Oxford Handbook of Early Christian Studies* (2008), has served as President of the North American Patristics Society and as a visiting scholar at Nottingham University, Central European University, Katholieke Universiteit Leuven, and Villanova University.

Mary M. Keys is Associate Professor of Political Science at the University of Notre Dame. She received her B.A. from Boston College and her M.A. and Ph.D. from the University of Toronto. Her research and teaching interests are in political theory and the history of political thought, focusing on Christianity, ethics, virtue, legal philosophy, and politics. She is the author of *Aquinas, Aristotle, and the Promise of the Common Good* (2006), and of articles appearing in the *American Journal of Political Science*, *History of Political Thought*; and *Perspectives on Political Science*. She has received fellowships from the National Endowment for the Humanities, the Earhart Foundation, and the Notre Dame Institute for Advanced Study, and has been a visiting scholar at Harvard University and the University of Chicago.

Mathijs Lamberigts is Professor of Church History in the Faculty of Theology and Religious Studies at Katholieke Universiteit Leuven, where he also obtained his M.A. in Classics as well as his Ph.D. in Theology (with a specialization in Church History). He is also Research Fellow of the NCU at Toruń, he is also the editor-in-chief of the internationally renowned *Revue d'histoire ecclésaistique*, as well as the Director of both the Augustinian Historical Institute and the Conciliar Center for the Study of Vatican II. He has published extensively on the Pelagian controversy, with a special focus on the role of Julian of Aeclanum in this debate. He has also written numerous articles on the role of the Belgian bishops and theologians during the Second Vatican Council.

David Vincent Meconi, S.J. is Professor of Historical Theology as well as the Director of the Catholic Studies Centre at Saint Louis University. He holds the Pontifical License in Patrology from the University of Innsbruck and his D.Phil. from the University of Oxford. His published works on Augustine include the *Annotated Confessions of Saint Augustine* (2012); and *The One Christ: St. Augustine's Theology of Deification* (2013; pbk. 2018), he has co-edited (along with Eleonore Stump) the *Cambridge Companion to Augustine* (2014), and most recently, *Reading Augustine: On Self-Harm, Narcissism, Atonement and the*

Vulnerable Christ (2019). He is also a regular visiting Professor of Patristics at Kenrick-Glennon Seminary in St. Louis, at Franciscan University in Steubenville, Ohio, as well as the editor of the *Homiletic and Pastoral Review.*

Isabel Moreira is Professor of History at the University of Utah. She is the author of numerous studies of religion and society in late antiquity and the early middle ages, including *Dreams, Visions, and Spiritual Authority in Merovingian Gaul* (2000); and *Heaven's Purge: Purgatory in Late Antiquity* (2010; pbk. 2014). Dr. Moreira is also co-editor, with Margaret Toscano, of *Hell and Its Afterlife: Historical and Contemporary Perspectives* (2010). She lives in Salt Lake City, Utah, with her husband and two daughters.

Oliver O'Donovan is Emeritus Professor of Christian Ethics at the University of Edinburgh. He was educated at University College School, Hampstead, at Balliol College and Wycliffe Hall, Oxford, and at the University of Princeton, and then went on to teach at Oxford and the University of Toronto before being named Regius Professor of Moral and Pastoral Theology and Canon of Christ Church at the University of Oxford from 1982 to 2006. From 2006 to 2012 he was Professor of Christian Ethics and Practical Theology at the University of Edinburgh, and has been an Honorary Professor of Divinity at the University of St. Andrews since 2013. Dr. O'Donovan has written on the ethical theory of St. Augustine, the theological basis of moral concepts, contemporary bioethical dilemmas, political theology, and the ethics of war. He has served the Church of England as a member of the Board for Society Responsibility, the Doctrine Commission, the Faith and Order Advisory Group, and the General Synod, and most recently convened the Archbishops' review of the Crown Nominations Commission. He is a former President of the Society for the Study of Christian Ethics, a Fellow of the British Academy since 2000, and a Fellow of the Royal Society of Edinburgh since 2007. He is married to Joan Lockwood O'Donovan and they have two sons.

Michael Sweeney is Professor of Philosophy at Xavier University. He received a B.A. and an M.A. in Philosophy from Marquette University, an M.A. in Medieval Studies from the University of Toronto, an S.T.B. from the Pontifical Gregorian University in Rome and a Ph.D. in Philosophy from the Catholic University of America. He was a Fulbright Scholar in Moscow, Russia from 1998 to 1999. He is the author of two books: *Srednevekovaya Khristyanskaya Filosofiya* [*Medieval Christian Philosophy*] (trans. A. K. Lyavdanski, 2001); and *Politicheskaya Filosofiya Srednikh Vekov* [*Political Philosophy of the Middle Agesi*] (trans. A. K. Lyavdanski and M. B. Kravchenko, 2006). He is the editor of *Justice through Diversity? A Philosophical and Theological Debate* (2016).

Christian Tornau is Professor of Classical Philology at Würzburg University in Germany. His main research interests are ancient philosophy, rhetoric, and the literature of early Christianity. He has published widely on Neoplatonism, especially Plotinus, and on Augustine. His monographic studies include a commentary on Plotinus, entitled *Plotin, Enneaden* VI 4–5 [22–23]: *Ein Kommentar* (1998), as well as an inquiry into the relationship of rhetorical strategy and philosophical content in Augustine's *City of God*, namely, *Zwischen Rhetorik und Philosophie: Augustins Argumentationstechnik in De civitate Dei und ihr bildungsgeschichtlicher Hintergrund* (2006).

James Wetzel is Professor of Philosophy at Villanova University and currently holds the Augustinian endowed chair. His work on Augustinian themes broadly concerns the transmission of a wisdom tradition through Platonism. He is the author of *Augustine and the Limits of Virtue* (1992); *Augustine: A Guide for the Perplexed* (2010); and *Parting Knowledge: Essays after Augustine* (2013). He is also the editor of *Augustine's City of God* (2012), a volume in the Cambridge Critical Guide series.

Jonathan P. Yates is Professor of Historical Theology at Villanova University and an alumnus (Ph.D.) of the Katholieke Universiteit Leuven. His research focuses on North African Christianity's relationship to its sacred texts. Jonathan has published numerous peer-reviewed articles, book chapters, and edited volumes in addition to editing Augustinian Studies for a decade. He is currently co-editing a two-volume handbook entitled *The Reception and Interpretation of the Bible in Christian North Africa* for DeGruyter. Part 1 was published in 2020. Part 2 will appear in 2022.

Preface

This volume is a unique collection of essays addressing the many diverse and rich themes found throughout Augustine's *City of God* (*ciu. Dei*). When Alaric had traveled southward to sack what had been the glory of Rome, he upturned not only city and street, but psyche and perception as well. Rome's importance had by now grown old and, although it was felt by many, Rome's splendor was still being celebrated by its loyalists in poetry, history, and hymnody. Alaric had, however, exposed Rome's mortality, and news reached African shores from those fleeing persecution. The Bishop of Hippo was aware of the anti-Christian fallout after Rome's own fall. He therefore set out to address the accusations that Rome had fallen because this new sect called Christian had forsaken the empire's customary deities. For Rome's traditionalists were blaming *tempora christiana* for the blight of *romanitas*: having abandoned the ancient religions, Christians were now incriminated for failing to worship rightly. In response, and for over a decade, Augustine set to work to show not only what had been inherently wrong with Roman religion for centuries, but also why the God of Jesus Christ is the only solution to a society's, not to mention a soul's, ills. All experts in the kaleidoscopic thought of Augustine, fourteen scholars from the areas of philosophy, theology, classics, and political science have been brought together in this one volume in order to bring out the major ideas of each of the books of the *ciu. Dei*, and to show how each book contributes to Augustine's overall argument that two loves faces each of us, the love of self as opposed to the love of God, the earthly city against the City of God.

Abbreviations: Works by Augustine

Abbreviations	Latin titles	English titles
adn. Job	*Adnotationes in Job*	*Comments on Job*
agon.	*De agone Christiano*	*On the Christian Struggle*
b. conjug.	*De bono conjugali*	*On the Good of Marriage*
b. Faust.	*Contra Faustum Manicheum*	*Against Faustus, a Manichee*
b. vita	*De beata vita*	*On the Happy Life*
bapt.	*De baptism*	*On Baptism*
c. Acad.	*Contra Academicos*	*Against the Skeptics*
c. Gaud.	*Contra Gaudentium Donatistarum episcopum*	*Against Gaudentius, a Bishop of the Donatists*
c. Jul. imp.	*Opus imperfectum contra Julianum*	*Against Julian, an Unfinished Book*
c. mend.	*Contra mendacium*	*Against Lying*
c. Prisc.	*Contra Priscillianistas*	*Against the Priscillianists*
c. Sec.	*Contra Secundinum Manicheum*	*Against Secundinus, a Manichee*
cat. rud.	*De catechizandis rudibus*	*On the Instruction of Beginners*
civ. Dei	*De civitate Dei*	*City of God*
conf.	*Confessiones*	*Confessions*
cons. Ev.	*De consensu Evangelistarum*	*On Agreement among the Evangelists*
cont.	*De continentia*	*On Continence*
correpț.	*De correptione et gratia*	*On Admonition and Grace*
dial.	*De dialectica*	*On Dialectic*
div. qu.	*De diversis quaestionibus octoginta tribus*	*On Eighty-Three Varied Questions*
doc. Chr.	*De doctrina Christiana*	*Christian Teaching*
en. Ps.	*Enarrationes in Psalmos*	*Explanations of the Psalms*
ench.	*Enchiridion ad Laurentium de fide spe et caritate*	*A Handbook on Faith, Hope, and Love*
ep. (epp.)	*Epistulae*	*Letters*
ep. Rm. inch.	*Epistulae ad Romanos inchoata expositio*	*Unfinished Commentary on the Letter to the Romans*

(*cont.*)

Abbreviations	Latin titles	English titles
ex. Gal.	*Expositio Epistulae ad Galatas*	*Commentary on the Letter to the Galatians*
ex. prop. Rm.	*Expositio quarundam propositionum ex epistula Apostoli ad Romanos*	*Commentary on Statements in the Letter to the Romans*
f. et symb.	*De fide et symbolo*	*On Faith and the Creed*
f. invis.	*De fide rerum invisibilium*	*On Faith in the Unseen*
Gn. adv. Man.	*De Genesi adversus Manichaeos*	*On Genesis, against the Manichees*
Gn. litt.	*De Genesi ad litteram*	*On the Literal Interpretation of Genesis*
Gn. litt. imp.	*De Genesi ad litteram imperfectus liber*	*On the Literal Interpretation of Genesis, an Unfinished Book*
gr. et lib. arb.	*De gratia et libero arbitrio*	*On Grace and Free Will*
gr. et pecc. or.	*De gratia Christi et de peccato originali*	*On the Grace of Christ and Original Sin*
haer.	*De haeresibus*	*On Heresies*
imm. an.	*De immortalitate animae*	*On the Immortality of the Soul*
Jo. ev. tr.	*In Johannis evangelium tractatus*	*Tractates on the Gospel of John*
lib. arb.	*De libero arbitrio*	*On Free Will*
mag.	*De magistro*	*On the Teacher*
mend.	*De mendacio*	*On Lying*
mor.	*De moribus ecclesiae catholicae et de moribus Manichaeorum*	*On the Catholic and the Manichaean Ways of Life*
mus.	*De musica*	*On Music*
nat. b.	*De natura boni*	*On the Nature of the Good*
nat. et gr.	*De natura et gratia*	*On Nature and Grace*
ord.	*De ordine*	*On Order*
pecc. mer.	*De peccatorum meritis et remissione*	*On the Punishment and Forgiveness of Sins*
perf. just.	*De perfectione justitiae hominis*	*On the Perfection of Human Righteousness*
persev.	*De dono perseverantiae*	*On the Gift of Perseverance*
praed. sanct.	*De praedestinatione sanctorum*	*On the Predestination of the Saints*
qu.	*Quaestiones in Heptateuchum*	*Questions on the Heptateuch*
qu. Ev.	*Quaestiones Evangeliorum*	*Questions on the Gospels*
qu. vet. T.	*De octo quaestionibus ex Veteri Testamento*	*On Eight Questions from the Old Testament*

(cont.)

Abbreviations	Latin titles	English titles
quant.	*De animae quantitate*	*On the Greatness of the Soul*
retr.	*Retractationes*	*Reconsiderations*
rhet.	*De rhetorica*	*On Rhetoric*
s.	*Sermones*	*Sermons*
s. Dom. mon.	*De sermone Domini in monte*	*On the Lord's Sermon on the Mount*
Simpl.	*Ad Simplicianum*	*To Simplicianus*
sol.	*Soliloquia*	*The Soliloquies*
spec.	*Speculum*	*The Mirror*
spir. et litt.	*De spiritu et littera*	*On the Spirit and the Letter*
Trin.	*De Trinitate*	*The Trinity*
util. cred.	*De utilitate credendi*	*On the Advantage of Believing*
vera rel.	*De vera religione*	*On True Religion*

1 Introduction

DAVID VINCENT MECONI, S.J.

Studies treating Augustine's *City of God* normally begin with the year AD 410 and Alaric's infamous Sack of Rome. Yet, might it not be more accurate to start in AD 380 when the Emperor Theodosius (d. AD 395) presented himself for Christian baptism at fifty-three years of age in the middle of a severe sickness? Upon recovering, this new and grateful Christian issued the Edict of Thessalonica, *Cunctos Populos*, along with the Emperors Gratian (d. AD 383) and Valentinian II (d. AD 392), now making Catholic Christianity the official religion of the the Roman Empire. Furthermore, in just a decade thereafter, in AD 391, the ancient rites would be banned, and the old ways authoritatively denounced. It was a truly watershed moment. The strength of the reliable Roman pantheon had been replaced with the weakness of religious novelty professing faith in a humbly vulnerable God-man hanging on a cross.

For centuries Rome had stood as the means by which other civilizations were measured. Its grand structures were considered not only to surpass all other architecture but even was even perceived as otherworldly: "In great buildings as well as in other things the rest of the world has been outdone by us Romans. If, indeed, all the buildings in our City are considered in the aggregate, and supposing them – so to say – all thrown together in one vast mass, the united grandeur of them would lead one to imagine that we were describing another world, accumulated in a single spot."[1] Even time was based on Rome: most often historical dating was calculated by naming the two consuls who held office that year, but later the legendary dating of Rome's founding as 753 BC (*ab urbe condita*) became the basis for a common dating of events. Such prominence is no doubt why even as late as the 5th century AD, the poet Rutilius Claudius Namatianus could compose a nostalgic *De Reditu Suo* and cry out to his beloved city, "Listen to me,

[1] Pliny, *Natural History* §36.24.101–10.

Rome, most lovely queen of all your world, most welcome in the star-filled heavens! Listen, nurse of men, and mother of the gods! Thanks to your temples we are close to heaven."[2]

When he inked those lines, Rutilius' poetic nostalgia failed to convey that it was actually forbidden to pray at those temples, punishable even to stop and gaze upon one of its many ornate statues of some ancient Roman god or goddess.[3] In fact, by the time Rutilius wrote of his voyage in AD 416, the great capital of Rome had ceased being the world's crown for quite some time. In AD 285, Emperor Diocletian halved the empire into eastern and western sections and in the following year, AD 286, the western capital moved to Milan as Maximian's seat of power, with Diocletian himself taking up residence in Nicomedia. Diocletian next introduced the tetrarchy in AD 293, appointing two *Caesares*, serving under two co-emperors, *Augusti*, only diluting any sense of Roman centrality even further. With a massive insurgence of Visigoths continuing into Italy at the beginning of the 5th century AD, the emperor moved still again. In AD 402 the imperial court left the sprawling metropolis of Milan for the more defensible seaport town of Ravenna. Despite these decades of massive transition, Rome still stood strong as the spiritual mecca and the symbolic meaning of all that was the great empire. So when Alaric and his men entered its city walls, even Jerome would write that, "The city which took the world itself has now been taken."[4]

When the Visigoth army first moved easily through Gaul and Spain, encountering enervated Roman troops and leaders bereft of a common strategy, they were placated with large amounts of land. When Alaric then asked for Noricum just north of the Dolomites (mainly modern-day Austria) along with 4,000 pounds of gold, his demands were rudely rebuffed, only piquing his desire to embarrass the last vestiges of the great empire. In August of AD 410, then, Alaric and his men blocked off any voyages up or down the Tiber, surrounded all thirteen gates of the Rome's city walls and, although initially surprised, defeated the 6,000 imperial soldiers sent down from Ravenna. On August 24, Alaric had waited long enough, and he ordered an enemy army to march onto Roman soil – something which had not happened for over 800 years, ever since the Gallic Senones had taken Rome in c. 390 BC.

[2] On his Voyage Home to Gaul, 47–50; see Malamud, M., ed. (2018). *Rutilius Namatianus' Going Home*. London: Routledge Later Latin Poetry.

[3] See the decree "Nemo se hostiis polluat" as in *Codex Theodosianus* xvi.10.10.

[4] Jerome, *ep*. 127.12 to Principia.

Disaster demands details; a defense thus had to be given. Why did such a symbolic shift occur at this time in Roman history? The traditionalists turned to the ascendancy of Christianity to explain imperial decline, and they could easily look back over the last century to highlight where and how true Rome had been abandoned: Constantine's legalization of Christianity in AD 313, the removal of the Altar of Victory from the Senate by Constantius II in AD 357, Theodosius' implementation of Catholic Christianity in AD 380 and the subsequent outlawing of traditional rites in AD 391. With such a dramatic loss of civic religion, of course the gods and goddesses of Rome would withdraw their support from Rome and its peoples. But this is precisely the Christian retort: the Roman pantheon was never able to secure true felicity because it itself is based on divine deception and military might.

Immersed in the Donatist controversy, Augustine began the massive *City of God* (*ciu. Dei*) in late AD 412 or early AD 413 and worked on it intermittently until AD 427. By his own account, it is a *magnum opus et arduum* (*ciu. Dei, praef*; CCSL 47.1) nearly 900 pages in the Latin. Taken from the Psalms of David, the title serves throughout as the antithesis of the "earthly city" (*ciuitas terrena*; often times translated "City of Man," a term which Augustine himself never uses). Early on Augustine uses the image of the *ciuitas* for varied ways of human living: "there's a certain godless city, described as consisting of a kind of conspiracy of human godlessness throughout all countries, and it is mystically called Babylon in the scriptures. Again, there is a certain city, an alien wanderer on this earth, consisting of a conspiracy of godliness, and this one is called Jerusalem" (*s.* 299A.8). Ultimately there are two of these cities, the heavenly and the earthly, the deified and the diabolical (cf. *de patientia* §14), and whereas the first is characterized by "love of God," even to the point of contempt for self, the latter is "the love of self, even to the point of contempt for God" (*ciu. Dei* 14.28; Babcock 2.136). Citizenry is thereby determined not by family lineage or even by birthplace itself, but by one's loves. As such, it is not so easy to contrast, say, Cain with Abel, Jerusalem with Babylon, or even the Church against the world, as no one collective can exhaust the mystery of God's providence and the secret depths of the human heart. Augustine must therefore transcend present human history as the story of two mutually opposed loves, reflected and corroborated by contrasting social organizations, what will ultimately prove to be the worldly and the heavenly – the *ciuitas terrena* versus the *ciuitas Dei*.

The bifurcation of human history into two mutually contradictory parties is an ancient image in Augustine's mind. It is biblically clear in

Matthew 25 and the Lord's dividing all humans into those who served him in others and those who failed to recognize the Christ. It also becomes the way Augustine understands the post-lapsarian condition: in Adam all were one, but after we fell, some continued to choose to live as earthly, while others surrendered to Christ to become heavenly. "The whole human race, whose life lasts like that of one man from Adam up to the end of this age, is so regulated under the laws of divine providence that it is manifestly divided into two kinds" (*uera rel.* 27.50; Hill, I/8, 62). These two kinds of people get casted into the metaphor of two cities early on as well. For example, on his commentary on Psalm 9, we learn that the vicious make up a "city [where] all the self-indulgent desires and unsettling emotions of the mind whip up insurrection within a person every day" (*en. Ps.* 9.8; Boulding, III/15.145). The Fall has thus brought about two types of people, exemplified and embodied in two types of cities, one built on the ways of pride and ambition, another built on the ways of God. The first is largely visible, while the second labors most often secretly in the hearts and minds of those intent on truth.

The pages of *ciu. Dei* are dedicated to a Roman envoy, Marcellinus, who was dispatched to Carthage by the Emperor Honorius to preside over the Council of Carthage (seeking to put an end to the Donatist schism) in AD 411. Marcellinus took this opportunity to ask the renowned Bishop Augustine of Hippo for an apologetic to refute the pagan critique that Christians were responsible for the fall of Rome. This in fact had been a long-standing critique: that foreign religious groups caused the enervation of the empire by refusing to honor the ancient Roman deities (cf. *epp.* 135–138), the exculsivising monotheistic Christians above all. To meet this request, Augustine went to work on when he had the available time between AD 413–AD 427. What resulted in the twenty-two books of the *ciu. Dei*, which (as he explains in very careful detail in his *retr.* 2.43) is best read in either one of two ways. In fact, the *retr.* make quite clear the purpose and structure of *ciu. Dei*:

> In the meantime, Rome was devastated by an assault on the part of the Goths acting under King Alaric and by a most destructive invasion. Worshippers of the many false gods, whom we usually call pagans, attempted to impute the devastation to the Christian religion and began to blaspheme against the true God with more harshness and bitterness than usual. I started to write the books *On the City of God* in answer to their blasphemies and errors.

> This occupied me for a number of years, because many other matters interfered that it would not have been right to put off, and I had to use my time to address them first. But finally this vast work *On the City of God*, in twenty-two books, was finished.
> (*retr.* 43 (70); Hill, I/2.148)

He then goes on to tell his readers that Books 1–5 show why it human prosperity in no way depends on worshipping false deities, while Books 6–10 are dedicated to showing how pagans remaining in the empire are fooling themselves thinking there have not been massive tragedies and losses of all sorts before AD 410.

Realizing that he could not win many over simply by refutation and rejection, Bishop Augustine admits that he must also present the only real alternative to Rome's faulty narrative, the teachings of Christ's Church. Therefore, Books 11–22 are devoted to a ponderous explication of the Christian narrative beginning with the moment of creation, tracing the advancement of God's city, and concluding by showing the fitting end of this cosmic love story: "Of the next twelve books, then, the first four (11–14) deal with the origin of the two cities, of which one is God's and the other is the world's; the second four (15–18) with their development or trajectory; and the third four (19–22), which are the last, with their merited ends" (*retr.* 43.(70)). So, after critiquing the pagan vanity of thinking that their gods and goddesses are able to bring about civic justice as well as true human felicity, the *ciu. Dei* advances the Catholic counter-narrative that God lovingly created the world *ex nihil* for his glory, and after his own imaged persons selfishly turned away from him, he sent his Son into the world to found his Church and so to redeem all who are humble enough to embrace this savior. While the first half reads as an encyclopedic "who's who?" in Roman history, the second serves more as a many-tiered biblical commentary, providing some of Augustine's most mature views on the love of God, the role of angels, the goodness of material creation, the design of the human person, the humility of Christ, miracles, the proper nature of ecclesial worship, and the nature of eternity.

Augustine composed the *ciu. Dei* in the post-Constantinian Church but with a sober distance from the enthusiasm that led others (e.g. Eusebius in the East, Orosius or Lactantius in the West) to praise the emperor's conversion as God's finally embracing the political-militaristic machine of Rome as a way to advance the heavenly kingdom. Augustine was of course glad that more of the aristocracy had come to Christ, but he refused to christen the empire for the very reason that Christ came not to establish the best political program but to win the heart freely; until all is eschatologically fulfilled in him, history remains conflicted, indecisive, and opaque. The Church, more than any organized group on earth, may best realize Christ's plan but even here – the *ecclesia permixta* – Augustine refuses to identify member and saint strictly. The Church has citizens heaven will never see and heaven has *electi* who never explicitly frequented the sacred liturgy while on earth. The end of any social organization, justice (which, Augustine strongly argues, Rome never realized because it failed to give proper worship to the one, true God), will come only where God reigns over and in every soul, when all creatures turn to him in humble praise, and where vice gives way to charity. Obviously there are many gems discoverable throughout the *ciu. Dei*, but its lasting significance lies in its argument that destiny is not a matter of ancestry or genetics but of one's free will. The ultimate meaning of human history is found not in the affairs of state but in every human person who submits to Christ so as to live with him and his citizenry forever in the City of God.

In drawing so centrally upon God's goal as *ciuitas*, one wonders why Augustine has made such a conscious choice to invoke the intended imagery of this major work as one of a city. His late antique Latin certainly offered other equivalent terms – *regnum, scaeptrum, imperium, urbs*, or even *societas* – but invoking a city of the redeemed emphasized not imaginary buildings and streets necessarily. For Augustine's readers, a *ciuitas* is immediately the result of *ciues*, those citizens who constitute the city, and this is where the God of Jesus Christ now dwells, in the human sanctified. We see this often in Augustine's pastoral approach, exhorting his parishioners to become the living things of God, the ultimate goal of all created things: "Be what you proclaim – and you will be his praise if you live rightly" (*uos estote quod dicatis. laus ipsius estis, si bene uiuatis*; *s.* 34.6; PL 38.211). He can therefore encourage Christians to "Be gold ... be God's riches" (*esto aurum ... esto diuites de deo*; *s.* 62.12; PL 38.420). "Be valleys" (*conualles estote*; *en. Ps.* 103. exp. 2.11; CCSL 40.1498). "Be chrism" (*oleum estote*; *s.* 19.6; PL 38.137). "Become God's living tree in secret" (*esto arbor uiua in occulto*; *s.* 25A.1; CCSL 41.341) and "Become Jerusalem" (*estote Ierusalem*; *en. Ps.* 147.7; CCSL 40.2144). In this mystagogical approach to the sensible goods found in nature and used especially in liturgy, the preacher Augustine can insist toward the end of his career that, "We ourselves are God's city, his most brilliant and eminent sacrifice" (*Huius autem praeclarissimum atque optimum sacrifi cium nos ipsi sumus, hoc est ciuitas eius*; *ciu. Dei* 19.23; CCSL

47.694–5).[5] In this way, Augustine's *ciu. Dei* canvasses the former and false ways humans tried to draw close to the divine and offers a counter proposal: in surrendering to the God revealed in the Old and New Testaments, and alive today most subsistently in his Church on earth, human persons can know the integrity and the joy intended for every created soul since the beginning of time.

The following fourteen essays come from today's top scholars of Augustine's works. Each chapter is meant to serve not only as a commentary on the given book(s) of *ciu. Dei*, but also as a guide through Augustine's theological macrostructure as well as the themes evident in his pastoral toward those for whom he had oversight. In "Rome's Crumbling and Consecration as the Beginnings of Augustine's Theological Historiography," I set out to show why the *ciu. Dei* came into being and the apologetic roots Augustine aims to give this work. He strategically begins by focusing our attention on the pagan concept of asylum. In seeking sanctuary, politically persecuted people have found in holy sites at least temporary safety from those mightier than they. Romans took advantage of sanctuary when Alaric's men took the city in AD 410; yet it is these very non-Christians who condemn Christ's Church for Alaric's ability to enter Rome unchecked and for the general loss of imperial honor since Constantine. This critique next forces Augustine to explain how divine providence can allow such evils for the salvation of souls. Those who refuse to know the God of Jesus Christ may see temporal loss as irrevocable misfortune but those who worship the Crucified see in pain and suffering an opportunity for greater purification of love. This purification is tried nowhere as strongly as in the cases of rape and in the act of suicide which many non-Christians saw as a possible antidote. This then leads the Bishop of Hippo to an extended discourse on human dignity and the condemning of suicide as an offense against both God and neighbor. Finally, Book 1 treats the dangers of Roman *luxuria* and how those who pilgrim in this world must keep their senses and soul always and everywhere affixed on the eternal Triune God.

The former Regius Professor of Moral and Pastoral Theology at the University of Oxford and currently Emeritus Professor of Christian Ethics at the University of Edinburgh, Oliver O'Donovan sees in Book 2 the failings of the Rome to impart morality to its citizens. Throughout its history, Augustine explains, Rome was perpetually suffused by

[5] Note CCSL's typographical error of "non" for this "nos" at line 182 on 47.694.

religion (*ritus*), but its religion utterly lacked the teaching of morals (*mores*). By Augustine's account, only three positive moralizing influences were at work in ancient Rome – the mystery religions, philosophy, and law – and none of these successfully transformed the public realm. The mystery religions lacked public buildings for instruction and only imparted moral teachings in secret to a mere few, and neither philosophy nor law could successfully overcome the influence of Roman religion. After all, Augustine points out, such *cultus* was never truly Roman, but a confiscation from Greek religion; it was never divine in origin, but merely a human fabrication.

Where order and form have existed in Rome, it came about only by the imposition of government policy, not by a true upholding of justice. Indeed, Augustine argues, Rome is founded not upon the upholding of justice but upon the fostering of injustice, with a religion focused not upon *mores* but upon *adulatio*. Even in its mythic origins, Rome came to be through the immorality of fratricide, with Romulus's killing of Remus, just as the earthly city did with Cain's killing of Abel, and it is this immorality and injustice which persists in Rome (and the earthly city as a whole) to Augustine's own day, symbolized by the veneration of Romulus as a demigod. Thus, contrary to Roman tendencies to idealize the Republic of the past, Augustine insists that true justice was inherently absent in Roman history, at least until the Constantinian revolution, in which Rome was presented for the first time with an opportunity to choose a radically moralized religion. Still, the Roman body politic remains of a divided mind, since divine laws and morals have indeed entered the public sphere through the presence of Christianity; yet the public sphere wavers by preferring the Roman religion which lacks in morals rather than the fully moralized and salvific religion of Christianity.

In "Rome's Woes before Christ: History and Rhetoric in *The City of God*," Christian Tornau, a classical philologist at Würzburg University, situates Book 3 in those earlier works of the Latin Apologists which had already countered the pagan complaint that Christianity's ascendancy caused the empire's neglect of the traditional polytheistic cults. In cataloguing catastrophes that had befallen Rome before the advent of Christ, Augustine moves on a field already well-plowed, but now needs to face this traditional complaint against the Church which had apparently gained new force after the Sack of Rome in AD 410, Augustine thus adapting a traditional theme to his own apologetic purposes. It is shown how he employs rhetorical pathos in order to deconstruct the idealizing view of early Roman history was canonized by the literary tradition and kept exerting influence on educated persons – both pagan and Christian – in his days. While he sometimes encourages an emotional response to well-known events that reverses the traditional evaluation, he also builds upon and exploits the pathetic representation of the civil wars available in Roman authors like Lucan or Florus. His reading of Roman history as an almost uninterrupted series of civil wars reveals the distinction – conceded to the pagan adversaries in the opening chapter (*ciu. Dei* 3.1) between moral and external evils as artificial and marks the Roman Empire as an avatar of the *ciuitas terrena*, which is inevitably divided within itself. The chapters on Numa Pompilius briefly touch upon the systematically important issues of the relevance of peace for happiness and the relation of religion and philosophy and help to anchor Book 3 in the overall argument of *ciu. Dei*.

As we have now seen in the first three books of *City of God*, Augustine begins to defend Christianity against those who blame it for the sacking of Rome. But by the time we reach Books 4 and 5, we are brought into Augustine's close reading of Roman religion, realizing a need now to cover a seemingly disparate range of topics, including discussions of fate, free will, the just emperor, and the proper role of the emperor. Dean Hammer's intriguing essay accordingly approaches Books 4 and 5 by way of Augustine's own complicated relationship to the Roman past. Books 4 and 5 read not as a break from this Roman past, but as a recasting of memory. Citing Roman sources along the way, Augustine detaches paganism from romanticized images of Rome's past, showing that traditional Roman religious practices not only fail to account for Roman successes, but also are the contrivance of elites used to conceal their criminality and justify domination. In the place of a pagan reading of Roman history, Augustine substitutes a Christian one. Augustine clears out the lingering Roman beliefs in fate, divination, prophecy, and will in order to provide a reading of the Roman past that shows the relationship between God's empowering will and human choice. What once was Rome's greatness has a corollary in the glory of the City of God. But in tearing away the façade of traditional Roman religious practices by showing them to be tools of corrupt elites used to foster their own desire for control at the expense of the community, Augustine justifies the repression of paganism. Christianity, not paganism, is the true vehicle of Rome's glory.

Books 6 and 7 comprise the work's most extensive discussion of the civil religion of the ancient pagan world: the "gods of the nations" generally, and in particular the gods of Rome. The University of Notre

Dame's Mary Keys masterfully shows how in treating the nature of civil religion, Augustine crafts a lengthy rhetorical dialectic on one of the central queries of classical political philosophy: What are the actual and rightful roles of nature and convention in civic life? Indeed, questions of nature's status, goodness, and sufficiency, and of civil religion vis-à-vis true religion, permeate the whole of Augustine's *ciu. Dei*. This chapter offers an interpretation of Augustine's dialogue in Books 6 and 7 with Marcus Terentius Varro on civil theology or civil religion, with a focus on nature, convention, their relation to religion and the possibility of their harmonization in the political sphere. The chapter's first two sections explicate Augustine's interpretation and appraisal in Books 6 and 7 of Varro's writings on Roman civil religion, its origins, meanings, truth, and practical implications. The chapter's third section reflects on implications of Augustine's appraisal of Varro's philosophic or naturalistic defense of Roman civil religion, for the right relation of nature and convention in political life more broadly. The conclusion reflects briefly on Varro's and Augustine's respective religious projects from the Ciceronian perspective of wandering and homecoming within one's own city.

In his usual expert fashion, University of Oxford's Mark Edwards explains how Books 8, 9, and 10 complete Augustine's examination of pagan culture and philosophy, here responding specifically to the Platonists Apuleius and Porphyry. In Book 8, Augustine strives first to demonstrate the superiority of the Platonists, tracing two streams of philosophical schools in antiquity, the Ionic and the Italian, and noting that Plato fused the two streams, thereby crafting the soundest theology in antiquity. Plato indeed attained to a remarkable proximity to Christianity, yet among the three sects which had arisen from Plato – the Peripatetics, the Academics, and the Platonists – it was the Platonists who had fallen away most from the truth which Plato himself had expounded. Apuleius, for instance, suggests that daemons both good and evil play an intermediate role between humans and God and that humans must appeal to these daemons through magic and theurgy. Augustine himself associates these daemons with the demons of the New Testament, arguing that neither they nor any of the venerable dead are suitable for worship. That is why Edwards shows how Book 9 recapitulates and expands upon Book 8, as Augustine continues contrasting the Platonists with other philosophical schools, particularly the Stoics. Augustine considers Stoic assertions regarding the passions, reckoning their account as similar to that of the Platonists, though they fall short of the Platonists particularly in their treatment of misericordia.

Yet while the Platonists count misericordia to be a divine attribute, Apuleius and the other Platonists fail to recognize that it is out of misericordia that God took on flesh, taking on the true mediatorial role in contrast to the demons. Finally, in Book 10, Augustine treats Porphyry's arguments in favor of theurgy, and he therefore explains the Christian understanding of the worship of God. Beginning by detailing the Greek and Latin terminology by which Christians speak of the worship of God, Augustine explains that the Christian notion of sacrifice far exceeds that of paganism. The Christian sacrifice is at once both external and internal, and it is accomplished by the Christian's own gift of self, only shedding any blood if they are called to suffer martyrdom for Christ. It is only the upright heart which is truly pleasing to God, not the sorcery and sacrifice performed by the pagans. Thus, in contrast to theurgy which is ultimately offered to the demons, the Christian is united with Christ, the one mediator and only sacrifice, so that he might offer true worship to God.

Villanova University's James Wetzel takes up Books 11 and 12 and masterfully details the eternal foundations of Augustine's two cities in the creation of the angels and the fall of the demons. Book 11 represents the pivot away from Augustine's polemical work against the pagans toward the City of God itself, and Augustine therefore begins with the love and humility of the city's founder, the Incarnate Christ. From here, Augustine turns to the Scriptures through which Christ communicates, as he offers an exegesis of the first day of the Creation narrative in Genesis 1. Treating the nuances of the Latin text, Augustine posits that the creation of light in fact indicates the creation of the angels and that the seemingly uncreated darkness indicates those angels who turned away from God. Here Augustine finds the very origins of the two cities, and it is this intermixing of the angelic and human stories which Wetzel seeks to elucidate.

From here, Wetzel proceeds in three parts. The first section considers the divine dividing of the two groups of angels, beginning with Augustine's allegorical explanation that the angels were created as Day, Evening, and Morning, but by their own will, some angels turned instead toward the de-creation of Night. Augustine therefore asks why some angels should have turned away, though he admits that humans are simply unable to conceive of why they might have parted from God and related instead to the void, as there is no efficient cause for such a decision but only what Augustine can name a "deficient cause." The second section considers whether the temporal status of angels and whether any time therefore existed between the creation of Lucifer and his minions and the moment at which they fell. In order to explain the apparently temporal change from Lucifer the good angel to the Devil the fallen angel, the section considers hypotheses offered by Augustine both in the *ciu. Dei* as well as in his *Literal Commentary on Genesis*, seeking to judge which Augustine might have favored. The final section asks how this eternal frame in fact founds the human inhabitants of the two cities, giving particular attention to the respective manners in which God, angels, and humans relate to time. Responding to the concern that humans are uniquely defined by their nonbeing before their earthly creation, the chapter concludes by explaining God's continual, intimate generation of his creations, that is, the coming to be of good things out of goodness itself.

In "The Incomprehensibility of the Fall and Its Consequences for Humanity," Professor of Church History in the Faculty of Theology and Religious Studies at Katholieke Universiteit Leuven, Mathijs Lamberigts, shows how Augustine uses Books 13 and 14 to discuss one of the most challenging if not incomprehensible issues in Christianity: how to explain that creatures revolt against a good God who created a harmonious reality in which all creatures could have lived in perfect happiness. Augustine develops his arguments in debate with pagan philosophies (confronted with the same questions about evil and disobedience but offering different answers). In Book 13, the focus is on the many forms of death as punishment for the fall of mankind. Augustine pays special attention to the status of the created body, an important question in light of the reply to the dualistic Platonic approach in which the body is a hindrance for the soul. Book 13 already preludes and offers the essential cornerstones for the Adam and Eve story treated next.

Thus, in Book 14, Augustine first contrasts the life according to the flesh (the earthly city) and that according to the spirit (the celestial city). Most of the book is dealing with Adam and Eve, their life in the paradise, their fall and the dramatic consequences for themselves and their progeny: suffering, mortality, vices, carnal concupiscence, in sum disorder and disobedience in the self are the result of the disobedience to God. Augustine very much concentrates on sexuality as the supreme punishment of the first human beings' disobedience, offering his most extensive view on sexuality outside the controversy with the Pelagian Julian of Aeclanum. Here Augustine has much to offer our contemporary world on the divinely intended meaning of gender, body, and the good of marriage as the place where male lust can be tamed, children can be loved, and the sacrament of Christ and his Church is manifested and lived out in this world.

Jonathan Yates, current professor of theology at Villanova University and former editor of *Augustinian Studies*, comments on the intricacies of Books 15 and 16 where Augustine continues his examination on Genesis, recounting salvation history so that he might locate the presence of the City of God in each stage of the post-lapsarian world. Though the texts seem to contain straightforward accounts of the rest of the book of Genesis, he raises interpretive questions throughout, regarding both those points which are difficult to understand and those passages which seem to support ethical improprieties. Even more, Yates demonstrates that Augustine here reads the book of Genesis through a distinctly Pauline lens, making sense of the "pre-Advent" history of the people of God in light of the authoritative "post-Advent" revelations of the New Testament. Thus, Yates observes, Augustine's recounting of the ages of the City of God is less driven by a historical impulse than by eschatological concerns, constantly pointing to the end toward which the two cities progress.

Book 15 therefore recounts the events of the first age, from Adam to Noah, beginning with the Cain's envy and murder of Abel, which founded the earthly city. As Augustine explains, Cain and Seth, the brother who replaces the slaughtered Abel, represent the progenitors of each city, and each line would continue through the righteous and wicked of each generation. Book 15 concludes by considering the identity and significance of the Nephilim as well as the events of the Great Flood. As with most events in Scripture, the Flood was indeed a historical event for Augustine, but the narrative also signifies the City of God on pilgrimage in this world through the Church. Book 16 addresses the second and third ages, from Noah to Abraham and from Abraham to King David. Throughout, Augustine continues to read the events both as the histories of each city, as well as the prophetic anticipations of their fulfillments. Within this continuing framework, Augustine gives the greatest attention to Abram, noting the three promises which God made to Abram for the sake of building up the City of God, as well as the purpose and use of circumcision under Abraham. Throughout the rest of the book, Augustine's primary goal remains to demonstrate the continuous presence of a spiritual people, the very predecessors of the Christian people.

Xavier University's Michael Sweeney takes up *ciu. Dei* 17 and 18 to show how Augustine argues that Old Testament prophecy refers not only to the suffering Christ but to the two cities whose courses define history and human choice, namely, the City of God and the City of Man. The prophecy concerning these two cities goes back to the twofold prophecy made to Abraham: a prophecy according to the flesh of temporal prosperity that is fulfilled is the single nation of Israel, and a prophecy according to faith that is a spiritual promise to all nations and that is fulfilled through Christ. Prophecy and kingship are inseparable because the earthly kingdom is itself a prophecy that points to something new and future. When the earthly Jerusalem ceases to be prophetic, it becomes nothing but the City of Man.

One of the least explored elements of prophecy in *ciu. Dei* 17 and 18 is the nature of prophecy itself. Augustine's understanding of prophecy here is "Platonic" inasmuch as it based on the relationship between an "image" and an "original." The image has the power to prefigure or foreshadow, but it can never be the original; the earthly Jerusalem foreshadows the heavenly Jerusalem, which it can never be. Augustine devotes considerable attention to the pagan attempts to divinize kings – to "originalize" and thus eternalize the image. The knowledge that one can have of the original through the image is limited; it is necessarily obscure, and so prophetic knowledge of the future is murky. On the other hand, once one knows the original, the meaning of the image becomes clear. When the future, i.e. the original, has become present, the past image becomes clear. Since Christ has come and his heavenly kingdom has begun, the past can be read with clarity. By contrasting Augustine's sense of prophecy with the Islamic philosopher Al-Farabi (d. AD 950), who also developed an account of prophecy based on the Platonic relationship between image and original, we see that religion is an image that can be like but never be identical to the original that is philosophy. Prophets create images that are imperfect copies of the eternal essences that belong to philosophy. For Augustine, the image is particular and temporal – a particular portion of time and history – that imperfectly copies the future original. Both image and original are within history, for the original is Christ who enters history. Yet, for Al-Farabi, the act of faith limits one to the image; for Augustine, the act of faith reaches the original. For Al-Farabi, prophecy is the gift of the philosopher to those incapable of understanding demonstrative proofs, while for Augustine, prophecy is a proof superior to philosophical demonstration.

Writing the chapter on the most studied book of the *City of God* has fallen to Andrew Hofer of the Dominican House of Studies in Washington, DC. Book 19, according to Hofer, gives Augustine's appeal for peace as our most desired end. All people want lasting peace, but where can it be found and how can it be attained? Understanding that Augustine has two distinct audiences in mind, non-Christian and Christian, Hofer stresses that Augustine's rhetoric of contrast is at the service of an overarching concern for salvation and of inculcating a sense of humility. Compared to the City of God, the earthly city cannot have an authentic, lasting peace. Even the best of the earthly city's philosophers admit that troubles are inescapable in this life. Augustine's engagements with the thought of Varro and Cicero, and to a lesser extent here Porphyry, provide the impetus for his appeal to his non-Christian audience to accept the offer of the true God's peace. Compared to the City of God at rest, even the Christian audience of the City of God has sheer misery in journeying. As Augustine came to express more sharply and repeatedly in the Pelagian controversies from his early writings, Christians are assailed by all sorts of temptations and other disturbances during this earthly sojourn. Every Christian, for good reason, daily prays, "Forgive us our trespasses." Christians should realize that the two cities are mixed, that they were first born into the earthly city's *massa damnata*, and that they would revert back to that city had they not perseverance. Augustine impresses upon them, and implicitly in his argument especially those attracted to Pelagianism, the need for a humble reliance on God's graciousness now for the peace of everlasting life. In short, both audiences are humbled by Augustine's rhetoric – in order to turn to the Lord who "resists the proud and gives grace to the humble" (see Prov 3:34, James 4:6, and 1 Pet 5:5). Only in heaven can we find the fullest and most certain peace that our hearts desire. Only by humbly turning in faith to Christ, and persevering in his grace amidst the trials of this life, can we attain the lasting peace we want so much as our end.

Isabel Moreira, Professor of History at the University of Utah, shows Augustine's intent in Book 20 as one of parsing out good and bad interpretations of scripture, in order that he might more accurately speak of the individual's fate after death, as well as our eventual judgment in the end times. The chapter therefore begins with an overview of Augustine's approach to the text of the Apocalypse of John, recounting the controversies and other exegetical voices to which Augustine is responding. Utilizing insights gleaned from the whole of Scripture, Augustine strives to provide a more effective key for interpreting the mysteries of the Apocalypse. The chapter thus recounts a number of Augustine's interpretive strategies, before turning to his responses to a variety of particular questions in regard to the afterlife. The chapter first recounts Augustine's rebuttal of the millenarian interpretations popular among the Donatists of North Africa, in which he interprets certain passages from the Apocalypse as referring not to the end times but to the present, earthly life.

Book 20 relies on a major theme developed throughout Augustine's episcopal career, namely the theme of the two deaths and two resurrections experienced by the individual Christian, the first being spiritual (death through sin and resurrection through baptism) and the second being physical (bodily death and resurrection). It then recounts Augustine's defense of the bodily resurrection of all the dead, whether destined for eternal reward or eternal torment, as well as his related explanation of the purifying, world-wide conflagration, through which the mortal world passes away and gives way to a transformed, immortal one. From here, the chapter traces some of the conclusions wrought by Augustine which remained influential for medieval interpreters, including his explanations of the justice of God, his measured acceptance of communal purification after death, his account of the communion of saints and the lack of communion for those in hell. Finally, the chapter concludes by situating Augustine's views on divine judgment within the context of the Sack of Rome.

Boston College's David G. Hunter turns to the final two books, *ciu. Dei* 21 and 22, arguing that a radical sense of materiality or corporeality permeates Augustine's discussion of the ultimate fate of the Two Cities. Book 21 examines the destiny of the damned in eternal fire; Book 22 explores the prospects of the redeemed in eternal beatitude. Augustine himself was aware of the considerable change that his thought had undergone, Hunter argues, as is evident from the review of his own writings that he undertook in the *retr.*, a work contemporary with the *City of God*. Focusing on the issue of corporeality, Hunter examines a succession of topics in Book 21 that required Augustine to acknowledge the importance of the unity of body and soul in the next life. For example, when confronting the problem of how a physical body might suffer eternal pain without dying Augustine argued that only an unbreakable union between body and soul could enable a person to sustain eternal punishment. God was justified in imposing an eternal penalty on all humankind, Augustine believed, because of the gravity of the original sin. If God chose to redeem a few out of mercy, it was God's prerogative to do so.

The centrality of corporeality is evident as well, perhaps to an even greater extent, Hunter claims, in Augustine's discussion of eternal beatitude. There was no absurdity in a resurrected body inhabiting a spiritual realm, Augustine argued, since heaven itself will be partly corporeal. The fact that miraculous acts, especially of bodily healing, accompanied both the ministry of Jesus and that of the apostles and the fact that they persist to the present day was evidence, for Augustine, that a bodily resurrection was possible. Human bodies would reach perfection, that is, they would attain "the measure of the age of the fullness of Christ" (Eph 4:13), approximately the age of thirty. Women and men would retain their unique sexual characteristics, though these would no longer serve to reproduce children, but rather to provoke praise of God for their beauty. The Christian martyrs would retain the scars of their wounds, even as their bodies were restored to health, so that they would be corporeal testaments to the glory of God. Even the vision of God, Augustine speculated, might be accomplished through the eyes of the body, gazing with wonder at the beauties of the recreated world. The "end" of the body, therefore, was only its beginning, for Augustine envisioned human corporeality as the precondition of both eternal beatitude and eternal punishment.

To regather these myriad and major Augustinian themes, the University of Notre Dame's John Cavadini offers readers a lengthy Epilogue. Cavadini insists that the architectonic nature of the *ciu. Dei* is a brilliant weaving of philosophy, biblical theology, political thought, and Christian pastoral concerns, as its ultimate concerns is to show the final end of all humanity as the City of God which transcends any civil arrangements or governmental institutions. The only distinguishing factor that in the end will matter is charity: two loves for two ends, two loves for two eternities. Such guidance Rome could never have offered, for Rome was never a true republic. All ages and societal structures outside of Christ could never really bring about true human excellence, because outside of God's becoming human, all ways of life ultimately fail to embody true justice, never giving the only true God his rightful worship. This is the entire point of the sweeping review of history offered throughout these twenty-two books: to present and defend the glorious City of God and to offer a way out of the limitations and brutalities that any other way of life inevitably brings.

Many authors of the essays which follow have used their own English translations of Augustine's Latin, while others have relied on William Babcock's excellent English translation available through New City Press. The Latin critical edition of *ciu. Dei* is found at Bernard Dombart and Adolph Kalb, *Sancti Aurelii Augustini De Ciuitate Dei*, 2 vols. CCSL 47 and 48 (Turnhout, 1955).

Finally, this collection of commentaries is dedicated to a *conciuis in ciuitate Dei*, Dr. Eleonore Stump of Saint Louis University. Many of us have learned from Eleonore's careful analysis of the themes covered in these pages. Many of us have learned from her judicious reading of Augustine, not to mention her many writings and lectures on Saint Thomas Aquinas as well as Dante Alighieri. Her gifts of wisdom and counsel have been selflessly given to both Academy and Ecclesia, shining through many of the words which here follow.

2 Book 1: The Crumbling and Consecration of Rome

DAVID VINCENT MECONI, S.J.

Opening his *City of God* is a heartfelt dedication from Augustine to his "dearest son" (*fili carissime*) Marcellinus, a Roman tribune and the imperial commissioner who was dispatched by Emperor Honorius to preside over the Council of Carthage in June of AD 411. Best known for his assistance to the Bishop of Hippo in bringing the Donatist Schism to an end, Marcellinus was not shy in asking Augustine questions by exchanging rich letters (*epp.* 128, 129, and 133) during this time. Furthermore, Augustine's *On the Merits and Forgiveness of Sins and on Infant Baptism* (*pecc. mer.*) and *The Spirit and the Letter* (*spir. et litt.*), both dated AD 412, are also dedicated to Marcellinus in response to some answers this theologically cultured aristocrat first posed to the great bishop. Overseeing the debates between Catholics and Donatists in AD 411 would eventually cost Marcellinus his life, yet win him the hallowed crown of martyrdom. The well-connected Donatists were able to convince Marinus, *comes rei militaris* of both Italy and Africa, that Marcellinus and his brother Apringius (cf. *ep.* 134), African proconsul in AD 411, were secretly plotting with the *comes Africae* Heraclinus to usurp imperial power. Despite Augustine's and other African bishops' intervention, Marinus ordered the brothers' beheading in mid-September of AD 413 on charges of high treason. However, a year later the imperial court realized that these charges had been fabricated. Emperor Honorius exonerated both brothers, produced evidence that Marinus had acted out of selfishness, and thereby referred to Marcellinus and Apringius with great honor, and had both celebrated as Catholic martyrs of the Donatist rebellion.

It is in this context of imperial intrigue and power grabs that Augustine set to work on the twenty-two books of his *ciu. Dei*. Here the aging Augustine aimed to answer the objection that the ascendancy of the Catholic Nicene Church is what brought Rome's greatness to an end. Augustine knew well that there were more profound factors at work. But, so strong was the sentiment in late antiquity that "so went

Rome, so went the world," even one as otherworldly as St. Jerome could ask: "Where is salvation if Rome perishes?"[1] Never one to be allured by temporal machinations and opportunistic politics, Augustine's expansive historiography argues that Roman religion was never able to bring true prosperity to its votaries because it was based on deceit, aiming ultimately to bring glory and victory to the state and not true worship and glory to God. This *libido dominandi* has run through the very core of Rome's history, and Augustine is ready not only to expose it, but to offer an alternative temporal structure as well.

As we learn in the work's prologue, this is where the two cities part: one moored in the glorification of the self, and the other in a graced surrender to the "King and Founder" (*Rex et conditor*). This designation of a new kind of civic leader and founder of a city immediately distinguishes the two vying images of the divine: "those who prefer their own gods" and the God of "ultimate victory and perfect peace." That is why – in his prefatory dedication to Marcellinus – Augustine immediately juxtaposes the two cities: the proud against the humble, arrogance versus grace, the inflated set against the meek. After this brief dedication, Book 1 proceeds in four major sections, and our comments will follow this pattern.

The first will treat Augustine's gambit that only Catholic Christians have honored the safety of "sanctuary." The *ciu. Dei* opens in this manner because Alaric and his Visigoth marauders respected the sacred catholic places in Rome and seemingly spared the lives of those who sought refuge there. The second section is an extended theodicy: "Why does God allow temporal travesties, like the Fall of Rome, to happen?" Questions of the problem of evil, sin, and divine providence thus arise as a Christian apology forms on why God allows some evils and what he desires arises from them. Augustine's third major point in Book 1 is to see the many factors involved in rape during war time and the resulting suicide which the ancient mind reserved as a final solution to this tragic reality. Augustine approaches the terrible wrong of rape not so much as a sexual crime as it is one against human dignity and a matter of inhumane torture. For the ancients, the injustices of rape could lead to the sorrow that is suicide. Here too, the Romans and the Christians diverged in thinking that there could ever be a justifiable reason to violate the commandment against charity and the taking of one's own life. Finally, Book 1 ends with the fourth key theme, the role

[1] Jerome, *ep.* 123.16.

of spectacles and the allure of extravagance in the later period of the Roman Empire.

What follows is neither the history of Rome, nor is it even a philosophical examination of history itself. Rather, it is a theological invitation to see that the only intelligible underpinning of world and personal experiences and movements is the providential and loving will of the Triune God. Apart from God's good creation, his work of redemption, and his desire to draw all nations into his own divine kingdom, history has no intelligible telos and certainly no definitive purpose. While governmental polities are brought into law and quickly pass away again, God's ways are eternal and offer the only real sort of lasting harmony among peoples. And, while the first can reflect the second in varying degrees, the two will never be wholly identifiable in this age. That is why the earthly city fails to provide true felicity, for it is based on human ingenuity and ultimately human power; the heavenly city, on the other hand, can alone offer what it is every person from the beginning of time desires, everlasting peace and intimate union with all persons – human, angelic, and divine. However, even though Augustine is loathed to speak of a "Christian Empire," a bishop whose entire life is based on the divinely intended goodness of creation, the incarnation of God fully into the human condition, as well as the restoration of a "new heaven and a new earth," has to see in this world some indication of the divine.

It is the presence of God in human history that interests Augustine, and this is the goal of the *ciu. Dei*: to help to clarify the relationship between those events which occur in time and those eternal verities which alone can give the human condition ultimate meaning. This is why the state is not necessarily synonymous with the City of Man and why the church is not wholly identifiable with the earthly city. While God is undeniably active in and throughout the temporal order, his actions are, for the most part, invisible and personal. The reign of God cannot be reduced to governmental legislation or even any temporal structure, however better one way of life might be over another or how holy any one political leader might be. This is why Augustine has to examine almost every facet of human living, every classical figure and text, and every religious devotion, carefully: for in all things the one true God has planted seeds of his own presence, but herein is therefore also discovered the battle between God and his rivals. For the war that concerns Augustine is not between Rome and its current enemies – that would be much too small for our author – but between God and the Devil, between the two eternal cities.

Accordingly, while defending Christianity from imperial accusations of betrayal, Augustine has also to take up much larger themes of theodicy, proper worship, salvation history, and the afterlife. As such, let us now turn to Book 1 and highlight the four major themes with which Augustine chooses to open this foundational text of all Christian literature.

SANCTUARY (1.1–7)

Of all the philosophical themes and classical figures Augustine could have used to open this sweeping work, his chosen gambit is the ancient idea of sanctuary. Found both in Oriental as well as Hellenistic cultures, here politics and religion clearly coalesce. Asylum first arose from sacred natural sites that were off limits to even the highest of human or quasi-divine authorities. Orestes, for example, seeks refuge in the Delphic Temple, running from the Erinyes after murdering his own mother, but the best Apollo can do at his own temple is delay the inevitable. It was not until the rise of the Catholic Bishop as a centralized civic leader that sanctuary became codified and nonnegotiable rules were set in place. Augustine strategically opens *ciu. Dei* with this concept of sanctuary because it serves as an apologetic foreshadowing for the rest of the work. How so? In this one concept, the intersection of divine providence and human interests is brought to the fore, themes of violence and misfortune appear, the alleged benefits of the Roman imperial cult are revealed for what they are, the obvious advantages of the *tempora christiana* can be celebrated, and the City of God as the only locale where persecution ceases and true peace is enjoyed is easily foreshadowed. Here the vulnerable are harbored and human harmony is preserved for all of humanity regardless of nationality, religious creed, or even moral rectitude.

The starting theme of sanctuary thus appears in the opening context of very strong martial imagery: enemies against one's polis, the need to defend one's life, fires and the burning of towns, and so on. This sets the tone for Augustine's argument that Roman civilization has all along been based on power and the ability to dominate but, in the face of greater Gothic power now that the empire is waning, Romans seek refuge in catholic places of worship, trusting that while these Arian Christians from the north may not have respected the polytheistic pantheon of Rome, they will respect Christ and his ecclesia. These deriders of the Christian faith:

> are so ungrateful for the obvious benefits of its redeemer that they forget they would not be wagging their tongues against it today if they had not, in fleeing the enemy's sword, found in the refuge of its sacred places the life in which they take such pride ... many escaped who now deride the Christian times and make Christ responsible for the evils that Rome endured.
>
> (*ciu. Dei* 1.1; Babcock, 1.2)

As savage as the Visigoths may appear to the supposedly more refined Romans, even they respected holy sites and the name of Jesus Christ. Apparently, Alaric's men did not ask for a profession of faith from those seeking asylum but simply respected the *nomen ipse* of Christ, honoring not the men and women inside as much as the one to whom the sacred site was consecrated. This ought to make a profound impression on the Roman mind: that Jesus Christ's name and those things associated with him inspire awe and restraint even during times of war.

This sort of respect was never afforded by the Romans. Augustine accordingly exploits Roman history to show that the gods and goddesses of the pantheon were never themselves respected to this degree. He wants to depict sanctuary in the pre-Christian world as a convenient expediency that was easily shunned when the powerful demanded the blood of the accused. In the end, pagan asylum was nothing more than a pious façade and Augustine wants to expose it as nothing more than a political pragmatism that had no real otherworldly authority, evidenced by how the once great temples were stripped for their spoils and not used to honor the divine but to be divided among the conquerors. This is the first way the Visigoths are different from the Romans and their progenitors: "There liberty was lost; here it was preserved. There captivity was imposed; here it was forbidden. There people were driven in for slavery by an enemy exercising dominance; here people were led in for freedom by an enemy exercising mercy" (*ciu. Dei* 1.4; Babcock, 1.5). In fact, from its beginning, Rome's history is littered with such failures of the gods and goddesses to grant peace: "Troy herself, the mother of the Roman people, was unable to protect her citizens from the fire and steel of the Greeks in the places sacred to her gods, even though the Greeks worshipped those very same gods" (*ciu. Dei* 1.4; Babcock, 1.5)

At this point Augustine employs a strategy he will use for the rest of *ciu. Dei*, namely: single out a figure from classical history and celebrate this person's natural virtue but then, just as quickly, illustrate how such human effort will inevitably fail. The first Roman Augustine highlights in this way is Marcus Marcellus (d. 208 BC), the general who took Syracuse in 212 BC, the sort of good man who "shed his own tears before he shed [the] blood of his enemy" (*ciu. Dei* 1.6; Babcock, 1.6). Even though this well-respected leader issued a command that no Syracusan free person (*liber*) should be harmed, "the city was sacked according to the customary practice of war, and nowhere is it reported that even this upright and compassionate commander prescribed that anyone who fled to this or that temple should be kept from harm" (*ciu. Dei* 1.6; Babcock, 1.7). This is an apologetic tactic Augustine will use throughout both the remainder of Book 1 and, strategically, the rest of *ciu. Dei*: Romans can certainly boast some noble and upstanding figures, but in the end their virtue is revealed for the disorder it ultimately is, apart from ordering all desires and actions to Christ. As Jennifer Herdt so accurately puts it: "This might suggest that pagans can be virtuous at a first-order level, insofar as they achieve this order in the soul and pursue virtue for its own sake. At a second-order level, though, that is, when asked 'Why act virtuously?' they give a wrong answer, that is, an answer other than, 'To order all things to God'."[2]

But a new type of morality has appeared with the advent of Christ. Once Augustine showcases a non-Christian example of someone who starts on the right path but who is not enabled to complete the task virtuously for a number of reasons – usually their own human pride – his tone changes. In an almost mocking manner, Augustine lets his audience know that, whereas the learned Greeks and the majestic Romans failed to maintain the consistent worship and honoring of their deities, the "savage barbarians" have recognized the true God and kept sacred his basilicas. This is a novelty which only shows the ability of Christ to renew what moribund civilizations have neglected, if not outright denied:

> What was quite new, however, and put a whole new face on things, was that barbarian brutality appeared in a guise so gentle that the very largest basilicas were selected and set apart to be filled with people who were spared. Here no one was to be slain; no one was to be dragged out; but many were led in by their merciful enemies to be set free, and none were led away into captivity by cruel foes. Anyone who does not see that this is to be attributed to Christ's name and to these Christian times is blind.
>
> (*ciu. Dei* 1.7; Babcock, 7)

[2] Herdt 2008, p. 49.

The Christian temples not only slowed Alaric's advances, they even brought his army to a complete standstill. Yet non-Christian Romans complain about the very reality that saved their lives: the *tempora christiana*.

PROVIDENCE AND THE PROBLEM OF EVIL (1.8–15)

While Augustine may open by touting the fact that Christianity helped to save non-Christian Romans from Alaric's steel, he must also humbly admit that there is, in fact, war, destruction, and loss even for those whom he claims worship God properly. While it is thus an easy claim to show that the *numina* of Troy and Rome failed to protect their people, it is a bit more complicated to now lay out how it is that the one true God allows his people to undergo hardship as well. Christ's faithful suffer just as severely as those who actively reject him, and so Augustine has to move quickly from the question of, "Why was divine mercy extended to the ungodly and ungrateful?" to the scriptural acceptance at Mt. 5:45 of the hard truth that God "sends rain on the just and the unjust" (*ciu. Dei* 1.8; Babcock, 1.7–8). To develop this theme of theodicy then, Augustine weaves a twofold argument through this middle section of Book 1.

The first strand of argument focuses our attention on the inscrutable mercy of God. Augustine's image of God in these paragraphs is one who loves all his children equally and labors so as to sanctify every human soul. It is an image of God who wills that both "temporal goods and evils of this life" be "common to both" the proud and the humble (*ciu. Dei* 1.8; Babcock, 1.8). Yet, in this equal offering of goods and ills, God will do what he can to use each to bring all into a loving union with himself. The second strand is his philosophical view of evil. Here he localizes all evil from some cosmic drama and places the reality into the divided heart. Evil for this former Manichean is no longer a separate force, contrary to the *Summum Bonum*; the struggle Augustine and all members of the human race find themselves in is no longer to be understood in terms of a conflict between two independent nations. Rather, it is a civil war in which rebellious children have turned away from their only true Father.

In these sections of Augustinian theodicy, his concern is ultimately an existential exploration into the reaction and intention of the individual soul in the face of hardships. That is, for the worldly, times of persecution and loss are seen as insurmountable; whereas, for the godly, the same misfortunes are invitations to purification and greater awareness that this world was never meant to be one's final destination, especially the Christian pilgrim:

> This does not mean, however, that when the good and the evil suffer alike, there is no distinction in what they suffer. Even when the sufferings are alike, the sufferers remain unlike; and even when virtue and vice undergo the same torment, they are not themselves the same. In one and the same fire, gold glows red but chaff smokes; and under one and the same flail, straw is broken up but grain is separated out; nor is the oil mixed in with the dregs, even though it is extracted by the weight of the same press.
>
> (*ciu. Dei* 1.8; Babcock, 1.8)

As such, it is not the divine dispensation of either causing good or allowing evil that distinguishes the City of God from the City of Man, it is rather how each person receives, and thus appropriates, these heavenly conveyances: "What is really important, then, is not the character of the suffering but rather the character of the sufferer" (*ciu. Dei* 1.8; Babcock, 1.8). And who is the sufferer? Every child of Adam.

In this post-lapsarian world, all of creation is "off" and perhaps Augustine seeks to find some convergence of experience between the Christian and the Roman Traditionalist by stressing this common fate: it is the very sins of all of humankind (*ipsa peccata*) that have caused an angry God to fill up this whole world with calamities (*Deus indignatus impleuit tantis calamitatibus mundum*; *ciu. Dei* 1.9; CCSL 47.8). Here Augustine does not venture to explain why that will be done when he turns to the disobedience of our protoparents in Books 13 and 14. *Ciu. Dei* instead opens with a metanarrative on the fact that God's good creation has turned away from him, with the result that no human person will escape the punishments of pride and arrogance.

In this presentation of temporal universal misfortune Augustine necessarily and, rightly, includes the Christians in the evils that accompanied the Sack of Rome. God uses adversity to purify the purified and to sanctify the sanctified, a lesson Augustine next internalizes as he turns to the Christian virtue of fraternal correction. This exhortation is placed here because it is through temporal sufferings that we experience a sort of "paternal" correction, as God uses all historical events to teach us something of his divine care. This is precisely why those faithful to God should not shy away from rebuking or correcting those perceived to be going astray. This, of course, is not always personally delightful, but it is an office of love (*officia caritatis*) which God asks for and relies upon to bring his church on earth to a state of greater union.

We are next presented with three areas where such counsel is most immediately needed: (1) the human propensity to find comfort in temporal riches, (2) the natural fear of famine, torture, and the resultant effect of substituting one's temporal life for avoidance of physical pain, and (3) the possibility of captivity and imprisonment which loomed whenever one political regime came into conflict with another. Augustine's first move in discussing the allure of riches is to bring all readers into a sort of *memento mori*, quoting 1 Tim 6:6–10 on leaving this world as we came and reminding us of the plight of poor Job. Augustine here reminds us that every human eye gazing upon this work of his will also one day be called from this life. But is there no Roman hero in this regard? Is there not anyone from classical civilization who has laid down his or her riches for the sake of the Kingdom of God? Perhaps not, and that is why Augustine now presents his readers with the story of Paulinus, Bishop of Nola (d. AD 431). In Bishop Paulinus Augustine sees the nexus between the loss of personal property and the possibility of imprisonment and torture.

Although they never met in person, the lives of Augustine and Paulinus overlapped: both were men of the world who forwent worldly gain to become bishops of relatively smaller sees, and both took an interest in the other through a rich epistolary exchange.[3] In practice, Paulinus did what Augustine only might have done in potential: Paulinus sacrificed a huge fortune to oversee his diocese with greater focus and integrity, and he and his wife Therasia chose to live celibately as brother and sister. Perhaps this is why Augustine admired Paulinus so much, having achieved that which Augustine had longed for so long as well – they both had to overcome the loss of a son, and both were drawn to the virtue of celibate chastity, the renunciation of worldliness, and the gift of rhetoric in the service of truth. The reader meets Paulinus in *ciu. Dei* for one key purpose, however, his purported prayer when the city of Nola was sacked during the siege of Italy in AD 410: "Lord, let me not be tortured for the sake of gold and silver, for you know where everything I own is" (*ciu. Dei* 1.10; Babcock, 1.12).

With that, Augustine can turn to the second temporal misfortunes of war time: torture and famine. Once again, at stake here is the manner in which those facing adversity receive their current situation. Those who lost riches, as well as those who had to undergo long days of hunger, differed in terms of not *what* they were experiencing, but *how* they were experiencing. That is, the godly are able to turn all circumstances in life "to their advantage by enduring it with godliness. Those whom the famine killed, it snatched away – like bodily disease – from

[3] All in all, we still possess twelve letters between these two bishops: see Lienhard 1999, pp. 628–629.

the evils of this life; and those whom it did not kill it taught to live more sparingly and to fast at greater length" (*ciu. Dei* 1.10; Babcock, 1.13). This is the constant theme throughout *ciu. Dei*: those who love the good can meet the good in any state in life, while those who love only themselves value their worth through those contingent goods, which, one day, they will inevitably relinquish anyway.

It is in this context of the hierarchy of goods that Augustine makes an illuminating metaphysical distinction, making clear that there are two types of good in the world. There is a species of goods that when distributed, it diminishes; conversely, there is a species of goods that when it is distributed, it actually increases. The ungodly forfeit a few more years on this earth for the first type of goods, unwilling to lie to hold on to their gold and silver. Yet there is another type of good, like truth, that when it is distributed it is magnified, and this is what Augustine sees in the confession of Christ's name under torture:

> For it is the height of wretchedness to suffer for gold and silver, regardless of whether they kept their wealthy hidden by lying or gave it up by telling the truth. For under torture, no one lost Christ by confessing him, and no one kept his gold except by denying it.
>
> (*ciu. Dei* 1.10; Babcock, 1.1)

In the City of Man, the act of lying results in a gain that is fleeting and necessarily private; in the City of God, confessing and thus giving away what is good and meant for all – even under the pain of death – results in eternal life.

A related point in this section on famine and torture is the obvious problem of properly taking care of the dead. In fact, this was a concern to Augustine during the time he wrote *ciu. Dei*, as he dedicated his *cura mort.* to Paulins of Nola in AD 422. While that work is full of theological accuracy and pastoral sensitivity –how to bury the dead, why the church prays for the dead, why the sacrifice of the Mass is especially advantageous and so on – Book 1 of *ciu. Dei* is more concerned with the immediate problem of what to do with unburied corpses being heaped one upon another during times of war (*tante strage cadauerum*; *ciu. Dei* 1.12; CCSL 47.13). Here the concern is more practical: "Will the beasts which devour the dead impede their resurrection?" Of course not, Augustine insists: "There were, then, many Christian bodies that earth did not cover, but no one has separated even one of them from heaven, or from earth, which is wholly filled with the presence of him who knows from where he will raise that which he created" (*ciu. Dei* 1.12; Babcock, 1.14–15).

The third misfortune under review is not the problem of those who did not die in the siege of AD 410, but of those who were placed in captivity. Augustine is quick to point out that this is not as serious a calamity for the Christian as it is for the Pagan because the follower of the one universal God can worship anywhere on earth, and in any situation, citing biblical stories recounting the captivity of Daniel and Jonah. However, it is a Roman to whom our author gives the most attention, Marcus Regulus: a story, albeit fanciful, which was especially popular with the Roman aristocracy. Marcus Regulus was a general in the Roman army when he was captured in 256 BC by the Carthaginians during the First Punic War.

Augustine relates the story that, most surely encountered in Horace's *Odes* (3.5), Marcus Regulus was held up as the paragon of civic virtue and a stellar example of the power of Roman oath-taking. As the legend goes, Regulus was a prominent general in early Roman history who was captured and held by the Carthaginians, themselves notorious for brokering the exchange of prisoners, always to their own advantage. As such, they sent Regulus, escorted by a detachment of their own soldiers, back to Rome in exchange for many of their own men who were being held captive by the Romans. Once back on his native soil, most Romans expected Regulus to denounce and even slay the Carthaginian ambassadors. To the surprise of the Roman Senate, however, Regulus asked to go back to Carthage, as he had promised he would if he could not successfully negotatiate the release of the captive Carthaginians. Upon his return, the Carthaginians "shut him in a narrow box in which he was forced to stand upright. The box was studded on all sides with the sharpest nails so that he could not lean in any direction without horrible pain; and so they killed him by keeping him awake" (*ciu. Dei* 1.15; Babcock, 1.17). Recalling this story not only allows Augustine to demonstate his admiration of the natural courage of the Romans – and perhaps win over a sympathetic reader – but also enables him to highlight the inefficacy of the Roman pantheon.

That is, it seems that if anyone were to be blessed by the gods and goddesses of Roman history, it would be the exceptionally heroic figure of Marcus Regulus. He fought valiantly for Rome, he kept his oath and was utterly loyal, and he went to his death bravely and with dignity. But, in the end, such piety failed him thereby only serving to reinforce Augustine's main arguments in these early books: "the gods are of no use to their worshippers so far as temporal happiness is concerned" (*ciu. Dei* 1.15; Babcock, 1.17). But, perhaps, our author can hear his detractors ask: "What if Marcus was rewarded with the perfect tranquility of the afterlife?" Perhaps, Augustine himself admits, but that only shows that the divine is not to be worshipped for the sake of external goods or temporal advantages. Perhaps, after all, *true* religion is meant for the pilgrim and not the politician. If so, Augustine's recalling of Roman virtue has helped his readers come one step closer to understanding the God of the Christians who promises no ease in this life but who will bless and hear the prayers of all those who are now "awaiting a heavenly homeland with true faith, know[ing] that they are pilgrims even in their own homes" (*ciu. Dei* 1.15; Babcock, 1.18).

RAPE AND SUICIDE (1.16–29)

Moving from Marcus Regulus to other Roman figures who have long perished, Augustine has now set himself up to discuss a particularly ugly form of death: suicide. A large portion of this segment of Book 1 is dedicated to the ugly tactic of the enemy's raping women during war time because such an evil raised the question of the liceity of a woman's taking her own life so as to avoid such an atrocity. While Augustine admits that this is not a situation that is explicitly addressed in the Christian scriptures, he understands – through the consistent teachings of the church and the support of his philosophical tradition – that both of these actions are inherently evil. While one is a sin against human dignity and the other against the giftedness of human life, both are contrary to justice.

Augustine begins this section by admitting that no vulnerable woman was spared during the Sack of Rome: married women, maidens intent on marrying, and even "women consecrated to the religious life" were violated by Alaric's men. However, Augustine is quick to assure his readers that, regardless of the horrific nature of the tales he is about to recount, neither faith (*fides*), nor godliness (*pietas*), nor even the virtue of chastity (*castitas*) can be wrested and ruined by a mere human (*ciu. Dei* 1.16; Babcock, 1.19; CCSL 47.17). In a rare admission Augustine warns his readers that this section is meant not for the non-catholic interlocutor but for "our own" (*ipsis nostris*). Why so? It is because the argument to be laid out has nothing to do with the proud Roman view of the body but everything to do with the Christian understanding that it is the holiness of the will that makes the body itself a temple of God: "so as long as the will remains steadfast and unshaken, nothing that anyone else does with the body or to the body – and that cannot be avoided by the person who suffers it without some sin on his own part – brings any blame to the one who undergoes it" (*ciu. Dei* 1.16;

Babcock, 1.19; CCSL 47.17). This is why a bishop can advise victims of rape that, even though they may have experienced some shame (*pudor*), they are in no way guilty for what they had done to their bodies while their minds remained resolutely the Lord's.

That is why the Roman proclivity to take one's life instead of undergoing the ignobilities of rape has to be addressed. In order to do this, Augustine will weave together the tragic example of Judas with Roman legal history. For it is telling that the next figure Augustine presents at this point is Judas, the famous suicide victim who chose his own sad departure over the Lord's forgiveness. Judas could have turned back to Jesus, contrite and sorrowful, but instead compounded his "vicious act of betrayal" by unnecessarily taking his own life: "he killed himself for one crime by committing another." How much more so should a person who is innocent of actively intending a criminal act not take her life. In fact, it seems this person commits an even greater crime; for Judas was guilty but the women who take their lives so as to avoid sexual violation take the life of an innocent person: "Why should she perpetrate on herself a sin of her own to keep another's sin from being perpetrated on her?" (*ciu. Dei* 1.17; Babcock, 1.19; slightly adjusted).

To reinforce this argument for innocence, Augustine dedicates an entire section (*ciu. Dei* 1.18) to the virtue of purity. Augustine argues that purity is a spiritual state, a gift to those willing to desire purity of heart. It is a gift that cannot be taken from anyone unwillingly. Whereas we cannot determine what happens to our flesh, our minds are presented here as mini-sanctuaries which no external marauder can invade. This purity of mind (*uirtus animi*) depends on neither bodily integrity nor created goods:

> What makes the body holy is not that its members are intact or that they have not been defiled by touch ... Let us rather learn from this that the body's holiness is not lost as long as the mind's holiness remains, even when the body itself is overpowered, just as, in contrast, the body's holiness is lost as soon as the mind's holiness is violated, even if the body itself is still intact.
>
> (*ciu. Dei* 1.18; Babcock, 1.20)

To make his point as appealing as possible to the widest audience possible, Augustine now transitions into a story held sacred by all Romans, the legend of the Roman noblewoman Lucretia.

According to Livy's *History of Rome* (1.57–59), Lucretia was raped by the Roman king's son, Sextus Tarquinius, in 508 BC. Instead of concealing this deplorable act, she told her husband Collatinus and her kinsman Brutus what had happened and they immediately sought revenge. But, in the meantime, the shame became too much for her; in her confusion she succumbed to suicide. Thus, Augustine poses the question: "Should she be judged adulterous or chaste? Who can think it worth laboring over the issue?" (*ciu. Dei* 1.19; Babcock, 1.21). As a pastor himself, Augustine's sympathy pours through these words, defending Lucretia's bodily integrity over and over; as a bishop, however, Augustine must also teach in the public court what is true and here is where his gentleness with Lucretia takes on a more critical hue:

> If someone were to bring this case before your tribunal, then, and it were proved to you that a woman had been put to death who was not only uncondemned but in fact chaste and innocent, would you not punish the person who had done this will all due severity? But this is exactly what Lucretia did: Lucretia – the much celebrated Lucretia – did away with the innocent and chaste Lucretia, the victim of violence.
>
> (*ciu. Dei* 1.19; Babcock. 1.21)

In Augustine's contemporary context, the act of suicide was widely condemned as both unnatural and unjust. It robs one from oneself and the goods of this temporal order. That is, the taking of one's own life is not only unnatural, it is also a grave offense against the community of organically united human persons.

Plato records Socrates proclaiming at the end of his life – when he was *being forced* to drink hemlock that: "A person must never kill himself until God sends some necessity such as the one which now attends me" (*Phaedo* 62c). Cicero views suicide as a fundamental contradiction against the natural law's inherent propulsion toward self-preservation, even for those who may find life in general, and their life in particular, a burden: "it is clear that even for the foolish, who are also miserable, it is appropriate to remain alive if they possess a predominance of those things which we pronounce to be in accordance with nature" (*De finibus* 3.60). Given such precedence, we might be surprised by Augustine's tactic when addressing suicide. For it appears that it is not a moral absolute.

That is, after treating all the factors involved in Lucretia's case, our bishop knows he has to take on his own biblical tradition. Here, three Old Testament stories are brought together: (1) the Akedah and Abraham's possible sacrifice of Isaac at Gen 22:114, (2) Japhthah's vow to kill his daughter at Jgs 11:30–40, and (3) the unique situation of the last of the Israelite Judges, Samson, as depicted in Jgs 13–16. These are what Augustine conveniently calls "certain exceptions" (*Quasdam uero exceptiones ... diuina auctoritas*) ordered by God himself. Augustine is employing all his hermeneutical strength to make sense of these biblical heroes who choose to take life in very exceptional circumstances. How could Lucretia or Cato be deprived the same divine dispensation?

The answer comes by way of the one true God's rightful ownership of *all* life and his ability to exonerate those who acted to carry out his commands. God is the supremely just judge to whom all are eternally indebted, and when he asks for the life of someone, all the fallen are already eternally beholden to him. There is no life that does not already belong to God. Thus, he can exact the life of anyone "either by a law he provided or by an express command applying to a particular person at a particular time." Presumably, what God could never do is command Adam to take the life of Eve before the Fall (a test case Augustine does not entertain here), but now that all have "died" in Adam, all life is subject to God's providential ways. As such, when these biblical figures took a life, and especially when Samson voluntarily killed himself during his slaughter of the Philistines, were acting "like a sword, an instrument in the user's hand" (*ciu. Dei* 1.21; Babcock, 1.24). The true faithful must trust that God is neither capricious nor a moral monster who simply – and, it could be said, fickly – calls for the death of whomever he wills. God is the author of all life, and in this context is even named "the fount of justice," and in secretly asking some to take innocent life, he is simply carrying out his inscrutable will.

The final two instances of well-known suicides are those of Theombrotus and Cato. The first represents the sort of philosophical fatalism which was popular in some circles in the ancient world, while the second represents Roman resoluteness and the unwillingness to be ruled by a dictator at whatever cost. Theombrotus (fl. 300 BC) was a Cynic philosopher who was renowned for his greatness of soul. However, as Augustine is keen to emphasize, magnanimity without wisdom is very dangerous. As the legend goes, after he learned about Plato's resolute stance on the soul's immortality, he promptly threw himself off a high wall, expecting to be freed from his body and thus enjoy eternal spiritual bliss. In a rather condescending tone, Augustine continues by stating that, if he had only read a little more Plato, Theombrotus would have learned all of Plato's directives against suicide and surmised that not all great acts are necessarily good acts; besides, if Plato would have encouraged such conduct, he himself would have certainly lead the way.

The life and death of Cato the Younger (d. 46 BC) is more illustrative. Whereas Theombrotus represents a sort of philosophical farce,

Cato was a political figure held in high esteem even in Augustine's own day. Known for his sense of justice and hatred of tyranny, Cato spent most of the last decade of his life attempting to wrest power from Julius Caesar on the grounds that it had been seized and not offered. Thus, when Caesar led the XIII Legion across the Rubicon in January of 49 BC, thereby declaring civil war and open hostility against the Roman Senate, Cato fled to Sicily in the hope of securing Rome's supply of grain. After years spent as a fugitive, a Roman militia finally cornered Cato in the Tunisian town of Utica where he fell on his own sword in a final act defiance of Caesar, stating that he would rather die than be ruled or even pardoned by such an autocrat. While many ancient authors regarded Cato – in some cases devoutly – as a man who was willing to die rather than serve a despot, Augustine concludes his treatment here by instead holding up two different kinds of hero: Marcus Regulus, a man willing to endure injustice "in servitude rather than to escape from them by dying," and the biblical hero Job, an individual who also "chose to endure horrendous evils in his flesh rather than to rid himself of all these torments by putting himself to death" (*ciu. Dei* 1.24; Babcock, 1.26). With this, Augustine has now made explicit the Roman acceptance of suicide and the Roman inability to live without comfort. Part of the Roman's sacred tradition accepted the taking – by free will – of one's own life as preferable to living with the perceived burdens of injustice or chronic loss. Since Augustine spends more than half of Book 1 discussing the issue of viewing suicide as a solution to personal degradation, this must have still been a popular choice during the Sack of Rome in AD 410. However, Augustine concludes that the fuel behind such destructive behavior is a more prevalent problem inherent in the Roman way of life, the desire for comfort and the drive to obtain a life free from the vicissitudes of basic human existence.

THE DANGERS OF *LUXURIA* (1.30–34)

The final five sections of Book 1 condemn the Roman love of pleasure, especially their penchant for theatrical games. We begin with Cato the Elder (d. 149 BC) and his famous phrase, "*Carthago delenda est*" – "Carthage must be destroyed."[4] In this call to arms Augustine hears only the Roman desire for temporal ease and self-indulgence without restraint. While confusing Scipio Nasica (consul in 191 BC) with his son

[4] Plutarch, *The Parallel Lives*, see The Life of Cato the Elder, §27.

Scipio Nasica Corculum (consul in 162 BC and 155 BC), Augustine's point is that Cato wanted Rome to live without any enemies, without any restraints, while Scipio (the younger), "your chief pontiff, the best of men in the judgment of the whole senate, opposed the destruction of Carthage" (*ciu. Dei* 1.30; Babcock, 1.32). Scipio Nasica, a man entrusted with a divine office, a man so highly regarded in the political arena, wisely saw how an unchecked Rome would lead to an enervating extravagance, further laying bare the inescapable Roman *libido dominandi*, a phrase used twice in this section alone:

> And the lust for domination – which, of all the human vices, is found in its most undiluted form in the whole Roman people – after winning the day in a few of the more powerful, oppressed the rest, worn out and exhausted, under the yoke of servitude.
>
> For, once it is embedded in the arrogant minds, where can the lust for domination come to rest until, by passing from office to office, it has reached despotic power? ... And what makes a people avaricious and extravagant is prosperity – the very thing Nasica, with great foresight, voted to guard against when he opposed destroying the enemy's largest, strongest and wealthiest city. His aim was to keep lust under the restraint of fear so that lust, thus restrained, would not indulge itself in extravagance.
>
> (*ciu. Dei* 1.30–31; Babcock, 1.32–33)

Augustine thus praises Scipio Nasica Corculum's foresight in understanding that, without an enemy to keep Rome alert and vigilant, the Roman predisposition for *luxuria* would inevitably flow unchecked. Perhaps, in the long run, civilizations bent on dominance need a foe whose mere existence requires them to be ever cautious and attentive to the higher things of justice.

As fulsome as the praise is here, Nasica is not without censure in Augustine's estimation. While he showed great prudence when standing up to Cato, he failed to suppress the very spectacles that only served to fuel Roman indulgence. One example of this unrestrained lust stands in front of every Roman still today, the rise of theatrical shows. Blood sport and theatrical ribaldry increased since the destruction of Carthage. Having lost the sense of battle and the resultant need for vigilance and valor, even during times of supposed peace, Rome has grown morally lax. But Bishop Augustine, a convert from sport and theatrical madness himself (cf. *conf.* 3.1–5), is critical not only the content of such shows – the games filled with bloodlust and the stage with sexual promiscuity – but even more so of the faulty theology which buttresses such spectacles.

Such a man as Corculum "would also have banished theatrical performances themselves from the city of Rome, if only he had dared to resist the authority of those he imagined to be gods" (*ciu. Dei* 1.31; Babcock, 1.33). Here again is a powerful reflection of the entire argument of *ciu. Dei*: spiritual excellence, a well-ordered society, and the proper worship of the proper God cannot be separated. Nasica Corculum was a good man who ostensibly thirsted for real virtue and risked public derision for doing so. Yet, he was blindly beholden to a religious system that demanded sport – both bloody and brutal – and the praise of theatrical folly. If only he would have come to "understand that these gods are actually pernicious demons" (*noxios daemones*; *ciu. Dei* 1.31; Babcock, 1.33; CCSL 47.32). If only Nasica had been a priest of right religion, he could have condemned sin correctly and he himself would have been freed "from the domination of prideful demons" (*a dominatu superborum daemonum liberaret*; *ciu. Dei* 1.31; Babcock, 1.33; CCSL 47.32) which is precisely the faulty theological foundation of Rome's own desire for worldly domination.

Augustine's critique of the Roman games mirror that of other contemporary scribes. Tertullian's *De Spectaculis* (c. AD 200) condemns the attendance of Christians to the empty allure of both amphitheater and the stage because such cultural attractions are ultimately based on idolatry. A pseudo-Cyprianic work of the same title (often attributed to the antipope Novatian; d. AD 258), teaches that the thrill of the spectacle and the energetic intimacy of community sought in the games can be even more intensely experienced in church's gathering for liturgy. Augustine continues this critique not by looking at the content of such activities but by pointing to the "unpunished extravagance" sought through pagan culture, applying the ancient forewarnings of Nasica Corculum to the Sack of Rome in AD 410:

> Scipio wanted you to live in terror of the enemy, so that you would not sink into extravagant living; but, even when crushed by the enemy, you have not suppressed your extravagance. You have lost the change of gaining from calamity; you have become utterly wretched while, at the same time, you remained utterly foul.
> (*ciu. Dei* 1.33; Babcock, 1.34)

But this is precisely why God has allowed the Romans to survive even invasion, and this is how they should view contemporary political events: always and everywhere as God's invitation to embrace their blessings in Christian gratitude, or to learn from their misfortunes through repentance.

CONCLUSION (1.35 & 1.36)

After all, cities and cultures come and go, but the human soul is eternal. This is where God's real concern lies, and this is where his locus of activity is discerned. Accordingly, the temporal misfortunes of people are ultimately to be read as an invitation for personal purification, something Augustine preached about increasingly after AD 410:

> Perhaps Rome isn't destroyed; perhaps it has been scourged, not put to death, chastised perhaps, not obliterated. Perhaps Rome isn't perishing, if Romans aren't perishing. I mean, they won't perish, if they praise God; they will, if they blaspheme him. What is Rome, after all, but Romans? I mean, we are not concerned with bricks and mortar, with high apartment blocks and extensive city walls.[5]

Augustine the Historian, Augustine the Bishop, Augustine the Christian now sets out – over the course of twenty-one more books – to make this specific point: that the City of God is better equipped to estimate the blessings and burdens of Roman history because its clear vision is obtained through its "participation in the sacraments" of Christ's church (*ciu. Dei* 1.35; Babcock, 1.25; *conexos communion sacramentorum*; CCSL 47). Even though still on pilgrimage, the City of God is united to the Eternal Truth of man created by God, and this connection is what defines any people rightly, and this alone provides history with intelligibility, integrity, and purpose. This is why Augustine trusts in God's help only in setting out "what should be said about the origin, the course, and the appointed end of the two cities" (*ciu. Dei* 1.35; Babcock, 1.25; *conexos communion sacramentorum*; CCSL 47). For it is clear that the old ways of Rome are clearly perishing, and its veteran voices are shouting out against Christian novelty and the supposed abandonment of the deities who have protected the empire for so long. However, we discovere that this proves to be a sort of inset into the entire work itself: Rome's gods and goddesses are not faithful because they are nothing other than proud demons, even though Rome is being used as a vehicle for the one true God's providential purposes and Augustine will help his readers see how the heroes and happenings of history are to be understood properly.

Augustine addressed four central themes in Book 1 of *ciu. Dei*. The first is the importance of sanctuary, a theopolitical strategy now universally afforded to asylum seekers, a right never consistently afforded in

[5] *s.* 81.9; Hill (III/3) 365.

the pre-Christian world. The second is a theological examination of the nature and role of divine providence, focusing on the issue, the "problem," of why God allows human suffering. This leads to the third – and most extensive – theme: the cruelties of war, as evidenced by the rape of innocent women and the resulting suicide of the victims so as to avoid – in their eyes – such degradation. Book 1 concludes with a critique of the Spectacles embedded in Roman culture as a covert form of idolatry and the fruit of spiritual sloth. In an attempt to emphasize these convergences between heavenly and earthly activity, Augustine draws from stories of both Roman heroes as well as Catholic saints to illustrate how the Logos of the Christians has been both the inspiriation as well as the goal of the Roman Empire's qusest for true virtue and happiness.

This strategy is aimed at winning the sympathies of all of his readers, hoping to not only attract like-minded Catholics but also convince those weeping over the carnage of AD 410 that this catastrophe could be a great blessing, if only united to the Cross. Rome is on the way but must eventually admit that it is not the Way. Augustine could certainly imagine Rome as a godly city, but it was clearly not the City of God. Instead, the Bishop of Hippo needs to continue his examination of all that Rome holds dear to show his readers how Hebrew perseverance, Greek wisdom, and Roman industry are all faint reflections of the fullness of reality found in the Triune God. For this, we now embark on a lengthy sojourn of history, philosophy, political records, and liturgical practices. In the books that follow, we must thus be ready to read both a review of the past and a promise of the future, a critique of culture without Christ and the promise of fulfillment of life in Christ, an aversion to *ciuitas terrena*, and a graced surrender to the *ciuitas Dei*.

FURTHER READING

Herdt, J. A. (2008). *Putting on Virtue: The Legacy of the Splendid Vices*. Chicago: University of Chicago Press.

Lienhard, J. (1999). Paulinus of Nola. In A. Fitzgerald, ed., *Augustine through the Ages*. Grand Rapids, MI: Eerdmans, pp. 628–629.

Webb, M. (2015). Samson, Abraham, and "Certain Holy Women": Augustine on Suicide and Rape in City of God 1.26. In D. Meconi, ed., *Sacred Scripture and Secular Struggle*. Leiden: Brill, pp. 201–234.

3 Book 2: Augustine on Religion without Morality

OLIVER O'DONOVAN

The predominant theme of *ciu. Dei* 2, which sets the course for Augustine's critique of ancient Rome, is the disastrous influence of a religion without public moral teaching to offer. In exploring his treatment of that theme, we must first pause over the word 'religion', which is ours and not Augustine's. 'Religion and morality' is the way we would naturally pose the question, and more commonly talk about morality without religion than about religion without morality. Augustine could also have expressed his question in our way. He uses the word *ritus* (plural), sometimes in phrases, as *ritus sacri, ritus religionis,* in ways that correspond sufficiently to our use of the term 'religion', and on one occasion he even refers to 'religion and morality' (*ritibus moribusque*; *ciu. Dei* 14.1). But he states the question in terms of the conduct of demons, really existing powers that are worshipped as gods in Roman religion, who have failed to provide the city with laws and its worshippers with moral instruction, and who have peremptorily demanded the homage of corrupting theatrical productions.

The first question an interpreter has to face, then, is how mutually convertible the two ways of stating the matter are. If a translation cannot be admitted, Augustine's primary contentions in this part of the *ciu. Dei* are out of reach for most contemporary Western readers, and discussing them is essentially an antiquarian task. If, on the other hand, it is possible to capture Augustine's interest within the categories of 'religion', the way lies open for his discussions to make a contribution to our own. We had better acknowledge that the translation is not a perfect one. 'Religion' is a generic category, capable of many instantiations. But Augustine does not generally speak about the class of religions; he speaks of one religious culture, which failed to communicate moral teaching, and one other moralised religious culture that supervened to replace it – the cultures of pagan and Christian Rome respectively. At various points he compares these with other historical religious cultures, the culture of Greece on the one hand and that of

Israel on the other, but never to draw out continuities and establish the generic characteristics of the category 'religion'. He ventures on no generalisations that could sum up the experience of all religions. He is more strictly historical in his interpretation of pre-Christian and Christian Rome than our reformulation allows us to be. By framing his proposition in terms of demonic activity, moreover, Augustine is able to make certain claims that our formulation does not allow to be made, especially that the morally debased character of Roman religion was the result of deliberate malice. By attributing agency to the demons he can construe the history of religion as a drama in which the Romans, however much they colluded, were imposed on and deceived, which in turn allows him to treat Roman history as something other than a lost cause. There is a point of purchase for him to plead for a self-critical awakening and a change of mind in the powerful appeal that forms the climax of the book (*ciu. Dei* 2.29). Romans may turn from their demoralised religious past without repudiating whatever was genuinely glorious about it.

In evaluating these historically contextual elements of his argument we are more or less bound to be onlookers rather than participants. Even if we agree to make no difficulty about the existence of demons, the demons of ancient Rome are not our own demons. Yet we should not conclude that there is nothing in his argument for us to appropriate. Our category 'religion' has sometimes been suspected of being a pseudo-category, on the ground that it groups together diverse and distinct cultural-historical experiences and pretends to treat them as a generic kind of thing that is actually too loose to describe. Augustine would not have accepted that, and there is no reason for us to. However diverse the members of the class 'religion' may be, it is constituted by certain recognisable kinds of practice (*ritus*), and may be subdivided into two types, in which those practices are, and are not, bound up with positive instruction and guidance on living the human life. Our welfare depends very considerably on which of the types we embrace. Up to that point both the reader and Augustine are capable of understanding each other very well, which is what makes his claims seem rather pointed and relevant, perhaps painfully so, to our own cultural condition.

The other key expression – 'morality' – presents less difficulty. It corresponds more or less comfortably to Augustine's word *mores*, which appears prominently in the announcement of the main theme of the book. Though lengthily prepared for, the announcement still bursts on Augustine's readers as a surprise. From the Confessions onwards,

Augustine's habit in his larger-scale works is to situate long introductions to individual books at structurally critical points, indicating the opening of a new major section of the work as a whole. The introduction to *ciu. Dei* 2 lasts three chapters in the conventional numeration. The first of these is one of a handful of fascinating methodological excursuses on the genre of apologetic, arguing that it should not consist merely of responses to objections and challenges as they arise, but should be a sustained exposition of a position. In the second chapter Augustine looks back to the first book and explains that the greater part of it, defending the amorality of historical disasters, was no more than a preliminary digression preparing the way for the main argument of the first part of the work, now to begin. That argument, addressed to historically illiterate critics of Christianity who conform to the old adage, 'When the rain doesn't fall, blame the Christians!', will catalogue the disasters that befell pre-Christian Rome from its foundation onwards, containing nothing unfamiliar to those instructed in Roman history (*ciu. Dei* 2.3). So much, then, to tell us where we are going. But it has not in the least prepared us for the opening words of *ciu. Dei* 2.4: *Primo ipsos mores* ... 'First among the disasters was their morality! Why did their gods refuse to take any steps to protect them against that?'

It is the public teaching of morality that concerns Augustine – which is to say, teaching capable of shaping the character of a whole society. He will not allow that the mystery-religions, those enclaves of devotees cultivating esoteric moral instruction could ever be a satisfactory substitute for a fully public religious morality (*ciu. Dei* 2.6). In the general enthusiasm of Augustine's interpreters of the last generation to mark the distance that separates him from the ideology of Constantinian Christendom (an enthusiasm which has some sound justification), it is important not to overlook his position as a defender and advocate of the public realm.[1] At the outset (*ciu. Dei* 2.4) he challenges the individualism that would view moral failure and success as a purely personal matter: *quod voluntate propria quisque malus est*. Moral failure is cultural, and moral teaching is an essential politico-cultural resource which 'the gods', as responsible for all public goods, must be expected to supply. He expects those shaped by a Roman culture to recognise that the

[1] We owe the trend supremely to R. A. Markus' *Saeculum* (Markus 1970) which transformed the discussion of Augustine's political thought, making its case more carefully, and with much greater textual richness, than most of its predecessors. The recent death of this humble and generous scholar invites the observation that he was the first to free Augustine's political thought from the shackles of the medieval *florilegia*.

privatisation of moral principles – 'concealing decency and exposing indecency', as he ferociously expresses it later on (*decus latet, dedecus patet*; *ciu. Dei* 2.26.1) – is a reproach to pagan religious culture. At the heart of his defence of the influence of Christianity on Roman culture lies its programme for the regeneration of public morals.

It is moral teaching, in the second place, that Roman religion had failed to give. The noun he uses most is *praecepta*, which we may interpret as 'commands' or, in contrast to *leges*, 'counsels', which will help the Romans 'live well' (*ciu. Dei* 2.4). Either way, the need is for prescriptive instruction. It is not that pagan religion was without demands. In ritual matters its claims were 'imperious and, to a degree, oppressive' (*ciu. Dei* 2.8). Nor was it without influence on the ordinary life of men and women. Closely associated with Roman religion in Augustine's interpretation of Roman cultural history was the institution of the theatre, with its enthralling models of passionate behaviour projected onto divine and heroic characters, deeply formative of Roman morality in practice, he believed, and with appalling effect. The explicit public displays at the annual ceremony of the Virgin Mother of Berecynthus taught decent Roman married women, looking at them through their fingers while pretending to hide their faces, the postures required for the more indecent types of sexual encounter (*ciu. Dei* 2.26).

There is a famous distinction originating with Aristotle between 'ethics' and 'ethos', between specific principles consciously adopted, on the one hand, and intuitive evaluations transmitted by cultural habituation on the other. Among recent moral thinkers it is common enough to meet the suggestion that 'ethos' is of greater formative value than 'ethics'. Augustine, who made no such distinction, would not have agreed at all. What he describes in pagan Rome is effectively a common ethos, a set of values assumed within the social and religious practices of Roman culture, transmitted by example and unconscious influence. Occasionally Augustine describes its mode of cultural transmission as *adulatio*: 'What rational ground do they have for choosing gods – especially these false ones? Is it not mere adulation, rather?' (*ciu. Dei* 2.15).[2] *Adulatio* does not fare well in English translation.[3] It is not simply a matter of fawning on figures of power and prominence, but a wide-

[2] Also at *ciu. Dei* 3.15, 10.4,11, and 21.30.

[3] English translators converge upon 'flattery', sometimes qualified as 'cringing' (Henry Bettenson) or 'servile' (George E. McCracken). But it is not at all clear how flattery could be a motive for preferring one god to another. What is in question is an irrational impressionability and subservience to received opinion. Wilhelm Thimme's German translation makes happy use of the resources of its language with *Unterwürflichkeit*.

ranging impressionability, a readiness to be shaped wholly by the iconic symbols of the culture, exercising no critical reflection on the norms that they embody. It covers partisan loyalty, crowd behaviour, the collective attachment of a gang to its leaders, the client-patron relationship, and, of course, the relation of stage-player to audience. One reason that pagan religion was disastrous for Rome, in Augustine's view, was that it suppressed the capacity for reflective criticism rather than developing it. It had no 'teaching', no principles, no rational communication of how human beings might order their lives to attain what he and they will have called 'happiness', i.e. 'fulfilment' or 'self-realisation'. Romans therefore lacked the essential ingredient of freedom, which was the capacity for rational self-direction. This lack was demonstrated by a rift of a most destructive kind within Roman culture between religion, on the one hand, and non-religious sources of morality on the other. Where rational and critical norms of conduct were introduced – always, Augustine insists, as external influences from Greece – these norms, philosophical and legal, lived in unhappy tension with the prevailing myths and aspirations of society.

For the Romans had by no means been without elements of sound morality. This book, like the fourth and fifth, is as much about the ambiguous character of the good moral instincts Romans did acquire as about the demoralising tendency of the religion which not only failed to promote them, but actually subverted them. The best Romans in history are presented as the most unhappily divided in their minds and inconsistent in their practice, notably two members of the Cornelius Scipio family – Africanus and Nasica – and their later admirer Cicero, that 'serious man and dabbler in philosophy' (*ciu. Dei* 2.27), whose example closes the book. Cicero's intellectual influence on Augustine, evident almost on every page, does not entitle him to be called a philosopher, for as a Roman statesman Cicero lacked the moral consistency that philosophy requires; his scepticism about Roman religion did not restrain him from laying on lavish games at a moment of political crisis. It is important that we should not overlook the significance of Augustine's repeated reference (*ciu. Dei* 2.4, 2.26) to his own youthful experience in attending the *spectacula* of the Heavenly Virgin and the Mother Berecynthia, which brought home to him personally, while still in his pre-Christian period, the moral tension created by publicly promoted obscenities. This tension is then projected back upon Scipio Nasica, who had been responsible for introducing the cult. Roman republican culture is depicted as an unresolved struggle between certain positive natural moral qualities (after *ciu. Dei* 1 Augustine avoids referring to them as 'virtues', as he explains in Book 5, just as he refrains from referring to 'justice' in connexion with ancient Rome; *ciu. Dei* 2.21.4) and the demonic deception that will bring these positive qualities to nothing.

The most sustained discussion in the first half of the book is that of the relation of Roman religion to the theatre (*ciu. Dei* 2.8ff.) The difference between the Greek and Roman treatment of actors and poets brings out eloquently the ambivalence which thoughtful Romans felt to public religion and the contradictions in which it involved them. In the ancient world theatre, even at its artistic height in Greek tragedy, was always framed as a religious performance, and Augustine, using the general term *spectacula*, nicely conveyed by the English 'shows', believes that its connexion with religion was tight and inseparable. The Greeks were consistent in treating actors as equivalent in status to priests. The Romans displayed no such consistency: they showed public disrespect for actors, depriving them of full citizens' rights, yet in no way applied the same strictures to the poets, the writers whose lascivious invention gave the shows their character. On the one hand, the Romans – unlike the Greeks – had strict laws of libel, and would punish publications that detracted from the good character of a citizen, yet the gods were not protected in this way from poetic libels. While Augustine does not immediately declare in favour of the Greeks or the Romans, he finally makes it plain – in *ciu. Dei* 2.29 – that the divided mind of the Romans brought them closer to the truth than the logical consistency of the Greeks. There was, however, another pattern that Greek consistency could take, and that was the lonely high-principled calling of the true philosopher, illustrated by Plato, who famously suggested (while no one listened) that poets would be banned from the ideal city. Much of Augustine's discussion is inspired by these remarks from Plato's *Republic*.

There are three positive moralising influences that Augustine allows to have been at work in ancient Rome, the mystery religions, philosophy and law. Mystery religions receive the barest and most contemptuous treatment, as 'whispers breathed into a few select ears and communicated by secret ritual for instruction in a decent honest life' (*ciu. Dei* 2.6). Such effects as they may have had on individuals were negligible within the public realm. The point is reinforced by a striking comment on the architectural legacy of pagan Rome: it left no public buildings dedicated to instruction. Public buildings were constructed as theatres to enable the public to watch performances, rather than as auditoria to enable public listening and learning (*ciu. Dei* 2.6). The difference Christianity made to the culture is seen in the visible presence of churches: buildings dedicated to reading and teaching.

Of the two non-religious moral influences he has broadly similar things to say: they were foreign borrowings from Greece, not original to Roman civilisation; they were of human, not of divine origin; the value of their contents was mixed, but with many positive features; their effect upon the Roman ethos was decisively subverted by religion. A feature of the mythical history of the early Roman republic that throws a harsh light upon its primitive character is that the city was supposed to have got along without any laws until the reign of Numa Pompilius, third in the line of kings. Augustine shows little inclination to criticise Roman laws as such, and some ancient Roman laws, including that which denied actors full civil status, command his admiration. But the political and cultural identity of the city was not strongly determined by its laws, and those laws were in any case not conceived to have divine sanction. It would have been altogether better for the culture to be founded on divine laws than on the ambiguous mix of ancient laws and customary practices which in fact shaped it.

It is the contrast between philosophy and religion that absorbs the greater part of Augustine's attention. Though of human rational devising and a mixture of truth and error that is liable to encourage pride, philosophy would have been a better occupant of the place given in Rome to religion. The divinisation of Romulus is discussed three times (*ciu. Dei* 2.15, 18.24, and 22.4–6), and Cicero's quietly sceptical treatment in *De Republica* lies behind all three. The first discussion is an ironic passage toward the end of our first section (*ciu. Dei* 2:15), where Romulus' claims to divine status are compared with those of Plato. The occasion for this is given by the obscure chronicler of religious lore Labeo, who informed Augustine that Romulus' status as 'demi-god' (*semideus*) put him in the company of such a very unexpected recruit to the Roman pantheon as Plato – a recondite piece of learning, indeed, since in practice Plato 'was not thought worth a single shrine', while Romulus enjoyed the extraordinary honour of a flamen, making him the match in dignity of only Jupiter and Mars. Given this alternative, Romans might at least have preferred the god who would have given them comprehensive laws and instructed them on resisting their cravings! In the light of a tissue of references to Romulus that run through *ciu. Dei* from first book to last this passage assumes a rather greater weight in Augustine's argument than might be apparent. The important point it makes is that the earliest and most decisive religious settlement in early Rome was not that of the cultic importations of Numa Pompilius, but was the city's original adoration of its founder.

While Roman law could be dismissed as a foreign borrowing, Roman religion lay at the heart of Roman identity, because the city was founded on its initial 'error of love' in deifying Romulus, a superstition with which it then grew up, 'drinking it in, as it were, with its mother's milk' (*ciu. Dei* 22.6). Rome began as it was to go on, free of the influence of legal or moral instruction, its cultic practices governed solely by *adulatio*.

Book 2 divides fairly clearly into two major sections (*ciu. Dei* 2.4–16 and 2.17–29), of which the first presents the uneven balance sheet of Rome's moral profit and loss. The second complicates the account by treating the question of religion and morality from a historical point of view. The aim is to show that it is impossible to construct a moral history of Rome without coming face to face with the profound injustice that reigned over its history from the beginning and the positive collusion of Roman religion with that state of affairs. The object of Augustine's critique here is a nostalgic narrative of decline: a Rome which began as a model of primitive virtue degenerated into self-indulgent partisan violence that finally brought the republican period to an end. This was a narrative popular in writers of the late republic, and is represented here by two of the most eminent and best known from the educational curriculum, the historian Sallust and the philosopher-statesman Cicero.

Augustine's response occupies the second half of the book, and proceeds in two steps: (i) the early period down to the Carthaginian wars, nostalgically dressed out as an age of natural virtue, was in fact as barbarous and destructive as any other period in Rome's history, (ii) the period after the fall of Carthage, generally allowed to be one of violent collapse, was as much governed by religious influences as any other period in Rome's history.

Sallust's sketch of Rome's moral decline from primitive natural virtue is treated somewhat cursorily, though the historian's admission that the virtue of Rome flourished only until the fall of Carthage lifted the restraint of fear, is put to shrewd use against him. Augustine has already exploited some of Livy's narratives of the primitive period in the first book, and he will make further use of others later, so that here a few choice examples of treachery and ingratitude suffice, along with the somewhat more substantial observation that the early Republic proved incapable of resolving the question of justice between the patrician and plebeian parties. Lurking in the wings, however, is the more complicated argument about the moral character of early Rome, concerning, again, the original foundation of Romulus. References to Romulus' foundation in *ciu. Dei*, while tending to be casual and allusive, are a regular occurrence, and all tend to point in one direction.

Founder-kings, like Romulus and Alexander impose form upon their cities *uoluntate consilio imperio*, by act of will, by policy and by government (*ciu. Dei* 12.26) – and not by justice! The point becomes focussed upon the asylum for Rome's earliest citizens, first mentioned at the end of the first book (*ciu. Dei* 1.34), where attention is drawn to the 'striking parallel' between the asylum offered by Romulus and Remus at the city's foundation and that afforded to Romans escaping into Christian churches during the invasion of AD 410. For Romulus and Remus it was a serviceable means to strengthen numbers and security in the infant city, while for the Goths it accomplished only the security of their enemies. Since Augustine will not represent the Goths as Christians and their actions as instances of love for enemies within the City of God, their restraint is simply a mark of their religious awe before the dignity of Christ. The repetition of the pattern, then, is simply providential; it signals the undoing of cruel customs of war that make no distinction between the innocent and the guilty, customs that reflect the spirit of Rome, which made no distinction between the innocent and the guilty in its foundation. Though it is not a major feature of the argument in the second book, one reference to it in particular should not be overlooked: in the peroration (*ciu. Dei* 2.29.1) Augustine makes a direct contrast between the foundation of Rome and the foundation of the heavenly city, both of them created by an 'asylum'. Where ancient Rome gathered a citizen body of criminals and desperados by concealing criminal acts within a policy of impunity, the heavenly city gathers its citizen body by accomplishing the 'true remission of sins'.

Thus, Rome began as a gang of outlaws. The fact is recalled in the famous discussion of the continuity between *latrocinia* and *regna* at *ciu. Dei* 4.5:

> I pass over the question how to classify the community Romulus gathered round him. The question is prompted by the policy they conceived as most advantageous, that there should be no more question of the punishments to which, in forming a civil association, their manner of life would make them liable. Fear of punishment would drive them to greater criminality, and the aim was to coax them into a somewhat more pacific approach to human relations.[4]

[4] '*Proinde omitto quaerere quales Romulus congregauerit, quoniam multum eis consultum est, ut ex illa uita dato sibi consortio ciuitatis poenas debitas cogitare desisterent, quarum metus eos in maiora facinora propellebat, ut deinceps pacatiores essent rebus humanis.*' The major problem in translating the sentence is to determine how the phrase *ex illa uita* is attached. Translators usually attach it to *dato* …

Suspending the rule of civil punishment, the policy of asylum made early Rome's commitment to justice ambiguous. Yet it served a civilising function, to make them 'somewhat more pacific' – the comparative form is eloquent. As I understand this sentence, there is no hint of a transformation of the brigands' way of life before the experience of life in a city has that taming effect. They are not civilised simply by the act of entering the civil association, as in the Hobbesian social contract. Their criminal way of life is a persistent fact that they bring with them into the city, and so far from bringing it under the control of law, the city simply incorporates into its founding charter the immunity from law and justice they had always asserted by their brigandage. So Romulus' kingdom remains the band of robbers that it always was. The morally compromised character of Rome is foundational; in the course of civilising brigands, it embraced a good deal of brigandage.

Inevitably the assassination of Remus contributes to this picture of the early foundation. 'Unable to tolerate a brother's partnership', Romulus is the prototype of Roman lust for glory through competitive domination. When in recounting the primal narratives of Genesis Augustine comes to the story of Cain and Abel, the comparison with Romulus and Remus is irresistible: 'The first founder of the earthly city was a fratricide ... and therefore it is hardly surprising that in the foundation of that city which was to be head of this earthly city ... we see a reflection, an event of the same kind' (*ciu. Dei* 15.5). Envy, the hallmark of the earthly city as such, was the hallmark of the foundation of Rome. Yet the comparison once established, Augustine is no less interested in the difference between the two events. In the one case, the earthly city's founder envied his brother who was on pilgrimage to the heavenly city, in the other case the two brothers were both founders of the city. The envy of Cain, then, had a primal character; it was a 'diabolical envy', the envy of evil for good. The envy of Romulus, on the other hand, was merely a supreme instance of that competitive greed for undivided power which may fracture every form of earthly

ciuitatis, suggesting a change from 'that' way of life to political association. But this requires supplying a verb that is not present, while to take *dato ... ciuitatis* of the admission of members to political society fails to accommodate *sibi*. *Ex illa uita* can only depend, then, on *debitas*. *Dato* is best understood in the logical sense of 'granted' (*Oxford Latin Dictionary*, do 16). On the presumption of a civic association, punishments are 'due' for their way of life. (Augustine assumes that crimes committed outside the association would be prosecutable within it.) The terms of this association, then, are indeed those of a *latrocinium*, in which criminality is not held liable to punishment.

community. The episode of Remus' murder is first mentioned allusively in Book 3, as a demonstration of the inadequacy of poetic myth in proffering moral explanations of divine conduct: if the gods were so upset at the crimes of Paris as to abandon Troy, why did they treat the crime of Romulus with complacency? (*ciu. Dei* 3.6) This, therefore, invites a suggestive speculation: what if, after all, Romulus was not guilty of his brother's murder? 'Since the crime demanded punishment', he replies, 'the city as a whole, not caring to prosecute it, was responsible'. Remus, too, was the city's founder and father, so one way or the other the city as a corporate entity was guilty of parricide. The 'error of love' that deified Romulus, then, was simply an extension of the 'conflict and competition' that had produced Remus' death.

Augustine is interested in the moral character of the city as a collective entity, and he is interested in showing how from its foundation it could subsist politically although wholly negligent of justice. It becomes the type for a great deal of further reflection on the earthly city's independence of true justice. The point is taken up theoretically in *ciu. Dei* 2.21, where Augustine moves toward the second step in his rebuttal of the narrative of decline by recalling the version of it presented in Cicero's *De Republica* through the voice of Scipio Africanus, the historical conqueror of Carthage in the 2nd century BC. Though Augustine will embrace Cicero/Scipio's notion of Rome as a 'wholly demoralised republic' – *flagitiosissima respublica* – he will not endorse the conclusion that the Roman republic effectively ceased to exist, a conclusion which, for all its sober appearance, evades the significance of the moral collapse for Rome's collective agency, and clings with a certain complacency to the illusory ideal of a virtuous and well-ordered Rome which was never in fact realised in history. The logical implication of the conclusion, he insists, is that the Roman republic never did exist, and that is a *reductio ad absurdum*.

He has it in mind to demolish Cicero's idealising definition of a republic as a society united by common justice and common utility, and, in a striking demonstration of his planning for *ciu. Dei*, gives advance warning of the extended discussion of justice that will follow at *ciu. Dei* 19.21–28. At this point, however, his aim is simply to refuse Cicero the opportunity to drive a wedge between the virtuous early republic and the later vicious non-republic. The 'republic' was equally active, and equally true to its character, in both early and later periods. The republic's religion shaped events equally in both periods. The suggestion (with a pathetic allusion to Virgil's depiction of the gods' abandonment of Troy) that Rome lost the support of its gods as a result of moral decline, is treated with scorn. Far from abandoning Rome, its gods were never more active than in fomenting civil war. The rehearsal of the horrors of the Social Wars emphasises the part played by religious phenomena in shoring up the position of the most brutal of Rome's military leaders (*ciu. Dei* 2:22–25).

Augustine's interest in the moral and religious history of Rome, needless to say, has in view its final stage, the impact of Christianity with the Constantinian revolution of a century before. This presented Rome for the first time with an opportunity for radical moral choice with the possibility of choosing a radically moralised religion. This theme forms the climax of the book in the exhortation of *ciu. Dei* 2.29: 'Set your hearts on this, you who are praised as the flower of Roman stock, you descendants of such as Regulus, Sacaevola, the Scipios and Fabricius!'. A real decision is possible, but is it to be made simply by individuals, or is it a collective decision on the part of the *respublica*? The answer to that delicate question affects how we understand the overarching conception of the two cities themselves, and Rome's relation to them.

The passage is anticipated earlier, at *ciu. Dei* 2.19–20, where he sketches what we may see as two alternative eschatologies of Rome's moral life, one of regeneration through the moral revelation of Israel and the Gospel, the other a logical extension of the moral outlook enshrined in the practices of Rome's religion, assuming that the divided mind would finally be suppressed and replaced by a hardened cynicism. On the one hand, there might have been a universal worldwide republic formed under the tutelage of Israel's prophets and the evangelists, and this republic, having secured the happiness of all its members on earth, would finally 'ascend' to reign eternally in universal happiness. Although this possibility is clearly intended as a counter-factual projection, it is well worth noting as the moment at which Augustine came as close as he ever did to envisaging and embracing the ideal of Christendom. Yet this hypothetical world-republic which might even have ascended to heaven is not, even in its earthly guise, identified with Rome. On the other hand, equally hypothetical though capable of sending a shock of recognition through modern readers, there is a description of the wholly contractual and hedonistic ideal envisaged by pagan religious adherents, 'worse than the Roman empire, worse than the palace of Sardanapalus'. The *respublica*, on this view, had no need of a morality; it needed only security and economic success, to allow the emergence of differential wealth sufficient for the power-base of the plutocracy on which stability depends. Gratification, not utility, is the measure of social goods, stability the only measure of political success. Legal restraint is minimal and focused on the defence of property. But with liberty of conduct maximised, liberty of critical thought is reduced to vanishing point. To speak critically of the social order is to threaten it, and that is the greatest crime, perhaps the only crime, it can recognise.

The concluding exhortation is addressed not to the *respublica* as a whole but to those 'praised as the flower of Roman stock', as distinct from 'degenerate fellow-citizens'.[5] The appeal is founded on 'what is naturally praiseworthy' in them (avoiding, again, the language of virtue), which needs to be 'purged and perfected' if they are to find the true ground of their praise in God. He calls on them to awaken from a half-waking state, to receive the claims of a fully moralised religion. What is this half-waking state? If the address were intended for the Roman republic as a whole, we might recall that in *ciu. Dei* 2.19 Augustine had stated that the Constantinian emperors had failed to carry the whole population with them in their adoption of the Christian religion. Is this, then, a call to full participation of the body politic in the heavenly city, the forging of a bond between *respublica* and church? I incline to think not. In the immediate context, the half-waking state is actually the Roman law that denied actors full civil rights. Augustine is appealing, then, to the divided mind about Roman religion that the best of the Romans had always displayed. The time has come to take those doubts seriously. On this reading neither here nor in Chapter 19 did Augustine suggest that the Roman republic might, as a complete body politic, collectively repent and be incorporated into the heavenly city. There is a continuity between Christian Rome and the best of Roman history, but it is not a political continuity, but a matter, simply, of the moral fulfilment and self-realisation of Rome's more morally sensitive citizens. The contested interpretative question of how closely or remotely identified with the earthly city the Roman political body is taken to be, should not, then, be influenced by this invitation to

5 Again, translation is hard pressed to capture the sense of Augustine's address to the *indoles Romana laudabilis*. For the concrete sense, 'flower of the Roman stock' (cf. *Oxford Latin Dictionary*, indoles 2b). My choice of 'praised', rather than 'praiseworthy', for *laudabilis* is contestable. In what follows Augustine is clearly somewhat detached in his view of how praiseworthy he thinks contemporary Roman pagans really are, and I am inclined to suspect a hint of irony in the first appearance of *laudabilis*. However, he may simply wish to address the 'most excellent flower of Roman stock' (*Oxford Latin Dictionary*, laudabilis 2).

Romans to enter another and different *patria* founded on another and different asylum.

The literary qualities of the *ciu. Dei* are many, and differ from book to book. While Book 2 has none of the delicate theoretical subtlety that impresses us in Book 19, the profound questioning of common human experience that remains with us from Book 14, the doctrinal adventurousness of Books 12 and 13 or the sustained and half-sympathetic engagement with hostile authors of Book 10, the reader is likely to come away from Book 2 impressed by the single-mindedness of its conception and the rhetorical power of its execution. Some of the most purely energetic writing Augustine ever did is found at *ciu. Dei* 2.20, and we may add, some of the most angry. Yet Book 2 is not merely a loud and resourceful orchestration of a single theme. It also deserves appreciation for the way in which it lays the foundations for the broader structure. While on the face of it the ground on which Augustine joins issue with the pagan history of Rome was not the obvious one, given the angle from which his critics were coming, it was very well chosen for the longer-term constructive ambitions of the work as a whole. One can see many later moves prepared for here – not only in the obvious case of Cicero's definition of a republic, but also the 'good qualities' of Rome that are not 'virtues', and the relative value of philosophy in general and of Plato in particular.

FURTHER READING

Dodaro, R. (2004). *Christ and the Just Society in the Thought of Augustine.* Cambridge: Cambridge University Press.

Markus, R. A. (1988). *Saeculum: History and Society in the Theology of St. Augustine.* Rev. ed. Cambridge: Cambridge University Press.

O'Donovan, O. and O'Donovan, J. L. (2004). *Bonds of Imperfection: Christian Politics, Past and Present.* Grand Rapids, MI: Eerdmans.

4 Book 3: Rome's Woes before Christ: History and Rhetoric in *The City of God*

CHRISTIAN TORNAU

The complaint that the rise of Christianity had caused a series of calamities due to the neglect of the traditional polytheistic cults had already been combated by the early Latin apologists. In cataloguing catastrophes that had befallen Rome before the advent of Christ, Augustine moves on well-trodden ground, though the traditional complaint apparently had gained new force after the sack of Rome in AD 410. Accordingly, this chapter explores how Augustine adapts a traditional theme to his own apologetic purposes. It shows how he employs rhetorical pathos in order to deconstruct the idealizing view of early Roman history that had been canonized by the literary tradition and kept exerting influence on educated persons – both pagan and Christian – in his days. While he sometimes solicits an emotional response in order to reverse the traditional evaluation of a well-known event (*ciu. Dei* 3.14 on the Horatians and Curiatians), he is also prepared to exploit the traditional pathetic representation of the Civil Wars, available in authors like Lucan or Florus, to make his own point. His reading of Roman history as an almost uninterrupted series of civil wars reveals the distinction – conceded to the pagan adversaries in the opening chapter – between moral and external evils as artificial and marks the Roman Empire as an avatar of the *ciuitas terrena*, which is inevitably divided within itself. The chapters on Numa Pompilius briefly touch upon the systematically important issues of the relevance of peace for happiness and the relation of religion and philosophy and help to anchor Book 3 in the overall argument of the *ciu. Dei* as a whole.

It was a traditional idea of Roman religion that the historical success of Rome, its economic prosperity, as well as its military achievements and the growth of the Roman Empire over the centuries, would not have been possible if the Romans had not been on good terms with their gods.[1] The "peace of the gods" (*pax deorum*), as it is sometimes called, was secured through *religio*, i.e. the correct and punctilious performance of rituals, sacrifices, and auspices; neglect or violation of *religio* resulted in military defeats, famines, and plagues.[2] The complaint, faced already by the first Christian apologists, that the rise of Christianity and the ensuing neglect of the polytheistic cults had caused an unprecedented series of calamities – and thus endangered the very existence of the Empire – owed its persistence largely to this tradition.[3] The Latin apologists combated it in various ways. Tertullian reversed the traditional idea by claiming that the Christians' prayers to the true God were more profitable for the emperor and the state than the pagan cults of non-existent gods;[4] Arnobius pointed out that calamities of all sorts, far from being a distinguishing mark of the Christian era, had been frequent throughout history;[5] Minucius Felix catalogued catastrophic events from pre-Christian Roman history such as Romulus' fratricide, the rape of the Sabine women or the lost battle against Hannibal at Cannae.[6]

When in AD 410 Rome was sacked by the Goths under Alaric, the pagans – so Augustine tells us in the *retr.* of *ciu. Dei* – tried to blame the disaster on the *christiana religio*.[7] Whatever the truth of this assertion, it is certain that the event caused considerable distress among the Christians in the North African communities, who either experienced or anticipated increasing pressure from their non-Christian environment; quite a few among them seem to have felt religious doubts themselves. The Roman nexus of religion and Empire, of *religio* and

1 Where I have not relied on my own English translation of Augustine's Latin, I have provided the page number as found in Babcock. For a classical statement on the *pax deorum*, see Cicero, *Natura Deorum* 3.5. For a Christian paraphrase, cf. Tert. *Apologeticus* [*Apol.*] 25.2. See Beard et al. 1998, vol. 1, pp. 313–363: "Roman religion and Roman Empire."

2 Livy's *Roman History (Ab urbe condita)* abounds with examples. For instance, Rome's defeat at Lake Trasimene in the Second Punic War was due to Consul Flaminius' neglect of the auspices (Liv. 21.63); see also, the parody in Aug. *ciu. Dei* 2.3: *pluuia defit, causa christiani sunt*; similarly, Tert. *Apol.* 40.1.

3 Cf., e.g. Arnob. 1.1.

4 Tert. *Apol.* 29.4–30,1.

5 Arnob. 1.2–6.

6 Min. Fel. 25.5; 26.1–4. Cf. already Tert. *Apol.* 40.8. For a different strategy (not always appreciated by later writers, see the criticism of Lact. *inst.* 5.4,3–5) see Cyprian's *Ad Demetrianum*, who transforms the apologetic discourse into an *exhortatio ad martyrium*. For a full account of Roman history in Tertullian, Minucius Felix and Lactantius, see Inglebert 1996, pp. 79–148.

7 *retr.* 2.43.1.

res publica, was a time-honored and powerful tradition that could not easily be brushed aside, if only because it was present in the works of Latin classics such as Cicero and Vergil whom the educated among the inhabitants of the Empire had imbibed at school. People who perceived themselves as both Christian and Roman may well have experienced conflicting loyalties. This is at least the impression that emerges from the sermons Augustine preached in the months immediately after the event.[8] In these he tried to comfort his flock by pointing out that the complaint that military calamities had increased in Christian times was not borne out by the facts of Roman history[9] but also by insisting that a Christian owed loyalty to the Gospel rather than to the Empire.[10] With its panorama of the calamities of pre-Christian Rome and its occasional hints at the Christian alternative,[11] *ciu. Dei* 3 continues this line of argument.

CIU. DEI 3: A RHETORICAL TEXT

Book 3 is of course not an occasional writing designed to silence the pagan polemics or the murmur of disloyal Christians in the years after AD 410. As Augustine succinctly puts it himself, the aim of the *ciu. Dei* is to "defend the City of God against those who prefer their own gods to its founder, Christ"[12] and to persuade the readers to enter the City of God (i.e. in this context, the Church) without hesitation and to stay firmly within it.[13] In other words, Augustine seeks to demonstrate that the only possible means of securing happiness, the end or *telos* of all human endeavor according to ancient eudaemonist ethics,[14] is membership in the City of God and to reveal the alternative ways to happiness

[8] See, e.g. *s.* 296.9 on debates between pagans and Christians; *s.* 81.7 on discussions among Christians; on inner doubts of Christians see *s.* 296.9: *iam adhuc uideo quid dicas in corde tuo: ecce temporibus christianis Roma affligitur, aut afflicta est, et incensa est: quare temporibus christianis? quis hoc dicis? christianus.* On the sermons of AD 410–AD 411 and their relation to the *ciu. Dei*, cf. O'Daly 1999, pp. 28ff.; Tornau 2006a, pp. 126–129 with further references.

[9] *s.* 296.9. Interestingly, there is a similar argument in a pagan historian (Amm. Marc. 31.5,11, on the lost battle of Adrianople). See Hose 2015, pp. 87ff.

[10] *s.* 296,11.

[11] C.f., e.g. *ciu. Dei* 3.9; 3.17. See further below.

[12] *ciu. Dei* 1 *praef.*: *defendere aduersus eos, qui conditori eius deos suos praeferunt.* For *defendere* and related terms, cf. *ciu. Dei* 11.1.

[13] *ep.* 2*.3: *quod ciuitatem dei persuadent uel incunctanter intrandam uel perseueranter habitandam. persuadere* also occurs in *ciu. Dei* 1 *praef.*

[14] See, with an interesting thesis on Augustine's attitude to ancient eudaemonism, see Wolterstorff 2012. For a perhaps more traditional interpretation see Tornau 2015.

offered by the ancient (Roman or philosophical) tradition, in particular those that involved acceptance of the polytheistic cults, as inadequate and dangerous.

In order to reach this twofold aim, Augustine organizes the long and complicated argument of the *ciu. Dei* as a "three-cornered dialogue"[15] analogous to a speech in court: A speaker (Augustine himself in the role of the defendant or apologist) addresses a "judge" (the readership of the work, which in Books 1–3 is represented by the dedicatee of the work, Count Marcellinus, and envisaged as Christian throughout)[16] and tries to persuade him by refuting the arguments of an "accuser" (the pagan adversaries of Christianity) who is almost invariably referred to in the third person and portrayed very unfavorably as an unscrupulous polemicist and potential persecutor of Christianity. This rhetorical and literary arrangement does not of course exclude non-Christians as readers of the *ciu. Dei*. But wherever this kind of readers are envisaged, they are implicitly and sometimes explicitly asked *not* to identify with Augustine's aggressive pagan opponent.[17] The latter is not a real person but is construed by Augustine in such a way as to suit his own argumentative purpose. To take but one example: His tendency to style contemporary anti-Christian polemic as a new persecution of Christianity[18] may strike us as exaggerated. Yet it is one of the central tenets of Augustine's theology of history that while the City of God during its residence (*peregrinatio*) on earth does "profit from the peace of Babylon" (*ciu. Dei* 19.26), it nevertheless remains a foreigner in a potentially hostile environment; the relationship of the heavenly and the earthly city can never be reduced to full harmony. Augustine's rhetorical construal of the opponent as a personification of the *terrena ciuitas* at its most hostile is thus fully in line with the overall logic and theology of *ciu. Dei*.[19]

15 I borrow this felicitous formula from Classen 1991.

16 See esp. *ciu. Dei* 2.1 where the reader is explicitly invested with the authority of a judge. Interestingly, Augustine addresses Marcellinus as *Christiane iudex* in a contemporary letter (*ep.* 133.2).

17 Cf. *ciu. Dei* 2.29; the case of 3.17 will be discussed below.

18 See esp. *ciu. Dei* 3.23; 3.31: *nullus talium, quales nunc patimur, nisi christianae religioni mala illa tribuisset* – a clear allusion to the phrase *persecutionem pati* familiar since the New Testament (Mt 5:10; there are eight occurrences in *ciu. Dei* itself).

19 For a fuller discussion of the rhetorical design of the *ciu. Dei* see Tornau 2006a, pp. 112–126; in English, Tornau 2006b, pp. 265–267; Pollmann 2009, pp. 311–314. Rhetoric had been crucial to Latin apologetics since Tertullian had styled his *Apologeticum* as a paradoxical plea before the persecuting Roman authorities, but

In Book 3 Augustine is particularly careful to make the quasi-forensic, rhetorical character of his text explicit. Though the book largely consists of a survey of Roman history from Romulus to Augustus, he denies that he is a writer of history like the Roman historians from whom he takes his material.[20] Instead, he describes his way of writing as "pleading a cause" (*causam agere*),[21] and he constantly keeps us aware of the presence of his opponents by reporting or anticipating their counter-arguments.[22] As history, Book 3 would indeed be inadequate: It is hardly informative (the stories referred to having repeatedly been told and discussed in classical literature), and the treatment is very uneven (while some events are broadly narrated, others are barely mentioned).[23] As rhetoric, however, it is highly effective. To reach this persuasive goal – to refute the traditionalist claim that before the rise of Christianity and the decline of the polytheistic cults Rome enjoyed the special protection of the gods who made her great – Augustine relies on the very evidence that was generally believed to support that claim: the conventional narrative of Roman history that was sanctioned by the classical authors and firmly rooted in his contemporaries' historical consciousness.[24] But while acknowledging the "facts" provided by that narrative, he challenges their conventional interpretation, the inconsistencies of which the agonistic rhetoric of the book relentlessly exposes (adopting the technical terminology of Latin rhetoric, we might say that his plea does not concern the issue of fact – *an sit, status coniecturalis* – but that of quality – *quale sit, status qualitatis*). By advocating a revisionist and realistic reading of Roman history, Book 3 aims at freeing Augustine's readership from the

times had changed since then: Tertullian could not have portrayed his "judges" as Christian, and while he needed to argue against persecution, for Augustine it suffices to represent his opponents as persecutors to disparage them.

20 *ciu. Dei* 3.18: *si enarrare uel commemorare conemur, nihil aliud quam scriptores etiam nos erimus historiae.*

21 *ciu. Dei* 3.3; 3.6. The rhetorical terminology is also present in the later parts of the work, cf. 21.7: *apud eorum, contra quos agimus, historicos legi.*

22 E.g. *ciu. Dei* 3.2 (*inquiunt*); 3.3 (*ut dicunt*); 3.4 (*dixerit aliquis*); 3.8 (*dixerit quispiam*); 3.14 (*quid mihi obtenditur etc.*); 3.14 (*inquiunt*); and 3.20 (*respondebunt*).

23 Contrast *ciu.* where Augustine, following Varro and the chronicles of Eusebius and Jerome, catalogues less well-known events for the sake of information.

24 Augustine comments on this strategy himself, see *ciu. Dei* 4.1. The rhetorical technical term for such acknowledged "facts" is *confessum*; see Quint. *Inst.* 5.12,2; for a list of possible *confessa* c, see also Quint. *Inst.* 5.10.12ff. (esp. 5.10.13): *si quid inter utramque partem convenit, si quid probatum est, denique cuicumque adversarius non contradicit.* The argumentative use of historical *exempla* is, of course, good rhetorical tradition see, e.g. Quint. *Inst.* 10.1.34.

constraints and prejudices of the classical tradition and at shifting their loyalty from the earthly city of Rome to a city that has incomparably more to offer to its citizens: the City of God.

HISTORY IN THE ARGUMENT OF BOOK 3

As indicated above, Augustine in Book 3 casts himself in the role of an advocate at court, as he does throughout *The City of God.* The traditional defensive attitude of the Christian apologist, however, is abandoned for a more aggressive stance: Augustine now poses as an accuser of the Roman gods and their modern "defendants." This begins in the opening chapter where he censures his opponents for insisting on the fact that the Romans, apart from the moral evils just discussed in Book 2, also had to endure "external" evils such as wars, famines and plagues. All reasonable persons, he contends, rate these evils infinitely lower than the moral ones because other than these they do not force those who suffer from them to become evil themselves; by contrast, the pagans, who only care about external but not about moral evil, thereby reveal themselves as "foolish" and "wicked."[25] Augustine's decision to deal with the moral evils in Book 2 before treating the external ones in Book 3 thus enables him to force his opponents onto the defensive from the very beginning, and he continues to do so throughout the book.[26] He repeatedly urges them to "defend" (*defendere*) the behavior of their gods and ridicules the "defenses" they allegedly advance;[27] as "defenders and excusers of the gods"[28] they are, he implies, pleaders for a hopeless and repellent cause (*causa turpis*),[29] which effectively adds to the tactics of moral denigration just described. In addition, he scores the ironic point that the gods, traditionally regarded as the "defenders of the city,"[30] are in need of defenders themselves. When in the concluding chapter he claims victory, he asks his adversaries to accuse the gods

[25] *ciu. Dei* 3.1; cf. 4.2. The hierarchy of goods and evils Augustine presupposes here originated in Greek philosophical ethics and was, at least in theory, universally accepted in Late Antiquity.

[26] For more on the rhetorical disposition of Books 1–5, see Tornau 2006a, pp. 362–365.

[27] *ciu. Dei* 3.3: *ut rursus a quibusdam defenduntur*; 3.15: *nisi forte quispiam sic defendat istos deos*; cf. 2.22: *an forte … illam sententiam, sicut solent, pro defensione deorum suorum opponere audebunt.* In Books 2 and 3 the verb *defendere*, which otherwise often denotes the goal of the *ciu. Dei* (1 *praef.*; 11.1; cf. 1.1; 1.12), is never used for Augustine's own argument.

[28] *ciu. Dei* 3.20: *defensores et excusatores eorum* (i.e. *deorum*).

[29] The term is from the ancient rhetoricians: cf., e.g. Quint. *inst.* 4.1,40.

[30] *ciu. Dei* 3.20: *illis defensoribus*; cf. *ciu. Dei* 3.7; 3.8 and already 1.3; 2.27.

instead of defending them, i.e. to do what he has been doing all along (and, implicitly, to join the Christian ranks).[31] In this rhetorical framework, the historical material deployed in Book 3 serves as incriminating evidence against the gods and is selected accordingly. Here is a synopsis:

- .1 Preface
- .2-.8 The mythical origins of Rome and the fall of Troy
  - .3b–.6 Excursus: Birth and fratricide of Romulus
  - .7 Excursus: The sack of Hellenistic Ilium in the time of Marius and Sulla
- .9–.15 The Regal period and the first consuls
  - .9–.13 The period of peace under Numa Pompilius
    - .13 Excursus: The rape of the Sabine women under Romulus
  - .14 The war against Alba Longa under Tullus Hostilius and the fight of the Horatians and Curiatians
  - .15 The deaths of the Roman kings from Romulus to Tarquinius Superbus
  - .16 The failings and sufferings of L. Iunius Brutus
- .17–.19 From the first consuls to the First Punic War
- .19–.20 The Second Punic War; the sack of Saguntum
- .21 From the Second to the Third Punic war
  - .22 Excursus: Mithridates' massacre of the Romans in Asia minor
- .23–.30 The period of the Civil Wars
  - .23 Preface
  - .24–.26 The violent death of the Gracchi, the construction of the Temple of Concord and the subsequent inner strife and external wars
  - .27–.29 Marius and Sulla
    - .28 After Sulla's victory: peace outdoes war in bloodshed
    - .29 *sunkrisis* of the Civil Wars and the disaster of 410
  - .30 From Marius and Sulla to Augustus; the violent death of Cicero
- .31 Epilogue: The inconsistency of the pagans who fail to attribute the immense and well-known calamities of the past to their gods while blaming Christianity for the comparatively small evils of the present

[31] *ciu. Dei* 3.31: *deos suos accusent.*

The chronological backbone of this argument is a survey of Roman history from the mythical origins to the reign of Augustus. But Augustine often deviates from chronology and gives some events (the Horatians and Curiatians; Saguntum; Mithridates; Sulla) disproportionate attention for strategical reasons. The Roman historians are, at least at first sight, mainly used as a quarry of information. As Harald Hagendahl and others have shown, though Augustine follows his authorities – Livy, Florus, and authors of handy overviews (so-called *breuiaria ab urbe condita*) such as Eutropius – sometimes word for word, he seems to have little concern for their aims and methods.[32] With one exception,[33] the only historian mentioned by name is Sallust, whose devastating judgments on Roman decadence had already been of great help to the argument of Book 2. However, half-way through the book, when after his comparatively full discussion of the foundation myths and the history of the kings Augustine interrupts his narrative to announce the more perfunctory treatment of the rest of Roman history, he pauses to reflect on the generic characteristics of historiography and on the use of history in the apologetic debate (*ciu. Dei* 3.17). He begins by quoting Sallust's verdict that the whole time between the institution of the *res publica libera* and the Punic Wars had been a crisis-ridden period of inner strife (Sall. *hist.* fr. 1,11) – at the face of it in order to justify his own omission of the period, but in fact to strike, again, the keynote that the distinguishing mark of all Roman history was civil war, for which Rome's famous victories offered small comfort.

He then asks the "good and thoughtful Romans" (*boni Romani prudentesque*) not to be angry at this assertion, since after all he is only saying what their own classics say whom they force their sons to read at school.[34] He then imagines two possible reactions from the Romans: While some of them will accept his argument or even see the point themselves, others will stubbornly keep up their polemics (the latter he confronts with another, even more explicit Sallustian quotation: *hist.* fr. 1,12). The second group are, of course, the familiar intransigent pagans who ignore the facts of Roman history and whose ignorance or

[32] Hagendahl 1967, pp. 631–649 (Sallust); 650–666 ("Livy and his epitomists"); Angus 1906, pp. 26–35; 42–49; Schindler 1989; Inglebert 1996, pp. 408–413; for a brief overview, O'Daly 1999, pp. 240–246; 248–250. A concise summary of Augustine's interest in the Latin classics and his strategies of quotation and allusion is given by Shanzer 2012.

[33] *ciu. Dei* 3.7 (a reference to a lost passage of Livy, possibly from second hand).

[34] For Augustine's usually sarcastic remarks on late-antique literary education see *conf.* 1.22; 28ff. and, memorably, *ciu. Dei* 21.14. Marrou 1958 remains basic.

dissimulation Augustine is keen to uncover from their own authorities. But the sheer mention of the first group suggests that at least some traditionalist readers might be prompted by his arguments to revise their view of history and to endorse the fresh reading of the sources he advocates.[35] Augustine does not explicitly say whether these are pagan or Christian, and with good reason. There was no binary opposition of pagans and Christians in Late Antiquity (the picture of late-antique Roman society as split into two clear-cut religious camps being largely a propagandistic fiction of the Church Fathers),[36] and the historical consciousness of many Christians probably kept to be influenced by the image drawn by the classics and handed down (and simplified) by tradition and education. One of the purposes of Augustine's revisionist reading of Roman history in Book 3 is to offer a Christian alternative to this overwhelming tradition. In our chapter he pursues this idea by distinguishing the attitude of a Christian and legitimate citizen of the heavenly city toward Rome from that of a Roman historian who *faute de mieux* is unconditionally loyal to his earthly city:

> Again, if those historians held that honorable freedom required them not to keep silent about the evils of their city, which in many places they were compelled to praise in grandiose terms because they had no other and truer city, whose citizens are to be chosen for all eternity, what is the right thing for us to do? Our hope in God is better and more certain, and to just that degree our freedom ought to be the greater, especially when people impute the evils of this present time to our Christ in order to estrange weaker and less well-trained minds from the one city in which life is to be lived in eternal happiness.
>
> (*ciu. Dei* 3.17; Babcock, 1.90)

Augustine skillfully plays off various generic expectations toward historiography against each other. On the one hand, truthfulness (*ueritas*), impartiality, and frankness of speech (*libertas*) were

[35] The passage links up with *ciu. Dei* 2.29 and related texts. Of course, *boni Romani prudentesque* may be ironic, but there are no unambiguous markers of irony in the text. The clue may well be that Augustine leaves the decision to the reader.

[36] For recent attempts to overcome this old dualism see Kahlos 2007, pp. 26–54 who introduces an intermediate group of *incerti*; Cameron 2011, pp. 176ff. who distinguishes between "committed Christians," "center Christians," "committed pagans," and "center pagans" and an undecided group in the middle; and Rebillard 2012, pp. 1–8 who points out that the importance of the identity marker "Christian" may vary in diverse situations in the same persons.

mandatory for an ancient historian.[37] On the other, especially Roman historiography was "exemplary" in the sense that it focused on memorable deeds of single men and women, which it recorded for later generations as paradigms or "monuments" to imitate or to avoid.[38] Praise and blame – i.e. not just the documentation of past events but also their evaluation – were therefore part of the historian's task.[39] Roman historians tended to lavish praise especially on the early periods of Roman history, the era of the *maiores*. Augustine highlights this tendency, together with the general patriotic outlook of Roman historiography, when he singles out "praise of Rome" as its main generic purpose.[40] With a surprising yet consistent move, he links this to the guiding issue of the first five books and indeed of the *ciu. Dei* as a whole, the question of happiness.[41] The Roman historians, he contends, had no choice (*compulsi sunt*) but to praise Rome because they had no other city from which they could expect happiness (a motivation analogous to that of the opponents of Book 1–5 and their insistence on the necessity of the old cults for political prosperity).[42] But even so, being good historians, they were not afraid of voicing frank criticism of Rome when appropriate. *A fortiori*, the Christians, who do have a choice because they know of the City of God and have access to it and to true happiness, should feel free to see the Roman tradition with the critical eye it deserves. This is the only explicit mention of the City of God in Book 3. It briefly, but unmistakably, indicates that if our religious life is going to be successful, we

[37] See Marincola 2009, pp. 18ff. with references. Augustine emphasizes Sallust's *ueritas* in *ciu. Dei* 1.5, where it matters to his argument that the Sallustian statement he quotes is reliable.

[38] Cf. Roller 2009 and for the monuments metaphor Liv. *praef.* 10.

[39] Cf. Marincola 2009, pp. 19–21.

[40] Cf. *ciu. Dei* 1.6. This may not have appeared self-evident to his readers: Theorists warned historians not to overdo it with praise for their own city because that endangered neutrality and transformed history into panegyrics (Luc. *hist. conscr.* 7). It should also be noted that Augustine considers "praise for Rome" as a generic marker of Roman historiography, not of historiography in general. Cf. *doctr. chr.* 2.44; *ciu. Dei* 6.7; 16.2; Müller 2004–2010, pp. 370ff.; Inglebert 1996, pp. 402–407; Bittner 1999, pp. 345–347. Contrast *ciu. Dei* 3.15 on the Cicero of the *Hortensius*: *disputator magis quam laudator fuit*.

[41] See above. *feliciter uiuendum* is a variation of the philosophical technical term *beata uita*, a translation of εὐδαιμονία.

[42] There is a similar remark on Camillus, one of the old Roman *exempla uirtutis*, in *ciu. Dei* 5.18: *Furius Camillus etiam ingratam patriam … a Gallis iterum liberauit, quia non habebat potiorem, ubi posset uiuere gloriosius.*

must detach ourselves from the traditional view that the Roman past is praiseworthy and exemplary. It may be possible to be Christian and Roman at the same time, but our Roman identity needs to be reshaped and reformed by Christianity.[43]

In addition, the passage explains Augustine's choice of sources in Book 3. Later on, the notion that praise of Rome is a generic marker of Roman historiography is applied specifically, in an anonymous but marked quotation, to a historian of the 2nd century AD, L. Annaeus Florus.[44] Florus is never mentioned by name, because he was not a school authority, but he is (with the possible exception of Sallust) the only historian that is consistently used throughout the book.[45] The reason is that he unites all the qualities Augustine needs: He expressly aims at raising admiration for Rome's exploits;[46] he is generous with both praise and blame and particularly deplores the disasters that befell Rome during the Civil Wars; and he cherishes a highly pathetic style of historical writing, i.e. he presents his evaluation in such a way as to display intense emotional commitment of the narrator. As we shall see later in more detail, emotional style is one of Augustine's key devices of literary composition in Book 3. By imitating and outperforming Florus in this respect, he can demonstrate and enact the appropriate reactions of a Christian to the Roman past.

RHETORICAL STRATEGIES

The first section of the book (*ciu. Dei* 3.2–8) deals with the Roman foundation myths: the sack of Troy and the reign of Romulus. This in fact forms the central question of *ciu. Dei* 3.2–3: Why did the tutelary gods of Troy, as Vergil (*Aen.* 2.351ff.) testifies, abandon this city to the victorious Greeks? Immediately two possible reasons are entertained: (1) divine wrath regarding the perjury of Laomedon (*ciu. Dei* 3.2, alluding

[43] This, of course, affects the issue – addressed *inter alia* in *epp.* 138 and 155 – of whether a citizen of the City of God can, and should, participate politically in the earthly society. See Dodaro 2012. For Augustine's views on the *Imperium Romanum*, which generally speaking are rather more nuanced than it appears in Book 3; see Szidat 2004–2010, esp. pp. 549–558, with further bibliography.

[44] *ciu. Dei* 2.19 = Flor. 1.22,1. Cf. Hagendahl 1967, p. 663. On Florus and his literary aims and methods see Hose 1994, pp. 62–137.

[45] The parallels are noted by Hagendahl 1967, pp. 176–179; they are found throughout chapters 3.13–28. Cf. also Angus 1906, pp. 42–50 and the notes at pp. 117–152.

[46] Flor. 1 *praef.* 3. The practical point that Florus covered exactly the same period as Book 3 (from Romulus to Augustus) may also have been relevant.

to Verg. *georg.* 1.502; *Aen.* 4.542)[47] and (2) indignation about Paris' adultery (*ciu. Dei* 3.3–5). Augustine refutes these suggestions without difficulty by pointing out the inconsistent behavior of the gods they imply. It is implausible that the gods condemn adultery because some of them – especially Venus and Mars, the divine parents of Aeneas and Romulus – are notoriously guilty of it themselves.

This hardly goes beyond the anti-pagan polemics of the older apologists, who liked to ridicule the traditional gods by rationalistically pointing out the logical incoherence and moral offensiveness of their myths.[48] The next step in the argument is more serious. If the gods cared about moral issues at all, they ought to have avenged Romulus' fratricide (*ciu. Dei* 3.6) or to have protected Hellenistic Ilium, the innocent successor of Troy, from being sacked by Marius' henchman Fimbria in 86 BC (*ciu. Dei* 3.7). They did neither because they are not gods but weak, unreliable and malevolent demons; it was hardly prudent to entrust them the protection of Rome (*ciu. Dei* 3.8). The argumentative disposition of these chapters allows Augustine to reintroduce moral categories into the discussion without breaking his initial promise (*ciu. Dei* 3.1) to focus on external evils (it is the adversaries who first come up with moral arguments to defend their gods) and to single out the most disreputable element of the Romulus myth, the fratricide, while concealing features that would seem to indicate special divine favor and protection, as, e.g. the *augustum augurium* and the apotheosis[49] (ostensibly, Romulus is only cited as a subsidiary argument in the debate about Troy).

In the classical authors the mythical motifs of the fratricide and of Laomedon had symbolized Rome's tragic plight and guilt in the Civil Wars;[50] their mention early in the book foreshadows Augustine's strategy of depicting the history of Rome as a continuous sequence of inner

[47] In the first passage Vergil actually suggests that the calamities of the civil war are the gods' revenge for the sins of the Trojan forebears: *satis iam pridem sanguine nostro/ Laomedonteae luimus periuria Troiae* (*georg.* 1.502ff., in the context of a prayer).

[48] Cf. *ciu. Dei* 3.17 on Jupiter whose love affairs did not leave him time to study medicine.

[49] Of course, it would not have been difficult for Augustine to dismantle these stories rhetorically had he felt the need at this point. On the apotheosis cf. *ciu. Dei* 3.15; 22.6ff., each based on Cicero.

[50] On Laomedon see n.49 above. For the fratricide see Horace, *epod.* 7,17–20; Luc. 1,93–95; Mankin 1995, p. 151. It is, of course, also exploited by the older apologists (Tert. *nat.* 2,9; Min. Fel. 25,2; Maier 1955, p. 103). In *ciu. Dei* 15,5 it returns in a comparison with Cain and Abel and stands for the inner dividedness of the *ciuitas terrena*.

strife and bloodshed, and the rapid chronological leap from Romulus to Fimbria enhances the impression that Rome had been haunted by civil war from its mythical origins down to the last days of the Republic.[51] All this is clever forensic rhetoric, but Augustine's decision to make his opponents rely on moral arguments despite their alleged immoralism is also philosophically interesting. In Book 2, where he takes up and reinterprets the old motif of Rome's moral decadence, he had anticipated the possible objection that moral criteria were irrelevant for the evaluation of a city or society and that the only things that counted were stability and power (*ciu. Dei* 2.20). This argument he had disarmed by means of a kind of thought experiment: Even a permissive society that does not set any moral standards but is exclusively ruled by the citizens' individual desires and the right of the stronger will not be able to stand unless it respects and guarantees its citizens' personal safety and property, i.e. a minimum of morality or, as Augustine puts it, of peace.[52] It would seem that in Book 3 Augustine wants to deepen this lesson by letting moral categories re-enter the picture even if they have officially been ruled out. For instance, the chapter on Sulla's victory (*ciu. Dei* 3.28; more on this below) with its horrifying description of a complete loss of peace and total disintegration of society shows that physical suffering and moral depravation go hand in hand; it reads like a hyperbolic continuation of *ciu. Dei* 2.20.

As befits a discussion of Rome's mythical past, *ciu. Dei* 3.2–8 abound with quotations from and allusions to Vergil. One of them occurs three times in this section and three more times later in the book: "they all have withdrawn, deserting shrine and altar, the gods by whom that empire had once stood firm" (Verg. *Aen.* 2.351ff.).[53] In *ciu.* 3.3 and already back in 2.22, where he first cites these lines, Augustine claims that they were actually adduced by pagan polemicists against Christianity. He does not say what the exact point of the quotation was,

[51] Cf. *ciu. Dei* 3.7 (*ciuilibus iam bellis scatentibus* and *parricidam Romanae rei publicae*) with *ciu. Dei* 3.6 on the responsibility of the entire city for the killing of Remus: *non iam fratrem, sed patrem, quod est peius, occidit*. Parricide as a metonymy for civil war is almost a cliché in Roman literature since the Augustans.

[52] On peace on Book 3 see the section on Numa below.

[53] *excessere omnes adytis arisque relictis/di quibus imperium hoc steterat*. The translation is from Babcock 2013 (see below). For comment, see Horsfall 2008, p. 291. The references in Book 3 are: 3.3; 3.7 (twice); 3.14; 3.15 (twice), plus a possible allusion in 3.25 (*discedente Concordia*). For a full list of quotations from Vergil in Book 3 see Bouton-Touboulic 2013, pp. 174–176. Audano 2009, pp. 113–134 has a careful interpretation of Augustine's use of *Aen.* 8.822ff. (on Brutus) in *ciu.* 3.16. On Brutus in Book 3 see also Harding 2007, pp. 80–82.

but Orosius states that after the sack of Rome in AD 410 the pagans complained that since the Christian emperors had forbidden the cults and closed the temples, "all the gods were gone" and had ceased to protect Empire (Oros. *Hist.* 6.1,23).[54] If this is correct, Book 3 gives us a rare glimpse at Augustine's way of dealing with an authentic piece of contemporary anti-Christian polemics. On the one hand, he re-situates the quotation in its original Virgilian context, the sack of Troy, where the gods' departure was obviously not due to a neglect of their cults. On the other, he asks where the gods had been when the cities they had migrated to after the destruction of Troy were in their turn sacked and destroyed. His first and most impressive example is Hellenistic Ilium, amid whose ruins, according to Livy, a statue of Minerva had remained upright – on Augustine's interpretation, not a divine promise of the city's future restitution,[55] but evidence that the gods were present but either unable or unwilling to protect the city (*ciu. Dei* 3.7). Later on he adds the examples of Lavinium and Alba Longa, cities the gods seem to have quit just in time before their destruction:

> Then, as the fruit of victory, Alba was destroyed – the third dwelling of those Trojan divinities after Ilium, which the Greeks overthrew, and Lavinium, where Aeneas had established his kingdom of wandering fugitives. But perhaps the gods, in their usual fashion, had already moved on from there as well, and that is why Alba was destroyed ... They had withdrawn, no doubt, now for a third time, so that Rome might be the fourth city entrusted – most prudently, I am sure – to their care.
>
> (*ciu. Dei* 3.14; Babcock, 1.84)

By contrast, when Tarquinius Superbus was crowned after having assassinated his predecessor Servius Tullius, the gods had no objections: they did not "quit their altars and shrines and were gone," and the city remained intact (*ciu. Dei* 3.15). Thus far from being majestic tutelary divinities firmly seated in the cities that are entrusted to them, the Roman gods become unreliable demons who lightheartedly abandon a city in danger to move to another one and who do greater harm when they are present than when they are absent. Possibly Augustine's

54 Cf. Oros. *Hist.* 6.1,11. It is of course not impossible that Orosius just extrapolated from *ciu. Dei.*

55 This explanation, which is explicit in Iulius Obsequens 56b (p. 173 Rossbach: *spemque restitutionis populo protendit*), is implied in Augustine's quotation of Verg. *Aen.* 9.247.

re-interpretation of *Aen.* 2.351ff. was partly inspired by a piece of philological scholarship on Vergil. As Servius and Macrobius report, some ancient grammarians claimed that the lines were an allusion to the archaic ritual of *euocatio*. Before capturing a besieged city, the Roman general would "call out" its tutelary deities and invite them to settle in Rome. When the conquest was successful, the deities received a (minor) cult at Rome.[56] This antiquarian observation may have helped Augustine to reverse the pagan argument by identifying its weak spot, *viz.* that even the oldest tutelary gods, which Rome had inherited from Troy, had often abandoned their cities and may have been seduced to do so by promises and bribery.[57] However this may be, the disquisition on *Aen.* 2.351ff. prepares the dilemmatic situation in chapter *ciu. Dei* 3.17, where a long and impressive list of historical calamities is accompanied by an anaphoric series of rhetorical questions to the effect: *Ubi ergo erant illi dii?* – "Where were the gods?" Whether they were in Rome or elsewhere, they could not or would not do anything to avert her woes.

As indicated above, a key device of Augustine's in Book 3 is pathos, i.e., the use of emotional language in order to stir the emotions of the audience, in particular, to arouse pity (*miseratio*) with the victims and indignation (*indignatio*) with the perpetrators of the atrocities of Rome's past, i.e., in the last resort, the gods.[58] He was not the first who wrote on Roman history in an emotional style, but as we shall see, he adapts his predecessors' literary technique and, at times, their concrete responses to his own argumentative purpose. Our first example is King Tullus Hostilius' conquest of Alba Longa and the fight of the Horatians and Curiatians (*ciu. Dei* 3.14). Augustine gives his description an emotional coloring from the outset by interpreting the event in terms of the leitmotif of civil war, evoked already in the previous chapter on the rape of the Sabine women (*ciu. Dei* 3.13) where he had aligned the conflict of Romans and Sabines with the civil wars of the 1st century BC by depicting it as a war between fathers-in-law and sons-in-law and by applying the proverbial opening of Lucan's *Bellum ciuile* to it.[59]

[56] Macr. *sat.* 3.9,1–14 (partly after Plin. *NH* 18.28); Serv. *in Aen.* 2.351ff. (1.277, 8–16 Thilo-Hagen). For the ritual see Beard et al. 1998, vol. 2, p. 248.

[57] This is at least what I suggest in Tornau 2006a, pp. 236–241.

[58] On these two basic functions of pathos cf. *Rhet. Her.* 2.48–50; Quint. *inst.* 6.1,9 and 6.1–2 in general.

[59] *ciu. Dei* 3.13: *quanto et quam iusto doloris instinctu Lucanus exclamat: bella per Emathios plus quam ciuilia campos/iusque datum sceleri canimus* [Lucan. 1,1]. *uicerunt ergo Romani, ut strage socerorum manibus cruentis ab eorum filiabus amplexus miserabiles extorquerent, nec illae auderent flere patres occisos, ne*

Similarly, his treatment of the Horatians and Curiatians pathetically focuses on the human costs of the fight and its aftermath. The story about two sets of triplets dueling each other in order to end a long and tiresome war and about the victorious Horatian, the only survivor of the fight, killing his own sister because she wept at the death of the Curiatian brother who had been her betrothed, had been told by Livy[60] and Florus[61] and was firmly rooted in Roman historical consciousness. It was considered exemplary in that it embodied the Roman virtues of endurance under hopeless circumstances and of postponing private, including familial, interests to the common good to which even the life of an apparently innocent woman had to be sacrificed whose behavior, though natural, risked to demoralize the troops. Florus highlights the tragic side of the incident when he says that Horatius "maculated his victory with a parricide" (Flor. 1.3.5)[62] but immediately reinstates the orthodox view by concluding that "his virtue did away with the parricide and his misdeed was beneath his glory" (Flor. 1.3.6).[63] By contrast, Augustine markedly privileges the human aspect, asking from his readers an emotional response in line with natural intuition; values like glory and victory, traditionally adduced to justify the deed, are impatiently brushed aside. The war between Alba and Rome was just another *plus quam ciuile bellum*, because just as earlier under Romulus and later under Caesar and Pompeius fathers fought sons, now the "daughter-city" fought, and killed, her "mother-city" (*ciu. Dei* 3.14).[64] The losses among their progeny should have caused grief in Venus and Jupiter themselves, he adds, ironically adopting the point of view of the polytheists and implicitly denouncing the demons' lust for bloodshed that not even spares their own children and grandchildren (a theme that will be developed later in the chapter with the gladiators metaphor).

The tragic fate of Horatia is thus deplored in an extended rhetorical *amplificatio* that relentlessly exposes the unnatural brutishness of her

offenderent uictores maritos. Augustine explicitly approves of Lucan's often-criticized pathetic style. It is rare that poets are quoted affirmatively in Augustine. Another allusion to Lucan. 1.1 follows in *ciu. Dei* 3.14.

60 Liv. 1.25–26.

61 Flor. 1.3. Like Augustine, beyond this story he has little to report about Tullus' reign.

62 *uictoria ... quam ille mox parricidio foedauit*. Livy's version is both more distanced and more affirmative.

63 *Citauere leges nefas, sed abstulit uirtus parricidam et facinus infra gloriam fuit.*

64 *cum ciuitate matre*, a translation of Greek μητρόπολις. As it was founded by the grandsons of Numitor king of Alba Longa, Rome had begun its life as a colony of that city.

brother and the surrounding Romans who sentenced her to death for a behavior that was praiseworthy rather than culpable even by Roman standards – witness the Vergilian and Livian *exempla* of Aeneas weeping for Lausus and Marcellus regretting the destruction of Syracuse in the Second Punic War.[65] No trace of this in the conflict between Rome and Alba; all natural human affection, morality, and other regard had been overthrown by the civil war, and Rome lusted for cognate blood no less than her demonic gods who watched the killing like the spectators of a gladiatorial game. Augustine's concluding sentence with its marked antitheses and parallelisms is pathetic rhetoric at its best:

> *quaeso ab humano impetremus affectu,/ut femina sponsum suum a fratre suo peremptum sine crimine fleuerit,/si uiri hostes a se uictos etiam cum laude fleuerunt.*
>
> *ergo sponso a fratre inlatam mortem quando femina illa flebat,/ tunc se contra matrem ciuitatem tanta strage bellasse/et tanta hinc et inde cognati cruoris effusione uicisse Roma gaudebat.*
>
> Please, surely human feeling will grant us that it is no crime for a woman to weep over her betrothed, killed by her own brother! But while that woman was weeping at the death of her betrothed by the hand of her brother, Rome itself was rejoicing that she had gone to war against her mother city at the cost of such slaughter and had won the victory at the cost of shedding all that kindred blood on both sides!
>
> (*ciu. Dei* 3.14, Babcock, 1.84; slightly adjusted)

Yet Augustine's procedure was perhaps not quite as revolutionary as it would appear.

The technique he employs, especially the strong stylistic effects and paradoxes, are reminiscent of rhetorical declamation, a popular literary genre of Late Antiquity that had originated, and continued to be, a school exercise that trained the pupils' ability to view a given case from different angles and to find and phrase compelling arguments even for seemingly counter-intuitive propositions. As Cicero tells us, the defense and, as we may presume, the accusation of Horatius after the killing of his sister was a common subject of declamation.[66] Let us imagine a pupil in the role of

[65] Verg. *Aen.* 10.821–832 and Livy 25.24,11 respectively. For Marcellus cf. already *ciu. Dei* 1.6.

[66] Cic. *inu.* 2.78ff.; Kohl 1915, p. 360. The rhetor Emporius (5th or 6th century AD) gives precepts on how to handle Lucretia, another famous *exemplum*, in deliberative speech and provides arguments *in utramque partem* (*Rhetores Latini minores* 572–574 Halm), at times coming close to Augustine's revisionist treatment of Lucretia in *ciu. Dei* 1.19. See most recently Franchi 2012. On Roman declamation

the accuser: To make his case, he could not possibly directly attack Horatius, a hero who had just secured victory for Rome single-handed, and denounce him as a murderer – the defender's reply would inevitably have been Florus': "his virtue did away with the parricide." What he could do was to abstract from the Roman, military and exemplary background and to appeal to the jury's human feelings by bewailing Horatia's undeserved death. Augustine, the former *rhetor*, is doing precisely this.

The declamatory style continues in Augustine's subsequent anticipation of the predictable defense of Horatia's death and Alba Longa's destruction as necessary for the military glory of Rome:

> Why are the words "honor" and "victory" held out to me as an excuse? Pull aside the veil of crazed opinion. Let the evil actions be examined in their naked reality, let them be weighed in their naked reality, and be judged in their naked reality.
>
> (*ciu. Dei* 3.14; Babcock, 1.84)

Augustine's rejection of the traditional values "glory" and "victory" as mere names and preconceived opinions is in line with his rhetorical tactics in this chapter and with his revisionary outlook on Roman history in general but has also a deeper significance. The opposition of "facts" (*facinora*) and "opinions" (*opiniones*) is reminiscent of philosophical ethics, especially of the Stoic doctrine according to which negative affections arise, not from the facts but from our unreasonable opinions about them. Taken by itself, "victory" means killing and being killed. There is nothing great or glorious about this; gladiators do the same,[67] even though in their case nobody would enjoy watching a duel between father and son whereas the Romans in their madness glorified the "daughter-city's" killing of her "mother." The "glorious" victory over Alba Longa is thus just another of the evils that befell Rome before the advent of Christ. As before in the case of Troy, Augustine asks for the cause (*causa*) that brought it about.[68] His first explanation is, as usual in Book 3 the influence of the gods or demons. His second answer concerns the human agents and their motivation and thus points beyond the immediate polemical goal of Book 3. If "glory" and "victory" are empty names, what motivated Tullus and his Romans to attack

see Bonner 1949; Kaster 2001; on its influence on Augustine, Ribreau 2015. See also Pernot 2005, pp. 151–157.

[67] For the comparison cf. *ciu. Dei* 4.4 with the famous claim that states without justice are no better than *magna latrocinia*.

[68] *ciu. Dei* 3.14: *causa dicatur Albae, sicut Troiae adulterium dicebatur.*

Alba Longa and start a civil war? Augustine replies: the lust for (tyrannical) domination (*libido dominandi*),[69] by which they were dominated themselves.[70] This explanation (almost a quotation from the general preface of *ciu. Dei*,[71] even though Augustine, true to his strategy in Book 3, now supports his diagnosis with the authority of Sallust) is systematically important for several reasons. First, according to Augustine's "intentionalist" ethics[72] the criterion of moral evaluation of an action is not its external success but the agent's internal motivation or intention. Hence the diagnosis that the Romans acted out of *libido dominandi* amounts to an uncompromising condemnation of war-waging Rome as an archetypal incarnation of the *ciuitas terrena*. Later in the work we will learn that lust for domination is a particularly repellent form of excessive self-love or *superbia*[73] which, as Augustine says in the famous concluding chapter of Book 14, is the distinguishing mark of the earthly city as opposed to the heavenly city's love of God.[74] The dualism of the Two Cities and its ethical foundation is thus adumbrated in our passage at an early stage. Second, the interplay of moral and external evils in the history of Rome, which repeatedly surfaces in Book 3, becomes understandable. People dominated by lust for domination act in such a way as to inflict external sufferings on others and on themselves; the strict separation of moral and extra-moral evils in history promised in *ciu. Dei* 3.1 (though already there Augustine had conceded it to his adversaries rather than endorsed himself) turns out to be impracticable. Augustine does however not address the relationship between human moral agency (or, rather, disposition) and demonic instigation. This question, which concerns the difficult issue of human responsibility and fate, is briefly touched upon in Book 3 in the chapters on Numa (*ciu. Dei* 3.10), but a full treatment is postponed until Book 5.[75]

69 See *ciu. Dei* 14.15: *libido dominandi, quam tamen plurimum ualere in tyrannorum animis etiam ciuilia bella testantur.*

70 *libido ista dominandi magnis malis agitat et conterit humanum genus. hac libidine Roma tunc uicta Albam se uicisse triumphabat et sui sceleris laudem gloriam nominabat.*

71 *ciu. Dei* 1.*praef.*: *de terrena ciuitate, quae cum dominari adpetit, etsi populi seruiant, ipsa ei dominandi libido dominatur.*

72 See, e.g. Mann 1999; Rist 1994, pp. 148–202 ("Will, love and right action").

73 Cf. *ciu. Dei* 5.13 on *cupido laudis* which, though a vice, is more tolerable than naked and brutal lust for power; 5.19; 19.14: *dominandi cupiditate ... principandi superbia*; Tornau 2006a, pp. 297ff.; Rist 1994, pp. 220–223.

74 *ciu. Dei* 14.28.

75 See the important section on divine foreknowledge and human freedom in *ciu. Dei* 5.9–10; Tornau 2006a, pp. 263–294; Perkams 2008. The systematic importance of this section of 3.14 is signaled also by the only explicit and verbatim quotation from

A different yet related strategy can be observed in the chapters on the civil war between Marius and Sulla, which Augustine depicts as the darkest moment in the dark history of pre-Christian Rome (*ciu. Dei* 3.27–29). Using all the resources of pathetic rhetoric and relying, again, heavily on Florus, Augustine draws a gruesome picture of the slaughter of innocent people not just in war but also in peace and of the total disintegration of society and state that followed Sulla's victory. As before, Augustine wishes to encourage his readers to rethink the conventional views of Roman history, but other than in the case of Alba Longa and the Regal period, he now attempts to reach his purpose while sticking to the traditional evaluation of the events. It was common knowledge that the civil wars of the 1st century BC had been horrible, and especially the sinister figure of Sulla was famous for his reckless cruelty.[76] Augustine's tactical means in this case are heightened pathos and new contextualization. He activates the traditional image in his readers from the outset by quoting two well-known passages from Cicero's *Catilinarians* and, once more, from Lucan that articulate the familiar view that Sulla's dictatorship and the proscriptions had outdone Marius' war in horror and gratuitous carnage (*ciu. Dei* 3.27, quoting Cic. *Cat.* 3.24, Luc. 2.142–144). After a list of prominent civil victims of Marius and his followers (*ciu. Dei* 3.27),[77] he goes on to depict the victory of Sulla (*ciu. Dei* 3.28), using as a leitmotif the paradox that though the civil war had been horrible, it was outdone in horror by the subsequent peace. The chapter is clearly based on Florus who had already treated the same topic in a highly pathetic manner:

> The slaughter of more than 70,000 men by Sulla at Sacriportus and the Colline Gate was a lesser crime: that was the war. But he ordered 4,000 unarmed citizens who had been surrendered to be slain in the Villa Publica: are these, slain in peace, not the greater number?[78]

the Bible in Book 3 (Ps 10,3). The quotation is not strictly necessary for the argument. The only two other references to Scripture are in 3.5 (a "footnote" on the giants of Gen 6:4) and in 3.9 (Mt 5:45; see below).

[76] For a modern assessment, see Steel 2014.

[77] The victims are partly familiar from Cicero, but the list is based on Florus (2.9,14–17). See Walsh 2007, p. 214; Hagendahl 1967, pp. 177ff.

[78] Flor. 2,9,24ff.; translation adapted from E. S. Foster: *Minus est, quod apud Sacriportum, apud Collinam septuaginta amplius milia Sulla concidit: bellum erat. Quattuor milia deditorum inermium civium in Villa Publica interfici iussit: isti tot in pace non plures sunt?*

Now consider Augustine's adaptation:

> Then Sulla entered the city victorious, and in the Villa Publica, not in the course of battle but simply by his command, he had seven thousand men cut down (*non pugnando, sed iubendo prostrauerat*), men who had already surrendered and therefore were certainly unarmed. Now it was no longer war but peace itself that was raging like a savage (*non iam bello, sed ipsa pace saeuiente*).
>
> (*ciu. Dei* 3.28; Babcock, 1.104)

Augustine is primarily interested in Florus' paradoxical antithesis of war and peace. He intensifies it by omitting Florus' comparison of the numbers and by introducing two mannered oxymora: "raging peace" (*pace saeuiente*) and "killing by command" (rather than in battle). The former, which is especially striking and almost unparalleled,[79] drastically shows that peace has taken over the role of war. The hyperbolic style of the sentence borders on tastelessness, and deliberately so: By a mimetic principle often operative in the use of paradox in antiquity, a world out of joint cannot be described adequately without one's language getting out of joint too.[80]

The notion of peace is also central to Augustine's strategy of recontextualization. As mentioned above, in Book 2 Augustine envisaged a disordered, permissive society that is kept from total disintegration only by retaining a minimum of unity and peace (*ciu. Dei* 2.20). At the end of Book 3 this minimum has gone. Peace itself becomes war, the cohesion of state and society is swept away by blood. In Book 2 Augustine had quoted Cicero's pessimistic remarks about "the loss of the Republic" (*res publica perdita*),[81] and he will do so again later in Book 3.[82] In the chapter on Sulla, Augustine demonstrates as concretely and with as much emotional commitment as possible what this diagnosis means in real life. Nor are the civil wars of the dying Republic an isolated misfortune or, as the traditional, especially Sallustian reading of Roman history would have it, the outcome of the later Romans' moral

[79] While the combination of *bellum* and *saeuire*/*saeuus* is common and even banal, there is no exact parallel for *pax saeuiens*. Cf., however, Tac. *hist.* 1.2,1 (*ipsa etiam pace saeuum*); *ann.* 1.50,2 (*saeuae pacis exempla*). There is no evidence that Augustine had read Tacitus (Hagendahl 1967, p. 669), but it is not by accident that he here comes close to an author who is notoriously fond of pathetic paradox.

[80] Cf. Lefèvre 1992, p. 209.

[81] *ciu. Dei* 2.21, quoting Cic. *rep.* 5.1ff.

[82] *ciu. Dei* 3.30: *bella ciuilia …, quibus illa res publica nec adflicta, sed omnino perdita iudicata est.*

decline. In the course of Book 3 Augustine has established civil war as the persistent evil of Roman history from the earliest times that accounts for most of the countless woes of Rome before Christ. Viewed from this perspective, and if we are prepared to regard history without prejudice (as Augustine urges us to do at *ciu. Dei* 3.14),[83] the carnage under Sulla differs from the rape of the Sabine women or the fight of the Horatians and Curiatians only in degree.

Moreover, the subsequent chapter (*ciu. Dei* 3.29) contains the only explicit comparison between Rome's woeful past and the Christian present. Drawing on the resources of rhetorical *sunkrisis* or *comparatio*,[84] Augustine skillfully opposes the horrors Rome had experienced when it was conquered by a Roman, Sulla, and the war-like but not excessively cruel behavior of the Goths, i.e. external enemies, during the recent sack of Rome.[85] Obviously, this comparison could not have worked had Augustine not endorsed and, with the help of Florus, dramatized the traditional judgment on Sulla and the civil wars. Nevertheless, he is steering a somewhat risky course here. Certainly, he does not infer from the comparison any more than that to blame recent calamities on Christianity when there were similar and much more terrible woes in the pre-Christian period is both silly and shameless.[86] However, in his concluding attack on the pagan opponents, putting the same idea positively, he goes so far as to say: "So then, let those who are ungrateful to Christ for his great benefits blame their own gods for these great evils" (*ciu. Dei* 3.31; Babcock, 1.106).

It is, of course, logically unsound to infer from the *fact* that Rome had suffered from heavier calamities before the coming of Christ than after that the improvement had been *caused* by Christianity. For a Christian in the time of Augustine, it was nevertheless tempting to draw this inference. Augustine usually resists this temptation, which would have run counter the whole logic of the *ciu. Dei*,[87] but as the passage just quoted shows, even he was capable of momentarily

[83] Cf. also *ciu. Dei* 3.31: *quisquis sine studio partium iudicat.*

[84] Quint. *inst.* 2.4,21: *exercitatio ... comparationis, uter melior uterue deterior.*

[85] Augustine's depiction of the Gothic conquest is in harmony with his more detailed plea at *ciu. Dei* 1.1.

[86] *ciu. Dei* 3.30: *qua igitur fronte quo corde, qua inpudentia qua insipientia uel potius amentia illa diis suis non inputant, et haec nostro inputant Christo?*

[87] This is generally acknowledged. See, e.g. the influential interpretation of Markus 1970, 45–71, and, for a recent reassessment, Wetzel 2012. Augustine is careful to deny any causal connection between Christian faith and earthly well-being from the outset (cf. *ciu. Dei* 1.8).

succumbing to it. Others were less scrupulous: Orosius' *Historia contra paganos* is entirely designed to collect evidence in favor of the inference.[88]

A WIDER PERSPECTIVE: AUGUSTINE ON NUMA

Numa Pompilius, the second king of Rome, receives a remarkably full treatment in our book (*ciu. Dei* 3.9–12). Due to the generic tradition, the historians were usually more concerned with periods of crisis and war;[89] accordingly they tended to give less weight to his peaceful reign than to the military achievements of a Romulus or a Tullus Hostilius.[90] By contrast, Augustine devotes four chapters to Numa but only one to Tullus;[91] Romulus is contemptuously relegated to two excursus-like passages.[92] There are several reasons for this reversal. First, Numa was the king whom history credited with the foundation of most of Rome's religions institutions and, as it were, with the completion of the Roman pantheon. This made him an important figure for the Christian apologists.[93] Second, the four decades of peace Rome enjoyed during his reign were usually explained as a gift from the gods in return to his devotion and religious expertise. Augustine, of course, needs to refute this explanation but in this case cannot, as in the rest of the book, point to historical calamities allegedly caused or tolerated by the gods. He must, while accepting the reality of Numa's peace, deny that the gods were responsible for it. This, in turn, raises the question about its true cause, which Augustine can only answer by referring to the providential care of the true (Christian) god. He thus needs to argue more subtly and to rely more heavily on Christian presuppositions than elsewhere in Book 3. Third, Numa was often represented as a kind of philosopher-king (Augustine briefly alludes to the tradition that connected him with Pythagoras).[94] This raises the problem of the relationship of religion

88 On Orosius and Augustine see Inglebert 2014, with further bibliography.

89 Cf. Tacitus' manner of advertising his *Histories* (*hist.* 1.2,1).

90 Livy devotes four chapters to Numa (1.18–21), eleven to Romulus (1.7–17) and ten to Tullus Hostilius (1.22–31). Florus' chapter on Numa (1.2) is considerably shorter than those on Romulus (1.1) and Tullus (1.3).

91 *ciu. Dei* 3.14 (discussed above), admittedly an important chapter.

92 *ciu. Dei* 3.6 and 3.13 (on the rape of the Sabine women; the deviation from chronology is probably intended to mark off the reign of Numa as an exception from the rule).

93 Cf. Maier 1955, p. 105 with n. 76 who points to Tert. *Apol.* 21.29ff.; 25.12; Arnob. 7.26.

94 *ciu. Dei* 7.35. For Macrobius, Numa ideally combined the active and the contemplative life, like the Greeks Lycurgus and Solon (*somn.* 2.17,8).

and philosophy, which will be the main subject of the second part of the work (Books 6–10). Augustine's arguments concerning Numa thus of necessity point beyond the immediate polemical aim of Book 3 and therefore deserve some closer inspection.[95]

Augustine opens the debate with the following resolute claim:

> Here, however, the question has to do with the benefits brought by the gods. Peace, of course, is a great benefit, but it is a benefit bestowed by the true God, and – like the sun, the rain, and other supports of life – it is commonly bestowed even on the ungrateful and the scurrilous.
>
> (*ciu. Dei* 3.9, paraphrasing Mt 5:45; Babcock, 1.77–78)

He flatly denies that the gods venerated by Numa were capable to guarantee peace and insists that the only giver of peace is "the true God" (*dei ueri*).[96] This wording, together with the near-quotation of a biblical verse[97] (the only one in this book except for the quotation of Ps 10:3 at *ciu. Dei* 3.14), marks the sentence as a specifically Christian conviction – quite unusually, because Augustine in Book 3 generally grounds his refutations on his opponents' own presuppositions. For the moment, however, he does not pursue this idea any further but returns to the agonistic style by arguing negatively that the peace under Numa cannot at any rate have been due to the pagan gods – had it been, they should have kept it up after his death, when thanks to Numa's religious policy their number had considerably increased (*ciu. Dei* 3.9).

He then goes on to anticipate and refute the objection that without continuous war Rome could never have been as great and glorious as it is (*ciu. Dei* 3.10). He retorts that it would have been better for Rome if it had been less great and less renowned but had lived quietly and in peace. The argument is parallel in structure and content to *ciu. Dei* 3.14 where Augustine brushed aside all preconceived opinions about greatness and glory and unmasked "lust for domination" (*libido dominandi*) – the counterpart of the "greed to win men's praise" (*auiditas adipiscendae*

[95] Bruggisser 2009 lists and briefly comments on seventeen Augustinian passages (from *ciu. Dei* and elsewhere) that mention Numa. On Numa as the founder of Roman religion in the *ciu. Dei*, see Harding 2007, pp. 83–85.

[96] The phrase *deus uerus* occurs three times in the chapters on Numa (3.9; 3.11; 3.12) but is absent from the rest of Book 3. Christ is mentioned five times (3.1; 3.17; 3.20; 3.30, and twice at 3.31).

[97] Mt 5:45: *qui facit solem suum oriri super bonos et malos et pluit super iustos et iniustos* (thus quoted in *ciu.* 4.2). Cf. already *ciu.* 1.8.

laudis humanae) of *ciu. Dei* 3.10 – as the questionable motive behind the Romans' military exploits. As at *ciu. Dei* 3.14, the argument is primarily designed to deflate Roman expansionism, but he phrases it in such a way as to bring up the issue of what makes a man and a city happy[98] and in his answer uncompromisingly opts for peace rather than for glory. Much later in the philosophical discussion of (moral) ends in Book 19, we will learn that peace is a universal ethical principle operative on all levels of reality that guarantees the well-being of both individuals and societies by preserving the harmony and the natural (hierarchical) order of the divergent elements. Supreme peace, i.e. the loving subordination of humans to God, is identical with true happiness.[99] At the present stage of the argument, where he is still dealing with an adversary who identifies happiness with political and military success, Augustine does not develop this point further. But the claim that peace is a necessary (and, perhaps, sufficient) condition for happiness is on the table, even if it remains somewhat shadowy and its implications are not spelled out.

Augustine's way of introducing the subject of philosophy is equally allusive. His first words on Numa in *ciu. Dei* 3.9 caricature him as an intellectual whom the gods or rather demons, profiting from his political leisure (*otium*, a synonym of *pax*), lured into experimenting with dark magic. For the details, Augustine refers to his forthcoming treatment in Book 7 (where we shall learn that Numa's practices included hydromancy and necromancy); he is however careful, as usual in Book 3 to base his claim on a Roman authority (in this case, Varro).[100] This is no doubt primarily an invective against Numa's religious reforms, but Augustine ascribes him a key characteristic that links him with the philosophers: curiosity (*curiositas*),[101] the very vice that in Book 10 induces the Platonists to neglect their correct insight into the nature of the transcendent God and to indulge in demonic cults and

[98] Cf. *ciu. Dei* 1.15: *neque enim aliunde beata ciuitas, aliunde homo, cum aliud ciuitas non sit quam concors hominum multitudo*; cf. 4.3ff. The word *beatus* is absent from *ciu. Dei* 3.10, but the opposition of *bonum* and *malum* is prominent.

[99] See esp. *ciu. Dei* 19.10; 19.13; O'Daly 1999, pp. 203ff. The fullest recent treatment of Augustine's theory of peace is Weissenberg 2005, esp. pp. 276–298. See also the numerous discussions of Augustine's views on war and peace, e.g. Holmes 1999; Burnell 2010; and Fuhrer 2011.

[100] *nam quid ille molitus sit et quibus artibus deos tales sibi uel illi ciuitati consociare potuerit, Varro prodit, quod, si domino placuerit, suo diligentius disseretur loco.* The cross-reference is to *ciu. Dei* 7.34ff.

[101] Let us however note that *curiositas* surfaces already in Tertullian as characteristic of Numa's *superstitio* (*apol.* 25.12).

theurgy[102] instead of accepting the mediation of Christ incarnate (the *Christus humilis*) – the only path that leads to God (Jn 14:6).[103] The link to philosophy becomes even clearer later on:

> Perhaps this is the reason why Numa Pompilius, enjoying abundant peace but neither knowing nor investigating who bestowed it, when he considered at leisure to what gods he should entrust the protection of Rome's sovereignty and well-being – since he had no idea that the true and all-powerful supreme God cares for these earthly matters, and since he remembered that the Trojan gods, whom Aeneas brought, were unable to preserve for very long either the kingdom of Troy or the kingdom of Lavinium founded by Aeneas himself – came to the conclusion that he must provide other gods, in addition to the earlier ones who either had come over to Rome with Romulus or would come over when Alba was overthrown.
>
> (*ciu. Dei* 3.11; Babcock, 1.80)

Augustine polemically connects Numa's new rites with the notorious unreliability of the tutelary gods of Troy and Rome but at the same time imagines him as a philosophical theologian pondering at leisure (*otiosus*; again the link with peace) on the nature and powers of the divine. Numa sees the importance of peace for happiness, and Augustine even seems to grant him, like the Platonists, some degree of awareness of the supreme God.[104] His mistake is to deny or simply to ignore God's providence – a view that links him to Epicureanism rather than Platonism and, from the point of view of a late-antique intellectual (whether pagan or Christian), disqualifies him as a serious philosopher.[105] Together with his curiosity, his failure to see that God cares for humankind and that he is the ultimate cause of all happiness and peace makes Numa an easy prey to demonic seduction

[102] According to Augustine theurgy is just a more pretentious name for magic (*ciu. Dei* 10.9).

[103] With *ciu. Dei* 3.9; cf. 7.34 (again on Numa); 10.26; 10.27; and 10.29 (all on Porphyry and the Platonists). See Labhardt 1996–2002.

[104] This is of course anachronistic as far as early and Republican Rome is concerned, but it reflects the fact that some kind of quasi-philosophical monotheism compatible with cultic polytheism was the default ideology of a pagan intellectual in Late Antiquity. Cf. e.g. Maximus *apud* Aug. *ep.* 16,1; Liebeschuetz 1999; Fürst 2008.

[105] Contrast *ciu. Dei* 8.1 on the Platonists: *cum et esse diuinitatem et humana curare consentiant. Epicurus or Epicureus* were used as abusive terms in Augustine's age (*ep.* 167,4; Julian of Eclanum *apud* Aug. *c. Iul. imp.* 3.48). See Erler 1996–2002 with further references.

and deception. Of course, the relevance of the pagan cults for "happiness after this life," i.e. happiness that does not depend on external and political events, receives full attention only later in the debate with the Stoics and, especially, with the Platonists in Books 6–10.[106] It is however significant that Numa, the first philosopher who makes his appearance in *ciu. Dei*, is marked by what Augustine considers philosophy's two worst aberrations, "Epicurean" practical atheism and magic.

CONCLUSION

Book 3 may appear to be one of the less attractive books of the *ciu. Dei*, and it is definitely among those least studied. Yet we have seen how artfully Augustine employs his rhetorical skills to finally discourage the idealizing reading of Roman history inherited from the Latin Classics that was still much *en vogue* among those of his contemporaries who had received a liberal education. After perusing the book, Christian readers will have felt excellently equipped for apologetic debate with their pagan neighbors, and the aesthetic appeal of Augustine's rhetoric will not have been lost on a public accustomed to appreciate declamatory showpieces. His pathetical style invites readers committed to traditional views on the exemplary value of the Roman past to respond to it with natural feeling instead of hardened prejudice – let us remember Augustine's rehabilitation of the emotions against the Stoics in Books 9 and 14 at this point.[107] The brief but weighty remarks that point toward a deeper interpretation of Roman history in terms of the theme of the Two Cities and of God's providential rule over all human history (whether sacred or secular) prepare the reader for the more detailed arguments to come and help to determine the place of Book 3 in the overall design of the *ciu. Dei*.

FURTHER READING

Hagendahl, H. (1967). *Augustine and the Latin Classics*, 2 vols. Göteborg: Elander.

Inglebert, H. (2014). Orosius. In *Augustinus-Lexikon* 4 (fasc. 3/4). Basel: Schwabe Verlag, pp. 398–403.

[106] For another foreshadowing of the discussion of *theologia naturalis* in these books cf. *ciu. Dei* 3.18.

[107] In particular, *ciu. Dei* 9.5; 14.9. See Wetzel 1992, pp. 98–111; Byers 2012.

Maier, F. G. (1955). *Augustin und das antike Rom*. Stuttgart: Kohlhammer.
Rist, J. M. (1994). *Augustine: Ancient Thought Baptized*. Cambridge: Cambridge University Press.
Tornau, C. (2006a). *Zwischen Rhetorik und Philosophie: Augustins Argumentationstechnik in De civitate Dei und ihr bildungsgeschichtlicher Hintergrund*. Berlin/New York: de Gruyter.

5 Books 4 & 5: Roman Religion and Just Power

DEAN HAMMER

In the first three books of *City of God*, Augustine begins to defend Christianity against those who blame it for the sack of Rome.[1] More specifically, Augustine is responding to both the written theological questions of the pagan Volusian, the proconsul of Africa (*ep.* 135), and Volusian's spoken concerns relayed by his Christian friend, Marcellinus (*ep.* 136), that Christianity and Roman citizenship were incompatible.[2] In his aim of exonerating the Christians from blame for Rome's fall, Augustine, as Markus suggests, speaks of Rome "as an outsider."[3] But Rome plays a more complicated role in Augustine's argument. For Augustine, we are a complex amalgam of experiences, memories, habits, affections, dispositions, and reason, all of which shape, both consciously and subconsciously, what we love.[4] "To have a past," as Wetzel observes, is "to admit grief into wisdom."[5] Augustine shares with his audience many of the same affective memories derived from his Roman upbringing and education.[6] One need only recall Augustine's recollection of how Virgil moved him to tears as a youth (*conf.* 1.13.20–21). Books 4 and 5 read not as a break from this Roman past, but as a recasting of memory. Citing Roman sources along the way, Augustine detaches paganism from romanticized images of Rome's past, showing that traditional Roman religious practices not only fail to account for Roman successes, but also are the contrivance of elites used to conceal their criminality and justify domination.

In the place of a pagan reading of Roman history Augustine substitutes a Christian one. Augustine clears out the lingering Roman beliefs

1 My thanks to Michael Kicey and Kerry Whiteside for their comments on earlier drafts of this chapter. All translations are lifted from Babcock.

2 For a translation of the letters, see Rotelle 1990, Pt 2, vol. 3.

3 Markus 1988, p. 57.

4 Hammer 2014, p. 396.

5 Wetzel 1992, p. 109.

6 See Hammer 2014, pp. 382–430 on the Roman influence on Augustine's thought.

in fate, divination, prophecy, and will in order to provide a reading of the Roman past that shows the relationship between God's empowering will and human choice. The immediate context is Rome's love of glory. Underlying this discussion is a view that all communities organize desire in some way; the only question is to what effect. In their love of something greater than themselves, Rome points the way toward what is possible among citizens of the City of God. The implication of this claim should not be overlooked. In the uncertain environment in which Augustine is concerned about the wavering commitment of the newly converted, Augustine is mitigating the divide between being a Roman and being a Christian. What once was Rome's greatness has a corollary in the glory of the City of God. But, and there is a big but, in tearing away the façade of traditional Roman religious practices by showing them to be tools of corrupt elites used to foster their own desire for control at the expense of the community, Augustine justifies the repression of paganism. Christianity, not paganism, is the true vehicle of Rome's glory.

THE PAGAN BACKDROP

Book 4 is directed at the variety of both imperial and local pagan rituals and cult practices that were employed by both the traditional Roman aristocracy and peasants. If one were to simply know Rome by way of Book 4, one would be left with the impression of struggling Christians besieged by a vibrant and politically powerful pagan community. In this first section I seek to contextualize Augustine's discussion by asking what was left of paganism by the beginning of the 5th century AD.

When Constantine I became the first Christian emperor (AD 306–AD 337), the immediate impact was to extend tolerance of Christianity across the empire. By any measure, including that of representation in imperial office, Christianity experienced a gradual and – but for Julian's brief reign – largely uninterrupted assent through the 4th century AD.[7] Peter Brown and others have gone far in revising our understanding of the relationship between the Christian elite and the traditional Roman aristocracy, pointing to a shared cultural identity that was as important as any religious divide.[8] Throughout the 4th century AD Christian and non-Christian elites mingled: they could be (as was the case for Augustine) from the same family, they corresponded with each other,

[7] See Barnes 1995; Haehling 1978.
[8] See O'Donnell 1979; Brown 2012.

and non-Christians appointed Christians to political offices and vice-versa. Augustine was inculcated in this exclusive literary culture and would have had interactions with this elite, particularly by way of the governors of Roman Africa who were drawn from the senate. The relationship between Augustine, Marcellinus, and Volusian (whose mother is Christian) is more representative than unique.

Although there were shared attitudes, there were also real divisions. The preceding centuries were marked by the periodic persecution of Christians because of their unwillingness to demonstrate their allegiance through cult observances to imperial authority, most recently under Diocletian at the beginning of the 4th century AD. But, as Christianity asserted itself both doctrinally and politically, the adherents of traditional Roman religion did not have a ready or coherent response. There was no "pagan party," as Bloch refers to it.[9] Traditional Roman religion was, if nothing else, pluralistic and adaptive, combining local and imperial cults and practices with indigenous religions and private cults. In North Africa alone, Roman deities and practices were mixed with Greek, Punic, and Libyan ones. It is precisely this amalgam of traditions that Augustine seizes upon in his romp through the variety of Roman gods (*ciu. Dei* 4.8–23). There was not an official religion, unified doctrine, or imperial policy. Roman religion operated more by what Rives describes as "a vague consensus" on what was acceptable.[10] In fact, the term "pagan" takes on a religious context only in the AD 370s. Originally used to refer to a civilian (as opposed to a soldier) who did not serve the emperor, *paganus* is employed by Latin Christians to denote their own exclusivity by identifying those not sharing in the honor of serving Christ, the "true emperor."[11]

Augustine would have been surrounded by reminders of paganism. The imperial landscape was dotted with baths, coliseums, porticos, temples, statues, dedications, and public squares that served as repositories of images of the ancestral past.[12] Each locale had its own public cults that were woven into the fabric of civic identity.[13] In addition, beginning with Augustus the ritual worship of deities associated with the state is connected with the emperor, who as both the *pontifex maximus* and as divine, becomes the central figure in assuring the

[9] Bloch 1945, p. 203.
[10] See Rives 1995, p. 245.
[11] Brown 2012, p. 102; also Cameron 2011, pp. 14–32.
[12] Freeman 2009, p. 257.
[13] Rives 1995, pp. 5–6, 246.

stability and prosperity of the state. The gods, by way of the emperor, could be appealed to through worship and sacrifice. Throughout the empire, temples to different gods – *Libertas*, *Pax*, *Victoria*, and *Felicitas* – were dedicated to emperors. Processions, games, and public banquets were all elements of this worship and important in instilling awe of – and a connection to – imperial authority. Aspects of the imperial cult, because it was so much a fabric of social power in the Roman world, continued to function even among Christian emperors (though absent blood sacrifice, which had been outlawed). For example, Constantine continued to promote the imperial cult to his family in Africa and Italy.[14] Constantine even issued a decree that if lightning strikes any public building, "the observance of the ancient custom shall be retained, and inquiry shall be made of the soothsayers as to the portent thereof" (*CTh* 16.10.1 [321]). Even as laws restricted pagan practices, the temples from which circuses and contests were performed were protected from demolition (*CTh* 16.10.3 [342; 346]).

The most significant interruption in the gradual assent of Christianity across the Roman empire in the 4th century AD came with Julian, who sought to return the empire to paganism, including decreasing the influence of Christian teachers of rhetoric by outlawing them in AD 362 (*CTh* 13.3.5 [362]) and restoring confiscated estates. After his short reign, subsequent emperors, though reestablishing the connection of Christianity to the Roman state, moved reluctantly toward any larger statement of the role of Christianity in the empire. In part the reluctance was a result of the focus on military engagements. For the emperors, securing the frontiers of the empire was more important than enforcing a uniform belief. The reluctance was also due to the unwillingness by emperors to create enemies among the wealthy landowners. For example, Jovian, following Julian, was Christian but also (as implied by way of a speech of Themistius, a senator) allowed for different Christian sects and even pagan practices (except for unacceptable sacrificial practices) (Them. *Or.* 5.70b). Valentinian in the West repealed Julian's unpopular law against Christian teachers of literature but issued laws guaranteeing freedom of worship as long as it did not harm the state. Theodosius, whose reign is seen by Augustine as marking a turning point in suppressing paganism, nonetheless showed a willingness to appoint and work with prominent pagans, including Symmachus, Albinus, and Flavian in the West and Tatianus and Proculus in the East.

[14] Lenski 2016, p. 128.

The push for establishing a unified Christian doctrine was, in fact, driven by ecclesiastical authorities, such as Ambrose, who resided in the imperial court at Milan, and later Augustine. There was a lot at stake. There was theological doctrine that did not admit of compromise. And there was also power. Imperial recognition had enormous impact on who would receive particular tax privileges. And recognition had significant impact on the competition for local influence. The traditional elite had styled themselves as "protectors of the people," not just in Rome but extending into localities across Italy, Sicily, and North Africa.[15] Now there was a new elite, the ecclesiastical authorities, who competed for local influence. And in this competition they would look to imperial help.

Paganism was slowly bled of its life: its practices curtailed, resources diminished, and its connection to political office and influence severed until once sufficiently weakened, it could be more assertively suppressed. Sacrifices were prohibited, as reiterated in AD 341 (though the law referred to is not extant) and largely ended by AD 385 (*CTh* 16.10.2 [341]; 16.10.5 [353]; 16.10.6 [356]; 16.10.7 [381]; 16.10.10 [391]). Temples were ordered closed (*CTh* 16.10.4 [356, 354, 356]), though enforcement was sporadic. The altar of Victory outside the Roman senate house, which had been a continuous site of a dedication on the opening day of the senate since established by Augustus, would become a bone of contention for decades. Constantius II initially ordered its removal in AD 357. Julian restored it, only for Gratian to remove it in AD 382 as well as banning the use of public funds for pagan temples. Symmachus famously appealed to Valentinian II two years later in AD 384 for the restoration of the altar (renewing his appeal from AD 382 that was denied an audience). The appeal precipitated a famous exchange between Symmachus and Ambrose that revealed just how different were their respective goals: toleration of traditional customs that had brought glory to Rome for Symmachus (*Rel.* 3.3; 3.5; 3.8–3.9); a strident rejection of anything not Nicene by Ambrose as evidenced in *epistula* 18.

With Theodosius one sees a more sustained effort against paganism. There is the first concerted attempt to enforce a Nicene orthodoxy through patronage and appointments, though enforcement did not go much beyond that. In AD 391, Theodosius ordered that the eternal flame of Vesta, a protector of Rome from its foundation, be extinguished. Sacrifices continued to be forbidden but in a series of three

[15] Matthews 1975, p. 20.

laws from AD 391–392 (likely in response to specific requests), there was a restatement of bans on sacrifice, a prohibition on entering temples (which would only affect priests and temple officials), a ban on the participation by officials in pagan ceremonies in the West that was consistent with previous legislation (*CTh* 16.10.9 [391]; 16.10.10 [391]), and a more comprehensive ban on all forms of pagan worship in the East (*CTh* 16.10.11 in the November AD 392 law from Constantinople).[16] The Olympic games were held for their last time in AD 393. In AD 399, the temples in Carthage were closed. In AD 407, Honorius ordered strong measures, placing particular pagan sects outside the law (*CTh* 16.5.40) and closing flourishing pagan temples in Africa. By AD 408, any buildings associated with the temples were transferred to public use and full power was granted to ecclesiastical authorities to enforce the ban on pagan practices (*CTh* 16.10.19 [408]). Honorius, in AD 408, banned pagans from imperial service (*CTh* 16.5.42), reiterated the requirement for officials to enforce laws against pagans (*CTh* 16.4.46), and forbade banquets (though banquets continued) (*CTh* 16.19.2–3). Exemptions were possible that allowed for some continued estate support for pagan practices: As late as AD 408, some of the African revenues supporting the pagan temples had not been reassigned.[17] In AD 410, Honorius banned any practice of paganism in Africa (*CTh* 16.5.51). In AD 415, Theodosius II banned pagans from imperial service (*CTh* 16.10.21).

The number of openly practicing pagans among the elite also dwindled. In AD 384, two prominent pagans occupied high-level posts, both appointed by the Christian emperor, Valentinian II: Praetextatus as praetorian prefect of Italy, and Symmachus as prefect of Rome. After Praetextatus' death in AD 384, Symmachus, the most prominent pagan official in the West, resigned his prefecture a year later and stayed largely out of the public eye (though appointed to the prestigious post of ordinary consul [*consul ordinarius*] in AD 391). His descendants, like others from the traditional elite, converted to Christianity. The priestly colleges, which established the dates of festivals and oversaw burial practices (and at one point advised the senate on religious matters), still active in the AD 380s, were all but irrelevant in the AD 390s and "simply faded away" as the senior members died.[18] As Cameron notes, no *pontifex* (AD 402), *augur* (AD 384), *quindecimvir* (AD 385), Vestal (AD 385), and *septemvir epulonum* (c. AD 385?) is known to have lived

[16] See Cameron 2011, pp. 60–61.
[17] See Cameron 2011, pp. 44–45.
[18] Cameron 2011, p. 167.

beyond AD 402.[19] Conversions, especially among officials, were accelerating. By the 5th century AD, even by Augustine's estimation in his headier moments, paganism was no longer a real threat to Christianity (e.g. Aug. *Contra Cresc.* 3.63.70).

Yet uncertainties abounded for Augustine. Although we often view Augustine now as exercising great authority among his contemporaries, as a bishop from Hippo his sway was limited: he did not share the social power enjoyed by the traditional Roman aristocracy (who were now flooding into North Africa with the fall of Rome); his ecclesiastical authority existed alongside of and had to be negotiated within an elaborate network of imperial and local authority; he did not have the ear of the emperor; and even among ecclesiastical leaders, he was at times ignored by them both in statements of doctrine and proposals for action.[20] Moreover, pagan celebrations still had popular appeal. Although pagan temples were closed and public practices officially ended, local festivals and private celebrations continued. The priests heading the provincial cults became more responsible for providing games, their functions remaining important even after any specific religious role was lost.[21] A law sent to the proconsul of Africa in AD 399 expressly provided for the continuation of banquets and games as long as the events were stripped of any pagan rituals (*CTh* 16.10.17 [399]). So popular were the games, outdrawing urban churches and festivals when spectacles were held at the same time, that a law in AD 400 outlawed spectacles from being held on Sunday (*CTh* 2.8.23). Adding to the anxiety of the time, there was of course the question of how true the religious convictions were of the aristocracy, many of whom converted as a way of maintaining political power. There had been some violent clashes between Christians and pagans in Africa, notably at Sufes in AD 399 (in which Christians were killed after overturning a statue of Hercules) and at Calama in AD 408 (in which a riot ensued, including the looting of Christian property, when Possidius tried to break up an illegal pagan procession). In AD 402, Claudian listed the omens and portents that are causing people to worry as Alaric advanced into Italy (though Claudian rejects these omens). In AD 405–406, with the invasion of Italy by Radagaisus and the Goths, according to Augustine Roman pagans were encouraged to call for restoration of sacrifice (see *ciu. Dei* 5.23). With the invasion of Alaric, the *praefectus urb*, Gabinius Barbarus Pompeianus, performed banned pagan rituals in an attempt to save the city.

[19] Cameron 2011, p. 165.
[20] See Leyser 2000, p. 3; McCarthy 2007.
[21] See Cameron 2011, p. 171.

According to some accounts, the act was inspired by visitors from the Etruscan town of Narnia who said that they had saved their city by offering prayers to their ancestral gods.[22] And one cannot overstate the feelings of vulnerability and humiliation among Romans with the disease and starvation from the blockade; the payment of bribes to Alaric by the senate; the desertion of Goths who had been enslaved by Rome (when they crossed the Danube in AD 376) to Alaric's army; the inability of Ravenna to provide aid; and the sacking of the city. Following on Symmachus' *Relatio* 3.9, in which he argued that traditional worship produced tangible results, after the sack of Rome one sees some relaxation of prohibition of pagan cults. In Augustine's own backyard, many of these pagan and newly converted elites fled to Africa, only compounding the ongoing struggle with the Donatists.[23] And now Christianity was being blamed for Rome's fall from glory. Augustine evinces some of this anxiety when he notes that he had heard that a reply to the first three books of *ciu. Dei* had been written by "certain persons" (*ciu. Dei* 5.26; Babcock, 1.181). In short, everything in these years looked like a setback for Augustine and Christianity as recent events kindled fond memories for Rome's pagan past.

The Corruption of Rome

Augustine opens Book 4 signaling a recasting of memory, citing Roman authorities (including Varro, Pompeius Trogus, Justin, Vergil, Cicero, and Scaevola) and history along the way: "In their ignorance, they imagine that the happenings of their own times are quite extraordinary and never occurred before in other eras in the past" (*ciu. Dei* 4.1; Babcock, 1.108). The statement is directed at those who blame the abandonment of the Roman gods for the Christian God on the humiliating sacking of Rome by the Goths. But the organization of Augustine's argument in answering who is to blame is at first confusing. He seems to shift from discussing Rome's failures, to Rome's corruption, to his famous riff, drawing on Roman authorities, on the contradictory, overlapping, and at times silly jurisdictions of the different gods (which was a common trope of Christian apologetic writing).[24] But I think we can understand the logic as follows: Augustine first rejects a providential reading of Roman history, which leads Augustine to ask what would lead the Romans to worship so many

[22] Recounted in Zosimus, *Hist. nova* 5.41. See Matthews 1970, p. 84; Matthews 1975, p. 290; Cameron 2011, pp. 190–211.
[23] Brown 1967, pp. 288–289; Courcelle 1964, pp. 58–67.
[24] See Arnobius *Adv. gen.* 4.24–29 and Lactantius *Div. inst.* 1.9–15.

gods who did so little. His answer is that it is the elites who perpetuate these beliefs in order to serve their own corrupt interests rather than to contribute to the formation of a just community. That is, paganism is not just a false belief; it is a politically motivated and dangerous one that (by the time we finish Book 5) justifies its repression.

The sacking of Rome precipitated not just anxiety, but also nostalgia for what had been depicted throughout the centuries as a new age of Roman peace and rule. Augustine turns his attention first to challenging these romanticized images of Rome's achievements. At the most general level, Augustine cites the North African (and pagan), Apuleius (AD 124–AD 170), in his translation of *On the Universe*, that "all earthly things are subject to change, alteration, and annihilation" (*ciu. Dei* 4.2; Babcock, 1.110). Augustine also notes the impermanence of any victory (*ciu. Dei* 4.3). None of these statements should be surprising since a continual refrain of Augustine is that all things on earth are temporal (*ciu. Dei* 4.7). But the argument takes an important turn when talking about the Assyrian empire that lasts longer than Rome's (*ciu. Dei* 4.7), thus raising the uncomfortable rhetorical question of whether the Assyrian gods are better than the Roman ones. Assyria and Rome may be similar in another way: they are indistinguishable from a den of thieves. Augustine suggests this in a deliciously ironic way. Augustine asks what gods helped Spartacus and (for Augustine) his literal den of thieves rise up and pose such a threat to Rome (*ciu. Dei* 4.5). As Augustine writes: "They broke the chains of their servile condition; they escaped; they evaded their pursuers; they gathered a large and exceedingly strong army; and, in their obedience to the plans and orders of their kings, they struck fear into the lofty power of Rome" (*ciu. Dei* 4.5; Babcock, 1.113). The passage previews an argument Augustine will make later in which he employs Cicero's definition of a *res publica* as a people united by a common sense of justice (see *ciu. Dei* 19.24). Absent justice, there is little that differentiates kingdoms from a large band of robbers other than the impunity of the kingdom. Augustine recalls a statement by a pirate who defends his thievery when captured by Alexander: "But because I do it with one tiny ship, I am called a robber; and because you do it with a great fleet, you are called an emperor" (*ciu. Dei* 4.4; Babcock, 1.112).

The suggestion here is that absent right, there is little that actually distinguishes Spartacus' gang from the Roman empire. Given what now emerges as Rome's own tumultuous past, Augustine asks:

> Why, then, was it necessary to worship and invoke such a throng of gods for the sake of these goods, whether of soul or of body or of

> outward circumstance? And I have by no means mentioned all of them, nor could the Romans themselves provide separate little gods for every separate little human good that they singled out. But why all that throng of gods, when, taking the short and easy way, the one goddess Felicity could have bestowed all these goods, eliminating the need to seek out any other god either to obtain goods or to ward off evils?
>
> (*ciu. Dei* 4.21; Babcock, 1.128; see also *ciu. Dei* 4.18 and 4.23)

Amidst the chaos of these gods, one theme emerges, and that is that the Romans in some sense recognized both the importance of *felicitas* and that it can only be given as a gift of a god (though they did not know the name of that god). "Let that God be sought," Augustine announces, which will require renouncing "the din of innumerable demons" that stand in the way of that happiness (*ciu. Dei* 4.25; Babcock, 1.133).

Augustine does not arrive at *felicitas* by accident. In the background of this claim is Augustine's view that all beings are oriented by love (*amor*), or a desire or impulse (*impetus*) that Augustine understands as a motion of the soul. That desire is directed toward possessing that which fulfills or satisfies one's being (*Trin.* 13.4.7; see also *Trin.* 9.2.2). Augustine characterizes that satisfaction to which all beings move as true *pax* (*ciu. Dei* 19.13; see also *ciu. Dei* 3.9; 12.5; 19.14). The peace that defines the aim of human beings is happiness: its perfect form (*beatitudo*) and its earthly form (*felicitas*). Both types are premised on the condition that it is enjoyed continuously and that one is certain of its continued enjoyment (*ciu. Dei* 11.13; see also *ciu. Dei* 19.1; *beat. uit.* 2.10; *lib. arb.* 1.4.10.30; *conf.* 10.21).

But no such happiness can be achieved because of the deceptiveness of Roman beliefs. Augustine's claim is connected to his depiction of the operation of the mind. The mind errs when it seeks to draw the surrounding bodies it loves into its own incorporeal nature. It can only do so by fastening together images "which it has made out of itself, and forces them into itself" (*Trin.* 10.5.7; see also *conf.* 10.8). In trying to make sense of things, one turns tangible things into intangible representations so that one's mind can operate on them: associating, combining, extrapolating, and judging. The will "snatches the deceptive images of corporeal things from within and combines them together by empty thought, so that nothing seems to it to be divine unless it be of such a kind of this; covetous of its own selfish possessions it becomes prolific in errors and, prodigal of its own selfish goods, it is emptied of strength" (*Trin.* 12.10.15).[25] The Romans in essence substitute the something that God has created with the nothing that they have created in their fantasies. That is Augustine's point when he suggests that the Romans created all of the different functions of the gods and goddesses which "they have imagined as they wished according to their own fancies" (*ciu. Dei* 4.21; Babcock, 1.127). They make "gifts of God into gods for themselves" by "their proud and obstinate self-will" (*ciu. Dei* 4.23; Babcock, 1.132).

That deception is in turn reinforced and endorsed by customs and habits of the mind: memories that orient one's will (*conf.* 7.17; 10.40; *doc. Chr.* 1.9.9). In confusing the world with one's fantasies, the soul becomes entangled in these images, "which it has fixed in memory, foully defiled by the fornication of the phantasy" (*Trin.* 12.9.14). We take the order of the world and turn it into "confused multitudes of phantasies, which contradict one another" (*conf.* 7.17) so that we must navigate like a ship in a storm-tossed sea (*ciu. Dei* 5.22). Augustine's portrayal of the pagan gods is meant to make precisely this point: the different and confused jurisdictions of the gods reveal the chaotic results of Roman fantasies projected onto the world.

Augustine draws on Varro and Scaevola's tripartite categories of the gods as mythical/poetic, natural/philosophic, and political to further make the case that the gods are both dangerous demons (or evil spirits) and used as tools of manipulation.[26] Varro and Scaevola have slightly different goals in their writings. Scaevola, the Pontifex Maximus, acknowledges the nonsensical portraits of the gods created by the poets as well as some of the dangerous claims of philosophers (*ciu. Dei* 4.27). For example, it would be dangerous if the people knew that pagan gods were simply deified mortals, which is a response by the apologists in part to pagan criticisms of Christianity as creating a blasphemous image of God through Christ as human.[27] Or it would be dangerous if people knew that the true God does not have bodily form. Scaevola argues that the gods promoted by statesmen, however deceptive, are important for the community. As Augustine remarks, "What a splendid religion! The weak may flee to it in order to be set free, and when they ask for the truth that will set them free, it is considered expedient for them to be deceived" (*ciu. Dei* 4.27; Babcock, 1.135).

[25] Augustine 2002.

[26] On demons, see *ciu. Dei* 8 and 9.

[27] See Kahlos 2007, p. 159; Tertullian *Ad nat.* 2.12–14.

Varro has several aims. One is to list the different functions of the gods so that the people will understand their power and which god to invoke (*ciu. Dei* 4.22). But this goal runs contrary to a second aim (or maybe wish) of Varro to harmonize civic religion with natural philosophy, namely, making the worship of the gods consistent with principles of nature (*ciu. Dei* 4.31). For Augustine, Varro comes close to revealing the truth about the gods, but ultimately accepts that the falsehoods perpetrated in civic religion are useful for civic order (*ciu. Dei* 4.22, 31–32).[28]

Augustine is interested in showing more than the falsity and inconsistency of these beliefs; he is focused on demonstrating the criminality and immorality of the theatrical shows that have their origin in the gods (on the origin of games, see *ciu. Dei* 4.1, 4.26; told in Cic. *Div.* 1.26.55, Livy 2.36.1–8, Val. Max. 1.7.4, though the story is likely from Varro). As Augustine writes:

> In these games, it is certain, poetic accounts of the gods' criminal behavior is publicly celebrate; and yet the games were restarted by order of the senate because the divinities compelled it. In those games, the vilest actors would sing and act out the role of Jupiter as the corrupter of innocence, and please him by doing so. If this was all a fiction, he should have been angry. But if he took delight in his own crimes, even if fictitious crimes, what is it to worship him but the serve the devil? Could this god really be the one who founded, extended, and preserved the Roman empire – a god who is more abject than any Roman, no matter how abject, who found such spectacles distasteful?
>
> (*ciu. Dei* 4.26; Babcock, 1.134)

At its best, such beliefs are perpetuated by custom rather than reason (*ciu. Dei* 4.31). Augustine suggests that if Varro "could have been free to withstand the prejudice of custom, he would have acknowledged and argued that one God is to be worshiped, the one God who governs the world by movement and reason" (*ciu. Dei* 4.31; Babcock, 1.140). He adds to his list the secrecy and deception of the rites and knowledge associated with the mystery cults. If paganism were only mistaken and ineffective then it might be possible to correct through teaching.

In fact, there is evidence that Augustine thought persuasion was preferable to coercion. But the stakes are higher for Augustine.

[28] There is debate about the origin of this tripartite scheme. See Pépin 1956. On its use in *ciu. Dei*, see Cardauns 1978, pp. 93–94. For the use of this scheme in the apologetic tradition, see Eusebius of Caesarea, *Praep. evang.* 3.17; 4.1; Tertullian *Ad nat.* 2.1–8.

Augustine uses Varro, Scaevola, and Cicero (*ciu. Dei* 4.30) to show that Roman authorities, in imitation of the gods, knowingly perpetrated the deception in order to maintain their power. The leaders used religion that they knew to be "mere illusion" in order to tighten "the bonds of civil society, as it were, so that they might likewise tighten their hold on their subjects" (*ciu. Dei* 4.32; Babcock, 1.141). License is encouraged as a tool of elite manipulation to bind people to the state – to create *ordo* by re-enforcing corrupt desires – justified under the guise of religion (*ciu. Dei* 4.32). Paganism emerges as a tool of elite manipulation that both deceives and corrupts the people. The claim will serve as the reason to look to imperial authority to suppress the practice.

FATE, FOREKNOWLEDGE, AND FREE WILL

But there is an elephant in the room. Despite Augustine's searing indictment of Roman practices, Rome did experience success, its dominion so expansive that many Christian writers placed their millennial hopes on its transformation into a Christian empire. If Book 4 is meant to discredit the pagan gods as an explanation for Roman successes then Book 5 seeks to explain why God, who wills all that exists (*ciu. Dei* 5.11), would give Rome its glory (*ciu. Dei* 5.*praef.*). Although there once again appears to be a confusing array of themes introduced in Book 5 that includes fate, prophecy, causality, foreknowledge, and will, there is actually a logic to the argument. Augustine must peel away habits of Roman thinking about prophecy and astrology as well as Stoic arguments about causality to reconcile God's foreknowledge with free will. This allows Augustine to understand Rome's success as both empowered by God's will and as an example of the possibilities and limits of human will.

Augustine begins by defining fate as events that happen "by virtue of some order governed by necessity" rather than by the will of God (*ciu. Dei* 5.1; Babcock, 1.144). Augustine wants to distance God's providence from fate because of its common association with astrology. It recalls Augustine's earlier invocation of Cicero's argument against divination (at *ciu. Dei* 4.30 and 5.9; see also Cic. *Div.* 2.3.8–72.150). Augustine's rejection of fate shares with Cicero (e.g. *De fato* 12.28–29) the sense that it encourages passivity: Why worship any god, or make any choices, if the stars control one's future?

As for prophecy, Augustine asks how one can explain diverse outcomes (such as in the different lives of twins) with the same placement of the planets and stars. Augustine argues, contra Hippocrates and

Posidonius, that the different experiences of twins (different health, for example) is likely attributable to different choices ("the mind's deliberate choice") about lifestyle (*ciu. Dei* 5.2) or, as he develops in his discussion of Esau and Jacob, different conditions (*ciu. Dei* 5.4). Even more striking for Augustine are twins of different sexes who are thus "utterly unlike in mode and matter of life" (5.6; Babcock, 1.149). Of the philosophic arguments about fate, Augustine suggests there is a similar deception used by political leaders to trick the ignorant (*ciu. Dei* 5.2). These philosophic arguments, especially of the Stoics, end up relying on such fine distinctions that any claim to being able to foretell an event becomes absurd. What in fact happens, Augustine suggests, is that people create their own destinies through the choices they make (*ciu. Dei* 5.7). In some sense, Augustine is replacing the sheer diversity that the Romans look to in their gods with an even greater diversity (of birth, growth, and decay) created by one God.

Of those who see fate as "the chain and sequence of all causes" (as do Seneca and earlier Stoics), Augustine simply folds that argument into a statement of God's omniscience and omnipotence in which he "know[s] all things before they happen and so leave[s] nothing unordered" (*ciu. Dei* 5.8; Babcock, 1.151). When Augustine returns to Cicero on divination, he is recalling a complicated Stoic argument about causality and necessity. For the Stoics, only bodies exist. When the Stoics contend that everything (or more specifically, all motion) is caused and (with perfect knowledge) comprehensible, they are referring to the relationship of bodies on other bodies. This includes the mind receiving an impression of an external object which is understood as a physical imprinting of the object on the mind. But the Stoics also distinguish between a "necessity" which involves a thing's nature and past events, and a "possibility" which involves the choice to act in terms of that nature (*ciu. Dei* 5.9). Cicero's argument against the Stoics is that if everything is both caused and known, then there is little place for free will (*ciu. Dei* 5.9). For Cicero, as Augustine writes, "if we grant this … the whole of human life is undermined. It is pointless to make laws, pointless to make use of reprimand or praise, of denunciation or exhortation, and there is not justice in establishing rewards for the good and punishments for the evil" (*ciu. Dei* 5.9). While rejecting the materialism of Stoicism, Augustine also rejects the incompatibility that Cicero sees between foreknowledge and free will.

There are two issues here for Augustine. First, human wills are part of the pattern of causation since the wills of individuals are the causes of human actions (*ciu. Dei* 5.9). There is no question that God, who has knowledge of the causes of all things, would not have knowledge of wills as among those causes. Augustine rejects Stoic efforts to distinguish between principal and proximate causes (see Cic. *De fato* 18.41), as well as Cicero's suggestion that the principal cause may lie in our own nature, and thus be a choice (Cic. *De fato* 19.45). Augustine argues that there are "no efficient causes of all that happens except voluntary causes, namely, causes stemming from that nature which is the breath of life" (*ciu. Dei* 5.9; Babcock, 1.155). God is that efficient cause.

There is a second aspect to Augustine's argument, which has to do with what Augustine even means by a will, that has both a theological and phenomenological component. God's will is a power (*potestas*) that creates an order of Good and empowers (and judges) wills to act according to this order. From God's perspective, our wills play a part in the order of causes since we are not only caused (as are all bodies) but also cause. From the individual perspective, it is by our own will that "we do whatever we feel and know we would not do unless we willed to do it" (*ciu. Dei* 5.9; Babcock, 1.154). That is, we have the experience of choosing. But this is not the choice of a will ordering itself but of a will consenting to the Good (see *ciu. Dei* 5.10–11).[29]

Although Augustine differentiates himself from Cicero in arguing that foreknowledge and free will are consistent, he agrees that it is a matter of living rightly that we affirm the power of our will to choose what is Good (*ciu. Dei* 5.10). That is why laws, prescriptions, approbation, and denunciation are all part of the picture. They are foreseen by God as important ways for us to live and act well. The discussion leads Augustine to an examination of the power by which Rome came to rule an empire, a power that (to extend our previous discussion) is always twofold: (i) the empowering by God and (ii) the power of the choices made by the Romans.

ROME'S GLORY AND THE ORGANIZATION OF DESIRE

Underlying Augustine's discussion of Rome's choices is an argument he develops in his other works about how desire is communally structured. We have already seen how for Augustine people seek happiness through the attainment of their desires. What we want is to make something our own. The desire "which is latent in seeking, proceeds from one who seeks, remains as it were in suspense and only comes to rest in the goal

[29] I am sympathetic to Schindler 2005. See also discussions of Augustine and the will by Dihle 1982; Wetzel 1992; Arendt 1996; and Harrison 2006.

toward which it is directed, when that which is sought has been found and is united with him who seeks" (*Trin.* 9.12.18). These desires are powerfully shaped by culture. The primary mechanism by which the Romans organized desire was by way of glory, the favorable judgment of others. "This glory they loved with a passion. It was for its sake that they wanted to live and for its sake that they did not hesitate to die. Their boundless desire for this one thing kept all their other desires in check" (*ciu. Dei* 5.12; Babcock, 1.159). The word translated as suppress (*premo*) is more accurately understood as shaping through pressure; not the suppression of desire but its organization by way of a stronger desire. What moves this desire, what directs it, arises precisely out of our social nature: the love of praise (*ciu. Dei* 5.13; 5.12) and fear of shame (*ciu. Dei* 5.12). One wants to be seen and talked about.

The Romans directed praise toward two actions: liberty (*libertas*) and dominion (*imperium*). The passion for *libertas* was born of the experience of kingship. Pointing to Rome's historical trajectory, Augustine notes that the royal state was regarded "not as the order imposed by a ruler or the benevolence offered by a counselor but rather as the arrogance of a despot" (*ciu. Dei* 5.12; Babcock, 1.159). It was in that time, when the memory of kingship was still fresh in the years following the expulsion of the Tarquins that Rome "accomplished so many wondrous things – things which were, beyond doubt, praiseworthy and glorious in human estimation" (*ciu. Dei* 5.12; Babcock, 1.160).

But how men judge sets in motion a dynamic in which no end is ever complete. One judges by way of one's temporally constituted senses, which measure the fulfillment of love by the amount of the desired object that is acquired. In the case of glory, which one measures by the marvelous deeds that are seen and admired (*ciu. Dei* 5.12), liberty by itself is not enough to sate the passion for glory; the measure of marvelous deeds is still grander once beheld by more people. So Rome coupled the love of liberty with a thirst for dominion, a love of ruling and commanding and subjugating extolled by Virgil, as Augustine notes (*ciu. Dei* 5.12).

The organization of desire requires not only direction – what is the object of love – but also a path – the means by which it is pursued or how is it practiced. Augustine quotes Sallust in saying that: "the good and the worthless alike seek glory, honor, and power for themselves, but the former strive on the true path, while the latter, lacking any good arts, compete by guile and deceit" (*ciu. Dei* 5.12, quoting Sall. *Cat.* 11; Babcock, 1.161). Augustine follows Sallust in identifying the role of fear – in this case, the fear of approbation – in channeling the pursuit of glory by the former path rather than the latter. But Augustine supplements Sallust's discussion (though in a very Roman way) by connecting fear to love: One fears losing what one loves. Fear focuses one's efforts, reminding one of what matters, which for the Romans was glory associated with liberty.

For Augustine, the experience of the Tarquins and the fear of their return lead the patricians to act "with just and moderate law" toward the plebs (*ciu. Dei* 5.12; Babcock, 1.162; see also *ciu. Dei* 3.17). But once the memory of tyranny recedes and the threat finally ends with the war with Etruria, "the patricians treated the commoners like slaves, abused them in the manner of kings, drove them from their lands, excluded all others, and exercised sole power" (*ciu. Dei* 5.12; Babcock, 1.162; see also *ciu. Dei* 2.18 and 3.16), giving rise to discord that ended, as Augustine writes in an earlier book, only from fear of Carthage (*ciu. Dei* 2.18). With the second Punic War, Augustine continues, "a deep fear began to weigh on Rome once again. A new and greater anxiety reined in their restless spirits from these disturbances and called them back to civic concord" (*ciu. Dei* 5.12; Babcock, 1.162). With the defeat of Carthage and the desire for power no longer suppressed by fear, as narrated at *ciu. Dei* 1.31, *concordia* gives way to civil strife and then bloody proscriptions. As glory becomes more fraudulently sought, Caesar being Augustine's example, the controlling effect of praise and blame are weakened, undermining the relationship between merit and public judgment: Praise could be purchased through bribes and inflated by the hypocrite and bad deeds could be disguised through deceit (*ciu. Dei* 5.12). Unrestrained by glory and liberty forgotten, love expresses itself as passion for domination, the desire to be like a god that is rooted in the illusion that one can transcend one's mortality (*ciu. Dei* 5.14).

Augustine makes clear the difference between a Roman and Christian perspective. As Augustine writes, a father would kill his sons "for the sake of liberty for men who were going to die in any case, and for the sake of desire for the praises that we gain from mortal man" (*ciu. Dei* 5.18; Babcock, 1.167–68). In contrast, a Christian does not kill one's sons but counts "Christ's poor among our sons" for "the sake of true liberty which sets us free from the dominion of iniquity and death and the devil" (*ciu. Dei* 5.18; Babcock, 1.167–68). But Augustine as much distances Christianity from, as appropriates, Roman history to suggest an affinity between Christianity and the uncorrupted aspects of the Roman past. Augustine draws on Roman *exempla* to build a bridge between citizenship in the two cities, partly because they are the examples he knows, and partly because Augustine wants to show to the Roman wavering in belief that these deeply imbedded cultural values have resonance in Christianity. That is, Augustine in a sense seeks to address the long-standing critique that the Christians were un-Roman. For example, Augustine compares the remission of sins in the City of God with the amnesty given for crimes by Romulus in Rome's founding (*ciu. Dei* 5.17). One can also see in the Romans the sorts of sacrifices that serve as models that remind Christians of their duties (*ciu. Dei* 5.18): Brutus and Torquatus' sacrifices of loved ones; Camillus' wrongful suffering and exile; Mucius' fortitude; Curtius and the Decii's sacrifices on behalf of the city; Marcus Pulvillus' dedication to the gods; Marcus Regulu's faith; and Lucius Valerius, Cincinnatus, and Fabricius' voluntary poverty. We get to Augustine's answer of why God grants such glory to Rome. It serves God's purpose by showing what is attainable in service to the even greater City of God. As Augustine writes, the Roman empire attained such glory "for the benefit of the citizens of the eternal city" so that they "might see how great a love they owe to their supernal homeland for the sake of eternal life" (*ciu. Dei* 5.16 and 5.18).

JUST RULE

The discussion of glory leads to a brief exploration of rule. The ambiguity of Augustine's formulations has led to widely divergent accounts of Augustine's conception of rule, from an aim of temporal peace,[30] to limited and coercive,[31] to harmonizing,[32] to offering an alternative political ethic.[33] In these final sections in Book 5, the focus is almost entirely on the happiness of the ruler and the good fortune of the people who happen to be subject to the just leader. Augustine is careful to separate happiness from any of the usual secular criteria for political success: longevity, a peaceful death, the perpetuity of rule through sons, or the vanquishing of external and internal enemies (*ciu. Dei* 5.24). As Augustine notes, pagans achieved these successes as frequently as Christian rulers did not. At a minimum, he who disregards glory and yet is eager for rule "outdoes even the beasts in the vices of cruelty and of self-indulgence" (*ciu. Dei* 5.19; Babcock, 1.172). Augustine singles out Nero as seeking to be exempt from the judgment of good men. But the

[30] Barr 1962, pp. 220–221: subordinate to the end of the City of God.

[31] Deane 1963; Markus 1988, pp. 133–153; and Weithman 2014.

[32] Dodaro 2004, p. 217.

[33] Milbank 1991: receptivity; Schlabach 2001: self-denying love; Gregory 2008: love and civic virtue. See also the excellent review article by Kaufman 2010.

happiest ruler is the Christian who acts with both piety and humility[34]: making their power "the servant" to God, acting with humility and restraint, inflicting punishment as necessary "for governing and defending the republic" (*ciu. Dei* 5.24; Babcock, 1.178), granting pardon in the hope of reform, seeing it as more important to rule over their base desires than over other states, balancing harshness (when necessary) with kindness and generous deeds, and doing it all out of a desire for eternal happiness. The virtuous individual disregards glory, but only because he is subject to the judgment of God. Augustine is careful to note that just rule is not an expectation a people might have. There is, for example, little difference between victor and vanquished except for empty glory (*ciu. Dei* 5.17). And a just ruler is not required, but a gift of God (*ciu. Dei* 5.19).

Augustine is wrestling with a deeper ambivalence toward political authority, though, in his discussion of rule. Christianity for centuries articulated a particular version of authority: the authority of Scripture with the clergy as its interpreter. And in the early history of the Christian church, that authority stood against imperial authority. Even as Christian authority itself grew in different communities, both with the role of bishops and the church councils, it identified itself with a different constituency: the poor and disenfranchised who often found themselves at odds with imperial authorities and the wealthy landowners the imperial authorities protected. Thus, local church authority self-consciously emerged as an alternative path of appeal, often intervening on behalf of the dispossessed. Christianity went from being a religion suspicious of secular authority to one that began to recognize the value of this authority to compel in ways they could not.

Augustine's discussion evinces some of his own ambivalence about authority. Augustine makes clear that imperial order was important for governing and defending. But Augustine had grown increasingly distrustful of human authority because of the limits of our knowledge, the proneness to error, and his own doubts about the value of coercion in changing belief.[35] Authority resided in the Scripture; and all other action, whether secular or ecclesiastical, was in service to that authority. It is in this context that we can appreciate Augustine's praise of Theodosius, who is not only aided by God, but is an example of a just ruler who offered Christianity to his enemies and refused to prosecute

[34] See Dodaro 2004, p. 217.

[35] See Markus 1988, p. 159 on limits of prophecy; Markus 1988, pp. 167–178 on his ambivalence toward politics and political programs; Leyser 2000, pp. 4–8.

personal enmities. Most importantly, Theodosius demonstrates the requisite "devout humility" (*ciu. Dei* 5.26; Babcock, 1.180). Augustine recounts how Theodosius was refused communion by St. Ambrose until he did penance for ordering out of anger the slaughter of a mob that had killed a governor in Thessalonica (*ciu. Dei* 5.26). When "corrected by the discipline of the Church, he did penance with such deep humility that the people, as they prayed for him, felt more grief at seeing the imperial majesty lying prostrate than they felt fear of the imperial wrath against sin" (*ciu. Dei* 5.26; Babcock, 1.180–81).

Augustine connects the humility of the just ruler back to happiness: the reward of these good works is not the illusory temporal goods which only "foolish people desire to have" but eternal happiness "which God gives only to those of the truly devout" (*ciu. Dei* 5.26; Babcock, 1.181). Augustine includes in these good works Theodosius helping "the Church in her struggle against the ungodly by issuing the most just and merciful legislation," including the destruction of pagan statues. That is, there are moments when a ruler must exercise authority to embrace "the power of the true God" over "the power of demons" (*ciu. Dei* 5.26; Babcock, 1.180). Augustine makes it personal, addressing "certain persons" who he heard had prepared a response to his first three books.

The model Augustine proposes for addressing these individuals – and it is a model that motivates Augustine's writing of *ciu. Dei* – is that of a teacher, urging consultation so that individuals can "be corrected by the prudent" rather than "praised by the impudent." But Augustine also suggests the limits of that correction when the response is "impudent babble" and "frivolity." In that case, "Anyone who counts himself fortunate in having license to slander would be far more fortunate if he had no such license at all" (*ciu. Dei* 5.26; Babcock, 1.182). That person could "put aside his empty boasting and, even at this late date, could pose any objection he wants as one eager for discussion and, in turn, he could hear what he needs to hear from those who, in friendly exchange, respond to his questions honestly, seriously, and candidly as best they possibly can" (*ciu. Dei* 5.26; Babcock, 1.182). Augustine comes full circle from Book 4. The model of authority is discussion. But faced with "foolishness," "obstinacy," "ill-will," a "disease" that is "invincible" and "incurable," and beliefs held with "destructive spite" (*ciu. Dei* 6.*praef*), the repression of the pagans and their demons becomes nothing less than a just act.

In this essay on *ciu. Dei* 4 and 5, I have revealed two ambiguities in Augustine's thought: (i) his relationship to his own Roman past and

(ii) his relationship to imperial authority. Far from decisively resolving these tensions, Augustine employs them, whether consciously or unconsciously, to mitigate the divide between Roman and Christian and to suggest the limits of political repression. It is within this space of indeterminacy that Augustine's work continues to resonate with us today.

FURTHER READING

Cameron, A. (2011). *The Last Pagans of Rome*. Oxford: Oxford University Press.

Hammer, D. (2014). *Roman Political Thought: From Cicero to Augustine*. Cambridge: Cambridge University Press.

Leyser, C. (2000). *Authority and Asceticism from Augustine to Gregory the Great*. Oxford: Clarendon Press.

Rives, J. B. (1995). *Religion and Authority in Roman Carthage: From Augustus to Constantine*. Oxford: Clarendon Press.

6 Books 6 & 7: Nature, Convention, Civil Religion, and Politics

MARY M. KEYS

In *ciu. Dei* 6 and 7,[1] Augustine turns from addressing arguments that Rome's traditional pagan cult is requisite for the this-worldly prosperity of the city and its empire, to the prospects of these rituals conducing to personal well-being after death. Books 6 and 7 form a bridge between Augustine's history of pre-Christian Rome in all its glory and its misery, and his consideration of philosophic or natural theology, especially accounts offered by the Platonic school, and the place it makes for traditional pagan worship. The main material from which this bridge is made, according to leading pagan intellectuals like Marcus Terentius Varro, is the traditional Roman civil religion. Varro variously presents Rome's traditional civil religion as framed by its founders for political utility on the one hand, and philosophic pedagogy on the other. Civil theology and its rites thus understood bind mythic pagan deities and popular views of their intervention on behalf of Rome to a naturalistic, pantheist account of God or the gods as the world itself or its soul. As Augustine interprets Varro, the latter lends his learned, public-spirited support to the civil cult, even while directing thoughtful readers beyond it to philosophic or natural theology. Varro is thus an indispensable interlocutor for Augustine in completing the political-historical-religious inquiry of *ciu. Dei* 1–5, and in preparing for the engagement with Platonic natural theology in Books 8–10.

In explicating Varro's two-part division of his *Antiquitates rerum humanarum et divinarum* [*Antiquities*] into discussions of "human

[1] All quotations from *ciu. Dei* are taken from the translation by William Babcock (2012 and 2013), modified occasionally in consultation with the Latin text as found at CCSL 47. The author wishes to thank Madeleine Filak, Colleen E. Mitchell, Jakub Voboril, and Melody Wood for their research assistance and Elizabeth C. Keys for her editorial assistance; and for their generous support of her research the National Endowment for the Humanities, the Strake Foundation, the Notre Dame Institute for Advanced Study, the University of Notre Dame Institute for Scholarship in the Liberal Arts, and the University of Notre Dame Program in Constitutional Studies.

matters" and "divine matters," and his three-part classification of theology comprising mythic, civil, and natural approaches to the divine, Augustine follows the eminent pagan scholar in broaching a critical question for classical political philosophy, that of the right relation between nature and convention in civic life and institutions.[2] While Books 6 and 7 constitute Augustine's most sustained reflection on this theme in *ciu. Dei*, the whole work is concerned with the meaning and status of nature vis-à-vis God, goodness, justice or right, evil, and grace.[3]

This chapter elaborates on Augustine's interpretative and critical engagement with Varro on nature, convention, religion, and politics.[4] The chapter's first section considers Augustine's reflections on these themes in Book 6; the second section, those in Book 7. The chapter's third section reflects on the implications of Augustine's appraisal of Varro's philosophic or naturalistic defense of Roman civil religion, for the right relation of nature and convention in political life. The conclusion reflects briefly on Varro's and Augustine's respective religious projects from the Ciceronian perspective of wandering and homecoming within one's own city.

[2] Commenting on Greek as well as Latin sources for the notion of *theologia tripertita*, and with special reference to Plutarch, Klauck writes: "[I]t is noteworthy that the triadic pattern can be overlaid by binary oppositions, when, for example, poets and legislators on the one side close ranks against philosophers on the other side ... Here we may see the much older [than Plutarch's life and works] antithesis of *nomos* (law) and *physis* (nature) or of *thesis* (convention) and *physis* still at work, which has been seen by some as the place of origin of the tripartite theology" (Klauck 2007, p. 337). See also Plato's *Republic* for Socrates' comment that there is "an old quarrel between philosophy and poetry" (607b; cf. 377b–383c, and Plato's *Apology of Socrates*, 20e–22c). For the *locus classicus* on nature and convention in politics, see Aristotle's *Nicomachean Ethics* Book 5, chapter 7, which opens: "What is just in the political sense can be subdivided into what is just by nature and what is just by convention. What is just by nature has the same force everywhere and does not depend on what we regard or do not regard as just. In what is just by convention, on the other hand, it makes originally no difference whether it is fixed one way or another, but it does make a difference once it is fixed, for example, that a prisoner's ransom shall be one mina, or that a sacrifice shall consist of a goat but not of two sheep, and all the other measures enacted for particular occasions (such as the sacrifice offered to Brasidas) and everything enacted by decree" (1134b18–24).

[3] On the role of nature and natural right or natural justice in Augustine's thought, see von Heyking 2001 and Keys 2013.

[4] Studies of Augustine's commentaries on Varro and Varro's works include Burns 2001; Clark 2010; Hagendahl 1967, vol. 2, pp. 589–630); Markus 1994; O'Daly 1994; and Rousseau 2009. For briefer considerations see also Ando 2010, pp. 75–78; Bobb 2010, pp. 74–76; Fortin 1996a, pp. 88–98; Klauck 2007, pp. 337–341; O'Daly 1999, pp. 236–238; and Silk 2004, pp. 863–865, 870–872. Other discussions of Augustine on Roman civil religion include Cavadini 2012, pp. 101–110; Fortin 1996b, pp. 15–18; Harding 2008, pp. 83–87; Hollerich 1993; and Vessey 2012, pp. 20–24.

THINGS HUMAN, THINGS DIVINE, AND THREE THEOLOGIES: BOOK 6

Augustine's dialogue with Roman luminaries on civil religion in Book 6 comprises two broad and intertwined themes: the first, "the gods of the nations" (*ciu. Dei* 6.1; Babcock, 1.184) and the natures of God, the gods, and human beings; the second, a classification of three theologies, and the relation of the civil theology to the mythical and natural theologies.

Regarding the first, Augustine opens with a lengthy discussion of the thought of Marcus Terentius Varro, the most learned among the scholars of Rome's divinities, religious institutions, and public cult.[5] Cicero's praise of Varro is deeply moving, and Augustine quotes it with respect:

> When we were wandering and straying about like visitors in our own city, your books led us back home, so to speak, so that we were at last able to recognize who and where we were. You made known the age of our homeland, the phases of its history, the laws of its religion and its priesthoods, the customs of its private and public life, ... and the names, kinds, functions, and causes of all divine and human matters.
>
> (*Acad. Post.* 1, 3, 9; quoted in *ciu. Dei* 6.2; Babcock, 1.187)

Yet, as if reversing Cicero's order, Varro in *Antiquities* had discoursed on "Human Matters" before "Divine Matters," these phrases serving as the titles of the work's two parts (*ciu. Dei* 6.3). Moreover, as Augustine notes a bit later, "human matters" in Varro's study mainly meant "Roman matters" (*ciu. Dei* 6.4; Babcock, 1.190).

Why should divine matters be preceded by human matters, to say nothing of Roman matters? Would not the reverse ordering be more fitting, as Cicero's eloquent prose suggests?[6] Here Augustine offers his interpretive key to unifying Varro's disparate analyses and making sense

[5] Marcus Terentius Varro (116 BC–27 BC) was a contemporary of Cicero. His life spanned Rome's late Republic and early Empire. Varro was renowned as a scholar on a myriad of topics. Most of his works, including those commented on by Augustine in *ciu. Dei* 6 and 7, are lost or extant only in fragments. See Burns 2001, p. 37, n.2, for bibliography involving the critical edition of Varro's extent writings. For interpretive and historical commentary on Varro's works see Rüpke 2012; Van Nuffelen 2010; and Vessey 2014.

[6] See also this telling passage from Cicero: "Homer invented these things and transferred human qualities to the gods. I would rather he had transferred divine qualities to us" (*Tusc. disp.* 1.26.65; quoted in *ciu. Dei* 4.26).

of Varro's counterintuitive ordering. Augustine takes his cue from a quote from "another" work of Varro, in which the learned late-Republican Roman writes "that, if he were himself founding a new city, he would have written in accord with the rule of nature, but since he found himself situated in an already-established city, he could do nothing but follow its customs" (*ciu. Dei* 6.4; Babcock, 1.190).[7]

Augustine applies this principle to the ordering of *Antiquities*, in which Varro's express purpose is to expound and preserve Rome's civil religion and its cult among the citizens (*ciu. Dei* 4.31). As Varro indicates, human matters precede divine matters in his *Antiquities*, "because cities came into existence first, and then these rites were instituted by them" (*ciu. Dei* 6.4; Babcock, 1.189). If Varro thought that the gods of the cities existed in truth and had a part in crafting the world and its peoples, it would have made sense to speak first of the gods and divine matters. Varro comes close to admitting this, according to Augustine, when he comments that if he were writing about "'the whole nature of the gods'" he would have written of them first. So in writing of the gods of the civil religion, it seems he is writing of just an element, or part, of the divine beings' natures. What could this mean, however, and how could even an "element" of the divine not merit primacy of place over what is human? Augustine judges that Varro in fact "rightly puts [an element of the nature of the divine] last, and therefore he is not writing of the divine at all" (*ciu. Dei* 6.4; Babcock, 1.190). In explaining his own ordering in an unconvincing way, moreover, Varro in Augustine's view indicates that he wishes able readers to grasp that he "did not want to put false matters ahead of true matters," and so "give[s] men priority over what men instituted, not the nature of men priority over the nature of the gods" or God (*ciu. Dei* 6.4; Babcock, 1.190).[8]

Augustine thus understands Varro to have bowed to his political community's customary beliefs, and indeed to have sought to purify and strengthen them by rationalizing their myths about the gods, as we shall

[7] Cf. *ciu. Dei* 4.31: "[Varro] he does not hesitate to admit that, if he were founding that city anew, he would instead consecrate the gods and their names according to the rule of nature. But as it is, he says that he feels bound, as one who belongs to an ancient people, to uphold the traditional account of the names and surnames of the gods as it came down from antiquity, and to make it the aim of his writing and research to encourage the common people to worship the gods rather than despise them."

[8] Cf. *ciu. Dei* 6.5: "In fact, this is the very reason why he wrote first about human matters and only then about divine matters – *because in writing about divine matters he was not following nature but rather the institution of men*" (emphasis added).

see in more detail later. Yet this was not Varro's sole aim in writing *Antiquities* and other religious works: "What, then, should we make of this, except that a man of the greatest acumen and learning ... who felt obliged to submit to the laws and customs of his city (*oppressum fuisse suae ciuitatis consuetudine ac legibus*), still decided, under the guise of commending religion, not to keep silent about the things that troubled him?"[9] (*ciu. Dei* 6.2; Babcock, 1.188; CCSL 47.168; see also *ciu. Dei* 4.31 and 6.9).[10] How this is so becomes clearer in the next segment of Augustine's study of Varro's writings on Roman religion, dealing with what the learned pagan termed Rome's "three kinds of theology" (*tria genera theologiae*; *ciu. Dei* 6.5; Babcock, 1.190).

The three theologies are the mythical, or fabulous; the physical, or natural; and the civil.[11] Varro's explication placed the first in the hands of the poets and the public space of the theatre; the second in the hands of the philosophers and the immense ambit of the world; and the third in the hands of the citizens and priests, in the temples of cities and towns (*ciu. Dei* 6.5). Varro explicitly opined that the mythic theology comprises many stories of the gods acting in a manner unbefitting of even a decent human being. In writing of the theology of the poets and theatres in his *Antiquities*, "where he could, where he dared, where he thought he could get away with it – Varro clearly stated, without even the least shadow of ambiguity, what a great injury is done to the nature of the gods by these lying fables. For he was speaking not of natural theology, nor of civic theology, but of mythical theology, which he thought that he could and should freely denounce" (*ciu. Dei* 6.5; Babcock, 1.191).

Varro nonetheless indicated that Rome's civil theology contains "not a few elements" of the mythical (*ciu. Dei* 6.6; Babcock, 1.194), and indeed that "the whole of the mythical theology" is consonant with

9 For Augustine's related concern regarding laws' and customs' oppression, that via the civil religion, learned and powerful elites effectively *oppress* the people and with lies keep them in check and bind them to the social order and regime, see *inter alia* *ciu. Dei* 4.27 and 4.32.

10 For reflection on Augustine's appraisals of "esoteric" and "latent" modes of writing and teaching, see Crosson 2005 and Kries 2010.

11 Augustine introduced the three kinds of theology in Book 4, there identifying "the most learned pontiff Scaevola" as an important source of reflection on them in earlier Rome (*ciu. Dei* 4.27). Analyses of the threefold theology in ancient Greek and Roman though include Klauk 2007; Lieberg 1984; and Rüpke 2012. For commentary on Scaevola, Varro, and Augustine on this subject, see Fortin 1996a and Klauk 2007, pp. 337–341. For a discussion of a related late-classical debate concerning "truth" and "utility" in Roman religion, see Riedl 2010.

and has become part of the civil cult (*ciu. Dei* 6.7).[12] The civil religion of Rome also "adopted" teachings from philosophic or natural theology. In his *Antiquities* Varro thus wrote, and Augustine quotes: "We shall describe, then, the elements that the civic theology has in common with each, along with those elements distinctive of it; but, of the two, we ought to keep company more with the philosophers than with the poets" (*ciu. Dei* 6.6; Babcock, 1.194). The "we" here appears to refer to the liberally educated readership Varro anticipated for his scholarly tomes. Augustine concludes that it cannot refer to "we the people," if only because Varro opined in another work that "the people were inclined to follow the poets more than the natural philosophers" (*ciu. Dei* 6.6; Babcock, 1.194). Varro considered that the common people are best shielded from the contested, often disturbing accounts of divinity offered by these natural philosophers, theories "which the ears can more easily bear to hear inside the walls of a school than outside in the forum" (*ciu. Dei* 6.5; Babcock, 1.191). Indeed, there are lies they should hear and believe, and truths they should not have the opportunity to learn (*ciu. Dei* 3.4, 4.27, and 4.31–32).[13] For Augustine, the irony here is that Varro seeks to protect the people in the public square from philosophic theology, but not from mythic theology's lies about divinity and humanity.

Augustine's Varro emerges from Book 6 as a patriotic and philosophic intellectual whose study of philosophy and history afforded him a certain freedom in thought, and also in his writing: freedom to criticize openly the vicious tales the myths or fables customarily held up as exemplary, as performed by gods among themselves and toward human beings. This freedom of expression was strictly limited, however, by the intellectual and educational possibilities of the common people and by the laws and customs of the Eternal City. Varro nonetheless sought to purify to the extent possible the public understanding of religion and to enlighten the liberally educated still further in the superiority of natural theology. If Varro's teaching concerning civil theology filtered down to the common citizens, it could ennoble their understanding and practice of the public cult as well, reinterpreting and rationalizing this worship

[12] Cf. *ciu. Dei* 6.8: "For the civic and the mythical theologies are both mythical and both civic. Both will be found to be mythical by anyone who prudently examines the vanities and obscenities of each, and both will be found to be civic by anyone who notes that the stage plays of the mythical theology are included in the festivals of the civic gods and in the 'divine matters' of the cities."

[13] For commentary on this aspect of Varro's thought on civil religion, see inter alia Bobb 2010, p. 75; Clark 2010; and Hollerich 1993, pp. 62, 66.

according to the order of nature. His civic-minded, liberally educated compatriots especially could glean from Varro that outrageous tales concerning gods and their envious, arrogant, lustful, contentious, foolish behaviors should not be taken literally. Rather, since they were entrenched in the public mind and heart through centuries of storytelling and public cult, they should be understood anew at least, as metaphors for the order of the cosmos, its elements, and its soul, which is what Varro especially terms God or divinity. Augustine elaborates this aspect of Varro's project at greater length in Book 7.

Augustine's initial survey, in Book 6, of Varro's threefold division of theology concludes with this reflection on Varro's civil religious writing:

> Who, then, is so slow-witted that he does not see Varro's aim in laying out and explaining the civic theology so carefully, in showing how similar it is to the unworthy and debased mythical theology, and in teaching clearly enough that the mythical theology is itself a part of the civic theology? It is quite obvious that *his purpose is to ready a place in human minds for the natural philosophy* which, he says, belongs to the philosophers. His approach is subtle: he denounces the mythical theology; and, even though he clearly does not dare to denounce the civic theology, simply by presenting it in the way he does he shows that it ought to be denounced. And so, once both have been rejected by the verdict of people who understand the matter rightly, the only choice left is the natural theology. And this I will discuss more fully, with the help of the true God, in its proper place.[14]
>
> (*ciu. Dei* 6.9; emphasis added)

CIVIL RELIGIOUS KNOWLEDGE, ANTIQUITY, AND "INVETERATE CUSTOM": BOOK 7

After Augustine has elaborated at some length, in Book 6, his sympathetic critique[15] of Varro's project of civil-religious revival, why does he

[14] See *ciu. Dei* 8–10 and 11–12.

[15] Burns 2001 and Rousseau 2009 similarly read Augustine's approach to Varro as one of appreciative or sympathetic critique, in contrast to other scholars who judge Augustine's approach to Varro to be chiefly adversarial or polemical (e.g. O'Daly 1999, pp. 101, 105). Burns writes that "Augustine's use of Varro differs from that of his [North African Christian] predecessors in a number of ways. He takes the text itself much more seriously by laying out its organization and by citing title and book

find it needful to continue it at even greater length in Book 7? Augustine explains that some readers might yet be unconvinced, since Book 6 treated mainly run-of-the-mill gods and goddesses, leaving unscathed Rome's so-called "select" divinities, namely the Olympians (by Latinized names) and others near them in grandeur, around whom Rome's public rituals revolved (*ciu. Dei* 7.1). At the close of Book 6 and again in the Preface of Book 7, Augustine identifies as the most difficult obstacle for such readers to overcome, not false conviction per se, but rather *"the force of inveterate custom"* which has been tenaciously rooted in the human and civic psyche (*ciu. Dei* 6.12; Babcock 1.205; emphasis added). In order to uproot such deeply ingrained false conventions, a sustained and repetitious engagement may be required. Augustine is willing and ready to make this effort, and launches into it in his seventh book.[16]

So, following Varro's order in *Antiquities*, Augustine in Book 7 moves from considering ordinary and more locally honored divinities, which Varro discussed under the classification "certain gods" and "uncertain gods," to treat the heart of Rome's civil cult, the public worship of its "select and principal gods" (*ciu. Dei* 7.1; Babcock, 1.207; see also *ciu. Dei* 6.2). Varro wrote of these in the last book of his *Antiquities*. Moreover, Varro prefaced his discussion of Rome's select divinities with a brief discourse on natural theology, suggesting a particular convergence here of philosophy with Rome's civil religion (see *ciu. Dei* 6.6; 7.17). This indicates further why Augustine cannot omit special treatment of Varro's rationalization of Rome's principle divinities and the rites performed in their honor, if these indeed especially exemplify the God or gods of nature. Throughout the bulk of Book 7, Augustine comments on Rome's "select" gods and goddesses, all together, one by one, or in small clusters (see *ciu. Dei* 7.2–4, 7–16, and 19–27), indicating how and why Varro's identification of these mythical divinities with phenomena of nature fails to persuade.

Two features of *ciu. Dei* 7 are especially noteworthy for this chapter's consideration of nature and convention in Rome's civil religion. The first is its introduction of a new facet of Varro's naturalizing project,

quite frequently. In addition to these formal differences there is a basic respect for Varro's views, which enables Augustine to be sympathetic yet critical" (Burns 2001, p. 41; cf. pp. 40, 42–43, 64).

16 On this aspect of Augustine's project, see also Rousseau (2009): "[Augustine's] task as a bishop was to shepherd men and women with deep historical roots into a realm that exceeded, without repudiating them, the expectations of their culture" (Rousseau 2009, p. 175; cf. pp. 162–163).

namely Varro's claim, apparently in his *Antiquities*, that the original intention of the founders of Roman religion included the representation and portrayal of nature and nature's God or gods through Rome's public rites and religious art. The second special feature is seen in Augustine's clear break in the flow of his argument on the select gods and goddesses of Rome's civil cult, about midway through Book 7, to pen two chapters highlighting Varro's skepticism about the true origins and meaning of these select divinities, and elaborating an alternative, more compelling interpretation, intimated by learned pagans as well.

ROME'S CIVIL RELIGION'S ORIGINS: NATURE AND/OR CONVENTION?

Early in Book 7 Augustine introduces a new account offered by Varro of Rome's civil religious institutions' original intention and meaning:

> In the first place, in commending these interpretations, Varro says that the ancients devised the images, attributes, and adornments of the gods such that, when those who had approached the mysteries of doctrine perceived them with their eyes, they might also see with their mind the soul of the world and its parts, that is, the true gods. He claims that those who made the images of the gods in human form seem to have been following the idea that the mind of mortals, which is in the human body, is very like the immortal mind.
>
> (*ciu. Dei* 7.5 Babcock, 1.212)

On this account, Rome's political theology was founded as an expression and pedagogue of philosophic or natural theology. Indeed, one might say that there was only one theology of note for the ancient citizen-sages who first formulated the civil cult: the natural theology.

Augustine does not call this contrast to his readers' attention explicitly, but the reflective reader will recall that an earlier quote from or paraphrase of Varro indicated precisely the opposite, that Rome's civil religion was not founded on philosophic reason. Varro wrote that, had he been founding a new city and its religious institutions, he would have written "in accord with the rule of nature" (*naturae formula*). As it was, he found himself a citizen of an already ancient city and so was compelled to follow its customs (*ciu. Dei* 6.4; cf. 4.31).[17] What is one to

[17] See Rousseau 2009, pp. 170–173 for a discussion of individual and community, nature and convention in Varro's *De lingua latina*, making evident the difficulty of interpreting Varro coherently on these questions. This passage quoted by Rousseau

make of this apparent contradiction: in one formulation, the originators of Rome's civil religion in fact followed the rule of nature; in another formulation, Rome's religious institutions compel Varro to write according to custom rather than nature?

We may surmise Augustine's possible reply from what he says explicitly in response to another question arising from Varro's argument that the ancient Romans intended to worship the divine soul of the cosmos through their civil cult and its images. Augustine notes that in a different work Varro opined that the earliest Romans worshipped without images, and that the introduction of the images that Varro in *Antiquities* interprets according to the order of nature, in particular with regard to the intellect or rational soul, in fact led Roman civil religion away from truer worship according to nature. Augustine's rhetorical remarks seem to suggest that, for Varro, the very "shadow of ambiguity" (*ciu. Dei* 6.5; Babcock, 1.191) and mystery shrouding Rome's beginnings, and so the origins and development of the civil cult, allowed him the freedom to advance for it multiple possible meanings, all plausible under the venerable protection of the "ancients" whom Augustine considers Varro's "authorities" in such matters (*ciu. Dei* 7.5).[18]

The title of Varro's major work investigating Roman religion, *Antiquities*, thus appears well chosen by its eminent author. Whether or to what extent the most ancient civil cult indeed followed nature, no one living in later eras can know. What Varro can and does know with solid certainty, according to Augustine, is that in Varro's own time, Rome's public religion required considerable reformulation and revision in order to move beyond mere convention and toward nature via philosophy. Varro seems to opine, moreover, that there was at least some error present in the civil theology from the beginning. Augustine construes this from a comment of Varro's, that the introduction of

nonetheless illuminates Varro's sense of *civitas* and civic compulsion, referenced with regard to Varro's political works by Augustine: "The people [Varro writes] has power over itself, but the individuals are in its power ... therefore as each ought to correct his own usage [*suae* ... *consuetudinem*] if it is bad, so should the people correct its usage. I am not the master – so to speak – of the people's usage, but it is of mine. As a helmsman ought to obey reason ... and each one in the ship ought to obey the helmsman, so the people ought to obey reason, and we individuals ought to obey the people" (Varro, *De lingua latina* 9.1(6), quoted in Rousseau 2009, p. 173).

[18] For a thoughtful argument that, in Augustine's view at least, Varro's deferral to ancient authority meant "denying himself genuine experience" of time lived in the present and its connection to eternity, and so of true religion, see Rousseau 2009, p. 164.

images of the gods "increased error in . . . cities" rather than introduced error, pure and simple. Augustine concludes from this choice of phrase that the learned Roman "obviously wants it to be understood that error was already present even before there were images" (*ciu. Dei* 4.31; Babcock, 1.139).

KNOWLEDGE, OPINION, AND SKEPTICISM

In Book 7 Augustine advances a second significant argument suggesting that Varro intentionally cast doubt on his rationalized account of Rome's civil religion. The central section of *ciu. Dei* 7, comprised of chapters 17 and 18, stands apart in its subject matter from the arguments regarding various select divinities that precede and follow it. This pair of chapters argues for Varro's acknowledged skepticism about the origins and natures of Rome's gods, and ultimately for Varro's disbelief in the naturalist explanations he himself offers concerning Roman civic cult's original intention and meaning.

Augustine opens chapter 17 by making reference to his previous analyses of Varro's discussions of the nature of the gods. He has just stressed anew, at the close of chapter 16, the many ways Varro's explanations contradict one another. The earth is said at one time to be Juno, another time the Great Mother, and yet again Ceres. Minerva is simultaneously identified with the highest heaven and with the moon, which dwells in the lowest heavenly sphere (*ciu. Dei* 7.16). Augustine sums up the conclusion Varro's contradictions point to, as he commences chapter 17: "Like the instances I have cited by way of example, their other interpretations *do not clarify but only confuse the issue*. Under the impulse of errant opinion, they are driven here and there, and they lurch forward and fall back so often, now in one direction, now in another, that Varro himself preferred to doubt everything rather than affirm anything" (*ciu. Dei* 7.17; Babcock, 1.223; emphasis added). How can Augustine be sure of Varro's doubts?

The penultimate pair of books of Varro's *Antiquities*, discoursing on Rome's "certain" and "uncertain gods," includes this disclaimer by Varro at the start of his treatment of the "uncertain" divinities: "I should not be held at fault if, in this book, I present doubtful views of the gods. For if anyone thinks that a firm conclusion should or can be reached, he may do that on his own, once he has heard what I have to say. As for me, *I can more easily be led to doubt what I said in the first book* [concerning 'certain gods'] than to bring what I am going to say in this one [on 'uncertain gods'] to any firm resolution" (*ciu. Dei* 7.17;

Babcock, 1.223; emphasis added). Augustine pithily notes that Varro thereby quietly conveys his uncertainty about Rome's certain gods, as well as the uncertain ones. Near the start of the third and final book of his *Antiquities*, just after a brief discourse on natural theology, Varro issues a similar disclaimer concerning his account of Rome's select divinities: "In this book" he states, "I shall be writing about the public gods of the Roman people, the gods to whom they have dedicated temples and whom they have distinguished with many marks of honor. As Xenophanes of Colophon writes, however, I will state my opinions, but will give no assured conclusions. For in these matters, man has opinions, but only God has knowledge."[19] (*ciu. Dei* 7.17; Babcock, 1.223; emphasis added). So Varro in his writings appears confident of the essentials of his natural theology, but utterly doubtful concerning the civil. He thereby once again indicates to thoughtful readers that his project of interpretive identification of these two theologies is most uncertain. This is the case, according to Augustine, not only because Varro's natural theology was itself incomplete and errant, but also because Varro was "weighed down by the authority of tradition" in "describ[ing] the things instituted by men" (*ciu. Dei* 7.17; Babcock, 1.223). Convention's force was in these matters much stronger than the force of nature.

Augustine continues in chapter 18 to propose a more plausible alternative, or rather, to echo one offered by other Roman philosophers and statesmen: that the civic gods did not begin as analogues for heaven, earth, and stars, but rather originated as men and women whose exploits were sung by the poets and whose post-mortem worship ordinary citizens, civic elites, and even malicious spirits encouraged (*ciu. Dei* 7.18). Augustine earlier references no less an authority than Cicero to support the hypothesis that these gods are really deceased human beings, deified by mortals due to public and/or elite admiration and civic pride (see *ciu. Dei* 3.15, where Augustine cites and interprets various texts by Cicero commenting on Romulus' disappearance, death, and subsequent deification by the Roman people; cf. *ciu. Dei* 7.28 and 18.18). Augustine's analysis suggests that civil theology's divinizing dead mortals may even have preceded and inspired the mythic:

> A more believable explanation of these gods is given when people say they were once human beings, and that sacred rites and

[19] Cf. Socrates on human wisdom's limits vis-à-vis divine wisdom in Plato's *Apology* 23a. For Augustine's understanding of Socrates and his famed "turn" to human things, see *ciu. Dei* 8.2.

> ceremonies were established for each of them, according to his talent, character, actions, and fortune, by those who, in their adulation wanted to take them as gods. Little by little, then, these rites seeped into the souls of men, which resemble the demons in their craving for public games and shows, and eventually spread far and wide as the poets adorned them with lies and deceiving spirits seduced men into accepting them.
>
> (*ciu. Dei* 7.18; Babcock, 1.223)

According to the civic cult and poetic myths, to give one of Augustine's subsequent examples, the highest god Saturn was overthrown by his son Jupiter and afterwards was represented with a sickle – symbolizing agriculture, Varro suggests. Augustine comments that perhaps at the actual origin of this portion of the tale was "that he [Saturn] who was a king at leisure in the earliest times became a hardworking laborer under his son's regime" (*ciu. Dei* 7.19; Babcock, 1.224; see also *ciu. Dei* 7.18 and 7.26). Augustine concludes that one should identify gods like Saturn, not with elements in the world, but rather with dead human beings or evil spirits, if one would have a more probable account of the origins of such civil religious matters (*ciu. Dei* 7.28).

NATURE, CONVENTION, AND POLITICS IN *THE CITY OF GOD*

What broader conclusions can be drawn from Augustine's dialogue with Varro on civil religion? In particular, what perspective does Augustine take on the respective roles of nature and convention in the life of cities and nations? Augustine does not dispute Varro's descriptions of the common people's propensity to keep company with the poets more than with the philosophers (cf. *ciu. Dei* 6.6), and so to follow convention more closely than nature. Neither does Augustine dispute Varro's prescription, to those able and willing, of the philosophic study of nature and endeavor to follow its guidance over that offered by myth (*ciu. Dei* 6.6). That nature – human nature and the nature of divinity or Deity – often is not, yet ought to be, followed in public life and in private, is not in question for Augustine or for Varro.

Based on his harsh critiques of poetry, or rather Roman theatre, Augustine may appear to be hostile to convention simply, to human invention in public life. This is not the case. Augustine judges that human nature itself, with its intellect and will, gives rise to discoveries of utility and to art, invention, and convention that over time may become widely shared, engrained custom (*consuetudo*) in cities, nations, and empires. If art and custom respect the basic guidance of nature toward good and away from evil, they may be accounted not only indifferent and permissible, but also useful, good, and even beautiful in Augustine's understanding (see *ciu. Dei* 11.22; 19.17; 19.19; 21.6; 22.19).

If Augustine recognizes the need human society has for convention and the naturalness, as it were, of its development, why is he so critical of the conventions of Rome's civil religion? There appear to be two chief grounds of Augustine's negative appraisal. First, some conventions have turned against nature, against what is good by nature for humans. Orgies, self-mutilation, glorification of war and victory, and other aspects of Rome's civil theology's fables and cult represent an assault on true humanity. The ascription of such behaviors to the gods and connection of them with the gods' desired worship, in the theatrical and ritual representation of these deviations in Rome's public temples, draw citizens away from ethical virtue and right relationships. Second, in addition to Augustine's moral critique of Rome's civil religious conventions, there is another yet more basic criticism, that these conventions do not and cannot conduce to true worship of the one true God. They lead their practitioners away from true religion (*uera religio*), and from rendering due honor to the only Deity.[20] And only from this true God, who creates the world but is not the world or its soul, who is possessor and giver of perfect happiness and fullness of being and life, can humans truly hope for eternal life (see *ciu. Dei* 4.21–25 and 6.12). As Philip Rousseau puts it, "Augustine stresses that a religious impulse destined to end in eternity (the joyful fulfillment of a well-founded hope) must have an origin that also transcends time – the one 'living, incorporeal, unchangeable being from whom we must beg the life of eternal happiness.'"[21]

Where this hope is precluded or stifled by public law and custom, an injustice is done by the political community to God and also to its members. Lack of hope in eternal blessedness issues as well in further earthly injustices, as humans grasp desperately for greater shares of power, wealth, praise, and material goods from which they hope to secure their lives on earth a little longer, win praise in the "eternal" city, or receive from a benevolent god to whom they sacrifice a better if

[20] On Augustine's understanding of the relationship among right worship (*latreia*), justice, and mercy, see Menchaca-Bagnulo 2019.

[21] Rousseau 2009, p. 164; quoting *ciu. Dei* 7.19.

still bad lot in Hades after death. Over a public square marked by Rome's religious rites and in the souls of citizens participating in them, death casts its dark shadow that cannot be fully dispelled.[22]

This brings us to a paradox of Augustine's respectful yet dissenting dialogue with Varro. At the outset of this dialogue, Augustine describes Books 6 and 7, together with Books 8–10, as intended precisely to "refute and instruct those who contend that the gods of the nations – whom the Christian religion is overthrowing – are to be worshiped not for the sake of this life but for the sake of the life which is to come after death" (*ciu. Dei* 6.1; Babcock 1.184). Yet at the end of his initial debate with the learned pagan, Augustine notes that Varro himself does *not* suggest that any of the gods and goddesses of Rome can or do offer "eternal life" to those who revere them (*ciu. Dei* 6.9)![23] Is Augustine being careless or duplicitous in this entire discussion?

Augustine's appraisal of Varro's natural theology may shed some light on this problem. As Augustine presents Varro's position, paraphrasing and quoting from what are now mainly lost works, Varro to a great extent shares Augustine's misgivings about the truth-value and moral impact of the civil religious cult. Some of Rome's rites, those most demeaning to gods and human beings, Varro simply passes over, refusing to call attention to them or to dignify them by philosophic reinterpretation (*ciu. Dei* 7.25–26). When Varro does present other elements of the public theology and cult as interpreting nature, Augustine understands him to be doing the best he can, with the lights he has, to mitigate moral harm and uplift the public mind toward truth about

[22] For a study of Augustine on the relationship of injustice, fear of death and diversion from this fear, and civil religion, see Dodaro 2004, pp. 27–71.

[23] See also the outset of Book 6, at the closing on chapter 1, immediately prefacing Augustine's engagement specifically with Varro. Speaking of "the men who divided up these temporal tasks and assigned them, little task by little task, to the gods" he observes that "even these men did not dare to claim that the gods could grant eternal life" (*ciu. Dei* 6.1). O'Daly also notes this omission, concluding that Augustine's "general intention is to make specific arguments superfluous. This gives the polemic against Varro a certain independence within the work" (O'Daly 1999, p. 101). At the end of his discussion of Books 6 and 7, O'Daly reiterates the absence of argument concerning the afterlife advanced by Varro and those holding similar theological positions. O'Daly concludes: "The thrust of Augustine's argument is that if the polytheists … hold contradictory views of the gods, these gods and the religious practices they assume can have no beneficial effects in this life, and by implication in the next" (O'Daly 1999, p. 109). This interpretation seems plausible to be sure, and yet may not be the only reason for Augustine's odd mode of proceeding vis-à-vis his stated intention in Books 6 and 7.

divinity. In other words, Varro concurs to a great extent with Augustine's two foundational critiques of Rome's civil cult.

In trying to bring civil religion into greater accord with nature, however, Varro's limited knowledge or erroneous opinion concerning the true nature of divinity, inclines him to be too accommodating of the civil-mythical theology and excessively modest in the hopes he can hold out to its practitioners, even from philosophy's standpoint as Augustine understands it. Early in Book 7, Augustine summarized Varro's natural theology in this way: Varro holds that the cosmos itself is the one divinity, by virtue of its soul. "Here," Augustine notes, "Varro seems, in a sense, to acknowledge that there is one God." Yet Varro further divides the cosmos into the spheres of heaven and earth, and each of these he divides and makes inhabited by lesser souls, still greater than human souls: "All these four parts, he claims, are full of souls ... immortal souls ... and mortal." The "heavenly gods" inhabit the upper regions; lesser gods dwell between the moon and earth's atmosphere. In this way, Varro's philosophic pantheism, a form of monotheism, can be interpreted as in accord with mythical-civil religion's polytheism.[24] Augustine observes that such pantheistic theology was not Varro's alone, but rather it was "favored not only by Varro but by many philosophers as well" (*ciu. Dei* 7.6; Babcock 1.213) – and also, as we learn at intervals throughout *ciu. Dei*, by philosophic poets such as Virgil (*ciu. Dei* 4.9; 4.11; cf. 6.9).[25]

Within a natural-theological paradigm that views the divinity as the soul of the world, a rational force or mind holding together and guiding all things that exist, what are the prospects for eternal life for human beings? Varro seems to classify the "rational soul[s]" of human beings as the highest among "mortal souls," but mortal nonetheless (*ciu. Dei* 7.5–6; Babcock 1.212–13). On this reading, there is no eternal life in which humans may hope for their souls, to say nothing of their bodies (cf. *ciu. Dei* 10.28–29 and 22.4–5, *inter alia*; see also Cavadini 2012).

[24] Clark (2010) observes that Varro's natural theology is a form of what she aptly terms "inclusive monotheism," common in late classical intellectual circles, and argues that Augustine does not interpret Varro's melding of this natural theology with civil religion with sufficient rigor. She nonetheless finds Augustine's critique of Varro to have some merit, especially politically but also theologically: "Pagan monotheism is too exclusive, because its teachings are accessible only to those who have financial and intellectual resources, and too inclusive, because its adherents continue to offer cult to gods behaving badly" (Clark 2010, p. 201). For other arguments that Augustine is less than fair in interpreting Varro's theological project, see O'Daly 1996, O'Daly 71–72 and Rousseau 2009, O'Daly 166–167.

[25] On Virgil and Augustine, see MacCormack 1998.

Alternatively, perhaps Varro understands humans' rational souls as comprising sparks or small shares of the one vast world soul, the mind moving and enlivening the whole cosmos. Also on this account, the prospects for personal life after death seem poor, even nonexistent: all human souls are really part of the one world soul, and after the body's demise cease to exist in a personal, individuated way. Varro is willing to stretch the truth and even lie to the common people, to revive the civil cult and render it respectable, and thereby reinforce his political community. He does not seem similarly to mislead people, however, as to what he thinks can reasonably be hoped, the greatest happiness he thinks can be attained by mortal men and women.

Augustine thus dialogues with Varro as to the nature and value of Rome's civil religion, and through it, the meaning and achievements of the philosophic or natural theology Varro expounds. This dialogue is meaningful for Augustine's task of persuading the noble Roman pagan that Christianity is not inimical to good citizenship for its refusal of Rome's civil theology. Augustine is thus primarily concerned with Varro as acting "in the political realm," or as a statesman (*ciu. Dei* 7.23; Babcock 1.228), not as a natural theologian. Yet his engagement with Varro in Books 6 and 7 is also meaningful and perhaps essential for Augustine's debate with the philosophic theology of the Platonists, in Books 8–10, and its rationale for upholding pagan cult for the common people. Varro's highest intention for his ablest, most reflective readers, as Augustine understands it, was precisely to lead them from civil to natural theology, as from falsehood to truth. *Antiquities* thus read appears as much more than a treatise on Roman religion. It also, as we have seen, comprises a protreptic or exhortation to philosophize about the cause or causes of things, about the divine: Which educated, attentive reader, asks Augustine, will not grasp that Varro's "purpose is *to ready a place in human minds* for the natural theology which, he says, belongs to the philosophers"? (*ciu. Dei* 6.9; Babcock 1.201; emphasis added).

Varro had worked for and come close to truth, Augustine emphasizes. Varro had perhaps lacked only the fortuitous encounter with Platonic wisdom from which Augustine himself had benefitted, to approach more clearly and fully to what human reason unassisted by revelation could grasp about God:

> The same extremely shrewd and learned author also says that, in his view, the only people who have rightly discerned what God is are those who believed that he is the soul that governs the world by

> movement and reason. In this regard, Varro had not yet attained the real truth, for the true God is not a soul but the author and maker even of the soul itself. All the same, however, it seems clear that, if Varro could have been free to withstand the prejudice of custom, he would have acknowledged and argued that one God is to be worshiped, the one God who governs the world by movement and reason. And so the only question remaining at issue with him in this connection would be his claim that God is a soul and not rather the creator of the soul . . . And perhaps, *being found so near the truth, he might easily have been prompted by the soul's mutability to recognize that the true God is an immutable nature which also created the soul itself.*
>
> (*ciu. Dei* 4.31; Babcock 1.140; emphasis added)

In the task of preparing able minds for philosophic theology Augustine aims to collaborate with Varro, to help those living after the learned Roman to go further on this philosophic quest than Varro himself had managed, for all his genius, and to reach a natural philosophy of the divine that makes room for human immortality, for a firm hope of life eternal in bliss. Augustine himself had been so helped by "certain books of the Platonists" (*conf.* 7.9.13; cf. 7.9.14–17), years after Cicero's dialogue *Hortensius* had first kindled in his heart a passion for philosophy (*conf.* 3.4.7–8). By clearly, as it were publicly, expounding for all what Varro quietly intimated for a select few, and in suggesting that even simple pagans longed for a felicity that transcended this mortal life (*ciu. Dei* 4.25; cf. 6.12), a felicity that the God of Varro's nature could not give, Augustine encourages readers to continue on with him to examine, in Books 8–10 of *The City of God*, Socratic and Platonic philosophy concerning the divine, which might in turn prepare them to receive the Gospel (*ciu. Dei* 7.29–33).

CONCLUSION: PILGRIMS IN THE CITY AND THE *SAECULUM*

And so we are brought back around to Cicero's moving praise of Varro's work with which Augustine commences his dialogue with Varro in *ciu. Dei* 6 and 7.[26] "When we were wandering and straying (*peregrinantes errantesque*; CCSL 47.167) like visitors in our own city, your books led

[26] Cicero's praise of Varro seems somehow a natural point of conclusion for commentators on *ciu. Dei* 6 and 7: see also Burns 2001, p. 64 and Rousseau 2009, p. 175.

us back home, so to speak, so that we were at last able to recognize who and where we were" (*Acad. Post.* 1, 3, and 9; quoted in *ciu. Dei* 6.2; Babcock 1.187). Augustine's task in *ciu. Dei* continues Varro's project of assisting readers to attain greater self-knowledge, even while challenging Varro's defense of Rome's traditional religious institutions and civil cult.[27] As Augustine understands them, Varro's conflicting naturalistic explanations of pagan religious conventions also intentionally suggest to careful readers that as human beings they cannot hope to be fully at home even in their own city. Varro's natural theology, explicated together with Rome's civil theology in his *Antiquitates* and other religious writings, reminds his compatriots that they are also citizens of the cosmos. Yet even this realization does not suffice, Augustine argues, for those seeking philosophic and religious truth, "[f]or, although the true God is God not by opinion but by nature, it remains true that all nature is not God" (*ciu. Dei* 6.8; Babcock 1.197).[28]

Augustine's *ciu. Dei* thus endeavors to go further along Varro's path, indicating how and why, even in this wide world, humans are by nature and by grace *peregrinantes*, wanderers or pilgrims in search of an everlasting city where perfect justice and peace prevail. With hope in this truly eternal city, the heavenly city or City of God existing albeit imperfectly as a "pilgrim society" (*ciu. Dei* 19.17) already in history, human wayfarers here and now are called to reside in and work for peace and justice in their political societies with patience and moderation, as they await their definitive homecoming.

G. K. Chesterton echoes beautifully this Augustinian theme for modern readers, writing of his own discovery of Christianity. A form of philosophy had persuaded Chesterton that he was only an animal being bound by nature and as such ought to feel fully at home in the world. Still he could not be at peace or happy until he discovered the Gospel, the call as Augustine puts it to become a citizen of the heavenly city on pilgrimage in this world (*ciu. Dei* 1, *praef.*; 2.29; 15.1; 19.17).[29] Then at last, writes Chesterton, "my soul sang for joy, like a bird in

[27] On Augustine's work in the tradition of Roman political thought, see Hammer 2014; O'Daly 1999, 382–430; and Harding 2008.

[28] See *ciu. Dei* 6.8: "But all these things [of the civil theology, according to Varro and others] ... have certain physical interpretations, that is, interpretations in terms of natural phenomena – as if, in this discussion, we were investigating physics rather than theology, which is an account not of nature but of God. For, although the true God is God not by opinion but by nature, it remains true that all nature is not God."

[29] On Augustine's *City of God* as a call to citizenship, cf. *inter alia* Burns 2001, p. 64; Dougherty 1979, p. 90; Roberts 2016; and Rousseau 2009, pp. 174–175.

spring ... *I knew now why...I could feel homesick at home"* (Chesterton 1908, 147; emphasis added).

FURTHER READING

Burns, P. C. (2001). Augustine's Use of Varro's *Antiquitates Rerum Divinarum* in His *De Civitate Dei*. *Augustinian Studies*, 32(1), 37–64.

Clark, G. (2010). Augustine's Varro and Pagan Monotheism. In S. Mitchell and P. van Nuffelen, eds., *Monotheism between Pagans and Christians in Late Antiquity*. Leuven: Peeters, pp. 181–201.

Fortin, E. L. (1996a). Augustine and Roman Civil Religion: Some Critical Reflections. In J. B. Benestad, ed., *Classical Christianity and the Political Order: Reflections on the Theologico-Political Problem*. Lanham, MD: Rowman & Littlefield, pp. 85–106.

Harding, B. (2008). *Augustine and Roman Virtue: Continuum Studies in Philosophy*. London: Continuum.

O'Daly, G. J. P. (1994). Augustine's Critique of Varro on Roman Religion. In A. H. Sommerstein, ed., *Religion and Superstition in Latin Literature*. Bari: Levante Editori, pp. 65–76.

7 Books 8–10: Augustine and Platonism

MARK EDWARDS

Books 8–10 of *The City of God* complete the polemical interrogation of pagan culture. As Augustine says, the last five of these ten are addressed to the philosophers whose connivance with the blasphemies of the civic cult exposes the insufficiency of reason as a means to the knowledge of God and the perfection of moral character. In the three books discussed here, his interlocutors are the Platonists Apuleius and Porphyry, one the foremost African man of letters before Augustine himself, the other a trenchant critic of the scriptures who had derided Christianity as the superstitious worship of a dead man.[1] Augustine's case against both is that, notwithstanding their adherence to a school which had come close to Christianity in its consciousness of the unity and sovereignty of God, they had returned to the most demotic form of polytheism, making human access to the gods depend on a race of aerial spirits who are inferior in piety and benevolence to the best denizens of earth. Augustine's aim is to show that their speculations are inconsistent not only with scriptural teaching on the origin of demons, but with the genuine traditions of Platonism, the confession of the ancient prophet Hermes Trismegistus and Porphyry's own intimations of the true nature of God.

BOOK 8

Having dismissed all philosophic palliatives to the folly and obscenity of the civic cults, Augustine proceeds in his eighth book to investigate the teaching of the philosophers themselves with regard to God and the ends of life. Noting that a philosopher is by etymology a lover of wisdom, he deduces that, as God is wisdom, the true philosopher must be a lover of God (*ciu. Dei* 8.1). This equation of God with wisdom,

[1] For Augustine on Porphyry see Magny 2014, pp. 99–147.

seemingly at odds with his earlier reasoning (in a more Platonic phase) that the object of wisdom must be superior to wisdom, is explained by the Christian tenet that the one through whom the Father made all things is also God. Thus we learn obliquely that the object of the true philosopher's love will be the Trinity, an inference which ensures that his chief interlocutors will be of the school of Plato. On first introduction they are pronounced superior to Varro because they extended the scope of natural philosophy beyond the world to include the God who created it. Here as elsewhere, Augustine seems to assume the literal reading of Plato's *Timaeus* which would warrant the application of this term to Plato's demiurge, though he is certainly aware that every Platonist since Plotinus had regarded the fashioning of the world by intellect as a process without any temporal beginning.[2]

To demonstrate the superiority of the Platonic system to all its precursors, he divides the schools of antiquity into two streams, the Ionic and the Italian, the first springing from Thales and the second from Pythagoras (*ciu. Dei* 8.2). As the one philosopher among the seven sages, Thales traced the origin of all things to a material element, water, for which his pupil Anaximander substituted the infinite. Anaximander's pupil Anaximenes made air the common substrate, but his two most illustrious students, Anaxagoras and Diogenes of Apollonia, both recognised the necessity of positing a divine intellect in addition to passive matter.[3] The pupil of Anaxagoras, Archelaus,[4] was in turn the teacher of Socrates,[5] who turned away from these uncertain reveries to the more fruitful study of the art of living (*ciu. Dei* 8.3). Nevertheless, his interrogative method was more suited to exploding false opinions than to establishing the truth, and it was left to his pupil Plato[6] to construct the soundest theology of ancient times by fusing the Socratic inquiry into the roots of action with the more contemplative principles of the Italian or Pythagorean school, which had always posited an immaterial and immortal soul (*ciu. Dei* 8.4). It is at this point that Augustine gives his own shape to the conventional

[2] See further Dillon 1989, pp. 50–72.

[3] Anaximander of Miletus died c. 547 BC; Anaximenes of Miletus died c. 525 BC; Anaxagoras of Clazomenae (also resident in Athens) died c. 428 BC; Diogenes of Apollonia seems to have been alive in 423 BC.

[4] On this shadowy figure see Hippolytus, *Refutation* 1.9, Plutarch, *On the Prime Cold* 21 and Porphyry, *History of Philosophy* Fr 12.

[5] The Athenian philosopher (469 BC–399 BC) had been a hero to Christians ever since Justin Martyr,

[6] On Augustine and Plato (c. 428 BC–347 BC) see van Fleteren 1999, pp. 651–654.

taxonomy – first attested for us in Diogenes Laertius, but confessedly not his invention[7] – which he has hitherto been content to accept by hearsay. From his own knowledge,[8] he can now assert that, although he often shields his insight behind the inconclusive quibblings of his master, Plato is understood by the best interpreters to have taught that there is one God, who is at once the cause of existence, the rationale of understanding and the regulating principle of life. These three conceptions of God correspond to the three divisions of philosophy – physics, logic (or rational philosophy) and ethics – which were perhaps more frequently ascribed in ancient historiography to the Stoics.[9]

This threefold apprehension of God as the cause of things, the teacher of truth and the donor of felicity suffices to prove the superiority of Platonism to the fabling of the poets and to the civic cults which had been observed from reverence to Numa, Rome's second king, until they found a sophistical advocate in Varro (*ciu. Dei* 8.5).[10] Again, it is clearly truer than those which seek the cause of all things in the elements, whether in water with Thales, in air with Anaximenes, in fire with the Stoics or in atoms with Epicurus. Paul's caricature of the Greeks as slaves of the weak and beggarly elements had already been extended to other nations by Aristides of Athens, Hippolytus of Rome and Firmicus Maternus;[11] the Platonists had been co-opted as theists and Trinitarians by Eusebius of Caesarea. But only Augustine credits them with the threefold merit of understanding God as the ground of natural philosophy (*ciu. Dei* 8.6), as the light of truth in rational philosophy (*ciu. Dei* 8.7) and as the ultimate goal of ethical philosophy (*ciu. Dei* 8.8). They have grasped, he says, what the angels perceive intuitively, that his being cannot be other than his life, or his life other than his intelligence, or his intelligence other than his blessedness (*ciu. Dei* 8.6).

In appearance this is a tetrad, not a triad, but the unnamed source of these terms is the Platonist Marius Victorinus,[12] who on converting to Christianity late in life, adopted the triad of being, life and mind from the successors of Plotinus, and correlated these terms with the Father,

[7] *Lives of the Philosophers*, proem.

[8] For his history of the decline and restoration of the Platonic school see *Against the Academics* 3.18–41, with Brittain 2001, pp. 242–247.

[9] Diogenes Laertius, *Lives of the Philosophers* 7.39.

[10] On this putative founder of Rome's religion and her calendar, see Livy, *Histories* 1.18–21; Plutarch, *Numa*.

[11] Gal 4:9; Hippolytus, *Refutation* 1.26.3; Firmicus Maternus, *On the Error of Profane Religions* 1.1; Pouderon et al. 2003.

[12] See Manchester 1992, pp. 207–222.

the Son and the Spirit, occasionally substituting blessedness for mind. Augustine does not follow him in this, either in the *City of God* or in *On the Trinity*;[13] the reason may be that, being aware of its provenance, he knew that this triad had been devised to account for the residual duality of subjective knowing and objective knowledge in the demiurgic intellect, which for Neoplatonists is not the sovereign principle. He also declines to pursue the obvious correlation of being with physics, intellect with logic and life with ethics, and hints instead that Paul unfolded a similar adumbration of the Trinity when he said to the philosophers of Athens that in God 'we live and move and have our being'.[14] It is only after crediting the Platonists with this triadic or tetradic notion of deity that Augustine commends their subordination of the sensible form of the body to the intelligible form of life, by which we are to understand the soul. As the discussion continues, he does not cease to remind us that God, for Platonists as for Christians, is the constitutive cause of the universe, the light of rationality and the fountain from which we imbibe felicity (*ciu. Dei* 8.10.50–51); in the shortest variant of this formula virtue, wisdom and felicity are the three supernal gifts (*ciu. Dei* 8.16.32).[15]

No other school deserves more than a deprecatory notice in a Christian survey of the Greek tradition. In contrast to the Platonists, the Stoics denied the existence of an intelligible realm and denied that anything can be known which is not a body.[16] Assuming, perhaps erroneously, that by body they meant on all occasions an object that is accessible to the senses, Augustine wonders how they can say that only the wise man is beautiful when the beauty of which they speak resides in his intellect and not his outward form (*ciu. Dei* 8.7). The Platonists show to advantage again in their understanding of the true end of life, for their rivals uniformly maintain that, whatever the good for humans is, it can be achieved by human endeavour. All are aware that certain goods pertain to the body and others to the soul; there are some – the allusion is to the Peripatetics[17] – who deem happiness incomplete without such external goods as rank, repute and wealth (*ciu. Dei* 8.8).

Only the Platonists see that to be blessed is to take satisfaction not in body or soul but in God himself – and not the satisfaction that we

[13] Thus at *Trin.*10.10 being, life and mind are characteristic of all three persons.
[14] *ciu. Dei* 8.10, quoting Acts 17:28.
[15] Where line references are given, these are taken from Dombart and Kalb 1954.
[16] See Long 1996, pp. 227–230.
[17] Aristotle 1999, p. 1098a, on the ground that such goods are necessary to the performance of noble works.

receive from ourselves or from a friend but that which the eye receives from light. Plato, in asserting that the true good is to live virtuously in the knowledge and imitation of God, fulfils the true definition of a philosopher as a lover of God. Augustine here invokes his own distinction between the objects of use and the objects of enjoyment, the latter being our absolute goods while the former are only the means by which we achieve them.[18] He also adopts the argument of Socrates that in seeking knowledge that we do not yet possess, we are moved by a love or desire for that object which is grounded in an inchoate knowledge of it;[19] in the ninth book of *On the Trinity*, the same premises enable him to correlate the three persons with *mens*, *notitia* and *amor* – mind, knowledge and love.[20]

No Christian, however ignorant, is unaware that philosophers are suitors of wisdom, or that Paul warns us not to be captivated by the wisdom of this world. The apostle who proclaimed the unknown God to the philosophers also denounced the cult of images which dishonours the invisible creator. If Plato saw further than others, discerning in God the foundation of causality in nature, success in reasoning and rectitude in conduct, we may reasonably ascribe this to some acquaintance with the scriptures. Like Clement of Alexandria, Augustine believed that Plato had visited Egypt, but he knows that he lived too late to have conversed with Jeremiah and too early to have perused the Greek translation of the scriptures (*ciu. Dei* 8.11). Nevertheless, he suggests that the *Timaeus* betrays some mediated acquaintance with the opening chapter of Genesis, for in Plato's cosmogony air and water hold the middle place between fire and earth, just as the Holy Spirit moves on the waters between the primordial heaven and earth in the Mosaic narrative.[21] Again, if Plato alone maintains the incorporeality of being, it is because he had heard of the passage in which God reveals himself from the burning bush as He Who Is (Ex 3.14). Augustine forgets that the incorporeality of the divine is a Platonic rather than a biblical tenet; in his defence, we may note that Origen had been guilty of similar reasoning, while Justin had paid equally little attention to the letter of either text when he charged the author of the *Timaeus* with various plagiarisms from the Pentateuch.[22]

[18] See further O'Donovan 1982, pp. 361–397.
[19] Plato, *Meno* 80d.
[20] *Trin.* 9.3.3ff.
[21] *Timaeus* 31b–32b; Gen 1:2.
[22] Origen, *On Prayer* 27; Justin, *First Apology* 59–60.

The recognised genealogy derived three sects from Plato, thde Peripatetics through Aristotle, the Academics through Speusippus and in Roman times the Platonists through Plotinus, Porphyry and Iamblichus.[23] Augustine professes to marvel that these last, who assumed the master's name, should have fallen away from his monotheism into the vulgar worship of many gods (*ciu. Dei* 8.12–13). Of course they did no such thing, for Plato himself, while he admits only one creator and one Good for all, does not deny the existence of the lesser divinities or their right to honour.[24] It was also he who characterised the daemon as a demigod, imperfect but immortal, though not yet as a ubiquitous mediator between the human and the divine, as his interpreters Plutarch and Apuleius did in the 2nd century AD.[25] While he may have been ignorant of Plutarch, Augustine certainly knew Apuleius as the foremost of African writers, in whose novel *The Golden Ass* the inquisitive hero accidentally casts a spell that deprives him of his human shape.[26] *On the God of Socrates*, by contrast, is an essay on the *daimonion*, or supernatural guardian, of Socrates, which follows Plutarch in recognising, along with our natal genii and the spirits of the dead, a third order of daemons, the purveyors of mantic dreams and tenants of shrines, who act as deputies to the gods and relay their oracles in answer to our prayers.[27] This third class, says Augustine, is known to Christians, but the demons of the New Testament are not intermediate beings, not emissaries of other gods, but fallen angels who avenge themselves by propagating the worship of the infamous dead, and have thus estranged the nations from their Maker (*ciu. Dei* 8.22). Both the angelology and the Euhemeristic theory that the gods of the world were once mortals are Christian commonplaces, eloquently expounded for Latin readers by Lactantius.[28] Augustine, in his own treatise on demonology, takes the conventional view that while (by divine consent) they possess some power to foretell the future and to

[23] Aristotle (384BC–322 BC) and Speusippus (c. 407 BC–339 BC) both taught in Athens; Plotinus (AD 204/5–AD 270) and Porphyry (AD 232–c. AD 305) were active in Rome, while Iamblichus (c. AD 245–c. AD 325) had a school in Syrian Apamea.

[24] See, e.g. *Timaeus* 40d–41a. On the moral superiority of the gods see, e.g. *Republic* 398b.

[25] *Symposium* 202b–e. On Plutarch (c. AD 50–c. AD 120) see Nesselrath 2010.

[26] See Augustine, *ep.* 102.

[27] Thomas 1970, pp. 6–35.

[28] Ogilvie 1978, pp. 50–57. On the origin of the theory that the gods were once infamous mortals see Athenagoras, *Embassy* 26 and Winiarczyk 2013.

cause us physical affliction, their usual and most efficacious weapon is subterfuge.[29]

Apuleius, himself their dupe and tool, has followed a method of binary division which he inherits from both Plato and Aristotle to arrive at the five defining characteristics of the daemon.[30] As Augustine notices, one of these, immortality, is shared with God and not with us; another, passibility, is shared with us and not with God; two, rationality and animation, are common to all three, while the fifth, the aerial body, is peculiar to themselves (*ciu. Dei* 8.16). The pagan author reasons that the gods, being incorporeal, cannot communicate directly with our gross organs but must deal with us through these tenuous intermediaries.[31] Augustine reminds him of what all Platonists know, that the divine is defined above all by its goodness (*ciu. Dei* 8.15); it would thus be absurd to suppose that a virtuous human had less access to their presence than a daemon who is encumbered by gross passions, simply because the latter's body is of a subtler constitution. If bodily excellence rendered a being more godlike, humans would find themselves lower in the cosmic scale than the many beasts which have the advantage of us in agility, strength or natural weaponry (*ciu. Dei* 8.16). Furthermore, their very irrationality prevents them from suffering the perturbations to which we are subject when our passions are in conflict with our reason. Philosophers of the Aristotelian school had drawn this contrast to illustrate the meaning of freedom;[32] Augustine uses it rather to forestall any argument for the superiority of daemons, who are equally subject to passion yet incapable of the moral amelioration which is possible for the saints. The doctrine that the angels who have fallen cannot repent, with its corollary that the unfallen are now incapable of sinning, had been defended by Augustine in his treatise *On Free Will*;[33] here he points out that it is corroborated by tales in pagan myth of demonic assaults on mortals, some prompted by enmity and some by lust.[34]

If the gods learn of us only through the daemons, what do they know of Plato's strictures on these myths? Do the daemons report them but conceal the fact they are the subjects of them? Or do they conceal both

[29] See Holt 2009, pp. 277–278.

[30] Apuleius, *On the God of Socrates* 13.

[31] *On the God of Socrates* 4, citing Plato, *Symposium* 203a.

[32] Alexander of Aphrodisias (c. AD 200), *On Fate* 14.

[33] *lib. arb.* 3.5.15.

[34] At *ciu. Dei* 8.13 he alludes to the abduction of the son of Titus Latinius, first recounted back at 4.26.

Plato's judgment and their own depravity? Do they, on the contrary, allow the gods to see both; or are they silent regarding Plato but unabashed in the *confession* of their own crimes? Of these hypotheses, all but the third imply that the gods are ignorant, while the third and fourth, if true, would make them accomplices of agents who are morally inferior the best humans (*ciu. Dei* 8.21). It is not the best humans who resort to magic, the necessary means to the evocation of a daemon; Platonists, as Augustine knows, prefer the term theurgy, but the imputation of magic to Apuleius is polemically astute because he himself had been forced to repudiate this illicit art[35] when he was accused of having used it to seduce a woman far above his station (*ciu. Dei* 8.19). We may add his own disclaimers to the admonitions of Cicero and the prohibition of magic in the twelve tables, the oldest of all Roman codes,[36] to show that no pious suppliant would wish his prayers to be borne to the gods by magic, or even by licit means if daemons were his instruments (*ciu. Dei* 8.19).

Reiterating his judgment that the daemons of the Platonist are the demons of the New Testament, and hence not fit objects of worship, Augustine summons a pagan witness, Hermes Trismegistus, author of a text with the title *Asclepius*, of which a complete Latin version survives with fragments of the Greek original. Like the other writings in the theosophic corpus ascribed to Hermes Trismegistus, the Asclepius purports to have been written at the dawn of Egyptian history by the deity or divinised philosopher whom the Egyptians knew as Thoth.[37] Although the Latin translation is ascribed to Apuleius,[38] its prediction of a day when Egypt's shrines would be empty of gods has been thought to prove that it must date in its present form from the reign of Theodosius I, who issued the first decree for the wholesale demolition of pagan temples.[39] Although this theory has been contested in modern times, we need not doubt that Augustine would have regarded the destruction of the Alexandrian temple to Serapis in AD 391[40] as a fulfilment of the prophecy, and hence as an affidavit to the inspiration of this pagan seer. For all their claims to Egyptian provenance, Hermetic

35 On the *Apology* see Harrison 2000, pp. 39–88.

36 Augustine may in fact be thinking of Pliny, *Natural History* 28.2.17. he also quotes Virgil, *Aeneid* 7.338, 4.492 and *Eclogues* 8.98.

37 On the Hermetic corpus, barely attested if at all before the 4th century AD, see Fowden 1993.

38 Thomas 1970, pp. 36–81.

39 For discussion of chapters 25–27 see Copenhaver 1992), pp. 213–214, 238–246.

40 See Butler 1902, pp. 410–424.

writings were of far more interest to Christians than to pagans, and above all to the Christians of Africa: Tertullian knows of Hermes as a philosopher, Arnobius numbers him among the strange authorities cited by certain 'new men' (*noui uiri*) among the pagans,[41] and Lactantius quotes profusely from the corpus as a testament to the antiquity of monotheism, the incorporeality of the soul, the invisibility of the creator and his manifestation through a second god.[42] Augustine, however, looks in the *Asclepius* not so much for a pagan witness to Christianity as for the witness of paganism against itself; it is therefore all the more remarkable that he seems to be unaware of the attribution to Apuleius.

In the first excerpt Trismegistus argues that the creation of sacred images by humanity was a fitting imitation of the divine handiwork in the cosmos;[43] he ascribes to these statues not only speech and motion, but the power of foretelling the future (*ciu. Dei* 8.23). The author thus appears to be an admirer (or, by his own account, a precursor) of Iamblichus, whose disciple Maximus won the favour of the Emperor Julian by causing a statue to move, thereby provoking the contempt of other Platonists who adhered to an older and more austere tradition.[44] Augustine takes notice only of the admission that even pagans know their statues to be mere artefacts, and appends a series of biblical animadversions on the futility of worshipping the creatures of one's own hands. Moreover, because the text of the *Asclepius* as he and we possess it is a palimpsest showing evidence of Platonic or Christian redaction, he can also produce a passage[45] in which Hermes admits that his grandsires were in error when they took to manufacturing their own gods (*ciu. Dei* 8.24).

This pagan testimony may persuade us that a daemon is associated with every pagan idol; it will not persuade us to kneel either to the daemon or to the idol, for the god that the artisan creates is a god for him alone, as Paul and the psalmists testify.[46] There are angels of another kind, but their closeness to God is demonstrated by their refusal of worship (*ciu. Dei* 8.25), as Augustine will go on to show at length in the following books. Endorsing the conventional theory that daemons propagate not their own cult but that of the dead, he can once again

[41] Arnobius, *Against the Nations* 2.13; see further Courcelle 1953, pp. 157–171.
[42] See especially *Epitome* 37.4–9, with Scott 1936, pp. 9–27.
[43] *Asclepius* 23, followed by a quotation from 24.
[44] Eunapius, *Lives of the Philosophers* 7.2.6–10.
[45] *Asclepius* 37.
[46] At *ciu. Dei* 8. 24 Augustine cites Psalm 96, Ps 115:5, 1 Cor 10.:0, and 1 Pet 2:5.

quote the *Asclepius* to prove that the supposed god of that name, the inventor of medicine, is a prisoner in his tomb (*ciu. Dei* 8.26). The veneration of martyrs is a Christian practice that he cannot deny (*ciu. Dei* 8.27), although his comments here as elsewhere suggest that, like Athanasius, he deprecates its excesses,[47] which he may have seen at first hand in the devotions of his mother.[48] Although inscriptions to the dead were legion in his time, he asserts that no priest who is offering a sacrifice in a martyr's name will suppose the martyr himself to be the recipient: the sole addressee of the oblation in every case is God (*ciu. Dei* 8.28).

BOOK 9

Book 9 is largely a recapitulation and expansion of the arguments presented in Book 8. Augustine notes at the outset that, while Platonists refuse to lay any evil at the door of the gods, them are some, like Apuleius, who maintain that there are both good and evil daemons (*ciu. Dei* 9.1–2). Since he admits at the same time that every daemon is subject to passion,[49] we must ask whether this does not render them inferior to the wisest of human beings (*ciu. Dei* 9.3). Philosophy in the Roman world was above all a training in the subjugation of the passions, but whereas the Stoics held up an ideal of *apatheia*, or perfect immunity from perturbation, the Platonists and Peripatetics argued that even the wise cannot hope to do more than preserve their virtue when they experience temptation: their watchword was therefore not *apatheia* but *metriopatheia*, or moderate feeling.[50] Augustine suspects that this is not a true difference of opinion but a quarrel over words (*ciu. Dei* 9.4). He derives his proof, as always, from a classic of Latin literature, the *Attic Nights* of the 2nd-century AD polymath and grammarian Aulus Gellius.[51] Gellius repeats a Greek anecdote that a Stoic was once observed to turn pale when the vessel on which he was travelling was in danger of being overwhelmed by a storm. When asked how such distress could befall a man who professed to acknowledge no good but virtue, regarding even life as a mere commodity which is morally

[47] Letters 22.1.6, 29.9 and 36.9.21. Cf. Athanasius, *Life of Antony* 90.
[48] *conf.* 6.2.2. See further Straw 1999, pp. 538–542.
[49] *On the God of Socrates* 12 is quoted at length.
[50] See further Dillon 1983, pp. 508–517.
[51] Aulus Gellius (c. 130 BC–180 BC), *Attic Nights* 19.4.

indifferent,[52] he showed his interlocutors a book in which Zeno, the founder of Stoicism,[53] had maintained that, while fearful or dolorous impressions from without cannot fail to stir the soul of the wise man, they will not command his assent or approbation. In short, concludes Augustine, the Stoics admit with the rest of the world that even the strongest constitution is susceptible to feeling, and the other schools agree with them that the goal of philosophy is the restraint of feeling. Whether the sage elects to call his life a good or a mere commodity[54] is a question of words.

The classicist Richard Sorabji demurs:[55] the Stoics, he argues, drew a clear distinction between emotions and inchoate perturbations, which Augustine has failed to grasp because he knows their doctrines only through Latin proxies. The charge is surely unjust, for Augustine is not betraying his ignorance but passing judgment on information competently gathered; he knows what the Stocis have said, but in common with Cicero, another able witness, he pronounces the distinction merely verbal.[56] Always more philosopher than philologist, he believes that any claim regarding the nature of our experience is open to correction in the light of our own experience; in addition, he has three theological reasons for insisting that the object of assent or dissent should be a definite, not an inchoate stimulus. The first is that he wishes the act of will to be not merely profitable to the building of character but meritorious in the eyes of God. The second is that the most momentous act of will that lies within our capacity is in his view the free assent to the offer of grace, which, as he explains in his anti-Pelagian work *On the Spirit and the Letter*, originates as a prompting from without that can have no other source than God.[57] His third and sovereign argument against all Greek endeavours to raise philosophy above the human passions is that Christ himself, the one perfect man since Adam, is said in the Gospel of John to have been troubled in spirit by his impending death.[58]

In the fourteenth book of the *City of God*, he regrets that the Stoics have countenanced only three *eupatheiai* (good passions) corresponding to gaiety, fear and hope, and have not recognised contrition for sin as the

[52] Augustine also quotes, through Gellius, his first reply, that his life was less easily spared than that of his questioners: see Diogenes Laertius, *Lives* 2.8.7.
[53] Zeno of Citium, taught in Athens (d. 264 BC).
[54] On this distinction see Cicero, *On Ends* 3, 69.
[55] Sorabji 2000), pp. 372–385.
[56] Cicero, *On Ends* 3.5.
[57] *spir et let.* 34.60.
[58] *eu. Jo. tr.* 60, on Jn 13:21.

philosophic counterpart of sorrow. In the present book, their fault is that, alone among the Greek schools, they reckon *misericordia* (pity) among the vices,[59] whereas Christians regard it as the sovereign virtue of God (*ciu. Dei* 9.5). Anger, fear and grief are not forbidden to Christians: we rather inquire (as Aristotle too would say[60]) in what manner and for what reason they experience these passions. Defying both Stoics and Platonists and following Lactantius,[61] he contends that God can feel anger, so long as this is understood, not as mere irascibility but as a dispositional hatred of sin which results in loving chastisement of the sinner. Even good angels feel the same compassion when they inflict such chastisement at his behest (*ciu. Dei* 9.5). In the saints carnal passions are tests of moral disposition and may be tamed or sanctified with divine assistance (*ciu. Dei* 9.5); in daemons, by contrast, they are present by nature and not to be overcome (*ciu. Dei* 9.6). The gods of whose delinquencies the poets sing, according to Apuleius, inhabit the middle region between the gods and earthbound mortals (*ciu. Dei* 9.7); yet he himself concedes[62] that human beings are distinguished not only by their lowly position but by their capacity for wisdom (*ciu. Dei* 9.8). Even if we did not have the historian Sallust[63] to teach us that the soul should be our master and the body our slave, we ought to perceive the futility of any intercourse between gods and daemons (*ciu. Dei* 9.9). Gods, by definition, are morally perfect, while the daemons who resemble them only in body resemble only their inferiors in soul.

That Platonists recognise pity as a divine attribute is proved by a quotation from Plotinus,[64] the founder of Neoplatonism, which is itself a quotation from the *Symposium of Plato* (*ciu. Dei* 9.10). In the myth which Plato attributes to Aristophanes our ancestors were globular until Zeus was obliged to forestall their plot to storm Olympus by

[59] Cf. Cicero, *On Ends* 3.35; *In Defence of Murena* 6, 9, 61. Augustine also quotes In Defence of Ligarius 12.37 in praise of compassion. Seneca, *On Clemency* 2.5 might also be cited, but, as Rome's foremost philosopher, as well as her most eloquent rhetorician, Cicero (106 BC–43 BC) is Augustine's chief informant on the opinions of the Stoics, which he often judged (with the caution of an Academic, or Sceptic) to be 'probable'.

[60] See, e.g. *Nicomachean Ethics* 1025b30–35 on anger.

[61] See Ingremeau 1982.

[62] *On the God of Socrates* 13.

[63] Sallust (c. 86 BC–c. 35 BC), *Catiline* 1.2.

[64] Plotinus, *Enneads* 4.3.12; Plato, *Symposium* 191b. Augustine quotes Plotinus with a frequency that seems to betoken first-hand knowledge of the Latin translation (probably by Victorinus', notwithstanding the arguments of Beatrice 1989, pp. 248–281, who believes Porphyry to have bene the sole author of the Platonic books which Augustine recalls at *Confessions* 3.5.27.

cutting them in half. It was after this that, 'taking pity' upon when he saw that they were dying from the pain of separation, he created the sexual organs which have made possible both the restoration of oneness and the survival of the race. As Plotinus applies these words, however, the object of divine pity is the soul, which is periodically liberated from the body by physical death. Augustine also credits the Platonists with the theory that certain daemons are souls of the dead, the more benign being those whom the Romans call Manes while the wicked are known as Larvae (*ciu. Dei* 9.11). This is the doctrine of Apuleius[65] rather than Plotinus, though the latter had spoken of the unhappy persistence of the unenlightened soul as an *eidolon* or shadow,[66] while his pupil Porphyry not only held that the souls of those who die violently continue to haunt their graves, but conferred the title daemon on those who liberate the soul by philosophic exercises.[67]

Augustine pursues his objections to the tricameral representation of the world in Apuleius, according to whom the daemons occupy a place between the immortality of the gods and the mortality of humans, between their exalted seats and our lowly dwelling-place on earth, between their impeccability and our moral imperfection (*ciu. Dei* 9.12). As to the first, says Augustine, there is no mean between the mortal and the immortal, and the daemon shares the eternity of the gods. Likewise there is no mean between the sinless and the sinful, and the daemons in their turpitude are as far from the gods as we are (*ciu. Dei* 9.13). Only in the topographic sense can we style them intermediate beings, and this does not equip them to act as mediators between our mortal wretchedness and the blessed immortality of God. This mediation can be achieved only by an exchange of adjectives between the two extremes, which will yield two categories, the mortal blessed and the wretched immortal (*ciu. Dei* 9.14). The daemons belong, of course, to the second category; if humans could choose they would embrace the other, and it was God the Word[68] who made this possible by his assumption of flesh (*ciu. Dei* 9.15). In this act he put on our mortality without renouncing the blessedness that belonged to him eternally and by nature; faithful to his own principle that all persons in the Trinity are

65 *On the God of Socrates* 15. See further Thaniel 1973, pp. 182–187.

66 *Enneads* 1.6.9.

67 Porphyry, *On Abstinence* 175.6–20 in Nauck 1986. For the liberated soul as daemon see *Life of Plotinus*.

68 On the inability of Platonists to understand this act of condescension see *conf.* 7.9.13–14 and 19.24–25.

equal,[69] Augustine stipulates that it is in his assumption of manhood, not in his character as the Word, that he effects this mediation.

The incarnation refutes the Platonic adage that divine beings cannot associate with mortals, for it is sin, not materiality, that is antipathetic to the moral purity of God. If the Platonists imagine that the mere proximity of matter contaminates the gods, how can they explain the fact that the stars look upon us every night and yet remain unsullied (*ciu. Dei* 9.16)? If seeing cannot injure them it is no more probable that they will suffer by hearing. It is evident that their purity remains unimpaired by contact with odours, for they delight in the smoke of sacrifices. This is a hackneyed Christian jibe, and Augustine has chosen not to remember that Porphyry, in his treatise *On Abstinence*, roundly denies that the gods are the authors of sacrifice or that they have any need of sustenance at our hands. Porphyry would have said what Augustine goes on to say, that since the gods have no bodies that require nourishment, there is no possibility of their being defiled by the taste of food. Pollution by touch is possible – perhaps Augustine is thinking here of Christ's words to Mary Magdalen, 'touch me not'[70] – but surely it would be possible for gods to forgather with mortals while avoid physical contact. There can be no doubt that the gods would prefer the company of those who were mortal but morally pure to that of the daemons whose immortality dooms them to perpetual wretchedness.

The futility of invoking daemons is obvious to students of the first treatise of Plotinus, by far the most famous and perhaps the only one to have been published in his lifetime. Echoing Homer, this laureate of the Platonists exhorts us to fly to our own dear fatherland, adding that the fleet which will carry us thither is the philosophic pursuit of likeness to God.[71] It was Plato who defined this as the goal of philosophy;[72] to Augustine, it is the rationale of the incarnation, in which the Second Person of the Trinity assumed our likeness in order that we might be fashioned into his. Anticipating the criticism of Porphyry in the tenth book, Augustine adds that Christ, by his own account, is the one true way to heaven (*ciu. Dei* 9.17). In this human guise he encountered the daemons (*ciu. Dei* 9.21), who, as Augustine never tires of repeating, are not intermediate beings but fallen angels. We should follow biblical

[69] See, e.g. *Trin.* 1.3.
[70] Jn 20:17.
[71] *Enneads* 1.6.8, wrongly ascribing *Iliad* 2.140 to the *Odyssey*.
[72] *Theaetetus* 176a.

usage in distinguishing the two classes of angels, rather than adopting the distinction between good daemons and evil daemons, which was introduced into Latin by Cornelius Labeo,[73] an antiquarian of the late 3rd century AD and perhaps a teacher of the *noui homines* of Arnobius (*ciu. Dei* 9.18–19).[74] On the other hand, we may endorse the Greek derivation of the noun *daimon* from the root which signifies to see or to know (*ciu. Dei* 9.19),[75] for when they encountered the God-man they exclaimed 'What have I to do with thee, Jesus of Nazareth? Hast thou come to destroy us?' (*ciu. Dei* 9.21).[76] The scriptures say expressly that these daemons are the gods of the nations;[77] only to one, however, do they accord the designation 'God of gods' (*ciu. Dei* 9.23). If it be urged that the term 'god' is so often conferred on humans that it must be all the more applicable to daemons, Augustine retorts that those who possess the likeness of God are worthier of this title, and that, like the unfallen angels (*ciu. Dei* 9.22), they manifest their proximity to him by seeking no cult for themselves (*ciu. Dei* 9.24).

BOOK 10

The chief aim of the tenth book is to refute the case that Porphyry had advanced on behalf of theurgy, the art – or magical artifice, as Augustine would say – of co-opting the aid of daemons in the emancipation of the lower soul.[78] This is the occasion for an excursus on the Latin equivalent of Greek terms for worship (*ciu. Dei* 10.1), comparable perhaps to the discussion in *On the Trinity* of the Greek and Latin terms for the single substance and three persons of the Godhead.[79] *Latreia*, a common terms for the devoirs paid to gods of all kinds, corresponds to Latin *servitus*, meaning the service of slaves to a master. Greeks, however, reserve this term for service to divine beings, so that in Latin its proper counterpart is *cultus*, understood in its strictest sense and not as when one employs the verb *colere* to mean the cultivation of an acquaintance or the occupation of a territory.[80] *Thrêskeia* is the counterpart to *religio*, and *eusebeia* to *pietas*, with the caveat that piety in Latin can be an

[73] Mastandrea 1979.
[74] Smith 1987, pp. 766–768.
[75] Plato, *Cratylus* 398a.
[76] Mk 1:24; Mt 8:29.
[77] Psalms 50:1, 136:2, 95:3, 96:4, 82:6, with 1 Cor 8:35–36.
[78] On the relation between the two thinkers see Theiler 1933.
[79] See *Trin.* 5.8.9–10.
[80] Citing Virgil, *Aeneid* 1.12.

attribute of God. The particular exhibition of *eusebeia* which the Greeks style *theossebeia* is on Latin *dei cultus*, the worship of God, who is of course our one true master and whom we cannot honour with any gift that is not already his own.

Augustine now asserts that Porphyry's cult of the lesser gods belies the teaching of Plotinus,[81] who acknowledges only one source of illumination, the divine intellect, which imparts its light to the soul as the sun imparts its light to the moon (*ciu. Dei* 10.2). Only his epigoni have turned to the lesser gods whom they call good daemons, though in scriptural parlance these are the angels or messengers, and thus servants, of the true God. In scripture we have the testimony of John the Baptists that there is but one light whereby we live.[82] Augustine now contrasts the worship, piety and religion of the church with that of paganism, which in the tradition of Latin apologetic is supposed to consist entirely in externals and above all in the maintenance of a priesthood for the bloody and futile business of sacrifice (*ciu. Dei* 10.3). Christian devotion is, by contrast, both external and internal: temples are raised to God, the one master of all, but every Christian makes a temple of his heart, in the assurance that the sacrifice which God desires is not the slaughter of beasts but, as the prophets declare, the immolation of our carnal appetites, the hallowing of all desire and action, the relief of need and suffering at our own material cost. The only bloody oblation that God accepts is the dedication of our lives to the point of death;[83] the one feast that he sanctions is the eucharist, in which he vouchsafes his own flesh and blood to his worshippers, in order that they may be strengthened in obedience and grow into his likeness. It was common for Christian preachers of this time to exhort their hearers to seek in Christian rites and practices the gratifications which they had been wont to receive from the devil;[84] Augustine's eulogy of his co-religionists is no doubt also an exhortation to the double-minded. His appeal is all the more piquant because he argues in a style more suited to the age of martyrs, nowhere intimating that under Christian rulers clerics have come to think of themselves as priests and *sacrificium* is now an accepted designation for the eucharist.[85]

[81] *Enneads* 5.1.2–3 and 10.
[82] Jn 1:6–7 and 1:16.
[83] Cf. 2 Cor 3.15–16.
[84] Proclus 1904.
[85] See Hanson 1985, pp. 83–112; Ramelli 2015, pp. 349–375.

It is clear then that the good daemons whom we call angels will demand no sacrifices (*ciu. Dei* 10.4), for they are acolytes, not masters, and the Master himself disdains all altars but the upright heart (*ciu. Dei* 10.5–6).[86] Through them, and for his own glory, he foretold to Abraham the birth of Isaac and the destruction of Sodom, rescued Lot from the ruin of that city and spoke to Moses from the burning bush (*ciu. Dei* 10.8). Recalling that the miracles of the bible had been unfavourably compared with those of pagan magicians, Augustine scoffs that Pharaoh's minions failed to undo the third of the plagues which Moses inflicted on Egypt, and that no device of pagan thaumaturgy has been able to match the miracles which he subsequently wrought by word and prayer. Applying the invidious name of *goêteia*, or sorcery, to the discipline which Porphyry calls theurgy (*ciu. Dei* 10.9, line 9), he accuses him of commending in some of his works the arts that he condemns in others.[87] Of the two works to which he alludes here, the more sceptical is the *Letter to Anebo*,[88] also summarised by Eusebius and ascribed again to Porphyry, while Iamblichus the Platonist refutes long excerpts from it in his treatise *On the Mysteries*, without identifying his teacher Porphyry as the author.[89] The more credulous work, and the principal whetstone of Augustine's argument, has the 'return of the soul' for its subject;[90] if this is also its title, it is otherwise unknown, but it evidently had much matter in common with a work in three books, entitled by Eusebius the *Philosophy from Oracles*, which is quoted in *ciu. Dei* 19.[91]

Whatever its title, the work on the return of the soul described the purificatory rites by which the lower soul can be freed from its bondage to the material. According to Augustine, it denied that the liberation of the rational, or intellectual, soul can be accomplished by theurgy, if liberation is understood to mean eternal freedom. It also warned that the offices of the good angels who assist us in these rites can be counteracted with success by malevolent daemons; by way of example,

86 Augustine cites Ps 15:2, Ps 50:18–19, Ps 49:12–14, Mic 6:6, Heb 13:16, Hos 6:6, Sir 30:24, Rom 6:13 and 12:1, Ps 72:28, all affirming that God seeks only devout adherence.

87 For condemnations of magic in the Roman world see *Theodosian Code* 9.16.3 and *Justinianic Code* 9.18.4.

88 Reconstructed by Sodano 1958.

89 Clarke et al. 2003.

90 For this locution, *de regressu animae*, see X.29.62 and X.32.6. The fragments are assembled in an appendix to Bidez 1913.

91 Hence the two works are identified by O'Meara 1959. See also Augustine, *ciu. Dei* 19.23.1.

Porphyry records the complaint of a good man among the Chaldaeans, who had been prevented from an envious rival from achieving liberation (*ciu. Dei* 10.9, lines 50–54). From this Augustine infers that even the gods (that is, the angels) are subject to the passions and perturbations that Apuleius imputes to daemons and human beings – which is only to say that they are not true gods, whether they succumb to strength or to guile (*ciu. Dei* 10.10). The powers invoked by theurgy are in reality manifestations of the devil, who is known to disguise himself as an angel of light.[92] Polemical as it is in expression, this is likely to be a fair synopsis, for we know from other witnesses that Porphyry believed in two orders of daemon, one of which sustains the soul after death in its flight from the body, while the other draws it back to the nether regions.[93] The unfortunate Chaldean is perhaps to be identified with Julian, the author of the so-called *Chaldean Oracles*,[94] on which more will be said below.

Augustine now reinforces his strictures on Porphyry with a paraphrase of the letter to Anebo, in which Porphyry himself expresses surprise that the Egyptians should presume to coerce the gods by sacrifice and incantation (*ciu. Dei* 10.11). Whereas the treatise *On the Return of the Soul* had assigned the aether as a seat to the gods in contrast to the air which supports the daemons, the *Letter to Anebo* draws a more profound distinction between the incorporeality of one race and the subtle corporeality of the other. Hence it is all the less probable that the gods can be cajoled or compelled by material forces, whether these be extorted by the soul or by certain spirits.[95] It is equally unintelligible that honours should be paid to a class of beings who are known to be protean in shape, insatiable in greed and deceitful in communication. Lascivious in their own practice, these hidden parasites demand chastity in their human servitors;[96] drunk as they are with the odour of sacrifices, they forbid their priests to eat meat, and, while they themselves are worshipped in graveyards, they decree that those who have touched a corpse are impure.[97] We read with consternation in Chaeremon,[98] a priest of Egypt writing in Greek, that sorcerers

[92] 1 Cor 11.14.
[93] Proclus, Commentary on the Timaeus, vol. 1, 77.17–23 Diehl.
[94] See Majercik 1989. Tradition dates the *Oracles* to the later 2nd century AD, although there is no certain quotation before the third.
[95] Cf. Iamblichus, *On the Mysteries* 1.11.37.
[96] Cf. Iamblichus, 4.11.195.
[97] Cf. *Iamblichus*, 5.1.1.
[98] On this Egyptian writer of the 1st century BC, see van der Horst 1984, with Iamblichus, *On the Mysteries* 8.4.

regularly bend the gods to their will with the threat of scattering their limbs as those of Osiris were c=scattered in the ancient myth (*ciu. Dei* 10.11.60–65).

The accuracy of Augustine's report is corroborated by our other witnesses, but he seems to express a doubt of his own when he wonders whether Porphyry is writing in the spirit of an inquirer or with the cautious indirection of a philosopher who knows more than he dares to reveal to the multitude. The persecutor[99] was wise enough to fear persecution, not wise enough to perceive that daemons sin by choice, not by nature (*ciu. Dei* 10.11.73), and that, while they impersonate both the gods and the souls of the dead, they frequently disclose their own characters to us without disguise. There are pagans who maintain that visible prodigies could not be the work of an invisible deity, but the Christians can point to the fabric of heaven and earth as the greatest of visible miracles, which at the same time proclaims the invisibility of its Author (*ciu. Dei* 10.12). Such is his power that he can make himself visible to those with faith, not in his essence (which we could never endure) but in a manner analogous to the revelation of a thought in verbal utterance. The simile reminds us that God is known above all by hearing,[100] and Augustine contrasts his legislation on Sinai with that of Lycurgus in Sparta,[101] which was thought to proceed from the gods on no other testimony than his own (*ciu. Dei* 10.13). Forestalling the objection that such things are no longer witnessed, Augustine explains that revelation unfolds in stages according to God's providential design, the sufficiency of which will not be contested by a disciple of Plotinus (*ciu. Dei* 10.14). He had long ago given the same reply when the Manichees asked why miracles had ceased;[102] as he goes on to maintain that scripture itself is the sovereign witness to its own providential origin, we can only guess whether he was aware that Plutarch had ascribed the decline of oracles to the progress of the intellect, which furnishes us with less doubtful and more permanent indices of the divine will.[103]

Since, however, God has elected to make himself known by miracles, Augustine must show that these were not superfluous, or doubtful, or mere replicas of the works attributed to pagan gods

[99] For a review of theories on Porphyry's work against the Christians see Becker 2015.
[100] See, e.g. the climax of the shared meditation in Ostia, *conf.* 9.10.
[101] Lycurgus, the legendary founder of the Spartan polity, cannot be dated. Plutarch, Lycurgus 5 records that his legislation was inspired by the Delphic oracle.
[102] *uera rel.* 25.47.
[103] Plutarch, *On the Oracles of the Pythia* 21–29.

(*ciu. Dei* 10.15). As to the first, such works are necessary so long as humans go on being deceived by the charlatanry of daemons; as to the second, we do better to place our faith in witnesses who seek only the glory of God than in those who enhance their wealth and fame by forbidden arts. Here, as elsewhere, theurgy is assumed to be a species of magic, and when he proceeds to demonstrate the inferiority of pagan miracles Augustine takes their diabolic origin for granted (*ciu. Dei* 10.16). Those which he enumerates[104] were evidently familiar to the educated Roman: the biblical episodes which he cites for comparison all bear witness to the sanctity of ark which contained the tables of the Law. First it was sheltered by the tabernacle in the wilderness, then the Jordan was parted to ease its passage to the land of promise, then it caused the collapse of the walls of Jericho, and finally, after its capture by the Philistines, it was brought home by oxen, miraculously guided.[105] Just as the law itself is a miraculous gift, dispensed by angels who have no thought of usurping the honours due to the donor,[106] so the sacrificial ordinances were designed to glorify no other god than the Creator, though in a manner not yet commensurate with his glory (*ciu. Dei* 10.17). The one condign sacrifice was that of God himself in Christ, and it is faith in this that communicates the power of working miracles to the saints.

There can be no doubt of the veracity of these tales for those who put them abroad were men who said, in the words of Ps 72.28, 'my good is to cleave to God' (*ciu. Dei* 10.18). Hence a Paul and a Barnabas[107] will die for Christ, the one mediator and our only sacrifice (*ciu. Dei* 10.20), but will not submit to be worshipped (*ciu. Dei* 10.19). The veneration of heroes was a characteristic of ancient religion, sometimes as a memorial to greatness, sometimes as a means of propitiating the unquiet dead. The heroes of the church, declares Augustine, are the martyrs, who have vanquished the daemons by their fortitude (*ciu. Dei* 10.22). Here he tacitly echoes Origen, while openly co-opting the passage in Virgil where Juno is said to have been vanquished by Aeneas.[108] Porphyry shows a distorted understanding of such victories when he imagines that a good daemon cannot dwell in us until an evil daemon has been

[104] For sources see Valerius Maximus, *Sayings* 1.8.7 (moving Penates); Ovid, *Metamorphoses* 15.322–475 (Aesculapius comes to Rome); Ovid, *Fasti* 4.305–348 (Claudia Quinta pulling a ship); Livy, *Epitome* 20 (Tuccia, the vindicated Vestal).

[105] Ex 25–31; Josh 3.14; Josh 6.4; 2 Sam 6.2–6.

[106] Gal 3.19; Acts 7.53.

[107] Acts 14.11–14.

[108] Origen, *Against Celsus* 8.34 and 8.44; Virgil, *Aeneid* 7.310 and 438–439.

ousted by theurgical ministrations; are we to deduce, protests Augustine, that the evil tenant is stronger than the good? As ever, he is repeating the genuine words of his interlocutor, but with his own gloss, as we learn from Porphyry's letter to Marcella.[109]

We may therefore put some faith in his veracity when he informs us that, just as Christians embrace the incarnate Word as their only mediator (*ciu. Dei* 10.22), offering no other sacrifice, so Porphyry too is acquainted with more potent rites than those which are dedicated to daemons or to such visible powers as the sun and moon (*ciu. Dei* 10.23). The highest entities in his theurgical system are God the Father and God the Son, whom he also styles the paternal intellect or paternal mind; at the same time he posits a third, whom Augustine suspects to be the Holy Spirit (*ciu. Dei* 10.24). He himself repeatedly asserts that the demonology of Porphyry is Chaldaean, not Platonic, and Pierre Hadot has argued that he was also indebted to the *Chaldaean Oracles* for his representation of the transcendent realm as a triad of triads.[110] The first of these constitutes being, the second the *dunamis* or power of being to communicate itself, and the third the nous or intellect in which this communication takes a form accessible to the understanding. Within each triad this structure is repeated, so that each contains all three principles, but being is predominant in the first triad, *dunamis* in the second and *nous* in the third. The details of this supracosmic architecture remain obscure, and we hear of another Porphyrian triad (unless it is a variant of the same) in which the third principle is not an intermediary but the joint offspring of the two intellects.[111] This no doubt is Augustine's pretext for equating it with the Spirit, which in his view proceeds from the Father and the Son.[112]

Theurgy is pernicious because its objects are as godless as the agents who procure them; they cannot acknowledge Christ as the *principium*, or foundation,[113] for that would be to acknowledge him as the sole author of purification (*ciu. Dei* 10.24.30–31). Augustine foresees the retaliatory argument that the Old Testament often promises worldly prosperity as a reward for the service of God and his commandments

[109] Porphyry, *To Marcella* 11 in Nauck 1986, p. 284.

[110] Hadot 1968, pp. 213–344. On that part of his reconstruction which depends on Victorinus, see Drecoll 2010, pp. 65–81.

[111] Proclus, *Commentary on the Timaeus* 2.154.4 Diehl, quoted by Edwards 1990, pp. 14–25 at 20. See also Arnobius, *Against the Nations* 2.25.

[112] For the suggestion that Porphyry exercised a formative influence on the Augustinian doctrine of the Trinity. See Dillon 2007, pp. 51–59.

[113] See Augustine, *ep. Jo. tr.* 1.8 etc.

(*ciu. Dei* 10.25). He replies that, even allowing for the more primitive character of the first dispensation, the goods of the heart – that is, of the self in its orientation to God – are understood in the Psalms to be nobler than those of the flesh.[114] Porphyry, who knows nothing of the humility of the paternal mind, locates his daemons in the empyrean, the highest circle of the heavens, whereas even Apuleius, conscious of their moral fragility, confines them to the air (*ciu. Dei* 10.26.27). Although he has some inkling of the difference between his daemons and the angels who perform God's work without envy, the Platonism of Porphyry is so debauched that he takes the Father, Son and Holy Spirit for three distinct gods (*ciu. Dei* 10.24 and 29).

Hence he knows less of Christ than the Roman Virgil,[115] who foresaw the birth of a glorious child to inaugurate a new age and remove the hitherto indelible traces of ancient sin (*ciu. Dei* 10.28). No wonder that, by his own testimony,[116] he has found no universal way for the purging of the soul (*ciu. Dei* 10.32.7). By this he meant perhaps that no one nation or philosophy had so perfected the discipline of theurgy as to require no supplement from another tradition (*ciu. Dei* 10.32); Augustine, however, seizing on his oft-repeated caveat that theurgy cannot liberate the intellect, insists that Christianity is this universal way because it frees not only the intellect but even the body, of whose salvation the Platonists have despaired. It is he who tells us that Porphyry departed from both Plato and Plotinus by denying the transmigration of human souls into animal bodies (*ciu. Dei* 10.30); whether or not this is true – our other witnesses do not seem to speak with one voice[117] – we can attribute to every Platonist the strange and revolting paradox that although the soul is immortal it can never hope for beatitude, enslaved as it is to a cycle of transgression and expiation which precludes its escape from matter (*ciu. Dei* 10.32). This argument, like the defence of the historicity of the gospels, is once again reminiscent of Arnobius;[118] but we look in vain in Arnobius for the two foci of Augustinian theology – the descent of the Word from glory into flesh as Jesus of Nazareth and the future adoption of our flesh into glory as the tabernacle rather than the dungeon of the soul.

[114] Quoting Ps 72.28, Ps 72.17–18, Ps 72.20–21, Ps 83.3, Ps 118.81.
[115] Virgil, *Eclogue* 4.4 and 13, also quoted by Lactantius,
[116] For the view that he was indeed seeking such a way, see Simmons 2015.
[117] See Smith 1984, pp. 276–284.
[118] *Against the Nations* 1.57.

FURTHER READING

Dillon, J. M. (1983). "Metriopatheia and Apatheia": Some Reflections on a Controversy in Later Greek Ethics. In J. Anton and A. Preus, eds., *Essays in Ancient Greek Philosophy*, vol. 2. New York: State University of New York Press, pp. 508–517.

(2007). What Price the Father of the Noetic Triad? Some Reflections on Porphyry's Doctrine of the First Principle. In G. Karamanolis and A. Sheppard, eds., *Studies on Porphyry*. London: British Institute of Classical Studies, pp. 51–59.

Hadot, P. (1968). *Porphyre et Victorinus*, vol. 2. Paris: Études Augustiniennes, pp. 213–344.

Magny, A. (2014). *Porphyry in Fragments*. Fanham: Ashgate, pp. 99–147.

O'Meara, J. J. (1959). *Porphyry's Philosophy from Oracles and Augustine*. Paris: Études Augustiniennes.

Theiler, W. (1933). *Porphyryius und Augustin*. Halle: Niemeyer.

8 Books 11 & 12: Angels and Demons: The Eternal Framing of the Two Cities

JAMES WETZEL

In the first ten books of *ciu. Dei*, Augustine makes his case for Christian beatitude against the worldly glory of pagan Rome. Book 11 is a pivot. There he tells us – and now "we" seem to be his Christian and not his pagan readership – that we know best of the City of God, that eternal thing that peregrinates through time, from the witness of sacred writings, Psalms especially (87:3, 48:1–2, 48:8, 46:4–5), and from the inspiring love of the city's founder.[1] Most of us, most of the time, mix self-interest into that love and obscure for ourselves the beauty of the beloved. The moral is not that love must be selfless or worse, self-loathing, but that sacrificial love, sensing what is holy, practices humility. The great mediator between heaven and earth, the Son of God, takes up a human life, his own, without ceasing to be God. His is the original act of humility – think of it also as first love – that speaks consistently through the Scriptures and renders them authoritative (*ciu. Dei* 11.3). While sin makes it impossible for a mind used to the dark to endure the relentless illumination of pure divinity (*incommutabile lumen*; *ciu. Dei* 11:2), Augustine reminds us that we have, by way of mediation, a text to interpret and a spirit of humility to bring to the reading.

Readers fed on a diet of thinking that prioritizes skepticism and a disposition to disbelieve, especially when it comes to claims about extrasensory realities, may well be disappointed that Augustine is so

[1] I have listed verses from the Psalms in the order of Augustine's citation of them in *ciu. Dei* 11.1; all translations are my own. The usual take on the place of Book 11 in the overall structure of *ciu. Dei* follows Augustine himself: in *ciu. Dei* 11.1, he designates the previous ten books as polemical, a broadside against the enemies of a properly sacred politics (*sanctae ciuitatis inimicis*); that leaves Book 11 to inaugurate twelve books dedicated to the origin, development, and fruition of the City of God. But Augustine never discusses the holy city and its peregrinating persona (*ciuitas Dei peregrina*) wholly apart from its shadow, the earthly city (*terrena ciuitas*), and he never fully distinguishes his disdain for the earthly city from his critique of the very idea of polytheistic philosophy. For a rich and subtle reflection on the (quieter) anti-pagan polemics of the latter books, see Bochet 2004, esp. ch. 6.

willing to revert to scriptural authority as his final court of appeal. Even granting his suggestion that the Christian scriptures command respect outside of Christianity (*ciu. Dei* 12.9), surely his resort to his own historically based faith lessens the universality of his vision of two antithetical cities, one holy and one not, both destined for some kind of totalizing, end-of-time resolution. The issue is too big for my purposes here, and so I cannot hope to reassure the skeptics. But it is worth underscoring nonetheless that Augustine, at least in the context of Books 11 and 12, shows himself to be anything but a dully literalist reader of the holy writ. Indeed one might say on the contrary that he is remarkably, if not wildly, inventive. Within the brief compass of the five opening verses of the priestly creation narrative, the doings of day one, Augustine will have managed to discern both the specific creation of the angelic host and the awful split of that host into two irredeemably opposed camps – angels of light (*angeli lucis*) and sin-wrecked deserters (*desertores; angeli peccatores*), the stuff of Dante and Milton.

Let's quickly review the priestly verses.[2] In the beginning, God created heaven and earth (*fecit caelum et terram*; Gen 1:1). The earth was formless and unseen (*incomposita et invisibilis*; Gen 1:2). God said, "Let there be light," and light was created (*facta est lux*; Gen 1:3). God saw the light, that it is good, and God divided light from darkness (*tenebras*; Gen 1:4). God called the light Day (*diem*) and the darkness Night (*noctem*). Evening was created (*facta est vespera*) and also morning (*facta est mane*), this being day one (Gen 1:5).

My disclosures of the Latin are meant to track what precisely is being created. It is very important to Augustine that we notice the lack of a *facta est nox* (*ciu. Dei* 11.7). Night, though named by God, is never designated a divine creation. It seems to come out of nowhere, from some unspecified prior darkness – and, tellingly, God never calls that darkness good.

But notice first of all that there is no mention of angels in any of those verses. Augustine is undeterred. He finds the creation of angels implied in two places. If we take "heaven and earth" in the first verse to include all there is other than God, then the angels, being something but not God, must be in there somewhere. But as few of his readers, believing in God's city, would be much inclined to idolize or negate angels, that conclusion is not so momentous. Augustine gets better traction

[2] Here I gratefully make use of James J. O'Donnell's reconstruction of Augustine's likely Latin text for Genesis 1.1 to 2.2 in volume three of O'Donnell 1992, pp. 344–345.

when he identifies angels with the light that is mentioned in the third verse (*ciu. Dei* 11.9). Since the familiar corporeal conveyors of light – the sun and moon – receive explicit mention later on, in verses 14 and 15 ("Let there be lights"), Augustine not unreasonably assumes that first light is more about wisdom than lumens or candlepower. The generative wisdom that brings all things into existence, though not wholly angelic, is at least partly so. Angels become, by participation, agents of the very illumination that informs them. They are the true dawning of day one's "Let there be light." But now conjoin verses 4 and 5 as Augustine would and bring to mind God's separation of light from darkness. Here we catch a trace of angels – most notably Lucifer the light-bearer – who undo their merger with original daylight and generate inconceivable darkness. They slip into the Night that mysteriously serves creation by standing forever apart from its wisdom.

Augustine is not unaware of the inventiveness of his scriptural angelology. About halfway into the thick of his speculation in Book 11, he pauses to consider "the obscurity of divine speech" (*diuini sermonis obscuritas*; *ciu. Dei* 11.19) and the usefulness of such obscurity for giving birth to a diversity of perspectives on the truth (*plures sententias ueritatis*) and bringing them all into the light of knowledge (*lucem notitiae*). Not every faithful reader of the Priestly creation narrative will be apt to share Augustine's penchant for angelic interpolation, and rightly so. That is still no reason for the value of his inventiveness to be discounted. As long as Augustine is honestly striving to make sense of what resists complete sense, his inventiveness remains a form of truth-seeking, and indeed, in this case, he is prepared to rest a great deal of explanatory weight on a strikingly speculative framework. For his principal aim in Book 11 – and continuing into Book 12, its companion study – is to use the notion of an angelic rupture (*angelorum diuersitate*) to account for the eternal origins of the two cities and to bring something like a stable perspective to bear on their strange mixing, if not outright confusion, on the earthly plane, where mutability rules (*ciuitates permixtas*; *ciu. Dei* 11.1, cf. *ciu. Dei* 1.35).

As I attempt to explicate Augustine's perplexing efforts to bring angels into the human story, I will want especially to convey two basic observations. The first is simply that Augustine's conception of the rupture that divides the angelic host into failed and authenticated light-bearers proves to be less than lucidly intelligible in its own right. It is therefore hard to apply his rupture idea in any straightforward way to what is similarly obscure but closer to home: our human tendency to confuse friends and enemies and then dig in. (At what point do the angels rightly give up their fallen kin and consider them demons? Is this not a question for our politics as well?) My second observation is more hopeful. It is that Augustine's difficulties in moving conceptually from angelic to human regimes of solidarity are instructive difficulties; they are not (solely) the product of overburdened speculation. In effect, we find Augustine imaginatively thinking through the notion of a political community whose solidarity, for as long as time remains, fails to require a final sorting out of the damned (the outsiders) from the saved (those within). The unstable but promising idea of mixed cities, where virtues evolve and suffer corruption and it is often hard to tell the difference, speaks to the alluring possibility of political humility.[3] This possibility is inescapably obscure, as Augustine will teach us, but not foreclosed, and therein resides the hope.[4]

AN INCONCEIVABLE PARTING

Augustine's angels bear a peculiarly intimate relationship to time.[5] There is no time before which the angels were not. They come into being, then, along with all the other things that make up the world (*mundus*), not at a particular point in time (*in tempore*; *ciu. Dei* 11.6) but *with* all of time (*cum tempore*), as if time were less the limiting

[3] The literature on Augustine's idea of mixed cities is extensive, but too often the idea is evoked more than it is explored. One large exception is the classic study of Robert Markus (Markus 1988). I discuss Markus and a few of the major responses to his construal of Augustinian two-cities secularity in my essay, "A Tangle of Two Cities": Wetzel 2012a, pp. 5–23.

[4] Think of humility in relation to humus, the soil that consists of decomposing organic matter. To be humble is to accept with gratitude and without despair that life on the way to further life passes through death and is under no human being's control. Such acceptance can be a political as well as an individual recognition. But the former is especially hard to come by. The earthly city, named for its debt to mortal clay (*terrena ciuitas*), actively resists humility, considers it a weakness, and cultivates a politics at odds with the most basic fact of mortal existence – that what begins in time also ends there. Meanwhile the unsettled City of God on earth (*civitas Dei peregrina*), living out of its hope for an end-of-time homecoming, risks overlooking or discounting heaven's embrace, via Christ, of mortal life; see *ciu. Dei* 10, esp. 10.5–6 and 10.20, for the relevant Christology. The obscuring of political humility in both cities has much to do with *superbia* – unsacrificial self-love ("pride") – having an other than earthly origin. Augustine's angelology speaks to that obscurity.

[5] My explication of Augustine's angelology focuses squarely on the conceptual knots of Books 11 and 12, but especially *ciu. Dei* 11, with some venturing into his literal commentary on Genesis. For a more comprehensive take on his abiding fascination with angels, see Klein 2018.

context of angelic life than the divinely midwifed progeny of angelic motion.

Recall that, for Augustine, the angels are not just bathed in first light – the light that fundamentally answers to the command, "Let there be light" – they are that light. They are the Day (*dies*). They are also, as time passes, the Evening (*uespera*). As Day, the angels see both themselves and the world as they exist together in the mind of God: intricately beautiful, fully determinate, without flaw. Augustine calls this celestial vision "daylight knowledge" (*diurna cognitione*; *ciu. Dei* 11.29, cf. *ciu. Dei* 11.8). As Evening, the angels will have subtly loosened their attention from the grip of divine wisdom in order to take a look at stand-alone things, all of which share the trait of not being God. There is still, despite God's unconstrained intimacy with all of being, something to be known here, but a something that remains opaque to a knowing mind. Augustine calls this less well-informed vision an "evening awareness" (*uespertina cognitione*). When the angels at vespers remember, as the good ones always do, to praise and venerate the creator for having created even the murky void of unformed earth, morning (*mane*) dawns within the contemplative mind, and the angels return, ecstatic, to their daylight knowing. It is precisely this motion from day to evening to morning and back again to day that, for Augustine, constitutes angelic motion, properly conceived.[6] Angelic motion is time's measure, a paradigm of periodic, orderly, and intelligible change; "without the angels," Augustine tells us, "time itself would not be able to be" (*ciu. Dei* 12.16).

But we have yet to contend with nighttime, the conspicuously missing piece in the procession of angelic perspectives. In Augustine's angelology, original Night, named but not created (Gen 1:4), stands forever opposed to knowing or being known. There is simply nothing to know here. To get a sense of why, imagine your way into a couple of dramatic possibilities. You are an angel at vespers. As you shift your perspective to frame the creature in itself and its being apart from God, you come across a reflection of yourself in a mind-pool of some sort, and, like Narcissus, you become captivated by the beauty of your own image. You know that you are not simply your own image, but you cannot pull yourself away. The other angels, well into their daily doxology, have already begun to process into the dawn. Meanwhile, your evening has grown considerably darker, but you seem not to have

[6] For an earlier description of these angelic forms of knowledge, not essentially different from the one found in *ciu. Dei* but set within an exegetical context, see Book 4 of *Gn. litt.*

noticed the passing of the light. Or, again, you are an angel at vespers. As you shift your perspective to frame the creature in itself, you find in your self-reflection a portrait of your worst fear – it is of you alone, abandoned by your maker, and lost in a darkening plane. It occurs to you that you should have never been able to break loose from the grip of wisdom, if only to glance at things in dimmer light. You long for a tyrannical creator, perfectly able to confine your attention to daylight beauties and their place in the grand plan. Your disappointment with the current state of heavenly security turns into an obsession with imperfectly bordered communities. You decide to break into Eden and wreck the peace there, just to show the old creator the folly of his design. The irony of your revenge will, sadly, be forever lost on you.

When I say that there is nothing to know here in this Night of decreation, where angels become something unoriginal and decline, I mean that there is no reason why the story of one kind of angel and not another would be closer to yours. There is no reason, to put the point more precisely, why you would be more akin to a fallen angel than to a steadfast light-bearer, and no reason, within the angelic realm itself, why some angels and not others would be moved to desert the light. While Augustine is happy to entertain solidarities between humans and angels on psychological grounds – where one combination clings to God, the other invests in ego – he has a hard time accounting for preferences: why, for any given angel or earthling, is there irrevocably a choice of one solidarity (*societas*) or city (*ciuitas*) over the other?[7]

But what would such an accounting look like, anyway? For Augustine does have an easy way to sort things. Citizens of the City of God are all God-clingers; they know that beatitude, a soul-satisfying happiness, is nothing other than a liberated disposition to adhere to God (*adhaerere Deo*). Citizens of the earthly city, by contrast, act as if such God-clinging were loathsome and oppressive; they stake their well being on self-love. It is a contrast that will be frequently invoked

[7] Peter Brown speaks eloquently of Augustine's inclination to bring humans and demons into a common psychology: "In Late Roman popular belief, the methods of demons were extremely crude: they would simply take on human shape to start a plague or a riot. With Augustine, by contrast, the nexus between men and demons was purely psychological. Like was drawn to like. Men got the demons they deserved; the demons, for their part, perpetuated this likeness by suggesting to the masses immoral and anarchic gods as symbols of divine power." See Brown 2000, p. 310; and cf. Muehlberger 2013, pp. 50–55. It is far from clear, however, whether the psychological nexus is similarly as thick between peregrinating saints, still struggling on earth, and the angels in heaven.

throughout *ciu. Dei*. If we construe its terms to be explanatory in some way and not merely stipulative (i.e. terms that merely tell us what to *call* the world of the happy person and what to *call* the world of the unhappy one), then members of God's city always have sufficient reason for their preferred citizenship, whereas their darkened counterparts, wading through a miasma of self-deception and misleading simulacra, never do.

But now press the question of why a whole city of reason-capable creatures, one part angelic, the other human, would ever be moved, apart from insanity and other inadmissible offenses to an original goodness, to abandon the brightly lit path of God-clinging and enter the darkness of self. Augustine ventures two kinds of answer to this question. One attempts, futilely as it turns out, to supply a reason; the other attempts, with less clear results, to end all attempts at supplying a reason.

Imagine, along with Augustine, what is for him a metaphysical oddity: a time out of time, when the angelic host, whose coming into being has been coterminous with time itself, has yet to fragment into two irreconcilable factions. Eventually there will be, down below, the angels who have fallen out of the *caelum caeli*, the heaven of heaven, and been rendered demonic, and, up above, the angels whose steadfastness has forever confirmed them in the light-bodies that radiate heavenly intelligence. While it is of course true that angels fall when they choose, while in a bardo-like state of existence, not to stick with God, Augustine offers us a chance to dig into the depth – if there is indeed a depth to be dug into – of such a choice.

Angels, no less than human beings, crave a blessed life (*beata uita*). Augustine identifies the two principal components of such blessedness as enjoyment of the one good that is unchangeably good (*bono incommutabili*; *ciu. Dei* 11.13) and perfect assurance, free from doubt and error, that true enjoyment never ends. If I am one of the fallen angels, I will, as an *angelic* being, know something of true enjoyment. Angels dwell in the daylight of God (*dies*) – the radiance of absolute goodness – before any one of them ever thinks to venture into the unknowing Night (*nox*). But as one of the fallen angels, I will also, as a *fallen* being, lack perfect assurance of everlasting goodness. God may be unchangeable; I am not. So what keeps me fixed in goodness? Any virtue that comes from me would partake in the instability of my *ex nihilo* being and consequently render me susceptible to doubt and delusion. It must be God and God alone who can supply me with the assurance that miraculously transcends my changeable nature and becomes, despite me, eternally and reliably mine. Augustine calls this assurance, which is absent from any angel who falls or who is susceptible to a fall, "prescience" (*praescientia*); it is a strange feature for beings coterminous with time itself to lack.

Let's be clear here. The desired prescience is of beatitude – a sacredly secured happiness – and such prescience is, for Augustine, part of makes happiness happy. If I am an angel with foreknowledge of my fall, then there is nothing blessed about my life. My self-awareness is already a kind of hell; there is nothing left for me to do but watch my self-diminishment perpetually unfold. The story here is not just (or even primarily) of vice and punishment but also of a void where God is supposed to be, the privation of Night. Fallen angels choose nothingness, but they do not invent it. The nihilum is one of creation's original possibilities.

But what about being an angel and not having either kind of prescience, heavenly or hellish? Something vital to beatitude would remain lacking. Augustine considers the happiness of Adam in Eden, before the serpent mixes things up. The Adam he envisions, a bit of animated clay untouched by death, knows more of delight than most mortals do, but with this exception: think of a fallen son of Adam in the throes of some bodily torment (*in quibuslibet cruciatibus corporis*; *ciu. Dei* 11.12); if it has somehow been made clear to him, not as a sentiment but a certainty, that he is part of God's city and has a place with the angels, then he is, despite his torment, more blessed (*beatior*) than his ancient father, who lives ambivalently in a garden paradise.

The security component of beatitude weighs heavily in this comparison. To come to enjoy life apart from the threat of self-sabotage or the violent intrusions of an unruly time is not simply to prolong a goodness; it is to constitute one. Augustine has given his indeterminate angels, pitched between their day jobs and the anomalous night, more than enough reason to want a beatitude richer than the blessing they have thus far been given. The problem is this: he may have given them too much reason. It is no longer obvious that the demonization of angels has to do with their culpable refusal to soak up divinely sourced light and not with their (understandable?) craving for a place in the shade, where God is less overwhelmingly present. At the end of his first foray into the inner life of the angelic fall (*ciu. Dei* 11.11–13; a specific meditation on Satan is still to come), Augustine closes shop on his imagination and reminds Catholic Christians of what they and he are simply enjoined to believe: that angels in heaven never fall; that demons in hell never rise; that the world has a beginning and an end; that God is the one true constant.

The rift in the angelic host that precipitates twin eternal cities and forecasts the fault line in the Adamic heart takes in, at imagination's end, an inconceivable parting. It is not that we have yet to know or perhaps will never know, being too puny of mind, what moves unstable reasoners, whether angelic or human, to part from God and relate to the void. Again, there is simply nothing to know here, no hidden treasure lying buried at the bottom of a well. Augustine underscores the breathtakingly uninformative quality of a soul's turn to privation and the absence of goodness when he speaks of the evil will's origination in deficiency (*ciu. Dei* 12.7): "Let no one seek an efficient cause for the evil will; because this will is itself defect, not effect, its cause must be deficient, not efficient."

Augustine sets out the logic of a deficient cause (*causa deficiens*) in three concise chapters of Book 12 (*ciu. Dei* 12.6–8). The logic is both simple and maddening. Good comes of good; evil comes of evil. When evil makes its appearance in the created order (the order of the good), its relation to goodness is always parasitic, never productive. A good will participates in goodness and lends it further articulation, as would be the case in an activity of nurturing or artistic creation. An evil will consumes without issue, as if hunger were to feed on hunger, constantly undoing satisfaction. If we were to press Augustine to account for the eruption of evil, like some flesh-eating virus, into an otherwise healthy place, he would doubtless avail himself of his logic: there is no good that can account for the undoing of goodness. But notice here what is fundamental to defective willing: not the choice of the lesser good over the greater, but the prior assumption that the good always presents itself in conflict with itself. My inner fallen angel tells me that I must undo the goodness of one good in order to enjoy the goodness of another; there are no exceptions. I undo God's goodness in order to enjoy the world; I undo the world's goodness in order to enjoy God. And I construe all of this undoing, perversely, as an ability: *posse deficere*, the power to uncreate, to unhook creature from creator, to nullify the goodness of what has been given up for the sake of something else. The logic of defect is also the logic of fruitless sacrifice.

Some commentators have seen in Augustine's notion of a deficient cause a way for him to account for the culpability of beings who have sufficient reason not to fall and who choose to fall anyway.[8]

[8] The best articulation of a deficiently caused moral culpability is still Scott MacDonald's "Primal Sin": MacDonald 1999, pp. 110–139. MacDonald is responding, at least in part, to William Babcock's influential critique of motiveless angelic transgression in "Augustine on Sin and Moral Agency": Babcock 1988, pp. 28–55. I share with MacDonald his sense of the moral psychology of

But however culpable Augustine imagines first sinners to be (and here one imagines: *very*), a deficient cause is far too slender a reed to hold the weightiness of moral responsibility. It is a notion that has little, if any, explanatory value. The real function of a deficient cause in *ciu. Dei* is to leave Augustine free not to have to account for the strange time-out-of-time developments that have resulted in a peculiarly intimate opposition between angels and demons. The angels are one for all of time and yet not. Augustine invokes an irreconcilable difference that reduces upon analysis to nothing at all – a lack, a deficiency, a shadow in the night. We begin to get a hint of the complex play between time and eternity that will define a human (but, alas, not an angelic) possibility of redemption.

THE DEMONIZATION OF TIME

Let's dig a bit deeper into the dread mystery of angelic "diversity" (*diuersitas*), here the kind of diversity that turns a virtuous light-bearer into a princeps of darkness and somehow leaves us still talking about the same angel: Lucifer or, as Augustine usually refers to him, the Devil (*diabolus*, the obstructer). The Devil is, in two senses, Augustine's paradigm of a fallen angel. In one sense, he is first among equals. The angels who fall all have the same degree of original blessedness, and all follow the Devil's lead. They do what he does. In the other, more intimate sense, the Devil paradigmatically introduces into angelic being the possibility of radical change. Lucifer is eternal Day become endless Night. The angels who enter into his strange paradigm of self-extinguishing divine light will appear to have become radically other to themselves, new beings even. Where once they were angels, now they are demons, and demons are, to say the least, not angels.

Recall that, for Augustine, angels come into being not at a datable moment of time but with all of time (*cum tempore*); this form of "birthing" – a birthing without a birthday – affords them an extraordinarily intimate relationship with the created order. They are its first light, the undying Day. Meanwhile, the demonic conversion of some angels, rendered most vividly in Lucifer's case, threatens to undermine the coherence, and indeed the very intelligibility, of angelic life. For if Lucifer's coming into being with all of time can include a moment when he becomes, for the *rest* of time, the Devil, how is he not born evil?

negligence – of not availing oneself of the reasons one has for acting rightly – but I don't think that this psychology holds much relevance for Augustine's angels.

His would be a strange kind of self-birthing, to be sure, in that he chooses from no part of his original goodness to become the Devil, but the problem for Augustine's angelology remains the same. Lucifer, the good angel, and the Devil, the fallen one, are the same angel and not. They are the same in that Lucifer's life, being coterminous with time, must include the Devil's emergence (the Devil's birthday, so to speak); they are different in that Lucifer's self-knowledge can never be of himself as the Devil – the Devil being essentially Lucifer's negation, his deficient cause (*causa deficiens*). The deeper problem for Augustine is that his angelic paradigm for gathering all of time into a timeless order ("daylight knowledge") risks turning temporally situated life – or life with a before and an after – into a form of self-undoing. The Devil's moment, unhinged from eternity, puts a curse on time itself.

Augustine, of course, resists this conclusion. In his great literal commentary on Genesis, a work that well predates his ruminations in *ciu. Dei* on the angelic fall, he boils the perplexing case of the Devil down to four possibilities.[9] One is that Lucifer does not in fact take a moment to fall and become the Devil; he falls instantaneously, at the very inception of his creation (*ab initio conditionis suae*) – essentially a timeless change, wrought in the eternal. Another possibility: Lucifer is the charismatic leader, the "archangel" (*archangelus*), of a group of inferior angels. These angels, unlike their superiors, inherently lack knowledge of their own hearts and so are assigned only mundane tasks to perform, or basically grunt work for angels. Resenting his less-than-stellar status, Lucifer defies his boss and sets up his own firm. (This scenario, by the way, is the one Augustine finds least likely to be true.) Yet another possibility: the holy angels spend some time with Lucifer and his minions, and during this time neither side has knowledge of being on a side. Everyone lacks prescience (*praescientia*) of the division that is to come. But once Lucifer does fall and along with him his minions, the steadfast angels, clinging to God, immediately win a boon; they now can see, to their everlasting joy, that their blessedness is failsafe. And finally: imagine that Lucifer and his minions lack stable self-knowledge and its internal guarantee of failsafe beatitude, but not because they are inherently inferior angels. Assume that they have the

[9] Here I am recapitulating and glossing *Gn. litt.* 11.26.33. Augustine began his literal commentary in AD 401 and finished it sometime in AD 415; he began *ciu. Dei* in AD 413 and finished it in AD 427, three years before his death. Book 11 of *ciu. Dei*, where we find him once again taking up the topic of Lucifer's creation and fall, dates from AD 417.

same capacity for reassuring self-knowledge that any angel does. It is just that for some unknown reason, albeit one fully in accord with justice, they begin their angelic careers in (interior) darkness. Think of this beginning as a period of probation. The suspect angels violate their probation when, with Lucifer leading, they give themselves over to an irredeemable act of self-promotion.

In their commentary on this part of Augustine's literal, if strikingly speculative, exegesis of Genesis, Agaësse and Solignac surmise that Augustine is setting out a *complexio*, a complete round-up, of all the possible answers to the question of Lucifer's fall.[10] The four hypotheses, being four different and in ways incompatible hypotheses, do not settle the question, but, as the constituents of a true *complexio*, they are meant to exhaust the relevant possibilities and include the one right answer. If we read Augustine this way, as circumscribing a question he has yet to be able to answer, it is natural to wonder what his hunch would have been about which hypothesis is right. According to Agaësse and Solignac, Augustine initially favors the notion that Lucifer takes no time to fall (the first hypothesis). He comes eventually, however, to prefer the thesis that the angels intermingle for a time and are not sorted out as good and bad until Lucifer makes his break, gathers his minions, and precipitates transfiguration in the angels that steadfastly resist him (the third hypothesis).[11]

Let's assume that Agaësse and Solignac are right (a reasonable assumption) and that Augustine does intend the listing in Book 11.26 of the literal commentary to be exhaustive. Before moving too quickly to a winning hypothesis, it is worth noticing just how strange the listing is. The first hypothesis, the one that removes any interval of time between Lucifer's beatific creation and his catastrophic fall, stands in stark contrast to the remaining three, all of which suggest in different (but not radically different) ways that at some impossible moment in angelic eternity, all hell broke loose.

Paul Griffiths, one of Augustine's most discerning readers, and one of his most inventive, advocates for the wisdom of the first hypothesis.[12] If Augustine reduces the time it takes for Lucifer to fall to no time

[10] Agaësse and Solignac 2001, pp. 545–553. They further point out that *complexio*, corresponding to Greek συμπλοκή, hails from Stoic logic.

[11] In *ciu. Dei* 21.1 and *corrept.* 10.27, writings that date from late in his career (c. AD 427), Augustine seems reconciled to the idea that all the angels prior to the angelic fall enjoy less than fulsome beatitude (*hanc plenitudinem beatitudinis non habebant*).

[12] Griffiths 2014, pp. 133–135.

at all (and, by extension, the time it takes for future demons to follow suit), Augustine will have avoided creating the false impression that faithless and faithful angels can share the same experience of time. Taking his cue from Augustine, or at least the Augustine of the first hypothesis, Griffiths contends that where sin knows only a corrupt experience of time – that of something unendingly divisible and subject to measure ("metronomic" time) – grace gathers time into an immeasurable density and iterates, like a heartbeat, time's movement into and out of contraction ("systolic" time).[13] The relevant point, for the purposes of my focus on angelic diversity, is that Augustine's other three hypotheses hopelessly mix up angels and demons.

I am inclined to make this point more sharply than Griffiths does, while being less impressed than he is about the wisdom of a timeless angelic fall. Return to the second and fourth hypotheses. These hypotheses grant knowledge of future beatitude, *praescientia*, to the (as it turns out) good angels, but not, of course, to the (as it turns out) bad angels. The bad angels lack, whether inherently or probationally, what the good angels have. But what exactly do the good angels *have*? In the third hypothesis, there are still implicitly good and implicitly bad angels, but no angel begins with self-securing prescience. If there is still a difference here between the angels, it is that the good ones are disposed to be trusting of God, while the bad ones are not. Notice what this says about what the good angels have, in keeping with hypotheses two and four, or will have, in keeping with hypothesis three: a security that exceeds their trust in God. If, as Augustine insists, perfect assurance of future beautitude remains essential to what beatitude is (recall *ciu. Dei* 11.13), then apparently it takes more than trust really to know that goodness lasts. It takes a skeptically tried knowledge and, to keep the skepticism honest, an obsessive willingness to nurture doubt.

Augustine's original angels prove to be, in effect, a referendum on love's security. The bad angels cast their vote squarely for mistrust, but even the good ones look for a heavenly confirmation of their vote of confidence. The untrusting side of most any desire for security works to dislodge love from knowledge and eventually renders the self-offering

[13] Griffiths explicates the difference between the two regimes of time in chapters 15 and 16 of *Decreation* (2014). I cannot do justice here to the subtlety of his efforts, but see my review: Wetzel, J. (2015). Death and Decreation: Tiptoeing (with Paul J. Griffiths) at the Limits of Speculative Theology. Syndicate: An On-line Theological Review. https://syndicate.network/symposia/theology/decreation/.

God into an alien but effective imposer in chief.[14] Angels who look to be imposed upon beneficially, to be made secure from without, revere will.

What more is there to be said, then, about the first hypothesis and the Lucifer who simply has no time to experience insecurity? Does the simultaneity of his creation and paradigmatic fall succeed at inoculating angelic life from demonic infection and a fatal confusion of two cities? Augustine's best and most telling rendition of Lucifer's insanely short life as an angel comes in *ciu. Dei* 11, where he takes up the explication of Jn 8:44, or Jesus on the Devil: "He was homicidal from the beginning and did not stand in the truth – because the truth is not in him."[15] The key to Augustine's explication turns on how he proposes to render the idea of a beginning: *ab initio*. If Lucifer is homicidal from the beginning of his *creation* (*ab initio, ex quo creatus est*; *ciu. Dei* 11.15), then Lucifer was never other than the Devil, logically or in time: the two are, in every frame of reference, the same being. Augustine is quick to reject this reading. It leaves the unfailingly good creator with no goodness in Lucifer to affirm (with a creative failure, in other words). When Augustine adds to his perspective another Johannine verse, 1 Jn 3:8 – "The Devil has been sinning from the beginning" – he settles on a Lucifer who sins from the beginning of his *sin* (*ab initio peccati*; *ciu. Dei* 11.15). Lucifer sins when he sins. This is undoubtedly hard to contest. But what sounds at first like an uninformative tautology is actually a good deal more complex.

Consider what is arguably the most important difference between Lucifer, the original light-bearer, and his minions, the eventual demons: while it is abundantly clear from Augustine's angelology that the minions lack *praescientia* – a view across time to a perfectly secured beatitude – it is not so clear that Lucifer does. It is of course true that Lucifer can never know of his redemption if he is in fact the first angel to abandon divine light and sink into eternal darkness – if, that is, Lucifer is the Devil. But what is at issue here is not some hypothetical moment on Lucifer's time-line where he has the chance to lock into light and irrevocably does not. Lucifer's beginning in time is the

[14] In the Priestly account of first things, God acknowledges the goodness that, once created, belongs to creation; he does not simply impose goodness from without, as a constraint on chaos or the void. In this regard, note Augustine's critique of Origen at *ciu. Dei* 11:23. Where Origen thinks of the material order of creation (bodies especially) as an external check on wayward souls, Augustine holds to the simple but profound idea that the good God creates good things.

[15] The explication begins in the middle of *ciu. Dei* 11.13 and extends through chapter 17.

beginning that he shares with all of time; his life is coterminous with time (*cum tempore*) and so is not bound in its beginning to a particular moment of passage, or a time within time. It is axiomatic for Augustine that the good creator creates only good things. Being a creature of God and being contemporaneous with time itself, there is no conceivable time at which Lucifer would know himself to be other than originally good and loved by his creator. He really *cannot* know himself any other way, and, in that respect, he cannot sensibly be said to lack prescience of his future beatitude; his times (past, present, and future), and his goodness, are all available to him in his beginning.

What I am describing here is fully in keeping with Augustine's core angelology; minions and good angels, no less than Lucifer, live lives that are coterminous with time (a kind of eternal life, to be sure, if only in its indifference to passage). If there is an incongruous part to this angelology, it lies with Augustine's suggestion that some of the angels, if not all, originally lack prescience. Such a strange lack (and Augustine does think it strange) implies lives that have been cast out of the fullness of time and into temporal disarticulation, where isolated moments rule. As a framework for framing a sinful fall, a Luciferian lunge, the framework comes too late. Angels do not sin and fall because they lack prescience and crave it by other than reverent means; they lack prescience because they sin and invite the alien night into the sunlit coherence of their interrelated perspectives.[16] The result is disarticulation – an undoing of connection.

It is tempting to want to know what sin is apart from its effect, but the most that Augustine manages to do with this aspiration is to tie sin to itself, as if sin were its own source of being. Thus he writes (*ciu. Dei* 11.15; cf. 1 Jn 3:8): "The assertion that *the Devil has been sinning from the beginning* should be taken to mean not that he sins from the inception of his creation but that he sins from the inception of his sin." Augustine will go on to associate the inception of sin, especially in Lucifer's case, with the eruption of pride (*superbia*), but this is to give sin a name, not a cause. (If pride can be said to cause sin, it would do so only as sinful pride.) We remain in the neighborhood of an apparent tautology, where Lucifer sins when he sins and at no time before.

[16] My language echoes that of M. B. Pranger in his extraordinary contribution to *Political Theologies: Public Religions in a Post-Secular Word* (Pranger 2006). See especially pp. 119–120 of Pranger's "Politics and Finitude: The Temporal Status of Augustine's *Civitas Permixta*," where he discusses the uncreated night ("invading, alien") of human and angelic sin (Pranger 2006).

Let's let the tautology stand. To make sense of it, even as a tautology, we still need to come to grips with sin's beginning (*ab initio peccati*), and here is where all the complexity comes in. The beginnings of creation and sin are not identical in Lucifer, but nor are they different moments. Augustine can be read here, and usually is, as if he were suggesting the closest possible proximity of two times. We might say, along the lines of this reading, that Lucifer falls into sin very quickly, so quickly, in fact, that he takes no time to do so. But we also might say, equally, that Lucifer takes his time, all of it, to sin – there isn't a moment that remains free of his turn toward demonic self-fixation. Either way of framing his case is equally good and equally bad. The badness comes of our being too quick to assume that when Augustine speaks of an *initium*, an origin or a beginning, he implies a corresponding moment in time. He clearly intends not to do that in the case of Lucifer's creation. Just recall his reading of the Priestly creation narrative and where he puts the angels. Lucifer, no less than any other angel, is created to be first light, to be part of the undying illumination of temporary things. And yet Lucifer still falls and becomes the Devil; Day unaccountably gives way to Night. It is admittedly harder here not to imagine a timeline, a compression of light into a moment of loss, and an irredeemably dark beginning to a count down.

Augustine encourages this kind of imagining when he reduces angelic prescience to prediction and entertains the possibility that the winners of a guessing game will have their relation to time and its indeterminacies forever altered. Angels who rightly guess that they are faithless creatures, scorned by their creator, become demonic beings and sink below the possibility of redemption. Angels who rightly guess that they are faithful creatures, beloved of their creator, become perfect beings and rise above the possibility of damnation. Whatever center it is that houses substantially different angels together simply doesn't hold. But all of this is only one strain of Augustine's angelology in *ciu. Dei*, and he develops it in a self-consciously tentative way. When he tells us what we, as his faithful readers, ought to believe, that the two eternal cities – one of demons, the other of angels – do not mix, he does not insist on our having a particular story that gets us to that conclusion.

But where, then, does that leave us? I try to imagine here, bearing in mind the austerity of Augustine's antithesis between Night and Day in Lucifer, the beginning of a story of redemption, or damnation, and not the end of one. But whatever this story may be, it cannot be Lucifer's. His beginnings, one in creation, the other in sin, are too much in sync for a conversion narrative to find traction or any narrative along the lines of, "I once was lost but now am found."[17] Narrative logic, while banking on memory – on the possibility of recollected time – still requires the past to be the past, and the future the future. The Lucifer who begins as Lucifer and, just as quickly, ends as the Devil has no time either to fend off his diabolical future or to consign his old, light-bearing self to a once upon a time. The emergence with and within time of this paradoxically sinning angel suggests metamorphosis without issue, or the illusion of a life that has plot and character development. There is none of time's usual remediation here, no room for Lucifer meaningfully to declare, "I am no longer the Devil," or for the Devil to admit, "I was once the Light-bearer." And yet the picture is not of an angel with an evil nature (*natura mali*; *ciu. Dei* 11.13) or even that of a good angel who squanders his birthright on deficient self-love and deprives heaven of a spectacular light.

Augustine's Lucifer, while fallen and everywhere hobbled by his self-fixation, retains the goodness of his original nature – his beginning without an end in time. Sin, then, has no power to corrupt or delay the goodness of creation's beginning; it merely co-exists with that goodness as its privation, as the quality of not relating to, and therefore of lacking, goodness itself. The Devil's problem is that he has one too many possibilities, and he identifies with all of them. He is Lucifer deprived of Lucifer.

THE TWO CITIES WITHIN

Augustine insists that no creature – not the angel unscathed by its fellow's fallenness, not the world unfazed, in its creator's eye, by Adam's folly – experiences time's abeyance the way that God does. "What vast stretches transpired before the human kind came to be I admit to not knowing, but I have no doubt," Augustine writes (*ciu. Dei* 12.17), "that nothing whatsoever creaturely is coeternal [*coaeterum*] with the creator." This insistence of his on God's sovereign and separate eternity is no small matter for his angelology and the extension of that angelology into the framing of the two cities, whose respective mixings of human and angelic constituencies seem to amalgamate, or just plain old confuse, different regimes of time.

[17] The quoted words are from Amazing Grace, written by John Newton, an Anglican poet and preacher, and first published in 1779. Their scriptural provenance is the Parable of the Prodigal Son, especially Luke 15:31.

For here is the great incongruency of two-city infrastructure, as Augustine conceives of it: the human being, collectively represented in the figure of the *adam*, the first earthling, comes into being, uniquely, at a moment in time; the angels, for their part, come into being when time comes into being.[18] There is no time at which the angels are not. In that regard, angels do seem to be eternal beings of some sort. They are not born into a world, and they never die out of one. The angels just are, just as the totality of the world, with all of its possibilities, just is. Meanwhile, there are oceans of time (Augustine can't say how many) that predate the advent of the human being and all of its subsequent individuations.

When we humans are moved to measure particular lives against the staggering expanse of angelic existence, we begin to see the possibility of a unidirectional eternal life. Of course it is too late for me, an indelibly particular human being, not to be born, and so all those indefinitely many oceans of prior not-me time will present themselves as, in effect, my nihilation. It is not too late for me, however, never to die. If the creator God is willing, out of a not unjust mercy, to furnish my mortal clay with some kind of metaphysical prosthesis, undoubtedly invisible to the naked eye, then I will be able to survive my (apparent) death and take my place once and for all with the angels, hopefully the good ones.

So far this "eternal" framing of the two cities does little more than frame the possibility of a piecemeal human redemption or, what comes to nearly the same thing, a piecemeal damnation. The problem here is that the beginningless time of each and every angel, when taken as a norm for time's fullness, tends to render the human start, a birth, as a loss of being, and really a terrible one. I enter the world at the cost of having my existence defined mostly by non-existence, by my own endless, uncreated night; redemption and damnation alike are destined to become for me, in this frame, matters of making up for lost time. But however tempting the idea of a unidirectional immortality may be,

[18] Augustine underscores the singularity of the human coming to be – unprecedented and unrepeatable – at a number of places: *ciu. Dei* 12.15, 12.18, and 12.21. He reads Adam, whose partner, the woman, emerges out of a part of him (Gen 2:21–23), as a synecdoche for the whole of humanity and a reminder of the solidarity that is so basic to human existence: see especially *ciu. Dei* 12.22. I refer to "the adam" rather than to "Adam," the name of a father figure, in order to emphasize the generic quality of Adamic existence: a form of being, male and female, that is of the earth, and, similar to the Greek notion of the ἄνθρωπος, a hierarchically defined form of being, pitched midway between the angels and the beasts. For Augustine, Adam is both Adam and the adam.

where to be good is to be secured in goodness, the idea neglects two of the major motifs, especially evident in *ciu. Dei* 12, of Augustine's reflection on the creator's uniquely eternal way of creating: one is that God creates not by imposing form on chaotic matter but by mothering souls and bodies wholly into being; the other is that God loves beginnings.[19]

Let's begin with the second motif. Imagine a world that altogether lacks novelty. Everything that exists in this world comes into being and goes into nothingness, and given enough time (there is always enough time), comes and goes again, with endlessly repetitive frequency. Augustine has sharp words for a group of savants that he loosely refers to as "philosophers of this world" (*philosophi mundi huius*; *ciu. Dei* 12.14); they advance the thesis of a cyclic, repetitive world – which seems, on the surface, to be a thesis in physics – as the answer to a theological question: namely, how does the creator of this world know the world?

Assume here, as these philosophers do, that nothing can be known that lacks finitude or boundedness; to know a thing is just to know what marks off that thing unambiguously from the thing or the sort of thing that it is not. The exclusionary limit – the "not this" that tells us, after exhaustive deployments, what the "that" is – is thus of the essence of the knowable. The infinite, as indefinite, either falls short of knowing or beyond it. (But here: short of it.)

Assume further, again as these philosophers do, that the creator who knows the (necessarily finite) world is always in the act of knowing it and that its act of knowing is everywhere perfect. If its act were imperfect, then an absolute knower would know the world only imperfectly. If its act were temporary, a one-time achievement, then an absolute knower would cease after a time to be in the knowing business. In neither case would an absolute knower be able to be known unambiguously as a knower, and so, by virtue of our first assumption, to be known as a knower at all.

Keep up the embrace between our two worldly, quasi-theological assumptions, and begin to notice what Augustine notices: that the world, when made to answer to unambiguous borders and exclusionary

[19] In *ciu. Dei* 12.26, Augustine draws out a sharp contrast between creation as the imposition of form on matter (artifactual creation) and creation as the interior formation that makes self-generating form possible (a giving birth). Augustine is so intent on ascribing the latter to God alone that he (regrettably) denies mothers their basic claim to generativity: "Nor ought we to call a woman the creator [*creatricem*] of her new-born child."

limits, is forever tearing itself apart to be known. Augustine associates this whole, painfully ironic conception of the knowing relation between God and world with "hellish mortality" (*tartareae mortalitati*), "culpable stupidity" (*turpi stultitiae*), and "contemptible suffering" (*exsecrabilibus miseriis*).[20] It turns out that "the philosophers of this world" are not just or even primarily an eclectic group of speculative cosmologists (e.g. Lucretius, Apuleius) who hold to some version of a theory of a cyclic mundanity, where history reboots and things are forever, albeit with much wear and tear, staying the same. They are the would-be theologians of the earthly city, and their deity, whose finitude is of the same order as the world's, only more oppressive, practices a violent form of knowing. It is a form that is familiar to dispirited psyches. It looks something like this: in order to know what true blessedness is for a creature such as myself, born to the swaddling earth, I rehearse the dismantling of beatitude in myself and others countless times, until I finally arrive at the place where my dissociation from beatitude, my desecration, is all that I will ever want or be willing to accept from worldliness. It's safer that way. But the logic, of course, is demonic.

Augustine would no doubt counsel worldly theologians and the rest of us to give up on trying to comprehend what has to be an infinite means of comprehension; games with boundaries and boundedness are of no avail here. Still, he does seem to have a rather precise sense of what piety demands of belief (*ciu. Dei* 12.21; cf. *ciu. Dei* 11.4): we are to believe that "it is not impossible" (*non esse impossibile*) for God to "create new things" (*noua facere*), things never before created, and we are to believe that God creates new things, the beginnings, in keeping with his "ineffable prescience" (*ineffabili praescientia*) and "without change in will" (*uoluntatem mutabilem non habere*). It is far from clear, however, whether novelty and prescience can be believed to play well together, for each seems necessarily to preempt the other – thus fueling an angst about boundedness that pervades Augustine's angelology. Here we do well to keep in mind that "prescience" is a bad translation of *praescientia*. It is bad not because there is a better translation to be had ("foreknowledge" is equally bad), but because *praescientia* is untranslatable. Augustine refers to God's *praescientia* as "ineffable" (*ineffabili*).

[20] Augustine soberly discusses the presuppositions of worldly philosophy in *ciu. Dei.* 12.14 and 12.18. His language becomes markedly more affective in *ciu. Dei* 12.21, where he sounds as if he is calling out an extremely dangerous and somewhat insane enemy. In *ciu. Dei* 12.21, the chapter from which I have lifted some of his phrasing, he makes a striking claim: if the implications of worldly philosophy are true, it would be "more learned" (*doctius*) not to know about them.

We are clearly not in the neighborhood of an explicable kind of knowledge, and *praescientia*, as an eternal way of seeing, is going to remain on the sublime side of the translation divide. But this is not to say that the notion has no mundane resonance. Combine ineffable prescience with immutable will, and we get from Augustine a gesture toward a perfection that, strange to say, invites novelty. This is a perfection that is of this world. We just need to learn how not to shut off our perception to its presence.

So now consider the other major motif of Augustine's reflection on God's eternal way of creating: that God acts "inwardly" (*intrinsecus*; *ciu. Dei* 12.21) as an efficient cause, as a nurturer of form, and not as an alien, if benign, will to keep material disintegration, or loss of form, in perpetual check. The analogy here is to gestation and childbirth, the most mundane of human beginnings and yet still somehow marvelous. In *ciu. Dei* 12.24, Augustine observes that those whose habit it is to measure divine creativity against the workings of familiar, everyday human experience tend to discount the earthling's creation in Genesis – a spit of mud, divinely animated (Gen 2:7) – and, even more so, the story of the woman's coming to be out of her partner's severed rib (Gen 2:21–22); they take the stories to be whimsical (*fabulosa*), a child's fantasy. And while they are right not to cast the sublime creator literally in the role of a maker who handcrafts material form, their misplaced sense of wonder keeps them from seeing the alternative. "The hand of God," Augustine writes, "is the power of God – the power to work even visible things invisibly." The God who works body and soul wholly from the inside, akin to a mother's birthing of a child, only more invisibly, adds wonder upon wonder; but it is necessary to be struck first with the wonder of the human beginning to begin to sense this. Clearly not everyone is.[21]

Augustine's conception of eternal creation – endlessly innovative, absolutely intimate – amplifies his most basic sense of what creation fundamentally is: the coming to be of good things out of goodness itself. Jesus of Nazareth, born of Mary and yet also God's son, has his own kind of goodness, even as he providentially checks the darkness of this world; sin, in its sometime retreat, is not the full measure of his offering. Adam too, progenitor of humankind, has his own goodness, but he is also

[21] I owe my sense of the importance of *ciu. Dei* 12.24 almost entirely to Catherine Conybeare's brilliant 2017 Augustine Lecture, "The Creation of Eve," given at Villanova University and soon to be published in *Augustinian Studies*. I also owe to her my sense of Hannah Arendt's richly Augustinian evocations of natality.

somehow the beginning of the two cities – "not yet in evidence, to be sure, but already there in God's *praescientia*" (*ciu. Dei* 12.28). The angels who follow Lucifer and live outside themselves, in stillborn ecstasy, fruitlessly wait for a son or daughter of Adam to incarnate the uncreated night. Theirs is one of the two cities. Meanwhile, the angels in heaven bend their love toward changing ground and celebrate birthdays. Theirs is the other. There is no real confusion possible here, not in Adam nor in Adam's descendents, for a true beginning always begins with something good. Otherwise there is no story to tell. Thus can Augustine end Books 11 and 12 with some justification, with Ps 25:10: "Compassion and realism, these are all the roads of God."

FURTHER READING

Bochet, I. (2004). *"Le Firmament de l'Écriture": L'Herméneutique Augustinienne*. Paris: Institut d'Études Augustiniennes.

Griffiths, P. J. (2014). *Decreation: The Last Things of All Creatures*. Waco, TX: Baylor University Press.

Klein, E. (2018). *Augustine's Theology of Angels*. Cambridge: Cambridge University Press.

MacDonald, S. (1999). Primal Sin. In G. B. Matthews, ed., *The Augustinian Tradition*. Berkeley: University of California Press, pp. 110–139.

Muehlberger, E. (2013). *Angels in Late Ancient Christianity*. Oxford: Oxford University Press.

Wetzel, J. (2012a). A Tangle of Two Cities. *Augustinian Studies*, 43(1), 5–23.

9 Books 13 & 14: The Incomprehensibility of the Fall and Its Consequences for Humanity

MATHIJS LAMBERIGTS

Books 13 and 14, written around AD 418, are part of a broader set of Books 11–14 which deal with the origin of the earthly and heavenly cities. Books 13 and 14 were written in the midst of the Pelagian controversy but also sought to tackle an issue Augustine invested much time and energy in, from the very beginning of his ecclesiastical career.[1] Furthermore, these two books can be read as commentaries on Genesis[2] on the one hand, and as philosophical tractates critiquing Platonic and Stoic tenets on the other. And while Books 13 and 14 focus on the fall of Adam and its consequences, Augustine does use this opportunity to attack Pelagian positions explicitly in this context.[3]

CIU. DEI 13

In *ciu. Dei* 12.21–26, Augustine discussed the creation of humanity in Adam. Augustine insisted that the creation of man was the work of God himself, the human soul being created in the image of God. Augustine stated that God had foreseen both the fall and redemption. In Book 13,

[1] Grossi 2015, pp. 333–366 at p. 334 suggests AD 417/18 for Books 11–14. Given Augustine's many activities in this period and the similarities in topics between *nupt. et conc.* and Books 13 and 14, I suggest that these books are written in AD 418, beginning AD 419. However, given the fact that Augustine accepts in *nupt. et conc.* 2.59–60 that carnal concupiscence could exist in the paradise, Book 14 must be finished before. The date of *c. adu. leg.* (AD 418–AD 423) is not really of help. In this book (cf. CCSL 35, l.452) it is said that Book 14 is finished before this tractate.

[2] The two books are part of Augustine's reflections as developed over the years: they should be read in relation to his three commentaries on Genesis and of *conf.* 11–13; see Pelland 1972. The theme will be an important one up to the end of Augustine's life; see Lamberigts 1990, pp. 373–410.

[3] In the period these books were written, Augustine also wrote works such as *gr. et pecc. or.* and *nupt. et conc.* However, as far as I can see, Augustine nowhere in *ciu. Dei* explicitly mentions Pelagius. Also, the term *inimici gratiae* is not found in this work. That topics, discussed in anti-Pelagian works, are present in *ciu. Dei* 13 and 14, is evident. See also Drecoll 2015, pp. 367–386.

which can be read as a short treatise on the subject of death in its own right,[4] Augustine deals with Adam's fall and its consequences, now focusing on death. Augustine first discusses the meaning of death (*ciu. Dei* 13.1–15) and then the status of the body (*ciu. Dei* 13.16–24), in a sense an anticipation of Book 22.[5]

Augustine starts his exposition by stating that God did not create men like the angels: for man, mortality is part of his nature, not in the sense that the first human beings had to die anyway, but in the sense that they had to die if they would sin. If the first human beings had not sinned, angelic immortality and blessed eternity would have been their reward (*ciu. Dei* 13.1). But they sinned and thus had to die.

FOUR MEANINGS OF DEATH

Augustine distinguishes four meanings of death: the death of the soul, the death of the body, the death of soul and body and the final death because of eternal punishment.[6] All these forms of death are related to the fall of Adam: because the whole human race was in Adam when he sinned, all participate in the punishments of Adam and thus all have to die. Augustine first paid attention to the death of the immortal soul, understood as the soul being abandoned by God. Just as the body dies when the soul abandons it, the soul dies when abandoned by God. This death of the whole human being is called the second death (cf. Rev 2:11, 2:18). It is the worst of all evils (*ciu. Dei* 13.4). It happens in the final and eternal punishment. While the first death (of the body) overcomes all, the second death will overcome those who have abandoned God. Because the soul is immortal, it confers life on the body that continues to have feelings which have a punishing character and cause pain (*ciu. Dei* 13.2).

DEATH AS PUNISHMENT

Augustine refutes the idea that the first death (the separation of body and soul) can be something good.[7] Augustine considers physical death as a punishment for Adam and Eve, a punishment in which also their

4 See Cavadini 1999, pp. 232–249.
5 O'Daly 1986–1994, pp. 970–1010, esp. p. 974.
6 On these distinctions, see Van Horne 1981, pp. 34–50, 34–35.
7 Augustine uses the Platonic concept of separation, but does not give it a positive meaning as the Platonists did; see Cavadini 1999, p. 237.

progeny is involved, even although physical death now occurs naturally in all people. Now, all are born from the mortal flesh of the sinning Adam, all are characterized by mortality and sinfulness. When he procreated, Adam was already a punished sinner, thus becoming the origin of sin and death for all. As adults, Adam and Eve, experienced their sin and its consequences, but the rest of humanity will start in a situation of infantile weakness and helplessness. God wishes that babies start their lives like whelps, reduced as they are to the level of irrational animals (Ps 48:13). Even worse, they are weaker than the most vulnerable newborns of the other animals. Through Christ's grace, babies are released from the bonds of sin and, as babies, can only suffer the first death (*ciu. Dei* 13.3). Referring to *pecc. mer.* 2.31.50–51,[8] Augustine repeats that baptism does not result in the gift of an immortal body, because otherwise faith, directed to and longing for a yet unseen future, would lose its power.

However, physical death can have a positive meaning, as becomes clear in the case of the martyrs. Their death is based on faith and described as a victory and a matter of glory (*ciu. Dei* 13.4). Thanks to the grace of the redeemer, the penalty of vice turns into the armor of virtue, and the punishment of the sinner now becomes the merit of the righteous. In other words, negative things such as death are reversed into positive aspects such as virtue. The righteous prefer to suffer for their belief what was suffered by Adam and Eve because of their disbelief. For martyrs, a matter of punishment and an evil becomes a matter of merit and they do no longer incur guilt: because of God's mercy it has become a good through which martyrs pass into life (*ciu. Dei* 13.4), having received remission of all sins because of this martyrdom, for martyrdom has the same effect as baptism.[9] Choosing this first death because of Christ, they avoid the danger of the second death (*ciu. Dei* 13.7–8). However, it must be said time and again: the physical death is not neutral, it is *contra naturam* (*ciu. Dei* 13.6).

How to Describe the Time of the Separation of Body and Soul?

In chapters 9–11 Augustine offers a long philosophical and philological/grammatical[10] reflection about death and its conditions. He is analyzing

[8] Often called *De peccatorum meritis et remissione*, Augustine speaks here of *De baptismo parvulorum*; this is also the title one will find in *ep.* 139.3. Elsewhere, one can find *Libri ad Marcellinum* (*nat. et gr.* 15.15; 23.25; *c. Jul. imp.* 1.68; 3.177).

[9] This was the conviction of the Early Church since the time of Tertullian. Augustine bases his argument on Jn 3:5, Mt 10:32 and 16:25; see *ciu. Dei* 13.7.

[10] See Bardy 1959, pp. 517–519.

the meaning of expressions such as *in morte* and *post mortem*, the first indicating a state, the second the temporal aspect, "after death," giving the impression that death no longer exists.[11] When people are dying, they in a sense are still living but going into the direction of death.[12] Once the impending death has arrived, we say that they are dead (*ciu. Dei* 13.9). Death inevitably accompanies all from the first day of their life: the span of this life can be described as a race toward death. It does not matter how long one lives, for "real time" is the same for all: the one who takes more time on his way to death does not travel more slowly, but travels a longer distance (*ciu. Dei* 13.10). With reference to Scripture (Sir 11:28) Augustine concludes: before death occurs, we speak about "before death"; when death has occurred, we speak of "after death" occurred, or of "in death."[13]

Augustine then offers a philological reflection about the deponent verb *moritur*, a verb which one cannot decline like similar verbs such as *oritur*. The past participle of *moritur* is *mortuus*. Linking it to adjectives such as *fatuus, arduus, conspicuus*, Augustine qualifies *mortuus* as an adjective, used in place of a past participle, as if one should decline what in fact cannot be declined. Artificial as the argumentation might be, it makes clear that the verb can no more be declined in speech than what it means can be declined in practice (*ciu. Dei* 13.11).

THE THREAT OF WHICH DEATH?

God's threat with regard to the (possible) disobedience of the first human beings in paradise is related to the four forms of death, for they all are part of the death as a whole (*ciu. Dei* 13.12). Disobedience to God caused disorder in the first human beings themselves, an issue Augustine will return to extensively in Book 14. The disobedience to God resulted in a disobedience of the flesh to the soul: the soul willingly deserted God (the higher) and thus is deserted by its servant (the lower). The desire of the flesh, opposing the spirit (Gal 5:17), starts with the fall and will also be the fate of all children of Adam. Our vitiated nature makes of our lives a battlefield (*ciu. Dei* 13.13).[14] Adam willingly depraved and justly condemned, procreated in this situation of

[11] Van Horne 1981, pp. 36ff.
[12] Van Horne 1981, p. 35; Dupont 2010, pp. 41–62, 49–50.
[13] See O'Daly 1999, p. 151.
[14] For Augustine, only a good thing can be vitiated; cf. *ciu. Dei* 11.17, *CCSL* 48, p. 336. On this important idea of the vitiated nature in Augustine's work, see Strohm 1955, pp. 184–203.

degeneration and condemnation. In Augustine's monogenetic view of humanity, all human beings were seminally present[15] in Adam when the latter sinned and his semen became vitiated. All are affected by a succession of miseries, ending into the final ruination of the second death, which will have no end, except for those who will be liberated by God's grace (*ciu. Dei* 13.14). It will be clear that Adam's responsibility is enormous: because he abandoned God, he was condemned to spiritual (God abandoning man) and mortal (the soul abandoning the body) death, and all were involved in this disaster (*ciu. Dei* 13.15). On this fall and its consequences, Augustine will return at length in Book 14.

DEATH: NO LIBERATION BUT PUNISHMENT

In the Platonic philosophy, the separation of body and soul has been considered as something good.[16] Liberated from all physical hindrances as caused by the body, the soul can fully and freely return to the world of immutability – the world of the Forms, the world of the divine – in order to enjoy perfect blessedness.[17] Platonic philosophers, like Porphyry,[18] thus ridiculed the Christian idea that the physical death is to be considered as a punishment.

Augustine replies by focusing on the dignity of the body, a good creation of a good creator. Since the fall, the body is corruptible and characterized by dead and carnal concupiscence. The corruptible body weighs down the soul (Wis 9:15) and Augustine appeals to Plato's very clear argument (*apertissime*) that eternal bodies were promised by the supreme god to the lower gods, proving that the gift of the body is to be considered a great benefit.[19]

[15] On the idea of the *ratio seminis*, see Lamberigts 1988, II,I, pp. 66–7; II,II, pp. 52–54, 59–60 (with further literature). In this regard, Solignac (1956, pp. 359–385, esp. p. 378) speaks of "schéma biologico-juridique" and also of "schéma juridico-biologique," indicating with juridical that we all are in Adam, with biologically in his seeds (p. 386).

[16] On this issue, see Miles 1986–1994, pp. 6–19, esp. 7–9.

[17] This idea was embraced with enthusiasm by Christian authors such as Ambrose; see Cavadini 1999, pp. 223–234.

[18] O'Daly 1999, p. 151; Bochet 2010, pp. 7–52, esp. p. 21. Augustine also discussed this topic in his sermons, let it be in a simplified way; see Bochet 2009, pp. 267–298, esp. at pp. 281–282.

[19] Cf. *ciu. Dei* 12.26; see also *s.* 242.8. On Augustine's evolution with regard to the interpretation of this Scriptural text, see Bochet 2016, pp. 27–43. Augustine quotes Plato's *Timaeus* 41a–b in the translation of Cicero, *Timaeus* 11,40. Augustine is very much dependent on Cicero when referring to Plato; see, e.g. Testard 1958, p. 281. On

Porphyry's critique is not only unfair to Christianity, but also contradicts his master's positions.[20] The bodies of these lesser gods are neither immortal nor indissoluble by nature, but exist because of the will of the supreme god. The fact that these lesser gods fear the separation of their soul and body is an argument that the body as such is not the cause of the struggle between it and the soul.

Augustine observes a contradiction in the Platonists' argumentation. On the one hand, they maintain that the earthly body, mutable, finite, and thus perishable, is causing disturbance and unrest. On the other hand, they consider the whole earth (and the earthly body is part of it) as a god, higher than the other gods (*ciu. Dei* 13.17). Further, Augustine does not understand why these philosophers are attributing qualifications such as eternal to the (earthly) world, that is considered to be animated with a rational or intellectual soul,[21] while rejecting the Christian idea of the resurrection of the body.

Of course, Platonists will consider the human body as part of the earthly reality to which this body must return. However, Augustine replies, what then with regard to the immortality of the body, promised by the supreme god to the lesser gods? In fact, if Plato's god is able to prevent composed gods (consisting of soul and body) from decline and transiency, why should such privilege and capacity be denied to the Christian God? In fact, prophets, instructed by God's Spirit in order to announce God's will, are better informed about the truth than the Platonists, basing their arguments on human presuppositions. Augustine concludes that in the resurrection bodily corruptibility and the like must be taken away, but not the body as such (*ciu. Dei* 13.17). Christ's resurrection and the future resurrection of the martyrs illustrate that the earthly body is not necessarily held down on earth, for it will be in heaven. Referring to natural phenomena such as metals, made by human beings – normally these metals sink immediately when placed in water, while vessels are able to float – Augustine concludes that what human beings are able to do, God can certainly also realize (*ciu. Dei* 13.18). All the more so, the highest God is able to take away corruption from the flesh and to give immortality to it, while leaving

Augustine's use of this text in the context of the resurrection of the body, see Counet 2013, pp. 80–81.

[20] In *ciu. Dei* 12.27, Augustine already refuted both Plato and Porphyry; on this refutation, see Alfeche 1995, pp. 95–140, 124–128.

[21] Cf. *Timaeus* 30b.

this created nature as such intact. Philosophical arguments against the resurrection of the body do not stand (*ciu. Dei* 13.18).

THE PLATONIC VIEW OF THE BODY IS INCOHERENT AND CONTRADICTORY

Augustine argues that nobody dares to suggest that the life of dying or dead pious and righteous people is to be ranked above that of immortal gods, whom according to Plato (*ciu. Dei* 13.16), was promised an eternal union with their own bodies. Further, referring to *Phaedo* 108c and *Phaedrus* 248c, Augustine observes that for Plato the separation of body and soul is the best outcome people can expect. However, they are received into the bosom of the very gods who never depart from their own bodies. As a result, the souls begin once more to long for a return to their bodies.[22] Not only those who lived a foolish life and thus return almost at once, but also the wise and pious start desiring for a body, neither being able to be permanently in their bodies (happiness being described as separation of body of soul) nor to persist without their bodies in eternal purity (*ciu. Dei* 13.19).

Therefore, Porphyry rejected the Platonic idea that the souls of the wise might return to the body, for they would enjoy eternal happiness. He also rejected the Christian idea about the resurrection of incorruptible bodies, maintaining that these souls would live for all eternity without any bodies at all (cf. *ciu. Dei* 22.27). At the same time, Porphyry was of the opinion that one could venerate gods who have a body. He did not dare to rank bodiless souls higher than embodied gods. Why then are these philosophers opposed to the Christian belief about the first human beings, the fall and its consequences on the one hand, and the promise to receive immortal life if they had persevered in obedience. The Christian resurrection of the body is not the result of a (negative) desire to return to the earthly body, but of a (positive) desire to get back those bodies, in which they have endured many hardships, but which once will be free of any corruption or distress. In this new situation, the body will become a spiritual body (1 Cor 15:44) and obey the soul with an eminent and marvelous easiness.

In that life to come, the spiritual body no longer needs food or drink as was still the case with Adam and Eve before the fall (*ciu. Dei* 13.19–20). In other words, the Christian view on eternal life (with body

[22] Augustine quotes from Virgil's phrasing of this Platonic teaching in *Aeneis* 6.750–51; see *ciu. Dei* 13.19. On the simplified presentation of Plato, see O'Daly 1999, p. 152.

and soul harmoniously being together) is to be preferred over the Platonist view of an eternal soul, separated from an earthly body. Therefore, the flesh of the saints rests in hope, while the soul is longing patiently for the resurrection of the body (*ciu. Dei* 13.20). For Augustine, the relation between body and soul is as such not a relation of tension or aversion, but, in the long run, of a recovered harmony on the spiritual level, characteristic for the life to come. In this life to come, our transformed bodies will be in a better situation than Adam and Eve before the fall.

SPIRITUAL INTERPRETATIONS OF PARADISE

Since *Gn. litt.* Augustine read the Genesis story as a historical story. However, he did not reject allegorical readings of the Genesis story, but warned for an exclusion of any reference to historical realities, a position that is confirmed here.[23] Augustine discusses the spiritual interpretation of paradise which considers it as a place that transcends the senses, thus suggesting that trees and fruit-bearing plants refer to virtues and moral ways of living. They did not really exist, but were intended to signify intelligible matters. Augustine does not reject this interpretation (*ciu. Dei* 13.21) as long as one also takes into account that these stories can have a historical origin, interpreted in an allegorical way. In that interpretation, paradise can also be understood as the Church, the saints as the trees, Christ as the tree of life (*ciu. Dei* 13.21).

THE SPIRITUAL BODY

Augustine reflects on the status of the resurrected bodies of the just. These resurrected bodies will not need any protection of a tree, nor any bodily food, for they will be endowed with the inviolable eternal gift of immortality (*ciu. Dei* 13.22). Also Christ himself in his spiritual – but still real – flesh ate and drank with his disciples (Lk 24:42–43). The resurrected bodies are sustained by a life-giving spirit and *can* eat and drink if they will but *do not need* it. So, while Augustine can insist that these spiritual bodies do in fact possess the substance of flesh, thanks to this life-giving spirit vivifying these spiritual bodies, they will suffer no longer from mental slowness or physical corruption (*ciu. Dei* 13.23).

[23] Cf. the use of *tamquam, quasi* and the like; cf. *ciu. Dei* 13.21 as at CCSL 48.404.

The body's nature remains essentially the same but it will undergo a qualitative, deifying transformation.[24]

On the basis of Paul (especially Romans 8 and 1 Corinthians 15), Augustine discuss the differences between the animal and the spiritual body, for that both exist is evidenced by Paul in 1 Cor 15:42–45. Adam possessed an animal body (cf. the need for food and drink) but had in him the potential not to die if he had not sinned, the spiritual body being the reward. But Adam sinned and the consequences are known: vitiated nature, death, conflict. Adam's disobedience resulted in a death of the soul (abandonment by God) and the body (the departure of the soul from the body), a death, common to all. Referring to 1 Cor 15:45: "The last Adam became a life-giving spirit," Augustine relates the spiritual body to the risen Christ. This spiritual body, preceding us in Christ, our head, will be received by Christ's members in the final resurrection (1 Cor 15:47–49). Through birth, we are animal, through resurrection we will become spiritual, for this is a perspective for which we now hope (*ciu. Dei* 13.23). Christ became man, clothing himself with the body of earthly mortality, in order to clothe humanity with heavenly immortality, resulting in full harmony of body and soul.[25] Augustine immediately adds that not all who die in Adam, will be members of Christ, for much more (*multo plures*) will die in Adam than will become members of Christ (*ciu. Dei* 13.23). Indeed, Augustine is of the opinion that God's salvific will is limited to those who are elected, not to all who are called (cf. Mt 22:14).

THE BREATH OF GOD OR THE HOLY SPIRIT

In the last (and longest) chapter of Book 13, Augustine discusses the correct meaning of Gen 2:7: "God breathed into his face the spirit of life, and man became a living soul." He disagrees with the view that Adam had already a soul, but that it was brought to life by the Holy Spirit at the moment indicated in Genesis.[26] Gen 2:6–7 makes clear that God formed man from the dust of the earth. The opponents suggested that Adam had already a soul, otherwise he could not have been called man. Augustine accepts that man consists of soul and body but also remarks

[24] O'Daly 1999, p. 153.
[25] Cavadini 1999, p. 245.
[26] It is suggested that Augustine might have in mind Origen's view on this matter; cf. *On First Principles* 1.3.6–7; *Contra Celsum* 4.37. See Theiler 1970, pp. 554–563; O'Daly 1999, pp. 153, 261–262.

that the word "man" can be used either for the soul or the body (cf. 2 Cor 4:16: the inner man [soul] versus the outer man [body]). In other words, one must distinguish between the man as made in the image of God and the man who is of the earth and to which he will return. For both, the term man can be used and thus one can rightly conclude that God breathed into man's face the breath of life and the man became a living soul (Gen 2:7). Clearly being in a philological mood, Augustine discusses the Greek equivalent of *Spiritus*, *pneuma* (*ciu. Dei* 13.24). In the Christian scriptures, *Spiritus* always refers to the Holy Spirit as part of the Trinity. However, where Genesis speaks of God's breath (Gen 2:7), it does not speak of *pneuma* but of *pnoè*, a word that Latin authors have translated by *flatus*, *spiritus*, *inspiratio* or *aspiratio*. However, Augustine argues with reference to a series of Scriptural texts, *pneuma* is always translated as *spiritus*. In the text under discussion (Gen 2:7), the author used *pnoè* and thus was not speaking about the Holy Spirit: Scripture thus makes clear that man received a rational soul through the breath of God and that there is no reason to interpret Gen 2:7 as an activity of the Holy Spirit.

At the end of this long chapter, Augustine, quoting 1 Cor 15:44–49, by way of inclusion (cf. *ciu. Dei* 13.1), repeats that the animal body in which Adam was made, was such that he could not die if he had not sinned, what he did. The future body will be spiritual and immortal and will not be able to die, just like the immortal created soul, although the latter's fate depends on either the condemnation to a second death or the participation in eternal life, co-citizenship with the angels, immortality without sin or corruption of mental slowness (*ciu. Dei* 13.24). At the end of Book 13 Augustine announces the content of Book 14: in this life, people are subjected to the law of sin with the unfortunate consequence that procreation is only possible through a lustful concupiscence. Augustine thus wonders how the human race could have been procreated before the fall of Adam.

BOOK 14

Book 14 first focuses on the life in the earthly city (a life according to the flesh) and contrasts it with the life in the City of God (a life according to the spirit). From chapter 10 onwards, it pays attention to Adam, Eve, the paradise, the fall and its consequences for the first men and their progeny. Augustine begins Book 14 by repeating how God gave human beings their beginning from a single person, Adam. Unlike Adam who was a radically new creation, having come from the dirt of the earth, Eve comes forth from Adam, a human from a human, in order that humanity's unity could be stressed and how we are all intended to be joined in a society formed by likeness of nature and joined together in unity and concord (*ciu. Dei* 14.1). God's plan with humanity was characterized by harmony, but because of the fall this initial harmony was deteriorated for all human beings, mortality and bondage of sin being their fate. All deserve the second, eternal death, but God's undeserved grace saves some (*quosdam*) from it.

Although Augustine is well aware of the rich religious, moral, and cultural variety among human beings, our history can, according to Scripture, be reduced to two cities, the first being the city of those who life according to the flesh, the second being the city of those who are living according to the spirit (cf. Gal 5:17–21).[27] For Augustine, human beings' life is bipolar: one either chooses for his/herself or for the creator. In Augustine's hierarchical view of history, true happiness is related to God, the creator of all realities. Disobedience to God results in chaos and disharmony.[28]

Scripture Is to Be Preferred over Philosophy

For Augustine, the difference between the living according to the flesh and the living according to the spirit is to be based on Scripture, not on the Epicurean view on the bodily lust as the highest good for man,[29] an idea shared by the common people. This way of living, like that of the Stoics, who put the highest good of man in the spirit (*ciu. Dei* 14.2) is, in light of Scripture, Augustine's highest authority, to be qualified as living according to the flesh, for all are living according to human standards, neglecting the divine standard of truth.[30] For Augustine, living according to the flesh in an evil way is to be understood as defined in Gal 5:19–21: "Now the works of the flesh are obvious: fornication, impurity, licentiousness, idolatry, sorcery, enmity, strife, jealousy, anger, dissension, heresies, envy, drunkenness, carousing, and the like.

[27] *ciu. Dei* 11.1 and the scriptural texts quoted there. Augustine does not accept a kind of third, neutral entity; cf. O'Daly 1999, p. 154; cf. also J. van Oort 1991, pp. 151–153.

[28] Augustine will substantially discuss these choices in *ciu. Dei* 14.28. See O'Donovan 1980; see also Rist 1994, pp. 188–191.

[29] With regard to Augustine's view of Epicurean philosophy, see Colish 1985; Erler 1996–2002, pp. 858–861. It is interesting to see that Augustine in *ciu. Dei* prefers the use of the classic *libido* over the Christian *concupiscentia*. In the book under discussion, *libido* is used thirty-nine times, *concupiscentia* only seven times, a clear indication that he also wants to reach non-Christians. Commentators seldom pay attention to this significant aspect; see, e.g. Drecoll 2015, p. 381.

[30] O'Daly 1999, p. 154.

I am warning you, as I warned you before, that those who do such things will not gain the kingdom of God." The vices described have to do with the pleasures of the flesh and of the mind. Indeed, idolatry, sorcery, enmity and the like are vices of the mind, ideas that very well serve the purpose of *ciu. Dei*, written against pagans and heretics.[31]

Augustine repeats from *ciu. Dei* 12.26 that not the flesh, created by God, is the cause of our vices (*ciu. Dei* 14.4), but its corruptibility. Against Virgil,[32] Augustine argues that a sinful soul is the cause of the first sin, the corruptibility of the flesh being a punishment. In fact, if one attributes all vices of an evil life to the flesh, one could no longer accuse the devil of sins, because he has no body. Living according to the flesh thus must be understood as living according to the self (*ciu. Dei* 14.3). The essence of the first sin is sinful pride and a choice for oneself. Living according to man is behaving like the devil, while living according to truth is living according to God who is the truth (cf. Jn 14:6). Like elsewhere,[33] Augustine insists that all human beings want to be happy, but that a choice for the self, is a choice for falsehood and results in unhappiness.

Augustine rejects the Platonic view in which the nature of the soul is praised as the highest good and the nature of the flesh is defined as evil. The Platonists do not detest the earthly bodies as the nature of evil, like the Manichaeans do, for they ascribe all elements from which the visible and tangible world is composed and its *qualitates* to God as their creator. However, by claiming that the souls are affected by earthly limbs and death-bound members, they put the sources of the soul's desires and fears, joys and sorrows in the body. For Augustine, these four disturbances (*perturbationes*),[34] commonly qualified as passions (*ciu. Dei* 8.17), do not stem from the body, but from their souls (*ciu. Dei* 14.5).

THE QUALITY OF THE WILL

Whether emotions are perverse or right depends upon the will's quality and attitude for emotions are nothing more than movements of the will

[31] When speaking of heretics he must have had in mind the Apollinarists as presented by the "orthodox" Christians, for, according to that orthodox position, the Apollinarists were of the opinion that Christ had no human soul. Cf. *ciu. Dei* 14.2. See also 10.27 and 14.9.

[32] Augustine quotes *Aeneid* 6.730–32; cf. *ciu. Dei* 14.3.

[33] See, e.g. *c. Jul. imp.* 6.26.

[34] See Cicero, *Tusculanae disputationes* 6.5.10.

(*ciu. Dei* 14.6).[35] Joy and desire are nothing else than a consent of the will to things we want, while fear and grief are nothing else than the will's dissent from things we do not want. As a result, living according to God results in loving the good and thus hating evil: the one who really loves the good and hates the evil will not hate the evil person, but the evil in a person, while loving the person as such: once the fault is healed, what a person loves will remain, while what he hated disappeared (*ciu. Dei* 14.6). It will be clear that for Augustine the real reference point is loving God and loving the neighbor as oneself (Mt 22:37–39). This love, qualified as *amor*, is more often described by Scripture as *caritas*. However, for Augustine, words such as *dilectio, caritas,* and *amor* are interchangeable. He disagrees with those who claim that *dilectio* has a positive meaning and *amor* a negative connotation. In fact, this distinction is also absent in secular literature. All these concepts can have a positive and a negative meaning (*ciu. Dei* 14.7).[36]

EMOTIONS, DESIRE, AND PASSIONS[37]

Augustine already discussed the passions of demons in *ciu. Dei* 9.4. Now he focuses on passions in human beings. He starts his presentation with a discussion of the content of the verb *concupiscere* and the noun *concupiscentia*. Like elsewhere,[38] Augustine insists that both can have a positive meaning, even although in our daily parlance they are associated with a negative connotation.

According to Augustine, the Stoics[39] state that in the mind of the wise person three dispositions exist instead of the three above mentioned passions, dispositions which in Greek are called *eupatheiai*,[40] and in Cicero *constantiae*: it is ac act of the will instead of a desire,

[35] On this position and its Ciceronian background, see Clark 2016, pp. 209–225, esp. 212–214, 217.

[36] Augustine quotes Ps 11:5; 1 Jn 2:15 and 2 Tim 3:2 to substantiate his argument; see *ciu. Dei* 14.7. For a profound discussion of the question in a broader context, see Bardy 1959, pp. 529–531; cf. also Clark 2016, pp. 218–219.

[37] On the passions, see Bardy 1959; and Thonnard 1969, pp. 531–534, 536–539 respectively (n. 20); O'Daly 1999, p. 155; Grossi 2009, pp. 105–126, 111–118; Grossi 2015, pp. 334–344 situates the issue in the broader context of Augustine's œuvre and discusses also some of Augustine's predecessors.

[38] See the examples as given in Lamberigts 2000, pp. 176–197, 179–180.

[39] See O'Daly 1999, p. 155.

[40] See Diogenes Laertius, *Lives of Eminent Philosophers* 7.116.

gladness instead of joy, and caution instead of fear.[41] For the Stoics, distress or pain cannot have a place in the mind of the wise,[42] who long for the good. Joy is the result of the good the wise attains. Caution avoids evil, something the wise person is expected to do. Grief is the result of evil that happened, and thus cannot have a place in the mind of the wise person. While the wise person possesses will, gladness, and caution, the foolish can only feel desire, joy, fear, and grief. The first three are qualified as constant dispositions, the latter four as disturbances or passions.[43]

Reflecting on the verbs *gaudere* and *laetari* (in scripture there seems to be a preference for *gaudere* when authors think of the just people [cf. Is 57:21 LXX], while *laetari* seems to be used for the joy of the unfaithful; *ciu. Dei* 14.8), Augustine disagrees with the Stoic idea that the will as such is longing for the good, for when one speaks of a good will (cf. Lk 2:14), this implies that also a bad will can exist. Augustine observes that in Scripture (cf. 1 Cor 13:6) like in secular literature (cf. Virgil, *Aeneid* 6,733.278) *gaudere/gaudium* can have a negative connotation, while *cupere* can be used with a positive connotation.[44] Writing against pagan critics, Augustine is eager to show that his own views are supported by pagan literature. In sum, will, caution, and gladness are common to both the good and evil ones and whether they are good or bad depends on one's behavior. Augustine adds that even grief can be found in a good person (with a long quote from 2 Cor 7:8–11).[45]

As in *ciu. Dei* 9.4–5, Augustine suggests that the Stoics focus more on words than on realities and that they are more interested in controversy than in the truth (*ciu. Dei* 14.9). Such an attitude is not present in the inhabitants of the City of God: in their pilgrimage on earth, they are guided by Scripture and the sound doctrine. The authority of Scripture can be supported by pagan sources but never undermined, for Christians, inspired by Scripture, want to live their lives *secundum Deum*. They experience fear and desire, pain and gladness, but because their love is oriented to the right direction, their feelings are also turned to it and they thus cannot be qualified as diseases or evil passions.[46]

[41] Cf. *Tusculanae Disputationes* 4.6.11–14; see Clark 2016, pp. 219ff.

[42] See Inwood 1985, pp. 173–175.

[43] With regard to Augustine's ambivalent relation with Stoic views and criteria concerning passions, see Byers 2012, pp. 130–148.

[44] Augustine refers to *Contra Catilinam* 1.2.4.

[45] However, Augustine does not deny that the Stoic claim that there is no grief in the wise is correct; see his argumentation in *ciu. Dei* 14; see also Byers 2012, p. 133.

[46] O'Daly 1999, p. 156.

The citizens of the holy city fear sin and eternal punishment. They desire eternal life and perseverance. They suffer because they sin. They are still groaning inwardly, waiting for adoption and the redemption of their bodies. They rejoice in good works and in the hope that once death will be defeated. The citizens of the holy city not only experience these emotions on their own account, but also on account of their co-citizens, as Paul himself did. Joy, hope, fear and pain receive a positive meaning in the context of the life in the holy city. These emotions and feelings, belonging to this life (*ciu. Dei* 14.9), spring from love of the good and of holy charity. They are expressions of the love of the image of God for the images of God, for all are His image. Augustine rejects the Stoic negative evaluation of emotions in light of their interpretation of *apatheia*,[47] referring to Christ himself, who had a true human body and a true human mind and showed these emotions.[48]

However, emotions are *relatively* positive, for they belong to this life, not to the future life we hope for, but are in this life a *necessary* weakness[49] of our human condition, for one cannot live rightly without feeling these emotions at all, and absence of emotions results in an inhuman mind and an unfeeling body. Augustine is thus of the opinion that one can desire for *apatheia* (Latin: *impassibilitas*) and that this can be good, for it refers to a life where there is no longer sin in human beings. In that life to come, *apatheia* will exist, together with love and joy, both being essential aspects of truth (*ciu. Dei* 14.9).

Since we must live a right life to reach a happy life, it follows that a right life will have all these emotions in a right way, a perverse life in a perverse way. Only in the life to come, the happy and eternal life, there will be no fear (for sin) and grief at all. In order to reach that life, one has to live in this life according to God, not man. This perspective is contrasting the life in the city of the ungodly, who worship false divinity, and follow the teaching of men or demons. This City of Men is characterized by pride and impiety. Citizens of this worldly city who claim that they are not stirred or excited or swayed or influenced by any emotion at all, are losing all humanity rather than gaining real tranquility (*ciu. Dei* 14.10).

[47] Whether Augustine has a correct understanding of the Stoic views in this matter, is not clear; see Byers 2012, p. 140.

[48] Augustine also pays much attention to Christ's emotions for Christ wanted to live a human life in the form of a slave, see *ciu. Dei* 14.9; CCSL 48.427.

[49] Only in the case of Christ, his weakness is to be regarded as an expression of his power; see *ciu. Dei* 14.9, CCSL 48.428.

EMOTIONS IN THE PARADISE

Augustine wonders whether our emotions were also present in Adam and Eve before the fall. Living in a situation dominated by love for God and each other, they lived a happy and perfect life in harmony, without disturbances of the mind or distresses of the body, for they lived in a situation characterized by absence of any sinful desire, previewing the conditions in the eternal life to come (*ciu. Dei* 14.10).[50] The first man, perfectly obeying to God's commend,[51] enjoyed (*frui*) God. He did not lack anything and could live in such perfect state forever. Food and drink were present. The tree of life kept away the decay of old age. No fear or disease from within or of injury from outside. Adam had supreme health in his flesh and complete tranquility in his soul. Between husband and wife, there was a faithful partnership of genuine love, an alertness of mind and body in true concord, and an effortless observance of the commandment. Procreation would have been characterized by complete obedience of the genitals to the will's command. No enticing goad of sexual heat would have embarrassed sexuality (*ciu. Dei* 14.26).

However, this ideal situation never existed. Augustine does not explain why the first human beings, living in ideal conditions, sinned.[52] He simply states that in God's masterplan, the fall of the first human beings was foreseen and did not disturb God's plan, for He knew how much good He Himself would bring forth from man. Any "possible" change in God's mind and plans is to be perceived as human projection (*ciu. Dei* 14.11). In his almightiness, God, the supreme and supremely good creator, can make use of the condemned human race to complete the fixed number of citizens that He had predestined for his city.[53] Since the fall, only God's grace saves those He wants to be saved. In his providence and omnipotence God distributes to each what is due to each. All are condemned, yet some, without any merit, by grace, are saved by a predestining God (*ciu. Dei* 14.27).

THE FALL AND ITS CONSEQUENCES

Augustine clearly puts the blame and guilt on Adam who chose for himself (*ciu. Dei* 14.11). Adam's choice against God was ontologically

[50] See also Wetzel 2012b, pp. 167–185, esp. 172–173.
[51] In this regard, see Bowlin 2012, p. 188.
[52] Bowlin 2012, pp. 186–204, esp. 188–189.
[53] See O'Daly 1999, p. 159, with further references.

possible because he was created *ex nihilo*, thus being mutable and free to choose either for God or for himself. The first human beings gave in to the fallen angel (*ciu. Dei* 11.13–15 and 12.6.9), who misled them by means of a serpent. The serpent deceived Eve, the lower part of the human couple, for the serpent presumed that the man, although not erring himself, would not give up his wife (even although Adam would put the blame on her and on God: the woman you gave me). While the weaker part believed the serpent, the stronger was unwilling to be separated from her, his only companion, even when it came to sharing in sin. However, this choice for his sinning companion does not make Adam less guilty: both Adam and Eve were taken captive by sin and entangled in the devil's snares (*ciu. Dei* 14.11).

Given the ideal situation of Adam and Eve before the fall, the consequences of their easy to avoid sin are dramatic, for the fall resulted in corruption, death, disturbance and conflicting emotions (*ciu. Dei* 14.11). The main reason for their sin was pride, the beginning of all sin (Sir 10:13).[54] Pride is an appetite for perverse exaltation, for a choice to become one's own principle. It is defecting from the immutable good which ought to please him more than he pleased himself. The turn to the self, the abandonment from God, is as it were a step toward nothingness (*ciu. Dei* 14.13), to degradation and destruction. Only devout humility makes the heart subject to what is superior, to God.[55] Augustine makes clear that in the City of God in this world humility – the highest form present in Christ the King – must be commended. It is a feature of this city being on pilgrimage in this world. It is a feature opposed to self-exaltation. Christ's humility is in contrast with the devil's exaltation. While the City of God is a company of the godly, the city of the world is a company of the godless. In the City of God, the love of God comes before all else, while in the City of Men the love of self dominates. Instead of becoming gods through obedience to God, the first human beings believed to become gods through a choice for themselves. Longing for more, they wanted to be self-sufficient and thus defected from God who alone is truly sufficient for human beings. Pleasing himself, he displeased God: "This evil came first, in secret, and the result was the evil that was committed in the open" (*ciu. Dei* 14.13; Babcock 2.120).

[54] In Augustine's Bible version, the text runs as following: "Initium omnis peccati superbia est." With regard to this text, see Green 1949, pp. 407–432, esp. 413; see also Markus 1990, pp. 245–259; Bowlin 2012, pp. 186–204, esp. 189–190.

[55] See Bowlin 2012, pp. 194–195.

LUST

Because of the fall, condemnation, physical and spiritual death, pain, suffering, harsh and bitter slavery, disobedience and loss of self-control became Adam's part. Disobedience is punished by disobedience. The soul is hindered by a lust for revenge, a lust for money, a lust to win at any cost, a lust for glory. Those who do evil must suffer evil (*ciu. Dei* 14.15). This suffering is most visible in human beings' sexuality and the accompanying sense of shame. Lust (*libido*) arouses those parts of the body that have to do with sexuality.[56] It not only dominates the whole body but also the soul. It gives more pleasure than any other bodily pleasure. This lust is such that when it reaches its climax, the mental alertness and the vigilance of the mind are obliterated. It does not serve one's mind and will and in fact is uncontrollable. It can come when it is not wanted and sometimes does not come up when the mind desires it (*ciu. Dei* 14.16).

Therefore, these parts of the body that are related to sexuality are called shameful parts. Nakedness, before the fall experienced as unproblematic, now became indecent and embarrassed the first men (cf. Gen 3:7). They became aware of the good they had lost and the evil that now overcame them. They made loincloths (*succinctoria*) or aprons (*campestria; ciu. Dei* 14.17). Since then, all over the world people cover these shameful parts of the body. Even the Indian gymnosophists, who practice philosophy naked, do cover their genitals.[57] That there is a problem with this lust is evident: it avoids the public gaze, not only in cases of debauchery, but also with regard to prostitution, a shame, legalized in the earthy city, but for which brothels provide separate places. Even the legal and honorable marital intercourse, for the sake of procreating children, thus part of a marriage contract, is done in a room, removed from witnesses.[58]

Platonic philosophers, closer to the truth, have argued that anger and lust, vice-promoting parts of the soul, are turbulent and disorderly emotions that stir to acts that wisdom forbids. They must be kept under control by mind and reason. These philosophers are aware of the fact that even in the case of wise and temperate men anger and lust incite to

56 See Lamberigts 2000, pp. 182–186.

57 Concerning these gymnosophists, see Plinius, *Historia naturalis* 7.22. The term is also known to Tertullian (cf. *Apologeticum* 42) and Jerome (cf. *Adversus Iovaninum* 1.42), who both add that they are found in India.

58 In the *Tabulae nuptiales*, the procreation of children is described as the proper task of marriage.

vice. Of the two, lust is the worst, for, while in case of anger and other emotions, the will sets them in motion by consenting to the emotions, thus controlling them, sexual lust takes itself the lead and control over the genitals. Anger, even unjust anger, can be accepted in public, sexual intercourse not (*ciu. Dei* 14.19), which is why the Cynics later gave up Diogenes of Sinope's idea that lawful sex between a man and his wife can perfectly done in public.[59]

THE DISTINCTION BETWEEN CONCUPISCENCE AND MARRIAGE

Augustine distinguishes between marriage (the procreation being the glory of marriage) and concupiscence, a punishment.[60] The glory of marriage was already given before the fall in order to procreate and fill the earth (cf. Gen 1:28; *ciu. Dei* 14.21–22). God created human beings as male and female, both with their own sex. This anatomy did not change after the fall. The way in which sexuality was experienced, however, did change. The goals of marriage should not be mixed with uncontrollable sexuality, for the love of partners for each other is to be distinguished from it. When Paul admonished men to love their wives, he had in mind this first couple in paradise (cf. Eph 5:25; Col 3:19; *ciu. Dei* 14.22).

Augustine clearly rejects the idea that the fall was needed to procreate in order to reach the number of the just. Without sin, marriage and procreation would have existed without the presence of any lust. The genitals could have functioned in complete obedience to the human beings will, just like other parts of our body like hands and feet. Referring to the now lost work of Cicero, *De re publica*,[61] Augustine insists that lust is more shameful because our soul is not able to control sexual lust. It is this (relative[62]) uncontrollability of lust which is the proof that something is wrong with it. The body, on a lower level than the soul, should obey the soul but resists. The conclusion is clear: the first human beings were given over to themselves because they choose for themselves, against God, thus abandoning God. Since the fall, people no longer live as they might wish to live (*ciu. Dei* 14.24). For a life in

59 On this development in Cynicism, see O'Daly 1999, p. 158.

60 Augustine devoted his *nupt. et conc.* (AD 418/19) to the distinction of the two elements.

61 Augustine also referred to this work in his *c. Jul.* 4.12.61.

62 It goes without saying that people can resist lust. The point is indeed that they cannot direct it in the way soul and will want it to be led; see *ciu. Dei* 14.23.

true happiness, the righteous (*ciu. Dei* 14.23) have to wait till the time of the resurrection (*ciu. Dei* 14.25). True happiness has to do with eternity.

AGAIN THE TWO CITIES[63]

Already in chapter 4, Augustine had observed that the existence of two different and mutually opposed cities can also be put in the following way: "[Their existence] is due to the fact that some live according to man and others according to God" (*ciu. Dei* 14.4; Babcock 2.103). Living according to God would result in becoming gods ourselves (*ciu. Dei* 14.4). That is why in the last chapter, Augustine focuses on the separation of the two cities: "Two loves, then, have made two cities" (*ciu. Dei* 14.28; Babcock 2.136). The City of Man is characterized by love of oneself and thus despising God, the City of God consists of those who love God and thus despise themselves. The earthly city is characterized by self-glorification, searching for glory from men, lust or domination.[64] In the earthly city, people do not venerate the creating God but created God; they are dominated by pride and human wisdom. The celestial city is characterized by glorifying in the lord. It is a praying recognition of God 's glory (Ps: 3:3; Ps 18:1). In this celestial city, leadership is characterized by loving service for God and the neighbor. The only wisdom known is piety, rightly worshipping the true God and looking forward to the reward that all saints are waiting for, "that God may be all in all" (1 Cor 15:28). The antithesis godly-earthly with all its characteristics will be developed in the next books in societal and political terms. But the basis remains the Bible. Indeed, the last sentences of Book 14 are dominated by scriptural quotes, describing the earthly or the celestial city.[65]

FURTHER READING

Cavadini, J. C. (1999). Ambrose and Augustine *De Bono Mortis*. In W. E. Klinshirn and M. Vessey, eds., *The Limits of Ancient Christianity: Essays on Late Antique Thought and Culture in Honor of R. A. Markus*. Ann Arbor: University of Michigan Press, pp. 232–249.

[63] See van Oort 1991, pp. 68–69.

[64] Augustine will focus on this political dimension in the following books.

[65] On this antithesis between the two cities, see also Griffiths 2012, p. 48. J. P. Martin (Martin 1991, pp. 283–294) suggests that we should pay more attention to the similarities in terminology and exegesis between Philo and Augustine, suggesting that this dependence of Augustine on Philo deserves more scholarly investigation.

Clark, G. (2016). Caritas: Augustine on Love and Fellow Feeling. In R. R. Caston and R. A. Kaster, eds., *Hope, Joy, and Affection in the Classical World*. New York: Oxford University Press, pp. 209–225.
Lamberigts, M. (2000). *A Critical Evaluation of Critiques of Augustine's View of Sexuality*. In R. Dodaro and G. Lawless, eds., *Augustine and His Critics: Essays in Honour of Gerald Bonner*. London/New York: Routledge, pp. 176–197.
Martin, J.P. (1991). Philo and Augustine, De civitate Dei XIV,28 and XV. *Studia Philonica Annual*, 3, 283–294.
van Oort, J. (1991). Jerusalem and Babylon: A Study into Augustine's *City of God* and the Sources of His Doctrine of the Two Cities. Leiden: Brill.

10 Books 15 & 16: Genesis, Paul, and Salvation History for the Citizens of God's City

JONATHAN P. YATES

Noted Augustine scholar J. H. S. Burleigh (d. 1985) once opined that Books 15–18 were "the least satisfactory section" of the entire *ciu. Dei*.[1] While acknowledging that these words are comparative not superlative, this chapter suggests that there are good reasons for disagreeing with Burleigh's assessment. Indeed, it contends that there is much to appreciate within this overtly "historical section" if one develops a sense for what Augustine is attempting within them.

To see Books 15 and 16 aright, one needs to recognize where they fall within the chronology of Augustine's life and theological career. By AD 420,[2] he had been thoughtfully reading the Apostle Paul for more than a quarter of a century.[3] And, by AD 420, he had completed the enormous interpretive compositions *Quaestiones in Heptateuchum* and *Locutiones in Heptateuchum*, projects which required him to make sense of the "pre-Advent" history of the people of God in light of the authoritative "post-Advent" revelations of the New Testament.[4] In other words, in Books 15 and 16, Augustine is not simply commenting on *Genesis*. Rather, having established the absolutely fundamental role that the events recorded in Genesis 3 played in (salvation) history in *ciu.*

[1] Burleigh 1949, p. 196. Cf. p.132 where Books 15–17 are called "somewhat tedious."

[2] According to van Oort 1991, p. 62, *ciu. Dei* 15–16, which very likely to date to AD 420, are among the most readily datable of *ciu. Dei*'s twenty-two books.

[3] Referred to by Augustine on some thirty occasions in *ciu. Dei* 15 and 16 as "the Apostle," Paul provided him with the necessary salvation-historical and theological frameworks for reading both Gen 4–8 (cf. Book 15) and the history of Israel from the Flood through the Patriarchs (cf. Book 16) as important chapters in the histories of the *ciuitas dei* and the *ciuitas terrena*. It follows that to truly appreciate Books 15 and 16 one must have a clear sense of the role that passages such as Rom 9, 1 Cor 7:4; 15:46; and Gal 4:22–31 – to name just four – played in determining these details.

[4] In attempting this, Augustine is heir to a tradition spanning back (at least) to Origen of Alexandria. As Tzamalikos 2007), pp. 83 and 92, observes, for Origen, "history *before* [the Incarnation] ... already had a teleological character: its course moved towards the advent of the Logos ... Once the Incarnation of the Logos took place, we know the meaning of movement in history thereafter" (emphasis in original; cf. 424 and 434).

Dei 14, books 15, and 16 go on to use Augustine's long-established Pauline "lens" to show how the rest of Genesis 4 through Gen 28:19, factor into that same history.[5] By any estimation, it is an enormous and exceedingly difficult task.

BOOK 15

In 15.1 Augustine lays out his plans for the remainder of *ciu. Dei*: "since enough has been said about the rise of [the] two cities . . . it seems to me that I should now undertake to trace the course that each has followed from the point at which the first two human beings began to have children down to the point at which humans will cease to have children" (*ciu. Dei* 15.1; Babcock, 2.139; CCSL 48.453).[6] Stated differently, Augustine's goal is to recount selectively the whole of human history. Less obvious, however, is the fact that this plan is actually driven by New Testament eschatological concerns. In claiming that he will trace human history until "humans will cease to have children," Augustine is alluding to Jesus's anti-Sadducean claim that "those who are considered worthy to attain to that age and the resurrection from the dead, neither marry nor are given in marriage; for they cannot even die anymore, because they are like angels, and are sons of God, being sons of the resurrection."[7] In the very next line, Augustine makes it plain that the course of the two cities necessarily "runs" through the present post-lapsarian age, clearly marked as it is by the physical death of the old and the sick and their replacement via children.

In the next paragraph, Augustine begins to discuss the specific destiny of individuals even as he maintains the two cities binary: Cain "belonged to the City of Men," while his brother Abel "belonged to the City of God." One might well expect that this clear distinction would propel Augustine into a textual commentary on the details of Gen 4. Instead, Augustine begins a theological commentary – via Paul and 1 Cor 15:46 – on the aforementioned binary which runs all the way through *ciu. Dei* 15.4.

In *ciu. Dei* 15.5, Augustine returns to his meditation on Cain, reminding his readers that "the first founder of the earthly city was a

[5] These ca. twenty-four chapters of Genesis are the focus of all of Book 15 and ca. 90 percent of Book 16. Although he was not a historian, Augustine does (anachronistically) qualify as a "historian of salvation" (cf. van Oort 2012, pp. 1–7).

[6] Other summaries of varying detail are available. The briefest occurs in Chan and Dupont 2016, pp. 55–78.

[7] Lk 20:35–36 (NASB); cf. Mt 22:29–31, Mk 12:24–25; and *ciu. Dei* 15.17; CCSL 48.479–480.

fratricide." Augustine then asserts that it was Cain's "envy" (*inuidentia*) that propelled him to murder Abel, "a citizen of the eternal city on pilgrimage on this earth."[8] Augustine never explains his conclusion regarding Cain's motivation; however, a few lines later he goes on to assert that "Cain's envy was ... the diabolical envy that the evil feel toward the good simply because they are good, while they themselves are evil" (*ciu. Dei* 15.5; Babcock, 2.143; CCSL 48.458). This envy is diabolical not only because it is evil *in se*, but also because it reflects Satan's "envy" at not being accorded the place occupied by God himself.[9] It is thus unsurprising to find Augustine attributing to the founder of the earthly city the same fundamental characteristic that marked Satan, that city's patron, or claiming that Cain's hatred was ultimately as baseless and irrational as were the sins of Satan and Adam.

Ciu. Dei 15.8 represents a major break in Augustine's narrative. *Ciu. Dei* 15.6–7 include a second round of theological commentary on Cain and Abel and what they respectively signify. But in 15.8, Augustine moves on to Genesis 5 and takes up the challenge of defending "the historical record so that scripture will not seem incredible" (*incredibilis*) in its rehearsal of the generations of each line as they descended from Cain and Seth, the one who replaced Abel as the progenitor of the City of God (cf. Gen 4:25).[10] Conspicuous throughout this section is Augustine's insistence that the Christian sacred texts are inspired. According to Augustine, the aim of the author of *Genesis* "was simply to arrive at Abraham through a succession of specified generations ... and then to go on from Abraham's seed to the people of God." Despite this restricted aim, we can rest assured that "the Holy Spirit was at work" in Genesis's author (*ciu. Dei* 15.8; Babcock, 2.148; CCSL 48.463). This is followed by a multi-chapter digression on the significance of the differences between the Hebrew textual tradition and that of the Greek, the chief concern of which is to explain the manifest differences in the genealogies of the earliest generations.

In *ciu. Dei* 15.15, despite having spilled much ink in its consideration, Augustine concludes that any speculation regarding the

[8] Note that Gen 4:5 does not specify that Cain's anger was rooted in "envy" or anything else. On the contrary, all we know is that "for Cain and for his offering [God] had no regard. So Cain became very angry and his countenance fell." However plausible the inference that Cain was overcome by envy may be, it is no more than that.

[9] Cf. *Gn. litt.* 11.14–16 (CSEL 28.346–349), where both the Devil's pride and envy are discussed. There Augustine concludes that the former begets the latter and, thus, that pride caused the Devil's "fall."

[10] In *ciu. Dei* 15, Seth is referenced by name almost three dozen times.

possibility that those who lived for hundreds of years might have some sort of delay in their "sexual maturity" (*serae pubertatis*) – a theory invoked by some to explain why *Genesis* assigned no children to some antediluvians until they are past 100 years of age – as an "obscure and unnecessary question" (*ciu. Dei* 15.15; Babcock, 2.161; CCSL 48.476).[11]

More significant for Augustine's defense of Genesis's reliability is the principle that it should not be read as a comprehensive account of every person born in each generation. The text's selectivity proves that its two authors – one divine and one human – intentionally adopted a salvation-historical approach to their chronicle.[12] Augustine plausibly asserts that "the Spirit of God did not wish to mark the ages prior to the flood by the generations of the earthly city ... [but, rather,] ... to mark them by the generations of the heavenly city, as more worthy of being recorded and remembered." At this point he also claims that "the aim of the writer of the sacred history was to mark the passage of time through the successive generations down to the birth and life of Noah," but, in doing so, he only listed "those who came in the relevant line of descent," not necessarily the firstborn (*ciu. Dei* 15.15; Babcock, 2.160–61; CCSL 48.475–476).

In *ciu. Dei* 15.16, Augustine acknowledges that the earliest generations of Genesis, if they are to be regarded as historical in any sense, must have been guilty of a major ethical impropriety: "since there were no other human beings but the children of [Adam and Eve], men took their sisters as wives." While this practice is "wholly reprehensible" (*damnabilius*) and "deeply repulsive" (*sic auersetur*) Augustine blunts this criticism by invoking what amounts to an evolutionary model for ethics: this practice "was fully respectable at that time, when necessity compelled it" (*ciu. Dei* 15.16; Babcock 2.162–63; CCSL 48.477–478).[13]

In *ciu. Dei* 15.17–20, Augustine reverts back to Seth and Cain and to their respective progenies, including a citation of Gen 4:18–22, which

[11] "*obscura et non necessaria quaestio*;" e.g. Gen 5:6–7 implies that Seth was 105 before having any children.

[12] For a brief discussion of the intersection of "myth" and "history" in the ancient mind and of how that mind did "not have a line between myth and history," see Longman III and Walton 2019, pp. 17–20.

[13] "*nec essent ulli homines, nisi qui ex illis duobus nati fuissent: uiri sorores suas coniuges acceperunt.*" Overlooked here by Augustine is how Cain, once exiled, settled in "Nod" and, apparently, took a wife from there (cf. Gen 4:16–17). Also conspicuous by its absence is any reference to Abraham (cf. Gen 12 and 20, esp. 20:12) taking his half-sister as his wife, much less that he did so in an age when such was not a "necessity." At *ciu. Dei* 16.36 (CCSL 48.540–541) Augustine acknowledges that Isaac, who in Gen 26:7 called his wife his sister, "did what his

records the first few generations of Cain's line, before opining that his city "has both its beginning and its end on earth, where there is no hope of anything more than can be seen in this world." By contrast, the City of God, which, again, is represented by Seth's line, lives "in hope" (*in spe*) and is "born of faith in the resurrection of Christ" (*ciu. Dei* 15.17–18; Babcock 2.165; CCSL 48.480).

In *ciu. Dei* 15.20, Augustine again addresses the significance of Cain's line in terms of authorial intent: the main reason that the writer recorded Cain's line only down to the time of the flood is that he wanted to show how "the whole race of the earthly city was wiped out" – at least temporarily (*ciu. Dei* 15.20; Babcock, 2.167; CCSL 48.482).[14]

Toward the end of this same chapter, Augustine makes a brief excursus in numerology. A chief claim here is based on the facts that, according to *Genesis*, Cain's line consists in seven generations, but the last, that of Lamech, also includes the names of four of Lamech's children, three of his sons and one daughter, bringing the total "number" of Cain's line to eleven. Presupposing that this cannot have been accidental, Augustine explains its significance by reminding his readers that eleven is "a number which signifies sin" (*quo significator peccatum*). Eleven signifies sin "since the law is designated by the number ten (from which stems the well-known Decalogue), the number eleven – because it goes beyond ten – obviously signifies the transgression of the law, and thus signifies sin" (*ciu. Dei* 15.20; Babcock, 2.170; CCSL 48.485).[15]

Book 15's last thematic break occurs at *ciu. Dei* 15.21. Over the course of its final seven chapters, two main topics are introduced and discussed.[16] In *ciu. Dei* 15.22–23 and the first portion of 15.24, Augustine takes up the notoriously difficult questions surrounding both the identity and the significance of the *Nephilim* that are mentioned in

father had done," but tones down Isaac's deed by observing that Rebekah was his "kinswoman, related to him by blood on both his father's and his mother's side." Cf. also *ciu. Dei* 16.19 and 16.30 (CCSL 48.522 and 535) as well as the discussion below.

14 "*Vsque ad diluuium, quo totum illud genus terrenae ciuitatis absumptum est.*" But Augustine immediately notes that the earthly city was reestablished from among the sons of Noah and, indeed, "cannot finally cease to exist until the end of the world."

15 Babcock observes that a very similar numerological discussion of the number eleven occurs in Augustine's *s.* 83.7 (Hill, III/3.385).

16 Despite citing Gen 5:1–2, *ciu. Dei* 15.21 is fundamentally a theological commentary. Here Augustine repeatedly asserts that "calling upon God," the somewhat enigmatic phrase found in Gen 4:26, is actually "the whole . . . and supreme business of the City of God . . . while it is on pilgrimage in this world." How this can be so is made clear via an elegant summary of Augustine's post-lapsarian anthropology: this city must "learn not to . . . trust in its own freedom of will," but to rely upon "God's help" (*diuino adiutorio*), the *sine qua non* for doing good.

Gen 6:1–4. Two notable aspects of Augustine's approach to this *crux interpretum* are: (1) to argue that, whatever the *Nephilim* were, they were human beings and (2) to delimit his discussion of their identity and significance by confining himself to the data made available in the canonical scriptures.

Book 15's final three plus chapters deal with Gen 6:5–6:20 and the impact of the Great Flood. As he has done consistently in Book 15, Augustine first discusses the event's historicity. Just like the period marked by the presence of the *Nephilim*, the Flood and all its attendant details actually happened in time and in history. However, to make that claim is to do no more than to scratch the surface of why it was included in *Genesis*. The Flood was first and foremost divine judgment upon humankind's sin. God's dispassionate anger (*ira Dei*), which, according to Augustine, is only an idiomatic expression included for the sake of the reader's comprehension, is what brought the Flood about.[17] Likewise, in keeping with the prior Christian tradition, Augustine, assigns figurative significance to both the ark's inhabitants, who represent the City of God on pilgrimage in this world, and to the ark itself, which represents the church.[18] Significantly, much of *ciu. Dei* 15.26 and 15.27 are dedicated to explaining how any figurative interpretation that is assigned to these details "must not be at odds with the rule of faith" (*ciu. Dei* 15.26; Babcock, 2.179; CCSL 48.494), and to highlighting what is a fundamental Christian exegetical principle for Augustine: before beginning the work of interpreting, one must believe "that the account was committed to memory and to writing for a wise purpose, that the events actually took place, that they signify something beyond themselves, and that what they signify pertains to prefiguring the church" (*ciu. Dei* 15.27; Babcock, 2.183; CCSL 48.497).

BOOK 16

In the very last lines of Book 16, Augustine recounts what he thinks he has accomplished in Books 15 and 16: "Just as the previous book covered that first age in the course followed by the City of God, so the present book covers the second and the third ages; and in this third

[17] *ciu. Dei* 15.25; Babcock, 2.178; CCSL 48.493. Here, Augustine explicitly notes that God's anger was "not any passionate upset of [God's] mind" (*non perturbation animi eius*).

[18] Cf. 1 Pet. 3:18–22. For more on the reception of this passage in Augustine and his Latin predecessors, see Yates 2018, pp. 492–510.

age ... the yoke of the law was imposed, an abundance of sins appeared, and the earthly kingdom [of Israel] had its beginning" (*ciu. Dei* 16.43; Babcock, 2.236; CCSL 48.550). Not immediately clear here is what Augustine means by "age" and how it is he intends to divide one from another. However, the careful reader will remember that, back in *ciu. Dei* 15.24, Augustine informed her that the interpretive key that he is following is actually an analogy: he is explaining the ages that divide the histories of the two cities by comparing it to a single human life.[19] For Augustine, the first three stages of life are: infancy, adolescence, and (young) adulthood. And these three life phases correspond to the three "key eras of time" that ran "from Adam to Noah," "from Noah to Abraham," and "from Abraham to [King] David" (*ciu. Dei* 16.24; Babcock, 2.213). If we plot these three eras onto the canonical biblical books, data for the first era is supplied by Gen 1–9,[20] for the second by Gen 10–11,[21] and for the third by (parts of) no less than a dozen books, from Gen 12 through 1 Chron 29:28.[22]

Interestingly, Augustine's narrative treatment in Book 16 is inversely proportional to the above schema. That is, in Book 16, he uses no less than eleven chapters to describe the "second age" that ran from Noah to Abraham – even though this is covered by *Genesis* in just two short chapters – and some twenty-three chapters discussing Abraham, whose story is, as noted above, the primary aim of the authors of *Genesis*. The lives of Isaac, Jacob and Esau, and Abraham's great-grandson Joseph are dealt with in just eight chapters, and the entire history of Israel from her enslavement in Egypt to the pinnacle of the monarchy under David are covered in a single chapter that requires less than three pages in English translation (cf. *ciu. Dei* 16.43).

In fact, 16.43 begins with "the death of ... Joseph" at the age of 110 in the land of Egypt (cf. Gen 50:26). Remarkably, both the life of Moses prior to the Exodus, including the episode of the ten plagues, the Exodus itself, and the Israelites' forty years in the desert are treated in one paragraph each. Then the entire history of Israel under Joshua and

19 At 2.213 and n.94, Babcock correctly notes that this "division of ages, in which biblical eras correspond to periods of human life, is frequent in Augustine." The earliest occurrence is in *Gn. adu. Man.* 1.23.35–37 (PL 34.190–191), a passage securely dated to the late 380s.

20 Noah is introduced as the son of Lamech in Gen 5:29; his death – at 950 years of age – is recorded in Gen 9:29.

21 Technically, Abraham, whose name at the time was Abram, first appears in Gen 11:26 as one of the sons of Terah. Abram's call by God is not recorded until Gen 12:1.

22 David's death is also recorded in 1 Kgs 2:10.

the Judges is covered in just seventeen (Latin) lines. However, in them Augustine does go out of his way to comment that the Israelites' "victories came to them not so much on account of the merits of the Hebrew people as on account of the sins of the peoples they defeated," and that, under the Judges, "success and failure in war alternated according to the sins of the people and the mercy of God" (*ciu. Dei* 16.43; Babcock, 2.235; CCSL 48.549). Implicit here is the Augustinian vision of God's character and, in particular, the way in which God's grace is always the *sine qua non* whenever good is manifested in the world.

Reverting to the beginning of Book 16, we find a similar theological concern dominant. Augustine begins by asking a question that he admits is difficult to answer unequivocally in light of the biblical record: Was the history of the City of God continuous, or was it occasionally interrupted by "intervening periods of ungodliness" (*intercurrentibus impietatis interrupta temporibus*) (*ciu. Dei* 16.1; Babcock, 2.184; see also CCSL 48.498)? He concludes that, with the possible exceptions of Noah's two sons, Shem and Japheth, "we find no one in the canonical books until Abraham whose piety is clearly proclaimed by the divine writings" (*ciu. Dei* 16.1; Babcock, 2.185; CCSL 48.498).[23] At the same time, Augustine is convinced that all the significant events from Noah's post-diluvian life as recorded in Gen 9:20–27 – including his drunkenness and the exposure of his "nakedness" by Ham, the father of Canaan – "are heavy with prophetic meanings and screened with prophetic veils" (*ciu. Dei* 16.1; Babcock, 2.185; CCSL 48.498).

Ciu. Dei 16.2 is important because it contains another exegetical principle. Having concluded his discussion of the prophetic meanings of Gen 9 and of the names of Noah's sons, Augustine explains his procedure:

> We search out these hidden meanings of Divine Scripture … always holding faithfully to the certainty that these things … are to be referred to … Christ and his Church, which is the City of God. From the very beginning of the human race there have been prophetic anticipations of that city … [and] whatever is said here

[23] "*in canonicis libris … non inuenimus usque Abraham cuiusquam pietatem euidenti diuino eloquio praedicatam.*"

> about those who are not citizens of that city is said [so] that the City of God may gain profit or prominence by comparison with its opposite.
>
> (*ciu. Dei* 16.2; Babcock, 2.187; CCSL 48.500–501)

The importance of this principle for this section (and, indeed, for almost all of Augustine's interactions with the Old Testament) can hardly be overstated.[24] Its acceptance is precisely what transforms the Bible from an ancient book reflective of the history and beliefs of just one of many ancient Mediterranean cultures into a book that both defines and guides the faithful, that is, the genuine members of the City of God, in all ages, including the present one.

Ciu. Dei 16.4 opens with an extended quotation from Gen 11 that exhausts what the author desired to report about the infamous incident at Babel and that purports to explain how human languages came to be so wildly diverse. Augustine's comments on Gen 11:1–9 extends through 16.7. For him, these verses offer more than just a mythological explanation; they record an historical event of profound theological and exegetical import.[25]

Augustine begins by asking "What could empty human presumption have achieved?" and "What harm … could any act of spiritual and physical pride do to God, no matter how high it might aim?" (*ciu. Dei* 16.4; Babcock, 2.192; CCSL 48.505). In other words, what could the builders of Babel have been thinking? Could they seriously have believed that their labors would somehow close the ontological gap between themselves and God?

Augustine begins his answer by linking Gen 11:1–9 with 10:8–10.[26] He notes that the latter asserts that Nimrod, a grandson of Ham, was a king in "Babel … in the land of Shinar," and a major instigator of the

[24] Although not explicit, Augustine seems to base this exegetical principle (and, by extension, portions of his view on [salvation] history) upon 1 Cor 10:11: "these things happened … as an example, and … were written for our instruction, upon whom the ends of the ages have come" (NASB).

[25] Augustine's chief concern is with the ambiguity of the Greek preposition "ἐναντίον" that occurs in LXX manuscripts of Gen 10:9. It can mean both "in the presence of" and "on the other side of." By extension, the latter can signify hostility or antagonism. For Augustine, Gen 10:9 conveys Nimrod's hostility to God. This, in turn, compels the conclusion that Nimrod's tower "signified … his own ungodly pride."

[26] Here, Augustine invokes *recapitulatio*, a technique that allows him to deal with tensions created by the fact that the Bible occasionally uses an order of composition that does not necessarily reflect the chronological sequence in which events actually happened. For another discussion of this exegetical technique, which includes the explicit admission that the Donatist Tyconius is his source, see *doc. Chr.* 3.36.52–54 (Hill I/11.194–196; CCSL 32.111–114). For analysis, see Denecker 2017, pp. 99–101; cf. also the discussion of *ciu. Dei* 16.15 below.

tower at Babel. Not unlike Cain, and by extension, Satan, Nimrod, because he wanted the tower, was guilty of "ungodly pride" (*impia ... superbia*) that deserved punishment even though his plan ultimately failed. God punished Nimrod and his conspirators by dividing their languages and scattering them across their lands. Exactly how God did this remains mysterious: in this case, his "means are hidden from us and beyond our understanding" (*ciu. Dei* 16.4; Babcock, 2.192; CCSL 48.505).

Significantly, *ciu. Dei* 16.8 includes Augustine's definition of a human being. In context, his concern is not with the biblical record *per se* but, rather, with reports from various sources that so-called "monstrous" races of human beings exist and that they might even be descended from Noah's sons.[27] While he dismisses belief in such races as probably needless, he does take this opportunity to assert that anyone who is human, that is, anyone who is born "as a rational and mortal being" (*animal rationale mortale*) necessarily "derives from [Adam] the original, first-created man" (*ciu. Dei* 16.8; Babcock, 2.195; CCSL 48.509–510).[28] Although the existence of such beings is never explicitly attributed to the effects of Original Sin, the implicit rationale for this assertion seems to be the effort to guarantee that, whatever position one adopts on the question of "monstrous" races, one also holds that, without exception, anyone who is human is necessarily subject to Adam's sin and, thus, stands in need of redemption by Christ.

Ciu. Dei 16.9 addresses what Augustine calls "the fable of the antipodes." This fable asserts that, even if the earth is round – a detail that Augustine does not contest – there are human beings who live on its opposite side. Although skeptical about the fable, Augustine's discussion contains yet another argument for the trustworthiness of the Christian scriptures: "there is no falsehood of any sort in Scripture, which proves that it is reliable in its narration of past events by virtue of the fact that its predictions of future events have been fulfilled" (*ciu. Dei* 16.9; Babcock, 2.197; CCSL 48.510).

[27] Examples of such races include: cyclopes, those without a mouth, pygmies, those with just one straight leg (aka "skiopods"), those without a neck, the dog-headed (also known as "cynocephali"), those with crescent-shaped feet, the androgynous or hermaphrodites, and, apparently, what are sometimes referred to as Siamese twins.

[28] "*ex illo uno protoplasto originem.*" The notion that all human beings, no matter where they live and what they look like, must be descended from Adam is repeated no less than three times in this relatively brief chapter. Likewise, the definition of human as "rational and mortal" is also repeated in this context. Babcock, 2.198 and n.50, notes that this "definition of the human person is consistently [maintained] through his writings," before providing five examples, the earliest being 1.27.52 of *mor.* (Teske I/19.55; PL 32.1332), which, having been started sometime in AD 387, is probably Augustine's earliest Christian composition.

Of even greater concern than the antipode fable is the lingering question of whether, among the various peoples that *did* populate the earth, it is possible to continuously trace "the City of God in its pilgrimage on earth" (*in terris peregrinantem*) among them. This issue, along with the related question of whether or not ancient Hebrew,[29] which Augustine believes to have been the only language spoken by ante-diluvian humans, was affected by God's punishment for Babel, dominates *ciu. Dei* 16.10–11.

Augustine believes that it is indeed possible to continuously trace the City of God in the history of the peoples who lived between the day that Noah emerged from the ark and the day that Abram/Abraham was called by God.[30] Here he repeats the claim that "we must follow the line of descent from Shem" if we wish to see with certainty God's redemptive work among the human race (*ciu. Dei* 16.10; Babcock, 2.198; CCSL 48.511). Augustine is open to the idea there may well have been descendants of Shem or Japheth who "held God in contempt" (*fuerunt contemptores Dei*), just as there may well have been descendants of Ham (and Canaan) "who genuinely worshiped God" (*cultores Dei*). And this "more credible idea," in turn, leads him to conclude that any (salvation) history worthy of attribution to the God of the Bible "must hold that there was never a time when the world lacked both kinds of people" (*ciu. Dei* 16.10; Babcock, 2.199; CCSL 48.512).

Ciu. Dei 16.11 includes the assumptions that before the flood all human beings spoke the same language (cf. Gen 11:1) and that that unifying language was ancient Hebrew. Indeed, the people of God, who, at this juncture were represented by the household of Heber (or Eber; cf. Gen 10:21), a son of Shem who lent his name to the Hebrew language, "should certainly have been exempt from that punishment." Heber's obedience allowed Hebrew to survive and that tongue's continuation, in turn, generated a social and theological oasis in which "the punishment imposed by the change of languages did not apply" (*ciu. Dei* 16.11; Babcock, 2.201; CCSL 48.514).

We meet Abram for the first time at *ciu. Dei* 16.12; he remains the book's primary subject for the next twenty-three chapters, or for almost

[29] For explanation of Augustine's advocacy for a "Hebrew-centered" model, which proves foundational for later ages of Western thought on language history, see Denecker 2017, pp. 77–82, 93–94.

[30] In Gen 17:5, God changed Abram's name to Abraham because God "made him the father of a multitude of nations." Cf. the discussion of *ciu. Dei* 16.26 below.

half of Book 16.[31] This chapter's link to the previous eleven is the issue of the City of God's continuity within the greater scheme of (salvation) history. Without obvious biblical support,[32] Augustine links Abraham to Noah by praising the piety of Abraham's father Terah. In his view, "only in the household of Terah ... did the Hebrew language survive ... [and] the worship of the one true God continue." Moreover, Terah's piety was such that, just as Noah's household had survived a literal flood inside the ark, so also Terah's household "endured as the one place in which the tender planting (*plantatio*) of the City of God was kept safe" amidst an equally dangerous "flood of superstitions" (*diluuio ... superstitionum*) (*ciu. Dei* 16.12; Babcock, 2.203; CCSL 48.516). Augustine even goes so far as to claim that "the household of Terah suffered persecution at the hands of the Chaldeans for their true piety in worshipping the one true God" (*ciu. Dei* 16.13; Babcock, 2.204; CCSL 48.517).[33]

In 16.15, Augustine again invokes the exegetical principle of recapitulation in order to avoid "an insoluble problem" (*ciu. Dei* 16.15; Babcock, 2.205; CCSL 48.518). This time, his immediate concern is to explain why *Genesis* records that Terah was seventy years old at Abram's birth (cf. 11:26), that Terah died at age 205 (cf. 11:32), but only later reports that Abram was seventy-five when he departed Haran for Canaan (cf. 12:4–5). Given Gen 11:32, Terah must have been alive – albeit 145 years old – and in Haran when the events of Gen 12:1–9 came to pass. The sections of 16.16–21 are oriented around the

31 Augustine's emphasis on Abraham, while thoroughly Pauline, also indicates just how theologically driven his reading was. For an overview of the role that Abraham played in Augustine's thought across his ecclesiastical career, see Mayer et al. 1986; s.v. "Abraham," by C. Mayer. L. Patterson (1967, p. 121) summarizes that, according to *ciu. Dei*, with Abraham, "there began to appear a spiritual succession of those who, recognizing the real intentions of God, looked forward in faith to a fulfillment of the coming of that city of which Jerusalem could only be an image."

32 Terah is mentioned by name just six times in Gen 11:24–32.

33 "*domum Tharae persecutionem passam fuisse a Chaldaeis pro uera pietate, qua unus et uerus ab eis colebatur Deus.*" Just prior to his comment on the persecution, Augustine cites Judith 5:5–9, verses that do not mention Terah specifically. *Judith* does, however, mention the "descendants of the Chaldeans" who were "told by God to go to the land of Canaan." While this could certainly include Terah, we know from Gen 11:31–32 that Terah, despite intending to leave Ur for Canaan, died in Haran, a detail that at least calls Terah's obedience to God's command into question. *Judith* was deemed canonical for Augustine (and all North African Christians) at the synod of Hippo held in AD 393 and at two Councils of Carthage held in AD 397 and AD 418, respectively. Cf. *doctr. chr.* 2.8.13 (CCSL 32: 39–40), where the contents of Augustine's biblical canon are listed.

three (according to Augustine's reckoning) promises that God made to Abram in Gen 12:1–3, 12:7, and 13:14–17, respectively. These are crucial for understanding Abram's import for the history of the City of God because, in them, "the oracles of ... the one true God ... begin to appear more clearly, oracles that have to do with the godly people (*populo piorum*) that prophetic authority foretold" (*ciu. Dei* 16.16; Babcock, 2.207; CCSL 48.520).

God's first promise is fivefold. God will: make Abram "a great nation"; "bless" him; "make [his] name great"; "bless those who bless" him; and make him a source of blessing for "all the tribes of the earth." Following Paul (cf. Gal 3:7–9), Augustine asserts that the most significant of these is the last. This is because it refers not to Abram's literal progeny, but to his "spiritual seed, through which he is the father not just ... of the Israelites but of all the peoples that follow in the footsteps of his faith" (*ciu. Dei* 16.16; Babcock, 2.207; CCSL 48.520).

God's second promise, which also involves a prophecy for Abram's "seed," is accorded a brief clarification. In this case, "seed" refers only to the literal Israelites who "would possess the land" (*ciu. Dei* 16.18; Babcock, 2.208; CCSL 48.522). Augustine devotes the rest of *ciu. Dei* 16.19 to Abram's famine-induced sojourn into Egypt (cf. Gen 12:10–16). Here, as in *ciu. Dei* 16.30,[34] Augustine treats Abram's decision to identify Sarai as his sister, not his wife, and the resulting deception of the Egyptians. Augustine's chief concern is to exonerate Abram from any charge of intentional deception. Abram's reference to his sister Sarai emphatically "was not a lie, for she was also that, since she was closely related to him by blood." Moreover, according to Augustine, Abram remained guiltless since he "did not deny" that she was his wife, but "simply kept quiet about it" (*ciu. Dei* 16.19; Babcock, 2.208–9; CCSL 48.522). Given that a straightforward reading of Gen 12:10–20 compels the conclusion that, at a minimum, Abram had waivered in his faith both in God's promises and in God's ability to deliver him from danger, the reader is not expecting Augustine to claim that Abram was in fact acting in faith. Nevertheless, Augustine strikes an apologetic tone by asserting that Abram "committed the defense of his wife's chastity to God, and ... took precautions against human treachery. For, if he

[34] *ciu. Dei* 16.30; Babcock, 2.221; CCSL 48.535: "at Gerar, Abraham did the same thing ... that he had done in Egypt to protect his wife; ... [and] when [Abimelech] upbraided him for not saying that she was his wife and for calling her his sister, Abraham revealed his fears and then added, 'Besides, she is indeed my sister, my father's daughter, but not my mother's.' For she was Abraham's sister by his father, through whom she was his kinswoman." Cf. Gen 20 and 26:6–11.

had not taken measures to guard against danger so far as possible, he would have been tempting God rather than putting his hope in God," a hope "vindicated by the outcome" (*ciu. Dei* 16.19; Babcock, 2.209; CCSL 48.522).

God's third promise includes the gift of the Promised Land to Abraham's seed forever. Adjunct to this promise is the idea that God will make the number of that seed "like the sands of the earth." Augustine claims that the referent to this use of the word "seed" is not entirely clear in that it could refer to his literal descendants or, if taken in a Pauline sense,[35] it could refer to his spiritual descendants or those who regard Abram to be their father in the faith. In either case, Augustine is certain that the comparison with grains of sand is "an instance of the figure of … hyperbole (*hyperbolen*), which is definitely … [not] literal" (*non propria*), which is used with regularity in the Bible and "occurs when what is said is far more sweeping than what the statement actually means" (*ciu. Dei* 16.21; Babcock, 2.210; CCSL 48.523). Not only does this reading of Gen 13:16 make the most sense, it also accords with Augustine's "remnant" vision for the actual number of God's elect.[36] He readily admits that he does not know the number of the elect, but he is certain that "in comparison with the multitude of the ungodly" the elect are not "more than a mere few" (*ciu. Dei* 16.21; Babcock, 2.210; CCSL 48.524).

Ciu. Dei 16.22 and 16.23 discuss important events from Abram's life including: his settlement in Hebron (Gen 13:18); his intervention in a war between several local kings in order to liberate his nephew Lot (Gen 14:12–16); his interaction with the priest Melchizedek (Gen 14:17–20); and the reiteration of the promise that his seed will be quasi-limitless (Gen 15:1–5). Augustine is quick to note that the reiteration is followed by the assertion that proved crucial to Paul: "Then [Abram] believed … and [God] reckoned it to him as righteousness" (cf. Gen 15:6).[37] According to Augustine, Paul's aim "was to commend God's grace," "to keep the circumcised from boasting and to keep them from refusing to admit uncircumcised peoples to faith in Christ," since, at this point, Abram, by God's grace, clearly possessed salvific faith, despite the fact that his circumcision was yet future (*ciu. Dei* 16.23; Babcock, 2.212; CCSL 48.525).

[35] Cf. Rom 4:9–18; 9:6–8; Gal 3:7–9; and 3:29.

[36] Cf. Rom 9:27.

[37] For Paul's own citations of Gen 15:6, see Rom 4:3 and Gal 3:6.

Ciu. Dei 16.24 continues the discussion of Abraham's character. Augustine specifically addresses the fact that, when God spoke to Abraham in a vision, Abraham was bold enough to ask God clarifying questions (cf. Gen 25:8). According to Augustine, these questions did not signal any "failure of faith" on Abraham's part (*non eum in fide defecisse*). On the contrary, it increased the patriarch's status and earned him a comparison with the Virgin Mary, who, according to Luke, asked questions, not because she was uncertain *that* what had been prophesied would actually happen, but merely in order to find out "*how* it would happen" (emphasis added). 16.24 also reminds the reader of Abraham's position within Augustine's schema of (salvation) history: the third age (*tertiam aetatem*) runs from Abraham to David and is the period in which the Israelite people collectively "reached adulthood" (*adoleuit*) (*ciu. Dei* 16.24; Babcock, 2.213; CCSL 48.527).

Contemporary readers might dismiss *ciu. Dei* 16.25 as special pleading on Augustine's part. His intent is to establish Abraham's innocence in having a sexual relationship with Hagar, the slave of his wife Sarah (cf. Gen. 16).[38] In the space of just a few lines, Augustine insists that "Abraham is by no means to be branded a criminal (*crimen*) with regard to this concubine"; that he did not "use her to gratify his lust" (*non ad explendam libidinem*); that "there is no lascivious desire (*cupido lasciuiae*) here"; that "guilty sensuality" (*culpae luxus*) was totally absent; and that "with Hagar, [Abraham was] not satisfying his own pleasure but rather obeying his wife's will" (*ciu. Dei* 16.25; Babcock, 2.215; CCSL 48.529). Augustine's description then culminates in unabashed praise: "What a man, who treated women in a manly way – his wife with honor, his maidservant out of obedience, and no one immodestly!" (*ciu. Dei* 16.25; Babcock, 2.215; CCSL 48.529).[39] Interestingly, Augustine's defense also incorporates several references to Paul.[40]

[38] Augustine frequently defends this aspect of Abraham's conduct. Cf., e.g. *ciu. Dei* 15.2 (discussed above), *c. Faust.* 22.30–32, and *s. dom. m.* 1.16.49. For an interesting rebuke of anyone who might appeal to Abraham's activities with Hagar "as an example in his own defense" (*in exemplum defensionis*), see *c. Faust* 22.25 (Teske I/20:316–317; CSEL 25.1.619–620). For Augustine's evolving (if generally consistent) views on the biblical patriarchs' sexual practices, see Hunter 2002b, pp. 317–335, esp. pp. 329–325, which discuss Augustine's claims from c. AD 410 onward.

[39] *"O uirum uiriliter utentem feminis, coniuge temperanter, ancilla obtemperanter, nulla intemperanter!"*

[40] Cf., e.g. Babcock, 2.212; CCSL 48.525. Also prominent in this context is Gal 4:21–31, which is first referenced at *ciu. Dei* 15.2 and occurs *passim* in Book 16. Cf. van Oort 1991, p. 313 and n.648. Cf. also Helleman 2013, p. 107: "On the basis of the Pauline allegory in *Galatians* 4, [Augustine] recognizes Sarah as 'our mother'. With a fifth

For example, just after asserting that Abraham's choice was rooted in his desire to obey Sarah, he cites 1 Cor 7:4 ("the husband does not have authority over his own body, but the wife does") in order to justify their relational dynamic. Remarkable for their absence in Augustine's comments are any consideration: (a) of Hagar's views on this arrangement, especially since, technically, she too was Abraham's wife (cf. Gen 16:3) and (b) that Abraham's complicity amounted to disobedience to God since he knew well that God's promise would be fulfilled via Sarah.

Like *ciu. Dei* 16.25, 16.26 begins with a substantial quotation of the biblical text: the reader is supplied with all of Gen 17:1–21, a passage which reaffirms God's covenant with Abram while also announcing that both Abram and Sarai would undergo a name change – from Abram to Abraham and from Sarai to Sarah, respectively[41] – and that the sign of God's covenant with Abraham will be circumcision, both for him and for all of his covenant-continuing descendants. Noteworthy is that Augustine's comments on this passage begin by distinguishing between "grace" and "nature": once again following Paul (cf. Rom 9:9 and Gal 4:23), Augustine asserts that "in Isaac ... the son of the promise ... grace is signified, not nature" precisely because of the miraculous circumstances under which Isaac was conceived and delivered into the world. For Augustine, in Isaac's existence, God's "grace is recognized the more clearly" (*euidentius intellegitur*) precisely because it is "when nature has failed ... that God's work is clear." Augustine then asserts that circumcision signifies "the renewal of nature by the removal of old age," even as its performance upon an eight-day-old child signifies Christ, who rose again on the eighth day (*ciu. Dei* 16.26; Babcock, 2.217; CCSL 48.530–531).

Lest the reader critique this reading of Genesis 17 via Paul and Christ's resurrection as illegitimate, Augustine quickly invokes an exegetical principle that had been a part of his repertoire for some twenty years:[42] "the names of the parents are changed; everything

century work like the *De civitate Dei* we might expect Mary, as the mother of Jesus, to be recognized as mother of the church, but ... [here] ... that role is taken by Sarah."

41 Cf. 16.28 (CCSL 48.533) where, after citing Gen 17:5b–6 and 17:16 together, Augustine returns to the meaning of Abraham's and Sarah's name change (though his comments remain only partially correct) and a further meditation on the miraculous nature of their ability to conceive.

42 See *cat. rud.* 4.8 (trans. Canning, *Instructing Beginners in the Faith*, The Augustine Series, vol. 5 [Hyde Park, NY: New City Press, 2006], p. 70): "in the Old Testament is concealed the New, and in the New Testament is revealed the Old." *Cat. rud.* was probably completed c. AD 400 (though some place it in 403). Cf. also *c. Faust.* 15.2,

rings with newness; and the new covenant is veiled in the old. For what else is that which is called the Old Testament but the hidden form of the New? And what else is that which is called the New Testament but the revealed form of the Old?" (*ciu. Dei* 16.26; Babcock, 2.217; CCSL 48.531).

Unlike the immediately preceding chapters, *ciu. Dei* 16.27 focuses entirely on Gen 17:14, which, in part, reads: "an uncircumcised male ... shall be cut off from his people; he has broken my covenant" (NASB). Augustine focuses on this verse since some readers might be disturbed by the apparent injustice of "cutting off" an eight-day-old infant from his people when the child was powerless to decide for himself. Augustine's solution again invokes Paul: after alluding to Rom 5:12 and citing Rom 4:15,[43] Augustine concludes that the only way that this "cutting off" could possibly be just is if the doctrine of original sin is true. He is convinced that "even infants ... have all broken God's covenant in that one man in whom all have sinned," and that "it would still be unjust for the soul of the uncircumcised infant to perish ... apart from his guilt due to original sin" (*ciu. Dei* 16.27; Babcock, 2.217–18; CCSL 48.531–532).

Ciu. Dei 16.29 and 30 selectively cover portions of Genesis 18 and 19. Genesis 18 records God's appearance to Abraham at the oaks of Mamre, God's announcement of Sarah's pending conception and delivery of Isaac, God's plan to destroy Sodom and Gomorrah, and Abraham's attempt to stay God's hand by negotiating with him regarding the requisite number of righteous people that these cities would have to contain for God to forestall judgement. Genesis 19 records the ultimate destruction of Sodom and Gomorrah and God's (partially successful) attempt to spare Lot, his wife, and his daughters.

The only detail from Genesis 18 that attracts Augustine's attention is God's manifestation to Abraham via three angels. While he is convinced that this was a genuine visitation of God since "these men were angels" (*ciu. Dei* 16.29; Babcock, 2.220; CCSL 48.534),[44] Augustine is keen to clarify that this manifestation in no way compromised God's immutability.

which probably dates to AD 408–AD 410, *ep.* 157.13–14, which was written ca. 414–415, and *qu.* 2.73, which immediately predates *ciu. Dei* 15–16 (as discussed on p. 188 above).

[43] Rom 4:15 says: "For the Law brings about wrath, but where there is no law, there also is no violation" (NASB).

[44] "*dubitandum non est angelos fuisse.*"

When he turns to Genesis 19, Augustine is unequivocal regarding why God's judgment fell upon Sodom and Gomorrah: the inhabitants of these cities were judged for their sexual habits, not for their lack of hospitality, a failure that Augustine does not mention when discussing their situation.[45] According to his reading:

> It was a place where sex between men had become so customary that it enjoyed the same license that the laws ordinarily give to other practices. But their punishment was also a precursor of the divine judgement to come. For what does it mean that those who were being delivered by the angels were forbidden to look back except that the mind must not turn back to the old life that it puts off when it is regenerated by grace, if we expect to escape the final judgment?
>
> (*ciu. Dei* 16.30; Babcock, 2.221; CCSL 48.535)

Here, even the infamous examples of the judgment of Sodom and Gomorrah and of the judgment that befell Lot's wife are extrapolated by Augustine into a general (and Pauline; cf., e.g. Rom 6:6; Eph 4:22; and Col 3:9) moral exhortation, namely, to completely "put off" one's old life once one has been given the gratuitous gift of grace. Just as interesting is that Lot's obvious moral failures, including his willingness to hand over his two daughters to the men of Sodom and Gomorrah (cf. Gen 19:8), his initial faithless hesitance to flee (cf. Gen 19:15–20), his drunkenness, and his incestuous fathering of sons by both of his daughters (cf. Gen 19:32–38), are not mentioned by Augustine.

Ciu. Dei 16.31–33 discuss the meaning and derivation of Isaac's name (16.31), offer an extended meditation on how Abraham was "tempted" (*temptatur*) to sacrifice Isaac, a few comments on Sarah's death (16.32), and the (Christologically) prophetic significance of Isaac's marriage to Rebecca, a non-Canaanite (16.33). These discussions are all based upon brief excerpts from Gen 21–24. In *ciu. Dei* 16.31, Augustine correctly notes that Isaac means laughter and he documents how the promise and eventual fulfillment of his birth caused both Abraham and Sarah to laugh, though he also acknowledges that it took time for Sarah's laughter, which was originally generated by her cynicism and unbelief at the prospect of ever conceiving and bearing a child, to be

[45] He does, however, acknowledge that both Abraham and Lot acted well in aiding the angels, whom they regarded merely "as mortals in need of human refreshment" (*tamquam mortalibus … humana refectione indigentibus*)." See Babcock, 2.220; CCSL 48.534.

truly marked by "exulting joy" (*ad celebrandum gaudium*) (*ciu. Dei* 16.31; Babcock, 2.222; CCSL 48.535–536).

In *ciu. Dei* 16.32, as he turns to the sacrifice of Isaac, Augustine is keen to highlight its purpose: while it was a genuine temptation for Abraham, Augustine is convinced that God did not tempt him for God's own sake; rather, God wanted Abraham's "devout obedience" (*pia … oboedientia*) to be tested so that it would be known "to the ages" (*saeculis*) (*ciu. Dei* 16.32; Babcock, 2.222; CCSL 48.536). In order to support this, Augustine is compelled to claim that Gen 22:12, which implies that this test was so that God might learn whether Abraham truly feared God, teaches that this test was actually intended to demonstrate Abraham's faith to others. It is also here that Augustine confirms the traditional belief that Isaac was a type of Christ since: (a) he carried the wood upon which he would be sacrificed just as Christ carried his own wooden cross; (b) he was, in a sense, raised or "restored" (*reddi*) from the dead (cf. Heb 11:19); and (c) despite his "beloved" and "only" son status, Abraham was willing to sacrifice him for a larger necessity.

Ciu. Dei 16.34 explains why Abraham took both a new wife and concubines (cf. Gen 25:1 and 25:6) after the death of Sarah. Here Augustine reiterates his conviction that "we should by no means suspect him of uncontrolled sexual desire, especially in light of his age and the sanctity of his faith" (*ciu. Dei* 16.34; Babcock, 2.224; CCSL 48.538). Moreover, we "should cast no blame on Abraham," since it could be that God included these details about him simply "to refute future heretics who would oppose second marriages" (*ciu. Dei* 16.34; Babcock, 2.225; CCSL 48.539). After all, if "the father of many nations" (*patre multarum gentium*) contracted a second marriage after Sarah's death, how could any similar choice be sinful? Although she did not damage Abraham's reputation morally, Keturah, the new wife, does not fare well on the typological plane. In Augustine's reading, she, along with her sons signify "carnal people (*carnales*) who think (*existimant*) they belong to the new covenant"; indeed all of the sons of Abraham's concubines, represent "heretics" and/or "carnal Jews" (*Iudaei carnales*) whose lack of correct faith will prohibit them from inheriting "the promised kingdom." Augustine establishes this fact by another appeal to Paul: the only true heirs will be those who, by imitating the correct faith of Abraham and Isaac, his only recognized heir, actually become "children of the promise" (*filii promissionis*; cf. Rom 9:7–8; and Gal 4:28) (*ciu. Dei* 16.34; Babcock, 2.224–25; CCSL 48.538–539).

Ciu. Dei 16.35–43 are dedicated to "how the times of the City of God unrolled through Abraham's descendants" (*ciu. Dei* 16.35;

Babcock, 2.225; CCSL 48.539): 16.35 affirms an ancient (Christian) typological reading of the significance of Isaac's twin boys, Jacob and Esau. Following an approving rehearsal of the Pauline idea that, on one level, they illustrate the mystery of God's election since "Jacob I loved, but Esau I hated" (Rom 9:13; cf. Mal 1:2–3), Augustine claims that "almost no one among us" has understood Gen 25:23's phrase "the older shall serve the younger," "to mean anything other than that the older people, the Jews, would serve the younger people, the Christians" (*ciu. Dei* 16.35; Babcock, 2.225; CCSL 48.540).

Ciu. Dei 16.36, which includes a long quotation of Gen 26:1–5, discusses Isaac exemplary character and how his life, though of lesser rank, parallels that of Abraham, even in terms of his near perfect sexual chastity. Isaac "had no other wife nor any concubine; he was content to have for his posterity the two twins he fathered on one act of intercourse" (*ciu. Dei* 16.36; Babcock, 2.226; CCSL 48.540). Similarly, *ciu. Dei* 16.37 is dedicated to the life of Jacob, though instead of being summarized in just one chapter, this patriarch's significance is discussed intermittently for the following five. As he did for Isaac, Augustine asserts and then defends Jacob's exemplary character. With Jacob, however, the apology goes so far as to exculpate him from both the questionable means by which he obtained Esau's birthright (cf. Gen 25:29–34) and the deceptive means by which he secured Isaac's blessing (cf. Gen 27:5–28:5). Instead of blaming Jacob for opportunistically taking advantage of Esau's hunger, Augustine censures Esau for a "blameworthy" (*culpandam*) amount of "unrestrained greed" (*auiditate inmodesta*). Likewise, although he must admit that Jacob's misrepresentation of himself as Esau in the presence of his (nearly) blind father was a "deceit," he also asserts that it wasn't a "fraudulent deceit" (*fraudulentus dolus*) (*ciu. Dei* 16.37; Babcock, 2.227; CCSL 48.541).[46] Augustine also highlights how the blessing that Jacob's non-fraudulent deceit obtained – and especially the aspect that "anyone who blesses you shall be blessed" (cf. Gen 27:29) – was prophetic insofar as it "foretells the proclamation of Christ to all peoples" (*ciu. Dei* 16.37; Babcock, 2.228; CCSL 48.542).

[46] Despite his frequent reference to Jerome's *Interpretation of Hebrew Names* in *ciu. Dei*, about which see, e.g. Denecker 2017, pp. 177–178 and the bibliography provided there, Augustine is unaware that "Jacob," which in context (cf. 25:26) is claimed to mean "one who grabs the heel," ultimately needs to be rendered "Supplanter" or even "Deceiver" in light of Jacob's later conduct. See, e.g. Arnold 2009, p. 232. On the contrary, Augustine's preconception was that Jacob's character must have been largely impeccable.

Ciu. Dei 16.38 opens with a quotation of Gen 28:1–4 and 10–19. Here, Augustine's intention is to differentiate Jacob from Esau; to explain the "oracle" (*oraculum*) that Jacob received in his sleep, which made him the rightful heir of the promises originally given to Abraham; and to defend his choice to maintain relations with four women (more or less) simultaneously. For Augustine, it is only Jacob whose seed belongs to the City of God. Likewise, it is Jacob's elect status that qualifies him to receive the oracle and to foreshadow prophetically the coming of Christ via deeds such as pouring oil on the stone he placed under his head (cf. Gen 28:18). Augustine's explanation for Jacob's polygamy is not new to *ciu. Dei*: while Jacob did father children with each of them, he "felt no illicit desire for any of them"; moreover, "he never sought any woman but the one [i.e. Rachel]," nor had he ever "made use of any except for the purpose of fathering children" (*ciu. Dei* 16.38; Babcock, 2.230; CCSL 48.544). In Augustine's reckoning, Jacob's polygamy was another instance in which the Pauline principle expressed in 1 Cor 7:4 was (proleptically) fulfilled: "[Jacob] kept his marriage vow, for he would not have done even this except that his wives, who had legitimate power over their husband's body, demanded it of him" (*ciu. Dei* 16.38; Babcock, 2.230; CCSL 48.544).

Ciu. Dei 16.39–43 signal a departure in both form and content from what has proceeded in Book 16. Into these five chapters Augustine condenses the remainder of the *Genesis* narrative, the enslavement of Israel in Egypt, their deliverance by Moses, Joshua's leadership, the times of the Judges, the repudiation of King Saul, and the accession of David. Despite their dizzying pace, these chapters contain several notable observations. In *ciu. Dei* 16.39, Augustine (detrimentally) leans upon Jerome's etymologies when he assumes that "Israel," the name Jacob received after wrestling God's angel, means "seeing God" (*uidens Deum*) (*ciu. Dei* 16.39; Babcock, 2.230; CCSL 48.545). 16.41, besides including the text of Gen 49:8–12, explicitly traces the lineage of "the Christian people, in whom the City of God is on pilgrimage on earth," from Abraham, through Isaac and Jacob, to Judah (*ciu. Dei* 16.41; Babcock, 2.232; CCSL 48.546). Similarly, *ciu. Dei* 16.42 once again (cf. *ciu. Dei* 16.35) interprets the twins Jacob and Esau typologically: "the older is a type of the Jews, and the younger a type of the Christians." This reading's significance becomes clear when, in the immediate context, Augustine cites Gen 48:19's prophecy that the "younger brother shall be greater than [the older], and his seed shall become a multitude of peoples" (*ciu. Dei* 16.42; Babcock, 2.233; CCSL 48.548).

Ciu. Dei 16.43 takes the reader from "the death of Jacob and ... Joseph" (cf. Gen 49:33–50:26) to the succession of David to the throne of Israel (2 Sam. 5:3–4) – a span of several centuries – in just over eighty lines of (Latin) text. Augustine summarizes Moses's life in approximately forty lines, the entire period under Joshua and the Judges in another seventeen, and then dwells for a few more on the significance of David's reign. Indeed, David "marks a turning point" (*articulus*) in which "the people of God begins to come of age and to enter young adulthood" (*iuuentutis*) having completed its "adolescence" (*adulescentia*) (*ciu. Dei* 16.43; Babcock, 2.235–36; CCSL 48.550).

It was already noted that, according to Augustine, Book 16 has covered "the second and the third ages" of the City of God, and that, in the latter, "the yoke of the law was imposed, an abundance of sins appeared, and the earthly kingdom had its beginning." Not previously noted, however, is that, in order to prevent his readers from becoming unduly depressed at this strikingly Pauline recapitulation (cf. Rom 3:20; 5:20; 7:7–9; and Gal 5:1), Augustine, by way of a coda, goes on to reassure them that, even during this age, "there was no lack of spiritual people" (*ciu. Dei* 16.43; Babcock, 2.236; CCSL 48.550).[47]

CONCLUSION

Admittedly, Books 15–16 of *ciu. Dei* do offer the reader an uneven treatment both of Genesis 4–50 and of the earliest phases of the history of Israel, not infrequently covering seemingly significant aspects in short order, via a brief gloss, or not at all. Worse still, when viewed from the perspective of the modern reader, these books are also marked – at least occasionally – by what most would regard as special pleading.

Nevertheless, *contra* Burleigh, these books are not unsatisfactory – even in the relative sense. Functioning as what later theologians would call salvation history, they treat what can be gleaned from *Genesis* about the presence of the City of God in our post-lapsarian world with clarity, insight, and acumen. To appreciate this in full, one must regularly recall that *ciu. Dei* 15–16 are not attempting a straightforward reading of the *Genesis* narrative. On the contrary, they use the Christian New Testament, and, in particular, Pauline formulations, principles, and assertions, to explain how (some of) God's redemptive

[47] *"ita duas aetates secundam et tertiam liber iste contineat, in qua tertia ... inpositum est legis iugum et apparuit abundantia peccatorum et regni terreni surrexit exordium, ubi non defuerunt spiritales."*

plans were made manifest prior to Christ's first Advent. In doing so, they present that history in ways broadly consistent with what late antique Christians had come to expect.

One must also keep in mind that, by AD 420, Augustine had been thoughtfully and carefully reading the Apostle Paul for more than a quarter of a century. For Augustine, the enormously-complex "pre-Advent" history of the people of God makes maximum sense when viewed through the "post-Advent lens" provided by the New Testament. His reading of Paul had convinced Augustine that God would intervene in human history in order to save *some* of those who had fallen "in Adam" – even if when, how, and exactly whom God would save were questions that remained largely mysterious. What was certain, however, is that the God of Abraham, Isaac, Jacob, Paul, and, indeed, of Augustine himself, would continue to guide human history providentially to its appointed end, a conviction that clearly served as an impetus for the composition of Books 15–16, if not also for the entirety of his *magnum opus et arduum*.

FURTHER READING

Chan, J. and Dupont, A. (2016). *Restauratio* in *De ciuitate Dei*: The Role of the Restoration Motif in Understanding Augustine's Theology of History. *La Ciudad de Dios*, 229(1), 55–78.

Carlson, Charles Paul. The Natural Order and Historical Explanation in St. Augustine's 'City of God'." *Augustiniana* 21 (1971): 417–447.

Denecker, T. (2017). *Ideas on Language in Early Latin Christianity From Tertullian to Isidore of Seville*. Leiden: Brill.

Fortin, Ernest L. Augustine's 'City of God' and the Modern Historical Consciousness *The Review of Politics*. 41/3 (1979): 323–343.

Fredriksen, Paula. Secundum Carnem: History and Israel in the Theology of St. Augustine. In *The Limits of Ancient Christianity. Essays on Late Antique Thought and Culture in Honor of R.A. Markus*. Edited by W. Klingshirn and M. Vessey. Ann Arbor: The University of Michigan Press, 1999, 26–41.

Lewis, Gordon. Faith and History in St. Augustine. *Trinity Journal* 3 (1982): 39–350.

Norris, John M. Augustine's Interpretation of Genesis in the City of God XI-XV. In *Studia Patristica* XLIII, ed. F. Young, M. Edwards and P. Parvis. Leuven: Peeters Press, 2006, 207–211.

Pulsiano, P. (1995). Language Theory and Narrative Patterning in *De Ciuitate Dei*, Books XV–XVIII. In D. Donnelly, ed., *The City of God: A Collection of Critical Essays*. New York: P. Lang, pp. 241–252.

11 Books 17 & 18: Prophecy as Proof in Augustine's *City of God*

MICHAEL SWEENEY

In *conf.*, Augustine recounts how he was led to Manicheanism, in part, by his repugnance to Old Testament passages in which a human-like body is attributed to God (*conf.* 3.7). Ambrose helps to release the grip that Manicheanism had on Augustine by showing him that it is not always necessary to read the Old Testament literally (*conf.* 6.4 and 7.1). In Books 17 and 18 of the *ciu. Dei*, Augustine both rejects the notion that all of the Old Testament is allegorical (the allegorical cannot negate the literal meaning, and sometimes the text is purely historical) and affirms that the most important meaning of the Old Testament is prophetic (*ciu. Dei* 17.3). The earthly kingdom in the Old Testament is inherently allegorical and prophetic. It is not a kingdom that is about or for itself; it is about and for the future heavenly kingdom. The work of the prophets is to prevent the earthly kingdom from being taken too literally – as a kingdom whose meaning is wholly in the present and in itself.

THE AGE OF PROPHECY: BOOK 17 AND PROPHECY IN SACRED HISTORY

Prophecy in the Old Testament precedes what Augustine calls the "age of prophecy." Book 17 opens with the interpretative key to understanding the prophetic nature of the Old Testament as a whole and the age of prophecy in particular, namely, the two-fold promise made to Abraham: a prophecy according to the flesh of temporal prosperity that is fulfilled is the single nation of Israel, and a prophecy according to faith that is a spiritual promise to all nations and that is fulfilled through Christ (*ciu. Dei* 17.1). The former prophecy refers to an earthly kingdom; the latter refers to a heavenly or spiritual kingdom. There are thus three kinds of prophecy in Scripture: prophecy concerning the earthly Jerusalem, prophecy concerning the heavenly Jerusalem, and the prophetic prefiguring that pertains to both (*ciu. Dei* 17.3). A correct understanding of prophecy in the Old Testament requires the ability to distinguish between these two promises and knowledge of when and how God fulfills them.

If the Old Testament is so thoroughly prophetic, what constitutes the "age of the prophets" and the focus on prophecy in Books 17 and 18? Prophecy in the age of the prophets is concerned with the relationship of the twofold Abrahamic promise to kingship among the Israelites (*ciu. Dei* 17.1). In particular, the central question for Augustine in the age of prophecy is how the promise of earthly and heavenly kingdoms to Abraham is fulfilled in David and his heirs. Although Noah, Abraham, and Moses are prophets, it is Samuel's anointing of Saul as king that inaugurates the age of prophecy by establishing the Israelite monarchy. Prophecy gives rise to kingship and prophecy exposes the failures of Israelite kings to obey the law and to govern according to the twofold promise made to Abraham. More important than the exposure of royal infidelity, the prophets show God's fidelity to kingship as the fulfillment of the promises made to Abraham. Prophecy in the age of the prophets is, therefore, political, inasmuch as it is directed toward creating, sustaining, and understanding kingship as promised by God to his people. This is not to say that kingship is merely political in Augustine's age of prophecy, but there must be a political foundation that supports the spiritual edifice of worship.

Simply living in the promised land is not sufficient to fulfill the promise to Abraham according to the flesh; full realization requires the indisputable possession of land signified by kingship, especially the independent kingship exemplified by David and Solomon (*ciu. Dei* 17.2). Neither physical presence nor military occupation of the land are equal to possession through political rule, which entails a politically independent kingship.[1] After the Babylonian exile, the Israelites will return and live on the same land, but neither the land nor their lives will be fully theirs because they will not have full political control. Only an Israelite monarchy totally independent from foreign powers guarantees the territorial control and temporal prosperity promised to Abraham. This particular land belongs to this particular people when it is ruled by their king and no other; no tribute or allegiance is to be owed to any other power. Samuel is the first of the prophets in the age of the prophets because his anointing of Saul and David begins the fulfillment

[1] "Thus, Abraham's seed according to the flesh – that is, the people of Israel – were now in the promised land and had now begun to rule there, not only by taking the cities of their enemies but also by having kings" (*ciu. Dei* 17.2; Babcock, 2.238–239).

of the promises to the descendants of Abraham through political dominion over the land of Canaan. While God has sovereignty over all the earth, the Israelites are granted sovereignty over this particular land through an Israelite monarchy.

The prophetic promise to David is that he will govern a unified kingdom comprising the totality of the land of Canaan (*ciu. Dei* 17.7). Peace is likewise part of the covenant with David and his heirs because war, whether from external or internal enemies, signifies division and a threat to possession of the land (*ciu. Dei* 17.13). Such security comes from strength so great that there is no enemy to fear. Finally, and most importantly, eternal succession is promised to David's heirs (*ciu. Dei* 17.6). The land will be fully possessed because the Davidic monarchy will be eternal. The prophecy of unity, peace and eternity to Israelite kingship through David and his heirs guarantees Israelite possession of the promised land.

On this political foundation, a more spiritual edifice is built – the temple of Solomon – and temple worship is the purpose of the Davidic monarchy.[2] Full possession of the land through monarchy makes it possible to construct the temple and for the Israelites to worship in peace. For Augustine, this worship is still part of the earthly kingdom promised to Abraham because it belongs to one particular nation and takes place through animal sacrifice. David wished to build the temple himself, but that privilege fell to his son, Solomon (*ciu. Dei* 17.8). The unity of prophecy, monarchy, and temple worship is reflected in the unity of prophet, priest, and king. Monarchy comes to be through prophetic anointing, and David is both king and prophet. Indeed, Augustine emphasizes the prophecy of David above all others in Book 17 because David is the greatest authority on the heavenly kingdom that will be established by the messiah as the ultimate fulfillment of the promises made to the Davidic line (*ciu. Dei* 17.15). David, on the other hand, is not a priest; only in the messiah will the roles of priest, prophet, and king be unified completely.[3]

[2] "David understood this, therefore, when he says in the Second Book of Kingdoms … For at that time he was about to father the son from whom his line of descent would be carried down to Christ, and it was through Christ that his house was going to be eternal and was going to be the house of God. For what makes it the house of David is David's line of descendants, but what makes it the house of God is the temple of God, a temple not of stones but of human beings, where the people will dwell eternally with their God and in their God, and where God will dwell eternally with his people and in his people" (*ciu. Dei* 17.12; Babcock, 2.263).

[3] Although David was not a priest, there are occasions in the Old Testament where David appears to act as a priest. He appears to wear the priestly ephod (1 Sam 30:6–10) and to offer sacrifice wearing it (2 Sam 6:12–15). Augustine does not consider these instances significant enough to mention. For Augustine, the imperfection of the

Almost immediately after the establishment of the monarchy, however, the relationship between monarchy and worship will be shaken by sin; worship of foreign gods and reliance on foreign powers will fracture the political foundation and lead to loss of Solomon's temple. At the very beginning of the prophetic age, Samuel expresses divine displeasure with Saul, resulting in the transfer of the royal line to David (*ciu. Dei* 17.7). Nathan's prophecy criticizes David's fidelity to God and predicts that Solomon rather than David will build the temple (*ciu. Dei* 17.8). Worship of foreign gods within Solomon's family shows that the earthly kingdom could never produce a worship equal to the heavenly kingdom, and thus prophecy becomes chiefly a critique of the earthly kingdom (*ciu. Dei* 17.8 and 17.10). Nevertheless, Augustine insists that the earthly kingdom promised to Abraham and his descendants is not the City of Man, for the latter is in rebellion against God. As soon as the earthly kingdom is inaugurated through prophetic anointing, the prophetic mission aims at preventing the earthly kingdom from becoming the City of Man.

The unity and peace promised to the Davidic monarchy is soon lost through the infidelity of the monarchy. Division in the kingdom arrives because of Solomon's sin.[4] As a result of Solomon's excesses, King Rehoboam, son of Solomon, rules only two tribes in the south, and the rebellious King Jeroboam rules ten tribes in the north. In 721 BC, the Assyrians invade and conquer the northern kingdom, whose tribes are dispersed and lost among the Assyrian empire. Infidelity thus leads to division; division leads to a loss of peace and ultimately to a loss of the land. When the land is lost, worship is lost. The southern kingdom, Judah, is eventually conquered and deported to Babylon (598/7 BC and 587/6 BC).[5] With this loss of land comes a loss of the temple, which is

earthly kingdom entails the non-identity of kingship and priesthood. Only in the City of God are kingship and priesthood truly one: "faith leads to God all who are predestined for the City of God, the house of God, the temple of God" (*ciu. Dei* 18.47; Babcock, 2.334).

[4] "We know, of course, that, due to Solomon's sin, Israel was divided in two during the reign of his son Rehoboam, and that the division persisted, with each part having its own kings, until the whole people was overthrown with great devastation by the Chaldeans and carried away into captivity" (*ciu. Dei* 17.7; Babcock, 2.255).

[5] "And this went on under God's growing indignation, until that whole people was not only crushed in its own homeland by the conquering Chaldeans but was also carried off in large part to the lands of the Assyrians. This happened first to the part called Israel, with its ten tribes, and afterwards also to Judah, when Jerusalem and its celebrated temple were overthrown, and the people then lived in captive inactivity for seventy years. After that time, released from their captivity and allowed to return, they restored the Temple that had been overthrown, and, although many of them still

destroyed. The temple will be rebuilt when the Persian king, Cyrus, who had conquered Babylon, allows the exiles to return, but the temple will not again be wholly theirs because the land will be governed through foreign powers until the second temple is destroyed by the Romans in AD 70.[6]

Augustine takes pains to argue that the loss of kingship through the infidelity of kings and people also resulted in a loss of priesthood and of prophecy itself. Augustine sees in the prophecy to Eli of the death of his two sons, not simply the literal death of two sinful priests, but the allegorical and prophetic death of the Aaronic priesthood (*ciu. Dei* 17.5). He sees in the prophecy of Hannah, the mother of the prophet Samuel, the allegorical birth of a new priesthood in Christ out of the barrenness of the old priesthood (*ciu. Dei* 17.4). Prophecy dies out with the loss of the monarchy: "But during the whole period following their return from Babylonia – after Malachi, Haggai, the Zechariah who prophesied then, and Ezra – the Jews had no prophets until the coming of the savior" (*ciu. Dei* 17.24; Babcock, 2.277). The age of prophecy begins with the prophetic anointing of the first king, and the age of prophecy fades with the loss of kingship. Prophecy can begin again only with a new kingly foundation for the worship of God.

PROPHECY AND PROOF

For Augustine, the account of prophecy in sacred history cannot end with human infidelity. The loss of kingship, land and prophecy cannot be greater than God's fidelity to his promises, especially the promise of an eternal rule to the heirs of David. Augustine's principal claim in Books 17 and 18 is that prophecy is proof of the truth of Christianity. Sin obscures the fulfillment of that prophecy only if we forget that the promise to Abraham was a twofold kingdom, and only if we forget the prophecy by David himself. Augustine calls Isaiah more of an evangelist than a prophet (*ciu. Dei* 18.29), since he most clearly foretells the

remained in foreign lands, at least they no longer had a kingdom divided into two parts with different kings for each part. Rather, they had once prince in Jerusalem and at certain fixed times, they all came to God's Temple there from all over the world, wherever they were and from wherever they could. Not even then, however, did they lack foreign enemies and conquerors; in fact, when Christ found them, they were already tribute-paying subjects of the Romans" (*ciu. Dei* 17.23; Babcock, 2.277).

6 "After this, from the rebuilding of the Temple down to Aristobulus, it was not kings who ruled over the Jews but princes" (*ciu. Dei* 18.36; Babcock, 2.319; see also *ciu. Dei* 18.45; Babcock, 2.330–332).

coming of a suffering messiah, and yet Augustine spends less time analyzing Isaiah and the other prophets than he does the prophecy of David. In Book 17, according to the Babcock translation, Augustine devotes almost sixteen pages to David's prophecy. In Book 18, a total of thirteen pages are devoted to the prophecy of Hosea, Amos, Isaiah, Micah, Jonah, Obadiah, Nahum, Habakkuk, Jeremiah, Zephaniah, Haggai, Zechariah, Malachi, and Esdras. Less than two of those pages concern Isaiah.

If Augustine's principal interest is to prove that the Old Testament prophets point to Jesus Christ, one would expect a far greater emphasis on Isaiah and the Hebrew prophets treated in Book 18. Augustine concentrates his study of prophecy on David for several reasons. Firstly, David embodies the connection between kingship and prophecy. As a king, he is the subject of prophecy by Samuel, Nathan, and prophets after his death. As a prophet himself, David is the greatest authority on the prophetic promises made to him and his heirs; he is the great interpreter of the connection between kingship and prophecy. Consequently, he is the best voice for answering the objection that Jesus Christ is not the heir to the Davidic promises. No one can reasonably be waiting for another messiah, if David has unambiguously pointed to a suffering messiah.

Augustine goes on to treat the more general objection of pagan skepticism toward biblical prophecy: the course of sacred history seems to militate against the historical fulfillment of the Davidic promises, given the loss of kingship, land and temple worship, and this failure of biblical prophecy would thus seem to prove the non-existence of the biblical God, or the disinterest of God in the fate of His people, or the power of human sin to frustrate the will of God. Augustine's contention is that, as a prophet, David clearly saw the connection between the promises made to Abraham and the Davidic monarchial line. Moreover, David saw that human sin was part of the divine prophecy and would lead to a fulfillment in the sufferings of a messiah.

It is essential to recall, Augustine notes, that the monarchy began with Saul and his subsequent rejection (*ciu. Dei* 17.6). Augustine sees this ambiguity in the inception of the monarchy not as a failure or as the correction of a mistake but as a prophecy that the earthly monarchy was never meant to be eternal: "Rather, he had prepared Saul's kingdom as a prefiguration of the eternal kingdom" (*ciu. Dei* 17.6; Babcock, 2.253). The disruption caused by sin is not an obstacle to prophetic clarity; it is an essential part of it. The repudiation of Saul shows that the decisive separation of the earthly kingdom from the City of Man could only come through its fulfillment in the heavenly kingdom established by

Jesus Christ.[7] Similarly, God's refusal of David's offer to build a permanent temple is proof that Nathan's prophecy of a temple "built by another" would be fulfilled in Christ rather than by Solomon's temple (*ciu. Dei* 17.8; Babcock, 2.256–7). Solomon's temple is itself a figure – a prophecy – of its replacement by a greater temple (*ciu. Dei* 17.8).

In general, rather than obscuring prophecy, the misdeeds of kings in both the southern and northern kingdoms serve to make clear that the earthly kingdom was meant to be temporary.[8] David prophesies that the earthly kingdom is temporary because the earthly kingdom is meant to prefigure and prepare for the spiritual kingdom; that is, David's prophecy insists that the earthly kingdom is itself prophetic inasmuch as it must always be pointing toward its future fulfillment in the heavenly kingdom (*ciu. Dei* 17.14). As soon as the earthly kingdom ceases to be prophetic and no longer points to the heavenly kingdom, it becomes the City of Man. The City of Man points to itself and is therefore not prophetic (*ciu. Dei* 17.7 and 17.16). The earthly kingdom cannot be identified with the City of Man because what was promised to Abraham was not the City of Man, but the kings who forget the prophetic nature of the earthly kingdom, and who thus forget that kingship is prophecy, turn the earthly kingdom into the City of Man and require prophets who remind them of the difference.

David's prophecy is found in the psalms, and Augustine considers David to be the author of all the psalms (*ciu. Dei* 17.14–15). David ruled the earthly kingdom as a prophet, and his prophecy in the psalms maintains the Abrahamic promise of earthly and heavenly kingdoms by seeing the earthly as foretelling the coming of a kingdom that will not be temporary. David's prophecy in the psalms thus points to Christ as his heir and as the fulfillment of the promises of a unified, peaceful, and eternal kingdom. The two kingdoms are physically united in Christ – David's heir – at the moment that the earthly kingdom gives way to the heavenly kingdom.[9] David prophesies in the psalms that,

[7] "Figuratively speaking, then, Saul represented the person of the people of Israel, the people that was going to lose the kingdom when Jesus Christ our Lord came to rule, not carnally but spiritually, through the new covenant" (*ciu. Dei* 17.7; Babcock, 2.255).

[8] "All these things came upon the maidservant Jerusalem, in which there also ruled some who were children of the free woman, governing that kingdom temporarily but holding in true faith to the kingdom of the heavenly Jerusalem, whose sons they were, and hoping in the true Christ" (*ciu. Dei* 17.10; Babcock, 2.260).

[9] "This people, I say, together with the true Israelites, who are Israelites both by the flesh and by faith, is the City of God, the city that also gave birth to Christ himself according to the flesh, at the time when it consisted of those true Israelites alone.

unlike himself, the king who will found the heavenly kingdom will be a priest as well as a king because his kingdom will establish perfectly and eternally the worship of God (*ciu. Dei* 17.17). This king will establish the perfect worship of God without a particular land or temple, and he will bring about his kingdom and worship through suffering. For Augustine, David unambiguously foretells the passion, death, and resurrection of the messiah (*ciu. Dei* 17.17–18). In David's prophecy, the Davidic line will not fail because a king will appear who rules eternally a kingdom that is universal (one that includes all peoples) and that eternally gives worship to God (*ciu. Dei* 17.13). David prophesies the fulfillment of the promises made to him in an heir who is a king that suffers, dies, and rises from the dead.

Augustine sees the prophecy of the Old Testament as orientated both to Jesus Christ, the suffering messiah, and to the church, the city that He founded. Sometimes the prophecy is directed exclusively toward Christ, sometimes to the church, and sometimes to both (see, e.g. *ciu. Dei* 17.15, 17.21, 18.29, 18.35, and 18.44). So complete is the Old Testament prophecy of a suffering messiah that it also prefigures the Jewish rejection of a suffering messiah. The question arises, however, if the prophecy was so evident, how is it that so many of the recipients of this prophecy could have failed to recognize the suffering messiah? Augustine's answer is the same principle explaining the failings of Saul, Solomon and so many of the kings: failure to distinguish between the earthly kingdom and the City of Man. They expect a messiah who does not die because they fail to see that the earthly kingdom is prophetic and preparing for the heavenly kingdom. Nevertheless, blindness to the "completely obvious" prophecy of a messiah who suffers, dies and rises from the dead is also prophesied; this blindness was foreseen and becomes part of the prophecy – it is part of God's merciful providence (*ciu. Dei* 17.8; Babcock, 2.257; cf. *ciu. Dei* 17.18). Through the rejection of a suffering messiah, salvation is opened to all the nations (*ciu. Dei* 18.27). Jewish rejection of Christ is not a failure of Old Testament prophecy but the fulfillment of it. Rather than obscuring the proof that comes from prophecy, rejection of the suffering messiah becomes a confirmation of it. Such rejection was an essential part of the transition from the earthly to the heavenly kingdom; without this rejection, both promises to Abraham could not have been fulfilled.

For it was from that city that the virgin Mary came, in whom Christ assumed flesh in order to become man" (*ciu. Dei* 17.16; Babcock, 2.268).

The end of the prophetic age is not, for Augustine, about the failure of kingship and the failure of prophecy; rather, the age of prophecy ends because it is fulfilled. Prophecy is orientated to the future (*ciu. Dei* 17.1). The prophetic age ends when the future to which it is orientated has become present. John the Baptist is the last of the prophets because he ceases to speak in the future tense: "last of all, John himself, who did not foretell Christ's future coming, since they were contemporaries" (*ciu. Dei* 17.24; Babcock, 2.277). Prophecy is proof when the future of which it speaks is present. The heavenly kingdom has arrived through a new foundation established by a suffering messiah. Human rejection of that prophecy only serves to confirm it because rejection of prophecy is essential to the ending of an earthly kingdom limited to a particular land with worship in a particular temple, which gives way to a universal spiritual kingdom with a perfect sacrifice and worship. Both Old Testament prophecy and rejection of that prophecy are proof of Christianity.

PROPHECY AND SECULAR HISTORY: BOOK 18 AND THE CITY OF MAN, PROPHECY, AND POLITICAL EVIL

Augustine introduces Book 18 by noting that Book 17 was focused on prophecy concerning the City of God. Book 18, he says, will treat the City of Man with respect to prophecy (*ciu. Dei* 17.1). Understanding prophecy with regard to the City of God supplies so much light that one can read the course of secular history as well as sacred history, including the evil within each, and thus Augustine traces the history of the Assyrians, Sicyons, Greeks, and Romans. A pattern quickly emerges. Pagan theologians are typically poets, whose work includes turning human beings into gods (*ciu. Dei* 18.14). Human beings who perform extraordinary deeds, especially ones that benefit the human race, are declared gods (*ciu. Dei* 18.8). Commonly it is kings who are declared gods. Augustine's account begins with the Egyptians: "In those times, Apis, the king of the Argives, sailed across to Egypt with his fleet; and, when he died there, he became Serapis, the greatest of all the Egyptian gods" (*ciu. Dei* 18.5; Babcock, 2.284). The course of the City of Man continues to make human kings gods down to the Latins (Aeneas), Sabines (Sancus), and Romans (the Caesars) (*ciu. Dei* 18.19 and 18.24). There is, therefore, no purely secular history. There is the history of the Jewish people, whose kings prepare for the coming of a divine king, and there is the history of the rest of the human race in which either the kings are gods or the gods to whom the human rulers answer are man-made gods. Such gods are "ungodly," and so the history of the City of Man is demonic, whereas the history of the City of God is truly divine (*ciu. Dei* 18.18; Babcock, 2.296; cf. *ciu. Dei* 18.12).

The fundamental political sin of the City of Man is to mistake the image for the original, the human for the divine; there is no such distinction in the City of Man between the earthly and spiritual kingdoms and thus no real distinction between present and future. In brief, there is no space for prophecy. Prophecy requires the twofold promise to Abraham in which there is a difference between the earthly and heavenly kingdoms, past and future. Since the present in the City of Man is not a preparation for the future, nothing really changes in the history of the City of Man. History is tediously repeating itself in the City of Man: war, conquest, and slavery are the constant story of the City of Man (*ciu. Dei* 18.2). Thus Augustine says that the two great empires are the Assyrians and the Romans, and all others are "appendages" of these, but these two empires are so like each other that we can call Babylon the first Rome and Rome the second Babylon (*ciu. Dei* 18.2; Babcock, 2.282). Only the City of God really changes because it is on a pilgrimage; it has a destination, and prophecy makes that destination known.

THE CITY OF MAN AS PART OF DIVINE PROVIDENCE

Even if the history of the City of Man is the story of its rebellion against God and prophecy, Augustine contends that it is entirely within divine providence and so within prophecy. History shows that the City of Man is an instrument of divine providence because it serves as an agent of both divine punishment and salvation. Three moments in history stand out as examples. The first is the Babylonian exile and return (*ciu. Dei* 18.25). The prophets, especially Jeremiah, foretold the punishment that would fall upon Jerusalem. Babylon serves as an agent of divine wrath, but also as Jeremiah prophesied, Cyrus, king of the Persians, serves as an instrument of salvation when he allows the Jews to return from exile and to rebuild the temple. Secondly, Rome destroys the temple in Jerusalem that had been rebuilt after the Babylonian exile (*ciu. Dei* 18.46). Rome is also an agent of salvation here, but to Christians. Divine providence had long prepared Rome for a central role in the history of salvation. The Jewish rejection of Jesus makes possible the heavenly kingdom with a universal opening to all peoples. The age of prophecy began at the same time as the rise of Rome (*ciu. Dei* 18.25). As the prophets prepared the earthly kingdom for the heavenly kingdom that would be established by Jesus Christ, so the increasing universality of Roman rule prepared for the universal announcement of the gospel. The universal empire of the City of Man served the universal invitation to the heavenly kingdom. Finally, Rome's punishment of the Christians through persecution served to advance the heavenly kingdom. On the one hand, it was the City of Man at its worst – at its most demonic – because the Roman persecution of the Christians was punishment of those in the heavenly kingdom (*ciu. Dei* 18.51). On the other hand, the persecution of Christians caused the church to flourish.[10] Jesus was a prophet when he foretold the persecution of Christians and through that persecution the service of the City of Man to the City of God (*ciu. Dei* 18.50).

Augustine sees the Greek empire as preparing for the coming of Christ and his kingdom as well. Alexander the Great conquers "all Asia and in fact almost the entire world" (*ciu. Dei* 18.42; Babcock, 2.326). That included Judea, which came to be ruled by the Ptolemies. Philadelphus, a Ptolemy, allows captive Jews to return and requests a Greek translation of the Hebrew Scripture, which becomes the Septuagint. Augustine considers the Septuagint "prophetic," even and especially when it differs from the Hebrew original. More importantly, the Septuagint prepares for the opening of God's kingdom to all peoples (*ciu. Dei* 18.42; Babcock, 2.326). Just as the universality of the Roman Empire prepared for the coming of the universal kingdom, so the universality of the Greek language prepared for the universal announcement of the gospel, and once again, the City of Man is at the service of the City of God.

Augustine also finds prophecy outside the earthly kingdom in the Erythraean Sibyl, a pagan prophetess whose poetry includes lines that form an acrostic spelling out in Greek "Jesus Christ, Son of God, Savior" (*ciu. Dei* 18.23; Babcock, 2.301–4).[11] The content of the poem is a prophecy of judgment to which all the kings of the earth will be subject. In general, however, Augustine emphasizes the indirect role that the

10 "Such people even turn out to benefit the true and catholic members of Christ by their very wickedness, for God puts even the evil to good use, and *all things work together for good for those who love God* (Rom 8:28). In fact all the Church's enemies, no matter how blinded by error or corrupted by malice, serve a useful purpose" (*ciu. Dei* 18.51; Babcock, 2.337).

11 Augustine takes this prophecy of the Erythraean Sibyl as authentic, although skeptics charged that the poem was a Christian forgery, as Augustine himself acknowledges: "Someone might say, of course, that the Christians made up the prophecies about Christ that are cited under the name of the Sibyl or under the name of others" (*ciu. Dei* 18.46; Babcock, 2.332). For a discussion of the authenticity of the poem, see Hooker 2008; and Brocca 2011.

City of Man plays in bringing about the City of God. Prophecy, such as that of Jeremiah and Jesus, is necessary to understand the role of the City of Man in divine providence precisely because it is not intended by those who are attacking Jerusalem or persecuting Christians. The prophet is able to see the good that will come from the evil suffered because he knows both the power of God to bring good from evil and the divine plan by which the politics of the City of Man is made to serve the City of God. Augustine believes that the fruitfulness of this suffering has come to pass and thus constitutes prophetic proof of the truth of Christianity.

CONCLUSION: THE NATURE OF PROPHECY

Platonism and Prophecy

To better understand Augustine's view of prophecy in Books 17–18 in *ciu. Dei*, it is useful to compare it to the perspective of another Platonic philosopher for whom prophecy is at the center of political life – the Islamic philosopher Al-Farabi (c. AD 870–AD 950).[12] For Al-Farabi, the object of philosophy is essence, which is one and which the philosopher attains through demonstrative reason. The object of religion – that which is believed – is images, which are many. The image can be like but never be the original, and so religion and faith can be like but never be philosophy; faith can be like what is reasonable, but it can never be reasonable, and so prophecy and religion will always involve something obscure and ambiguous. Most human beings, according to Al-Farabi, are incapable of demonstrative reasoning, and therefore most human beings can never reach reality – essences. Prophecy is the translation of essences into likenesses of reality that non-philosophers can imagine but never rationally understand. Prophecy is a human act because it is the human creation of images for those who, either by nature or by habit, cannot reason. Prophets are philosophers with the imaginative capacity to lower philosophy to the level of imagination. A prophet is superior to a philosopher in the sense that he possesses both the theoretical virtue of philosophy and the practical art of expressing philosophy through the lower reality of images, but the content of prophecy is inferior to philosophy.

[12] For Al-Farabi's account of prophecy, see Al-Farabi 1961, esp. nn.54 and 63; Al-Farabi 1993; Al-Farabi 1962, esp. nn.38–48; Al-Farabi 2001. See also Sweeney 2007, pp. 543–72; Sweeney 2009, pp. 819–847; Sweeney 2011, pp. 41–62.

Political life and philosophy are inseparable for Al-Farabi, since only the philosopher knows what is good rather than what is merely like the good. Philosophers cannot directly rule through philosophy because the vulgar many cannot understand demonstrative reasoning. In fact, rule or coercion would not be necessary, if the multitude were capable of reason; instruction would suffice. What unites philosophy and political life is prophecy. The philosopher must rule either through his own prophecy or through the law given by a prophet. Religion is the prophetic creation of an imaginative reality by which the ruler guides the multitude to the degree of goodness and happiness of which they are capable, and this happiness is the purpose of political life. Philosophers remain above this imaginative reality as essences are superior to images. Philosophers do not believe; they know. Philosophers are united in the common good that is essence, which is one and the same for all. Non-philosophers are limited to the images that form the nation, which cannot be one, and so religions and nations are many. Philosophers are united by universal reason. Believers are united by the faith of a particular nation, which is given to them prophetically through the force of religious images.

Augustine shares with Al-Farabi the notion that prophecy concerns the relation of image to original. In Platonic fashion, he calls the earthly kingdom an image of the heavenly kingdom: "In the same way, the kingdom of Saul, who was himself repudiated and rejected, was the shadow of a future kingdom that was going to endure for all eternity" (*ciu. Dei* 18.6; Babcock, 2.253). The earthly kingdom is a shadow of the heavenly; the temporal kingdom is an image of the eternal kingdom. In contrast to Al-Farabi, for Augustine it is not only that the temporal is an image of the eternal but the original itself comes to be in time: "Rather, he had prepared Saul's kingdom as a prefiguration of the eternal kingdom" (*ciu. Dei* 18.6; Babcock, 2.253). As the temporal is an image of the eternal, so the present is an image of the future. The eternal is not outside time but within time; the eternal will be in the future. Augustine says the same of David's kingdom: "As the City of God ran its course through the ages, then, David first reigned in the shadow of what was to come, namely, in the earthly Jerusalem" (*ciu. Dei* 17.14; Babcock, 2.264). The earthly kingdom is an image and prefiguration of the heavenly kingdom to come. With the coming of Christ, the eternal is no longer in the future, it is in the present.

Prophecy for Al-Farabi is not knowledge of the future; it is the timeless essence translated into a temporal image. The eternal can never be in time any more than the original can be the image. For

Augustine, prophecy is knowledge of the future through the present; it is knowledge of the original through the image, which, is necessarily obscure and ambiguous. Since the earthly kingdom is itself prophetic – since it is an image of the heavenly kingdom – its meaning is obscure. The prophets, including King David, clarify the prophetic nature of the earthly kingdom through their own prophecy with the result that Augustine claims that the prophecy of the Old Testament is "obvious."[13] The future was knowable through prophecy, although it was not clear exactly when the eternal would become present. The role of prophets is to resist the tendency to de-prophetize the earthly kingdom – to turn the image into the original; they resist the attempt to de-temporalize the earthly kingdom and so to reduce its meaning to the present, which amounts to a reduction of the earthly kingdom to the City of Man.

Augustine's claim is that the original (Christ) should have been recognized through the image (Old Testament prophecy) when the original became present. Likewise, once one has the original, the image is fully knowable.[14] For Al-Farabi, the original is the universal, unchanging, and necessary essence that is outside time. For Augustine, the original is something eternal – God and His heavenly kingdom – that became present in time. All the history of prophetic prefiguring becomes fully intelligible through Christ. Both image and original are now within history. The Old Testament and its prophecy are intelligible through the New Testament, so much so that we now know when to read the Old Testament allegorically and when to read it literally. The meaning of time is not outside of time but within time because the eternal is no longer outside of time. Augustine and Al-Farabi agree that the image is knowable through the original and the temporal through the eternal, but they disagree on where the original – the eternal – is. Prophecy, for Augustine, is not pointing to something beyond time and

[13] "And in that Psalm so many things are said which could not possibly apply to him, but which apply to Christ the Lord as clearly as can be, that it becomes obvious that in Solomon a figure of some sort is represented, but in Christ the truth itself is presented" (*ciu. Dei* 17.8; Babcock, 2.258).

[14] "Otherwise we might look fruitlessly and futilely for another, as do the carnal Jews. For they themselves understand full well that the son who – as they read in this passage – was promised to king David was not in fact Solomon; but they are so extraordinarily blind that even now, when the one who was promised has been made so completely obvious, they still profess to hope for another" (*ciu. Dei* 17.8; Babcock, 2.257).

human history but something that enters time and human history through Christ.

Superiority of Prophecy to Philosophy

Prophecy, for Al-Farabi, is essential to the likeness of happiness achievable by non-philosophers and thus essential to political life, but it proves nothing. Proof is possible only within the demonstrative reasoning of philosophy. What is believed can be proven only if one leaves belief and reasons philosophically. Faith cannot reach the original; it can only reach the image. Thus the philosopher does not and cannot believe. Since the philosopher knows essences, he has no need for images and, consequently, no need for religion or faith. What is one and true and intelligible is philosophy. Al-Farabi's prophet-king looks at the multitude of nations and sees how he can form them into an empire that resembles the unity and intelligibility of philosophy, but his political creation in history can only approximate the eternal and so will always frustrate. The matter of the nations can only receive a likeness of the philosophical form.

Augustine's faith, on the other hand, reaches the original. The prophetic image is an object of faith that allows one to recognize the original. By adhering to the original – to Christ – in faith, history, and all that was prophetically believed becomes an object of understanding, which is the purpose of Books 17 and 18. For Augustine, the contrast is not between image and essence or between faith and philosophy; that is, the contrast is not based on the epistemological divide between the cognitive abilities of philosophers and non-philosophers. Instead, the contrast is based on will – the moral choice between the City of God and the City of Man. Prophecy is a constant return to the twofold promise to Abraham, the memory of which prevents the earthly kingdom from becoming the City of Man.

Contrary to Al-Farabi, Augustine sees prophecy as superior to philosophy, and the proof of prophecy is superior to the proof of philosophy. In Book 18, Augustine treats philosophy as part of secular history viewed from the perspective of biblical prophecy, and he argues for the superiority of prophecy to philosophy in several ways. The first argument is temporal: biblical prophecy is temporally prior to philosophy and therefore superior to philosophy. The more ancient wisdom is superior, and, since Abraham and Moses were prophets, biblical prophecy precedes Greek philosophy (*ciu. Dei* 18.37–38). For Al-Farabi, it is the reverse: philosophy is superior to prophecy because it precedes prophecy, inasmuch as prophecy is the work of imaginatively rich philosophers. Secondly, the unity of prophecy is superior to the disunity of philosophy. Al-Farabi sees philosophy as one because essence is one; there is perfect unanimity among philosophers, and consequently Al-Farabi must – and does – argue for the unity of the philosophies of Plato and Aristotle.[15] Prophets and religions are many and must inevitably disagree. Augustine's judgment is the reverse. He elaborates the dissent among philosophers concerning such central issues as goodness, happiness, and immortality. Among the biblical prophets, on the other hand, there is consensus because the voice behind them is God, who does not contradict Himself. The consensus that Al-Farabi attributes to the philosopher, Augustine sees only in the City of God; the philosophers, by contrast, share in the dissension of Babylon.

Finally, for Augustine, prophecy is superior to philosophy because it is more perfect. Prophecy reaches that which is most real, namely, God Himself, because the central theme of prophecy is the coming of God's heavenly kingdom into time through Christ. In addition, prophecy explains more than philosophy. Prophecy reaches not only that which is most real but also that which is less real and renders it knowable. History, both sacred and secular, becomes intelligible through prophecy. Time is not an obstacle to intelligibility but that in which intelligibility comes to be, and through the coming of the eternal into time, the meaning of time becomes evident. It is likewise with evil: through prophecy, evil is not an unintelligible surd but a knowable part of divine providence. For Al-Farabi, history and evil are formed through the power exercised by the philosopher-prophet-king. For Augustine, history and evil are formed through divine providence and explicated by divine prophecy.

For Al-Farabi, prophecy represents, in part, human failure, as does the political life that depends upon it, since the image that is believed can never be the essence known by the philosopher; the political life achieved through prophecy is a mere likeness of happiness enjoyed by the philosopher. Augustine could agree that political life represents, at least in part, a human failure, although for Augustine that failure is moral rather than epistemological; political life is a consequence of Adam and Eve's sin rather than their ignorance. Nonetheless, in Books 17 and 18 of *ciu. Dei*, the earthly kingdom promised to Abraham and David was not a failure but a success. The success of the earthly kingdom depended upon its prophetic nature, which limited it in time

[15] See Al-Farabi 2002.

and purpose to preparation for the heavenly kingdom. Old Testament prophecy, for Augustine, was in no way a failure. The prophecy in the age of the prophets was a success even when it seemed to fail. Kingly misrule that governed the earthly kingdom as the City of Man was not able to undermine the prophecy that human sin would lead to a suffering messiah who would bring forth the heavenly kingdom. The earthly kingdom succeeded in preparing for the heavenly kingdom that came, and with that fulfillment of prophecy, all political history – secular and sacred, the City of Man and the City of God – became intelligible.

Since, for Augustine, prophecy is superior to philosophy, everyone is in need of prophecy. Prior to his instruction by Ambrose, Augustine saw the Old Testament as crude, ineloquent, and unessential for understanding Christ (*conf.* 3.5). Augustine argues, in Books 17 and 18 of *ciu. Dei*, that the prophetic nature of the earthly kingdom in the Old Testament eloquently speaks of the heavenly kingdom that comes through Christ. Philosophers need Old Testament prophecy to understand that eternity is to be found within time – within the course of sacred history. Christians need that prophecy to understand the long history by which they came to be. Non-believers need prophecy to understand the reasonableness of faith: Christianity is worthy of belief because its truth was foretold long before it came to be. There was necessarily some obscurity in its prophetic prefigurement, but it was clear enough to allow recognition of the coming of Christ, and now that Christ has come, the truth of Old Testament prophecy is evident and undeniable.

FURTHER READING

Al-Farabi, A. N. (1985). *Al-Farabi on the Perfect State*. Translated by Richard Walzer. Oxford: Oxford University Press.

Fakhry, M. (2002). *Al-Farabi: Founder of Islamic Neo-Platonism: His Life, Works and Influence*. Oxford: Oxford University Press.

Fazlur, R. (2011). *Prophecy in Islam: Philosophy and Orthodoxy*. Chicago: University of Chicago Press.

Seyyed, H. N. (2006). *Islamic Philosophy from Its Origin to the Present: Philosophy in the Land of Prophecy*. New York: State University of New York Press.

12 Book 19: The Ends of the Two Cities: Augustine's Appeal for Peace

ANDREW HOFER, O.P.

In Book 19, Augustine concentrates on leading two audiences, both beset by different forms of violence, unrest, and insecurity within and without, to accept God's offer of the peace that endures in heaven's everlasting life as the supreme good. Primarily, this appeal for peace has a protreptic quality to attract a non-Christian audience. Especially for their sake Augustine uses, in addition to the divine authority of Scripture, the reason of philosophical argument in Book 19.[1] Secondarily, the appeal has a didactic exhortation for a Christian audience to seek more ardently the peace of the heavenly Jerusalem.[2] Even the pilgrim Church has "sheer misery compared to the happiness we call ultimate" (*ciu. Dei* 19.10; Babcock, 2.364; CCSL 48.674).[3] Augustine makes his appeal for peace

[1] O'Daly writes, "The beginning of Book 19 marks a transition from authority to reason" (O'Daly 1999, p. 196). Similarly, Harding writes about Book 19, "[A]gainst the sacralization thesis, Augustine tells the reader that he will argue for his view on the basis of reason's testimony rather than divine authority." See Harding 2008, p. 108. But Augustine did not completely abandon the authority of Scripture in Book 19. He writes: "I shall proceed not only by appealing to divine authority, but also, for the sake of unbelievers, by appealing to reason as far as possible" (*ciu. Dei* 19.1; Babcock, 2.347; CCSL 48.657). See how he begins to respond by faith, in addition to reason, in *ciu. Dei* 19.4. Another transition in argumentation occurs at the beginning of Book 20, when he stresses the foundation of Scripture for that book's argument.

[2] For Augustine's change of defining Jerusalem as "City of Peace" to the common Greek Christian understanding of "Vision of Peace" after AD 394, and its influence on the West, see Scully 2016.

[3] Augustine later writes: "[W]ho would be so absurd, so deranged by sheer argumentative obduracy, that he would dare to assert that, amid the woes of this mortal existence, not just the holy people but every single one of the saints who is living, or will live, or has lived, lives this life without tears and sorrows? The holier a person is, and the fuller he is of holy desire, the more overwhelmingly his tears flow in prayer" (*ciu. Dei* 20.17; Babcock, 2.417; CCSL 48.728; cf. *ciu. Dei* 22.22). In preparation for the endless peace of heaven, the *beata uita* of the saint in this world has intense mourning. Possidius, at the end of the *Life of Augustine*, emphasizes that Augustine died praying the penitential psalms, weeping freely and constantly.

by humbling the peace of what each of the two audiences experiences. All people experience in this life on earth, in different ways, not only a broken society, but also a broken heart. But without recognizing that experience in humility, why would readers yearn for heaven's peace? To all, Augustine makes an appeal for what he calls *pax plenissima atque certissima* (*ciu. Dei* 19.10; CCSL 48.674).

To explain that thesis, this chapter proceeds in three parts before its conclusion. The first expounds the argument of Book 19 in regard to Augustine's rhetorical strategy of comparison and the distinctive teachings on peace that Augustine gives in that book. The second part situates that argument within the *ciu. Dei*'s structure and larger purpose of leading the two audiences to heaven's everlasting rest in the resurrection of the body. The third part provides a commentary of Book 19's main movements, with attention to the book's structure and detailed examples of how Augustine appeals for peace. For its conclusion, the chapter briefly summarizes how each of Augustine's two audiences is humbled – and how through accepting humility they can find God's peace.

THE ARGUMENT

A scholar studying the *ciu. Dei*'s history of reception can say that Book 19, of the twenty-two books of this massive and difficult work, is "the book now considered the most important."[4] And rightly so. It plays a pivotal role in Augustine's design of the *ciu. Dei* by propounding the proper ends of the heavenly and earthly cities: supreme good (*summum bonum*) and supreme evil (*summum malum*) – what is most to be sought and avoided.

The setting up of the ends of the two cities exemplifies a particular, expanded use of *synkrisis*/*comparatio* (or *similitudo*) used by Greek and Latin orators. This comparative technique has several varieties in rhetoric, and can be used to exalt one of a pair and humble the other in antithesis to persuade an audience to choose the better option.[5] Robert

[4] See Kent 2012, p. 232. Cf. O'Daly 1999, pp. 196 n.2, 209.

[5] Rhetorical handbooks have varying descriptions of *synkrisis*. It is treated eighth among topics in the extant preliminary exercises by (or attributed to) Theon, Hermogenes, and Nicolaus, and tenth by (or attributed to) Aphthonius. For English translations, see Kennedy 2003. For an example, Hermogenes says, "Sometimes we blame one thing completely and praise the other" (trans. Kennedy 2003, p. 84). For pseudo-Cicero's *Rhetorica ad Herrenium*, *similitudo* has four modes: through a contrary, in order to embellish; through negation, in order to prove; through a

Markus writes, "The exploitation of dramatic contrasts has always been one of the favoured devices of rhetoric. Augustine shared a liking for it with his literary contemporaries. There was something about the cast of his mind, however, which made dramatic contrasts a more than normally apt means of expressing his ideas."[6] Augustine maximizes contrasts in his early double treatise *mor.* (begun in Rome in AD 387) and uses it even more extensively in the *ciu. Dei.*[7] In that latter work, Augustine says in one place that antitheses are called most pleasing (*decentissima*) among the ornaments of style. There he uses that rhetorical device to elucidate how rational creatures who are morally evil still serve a purpose in God's creation for an eloquence not of words, but of things (*ciu. Dei* 11.18).[8] About those God foreknew would not be delivered, Augustine also writes: "[I]n a supremely beautiful and just ordering of the whole rational creation, he created them for the benefit of those who were to be delivered and for the sake of presenting a comparison (*comparationem*) between the two mutually opposed cities" (*ciu. Dei.* 17.11; Babcock, 2.261).

But it is not merely the establishment of two very different sets of peoples and their ends that primarily motivates Augustine. In the *ciu. Dei*, Augustine gives sets of antitheses as a bishop with an overriding concern for the salvation of people, from whichever city, who take note of his words.[9] The heavenly and earthly cities are mixed during this life on earth (*ciu. Dei* 1.35). All the inhabitants of the heavenly city are reborn in Christ from the *massa damnata* of the earthly city (*ciu. Dei* 15.1; cf. *ciu. Dei* 15.20), but all those who have been washed in baptism and made partakers of Christ's body and blood are not guaranteed to enter the kingdom of God (*ciu. Dei* 21.25; cf. *ciu. Dei*

parallel, in order to place before the audience's eyes; and through abridgement, in order to speak more clearly (*Rhet. ad Her.* 4.45–47). Quintilian says that *comparatio* is called *antitheton* by Rutilius Lupus (*Institutio Oratoria* 9.2), and that many things are proved by their contraries (*Institutio Oratoria* 12.1). For a consideration of *synkrisis* within patristic exegesis, see Sheerin 1998.

[6] See Markus 1970, p. 45.

[7] For the most thorough study of the sources of Augustine's two-city doctrine, see van Oort 1991. Augustine uses forms of *compar** eighty-two times in *ciu. Dei*, such as in the expression *in comparatione*, forms of *similit** 106 times, and forms of *contrar** eighty-nine times. Forms of the Greek loan word *antith** appear only in *ciu. Dei* 11.18, but the idea in this work is pervasive.

[8] Cf. Carruthers 2013, p. 158.

[9] For the most succinct and expressive line concerning Augustine's pastoral zeal for salvation, he preaches to his people, perhaps in AD 425 or later: "I don't want to be saved without you" (*s.* 17.2).

15.20).[10] Recognizing this blending on earth, fluidity, and precariousness can help us understand Augustine's mission to persuade by setting up stark contrasts.[11] Writing to Firmus, an avid admirer of the *ciu. Dei* but not yet baptized, Augustine gives its books the following double purpose based on two audiences:

> For their fruit does not consist in delighting the reader or in making someone know many facts that he does not know but in persuading a person either to enter the City of God without hesitation or to remain there with perseverance. The first of these is obtained by rebirth, the second by a love for righteousness. If these books do not produce this in those who read and praise them, what do they accomplish?[12]
>
> (*ep.* 2*.3; Teske, II/4.233; CSEL 88.10–11)

As Augustine develops several interlocking themes in Book 19's argument to persuade readers, he focuses on bringing them to yearn for lasting peace. The word *pax* in its various inflected forms appears over 140 times within Book 19.[13] The *Doctor pacis* himself suggests that Book 19 has peace as its most distinctive contribution.[14] When speaking about the overflowing abundance of peace for the heavenly city at rest, such that there cannot be any greater, Augustine plays in Book 20 on

[10] For Augustine's ministry to convert the earthly city into the heavenly city, see Lee 2016 and Lee 2017, pp. 75–94.

[11] On the *ciu. Dei*, van Oort writes, "It is the *antithesis* that is emphasized time and again, not so much the fact that the two *civitates* are intermingled in this present age" (original emphasis). See van Oort 1991, p. 153.

[12] Augustine writes at the beginning of the *ciu. Dei*: "Many of these [enemies of the City of God], once the error of their impiety has been corrected, do become quite worthy citizens of God's city" – while Augustine also recognizes that others who are corrected persist in their hatred (*ciu. Dei* 1.1; Babcock, I/6.2). Cf. the persuasion of the *ciu. Dei* mentioned in *retr.* 1.17(16). Johannes van Oort astutely observes that Augustine "not only *attacked* the pagans, he also *addressed* them. He defended, but he also intentionally gave a thetic explanation. It is particularly this characteristic of the *ciu. Dei* that has not received enough attention" (van Oort 1991, p. 89, original emphasis).

[13] This number includes instances of its verb *paco, pacare, pacavi, pacatus* – and excludes the chapter titles given in various editions of the text. More broadly, Donald Burt writes, "Peace is one of the central concepts in Augustine's thought. The word *pax* in one of its various forms appears more than 2,500 times in Augustine's writings." See Burt 1999, p. 629.

[14] Also, much secondary scholarship attends to Book 19 as Augustine's teaching on peace, especially in German after Fuchs 1926. For an Italian translation with long introduction and notes, see Piccolomini 2012. For a two-volume study in Spanish and English on applying Augustine's teaching on peace to today, see Dupont et al. 2018. I am grateful to Anthony Dupont for an advance copy of the first volume. The second volume is Dupont et al., 2019.

that image: "as we have *abundantly* discussed in the previous book" (*ciu. Dei* 20.21; Babcock, 2.425 [my emphasis]; CCSL 48.737).

Augustine appeals for peace from the perspective of the ends of the two cities: the *summum bonum* and the *summum malum*. A form of the dispute over what composes the blessed or happy life, this consideration *de finibus bonorum et malorum* (on the ends of the good and evil) continues a long philosophical discussion that can be traced back to Plato and Aristotle.[15] Augustine concludes Book 6 of the *conf.* by mentioning a discussion with Alypius and Nebridius *de finibus bonorum et malorum* (*conf.* 6.16.26), and how he would have preferred Epicurus's position – if Epicurus had believed that the soul continues after death.[16] *De finibus bonorum et malorum* is, in fact, a title of Cicero's work on the ethical perspectives of Epicureanism, Stoicism, and those of the Academy, which includes for him Aristotelian thought and that of Antiochus of Ascalon of the Old Academy.[17] Veronica Roberts Ogle rightly argues that this philosophical work by Cicero, skeptical of the certainty of the schools' teaching on how happiness is to be achieved, has not been sufficiently appreciated for its influence on the *ciu. Dei*.[18] While Augustine continues Cicero's critique, he changes it to a certainty that all philosophical approaches are tainted with pride, and need the Mediator who is Christ. In *ciu. Dei* 19's introduction, Augustine differentiates all the positions of the philosophers from that of the heavenly city with its twofold status of the *spes* (hope) of the pilgrim City of God and the *res* (reality) of that city at rest in the God-given happiness of glory (*ciu. Dei* 19.1; cf. *ciu. Dei* 19.20). All philosophers try "to make happiness" (*beatitudinem facere*) for themselves by discovering the supreme good and supreme evil within the vanity of this world, but they differ on where human fulfillment occurs: in the body, the soul, or both (*ciu. Dei* 19.1; CCSL 48.657; cf. *ciu. Dei* 8.8).

To build his case, Augustine focuses in the first three chapters on Cicero's brilliant contemporary Marcus Terentius Varro, often praised

15 See the examples of the analogy of the sun in Book 6 of Plato's *Republic* 507b–509c, and all of Book 1 of Aristotle's *Nicomachean Ethics* 1095a–1103a. For a discussion of Aristotle's reaction in Book 1 to Plato, see Shields 2015.

16 Augustine confesses that at that time he loved his friends for their own sake (not God's), and describes his state in terms of the restlessness of an insomniac. For commentary on Epicurus here, as related to *ciu. Dei* 19.1, see O'Donnell 1992 [2012 reprint], 2.388–389.

17 Book 1 treats Epicurean ethics, and Book 2 gives a Stoic response. Book 3 treats Stoic ethics, and Book 4 gives Antiochus's response through Cicero. Book 5 presents Antiochus's Old Academy, and a response is given to it.

18 See Ogle 2019.

and critiqued in the *ciu. Dei*. Specifically, Augustine turns to Varro's *On Philosophy*, no longer extant, with its taxonomy of 288 possible philosophical quests – with allusion to even further possibilities. For Varro, this bewildering multiplicity does not indicate fruitfulness in philosophical thinking, but rather points out the need to find the one right path in life; Augustine will make a similar argument. The plethora of schools of thought ponder the following: the possible objects of happiness (pleasure, repose, a combination of these, or the primary goods of nature); whether virtue is to be sought for the objects' sake, for virtue's sake, or the sake of both the objects and the virtue; whether the good is sought for oneself or for society; whether the good is certain (as according to the Stoics) or probable (as according to the New Academics); whether one ought to follow the mode of life of most philosophers or that of the Cynics (such as their dress and way of living habits); and, finally, the different types of life – contemplative, active, or a composite of the two. When all of these factors are multiplied ($4 \times 3 \times 2 \times 2 \times 2 \times 3$), we arrive at 288 possibilities.

Augustine uses Varro's own categories to summarize the Roman scholar's rejection and positioning of the happy life as especially enjoying virtues and the other goods of soul and body without which virtue cannot exist (*ciu. Dei* 19.3). Such a life is social, and Augustine knows from Varro and the other philosophers how the social aspect rises from one's own family, through the city and world, to all things of the universe, and claims that this life enjoys society with the gods. Given the completeness of this philosophical account, Augustine finds it contradictory that for Varro and the Old Academy, even if life becomes so unbearable that a person seeks suicide, that one still has the happy life on earth (*ciu. Dei* 19.4).

Book 19 certainly challenges the non-Christian philosophical ethics of all these schools, such as the ethics that would have attracted Augustine from his late teenage reading of Cicero's exhortation to philosophy, the *Hortensius*, now extant only in fragments. Augustine tells us that it began with: "We all certainly want to be happy."[19] But Book 19 does much more than challenge non-Christian approaches. It also offers a development from Augustine's early writings. Augustine came more sharply to express the difference between this life on earth and heaven's happiness in his anti-Pelagian writings, whose

[19] For Augustine's most famous recounting of his reading of Cicero's *Hortensius*, see *conf.* 3.4.7–8. For Augustine's quoting the beginning of that protreptic, see *Trin.* 13.4.7; CCSL 50A.391.

inauguration in AD 411/2 nearly coincided with his plan to write the *ciu. Dei*.[20] To exemplify how Augustine distances his position on the pursuit of the supreme good from his own early writings, we can see how he reviews his *s. Dom. mon.* (AD 393) in the *retr.* (AD 426–AD 427).[21]

Regarding this early work on Christ's first preaching according to Matthew's account of the Gospel, Augustine highlights two questionable uses of Matt 5:9, "Blessed are the peacemakers, for they shall be called children of God." In both Augustine contrasts the kind of peace that may be attained during this earthly life with the heavenly peace, twice called *pax plenissima* in this entry of the *retr.* (1.19[18].1–2). With respect to the first case, Augustine aligns wisdom with peace, but he does so to show his deeper realization at the end of his life that a perfect ordering in this life is impossible. He quotes his earlier work: "Wisdom belongs to peacemakers, in whom all things have already been set in order and there is no rebellious movement against reason, but everything submits to a person's spirit, just as he himself submits to God" (*retr.* 1.19[18].1; Ramsey, I/2.80; CCSL 57.55). Not well known in the reception of this passage, he comments, "The way in which I spoke is truly problematic. For no one can make such progress in this life that the law fighting against the law of our mind is utterly absent from our members" (*retr.* 1.19[18].1; Ramsey I/2.80; CCSL 57.55; cf. *ciu. Dei* 14.9).[22] The second instance is his assertion regarding "Blessed are the peacemakers" that "these things can certainly be realized in this life, as we believe that they were realized in the apostles" (*retr.* 1.19[18].1; Ramsey I/2.80; CCSL 57.56). In his retraction, the Bishop of Hippo now emphasizes that our hope lies in a peace beyond this world: "Thanks to that utter peace [*pace plenissima*] for which we hope, when it will be said, *Where, O death, is your strife?* (1 Cor 15:55)" (*retr.* 1.19 [18].2; Ramsey I/2.81; CCSL 57.56). What the apostles experienced during their lives can also be experienced in life now, but such is still quite far from heaven's peace.

Also, although Augustine does not retract the famous stages of spiritual progress outlined in *doc. Chr.* 2.7.11, his position in the *ciu. Dei* differs from this early view as well. Writing on the seven Gifts of the

[20] For a recent treatment of the work's anti-Pelagian context, see Dupont, forthcoming.

[21] Other pertinent revisions showing Augustine's more pronounced difference between what can be expected in this life and in the next include: *retr.* 1.2 (*b. vita*), 1.4.3 (*sol.*), 1.7(6).4–5 (*mor.*), and 1.14(13).2 (*util. cred.*).

[22] For an example of reception without expressing awareness of Augustine's retraction, see Thomas Aquinas, *Summa Theologiae* II-II, q. 45, a. 6, *sed contra*.

Spirit (Isa 11:2–3 LXX), Augustine comments that when one arrives at wisdom, "one thoroughly enjoys having been made peaceful and tranquil" [*pacatus tranquillusque perfruitur*] (*doc. Chr.* 2.7.11; my translation; CCSL 32.38). Such a description aligns with what Augustine said before *doc. Chr.* about the wise, but hardly captures his position on peace and tranquility in the *ciu. Dei*. For example, he says there: "And who is so fully wise that he no longer has to engage any struggle against his fleshly desires?" (*ciu. Dei* 19.4; Babcock, 2.356; CCSL 48.666).

Augustine often reminded his people of this experience after he had encountered Pelagianism's refusal to account for the frailty of human nature after Original Sin, even in baptized Christians who still struggle against concupiscence. Indeed, the penultimate chapter in Book 19, summarizing the appeal for peace, has this:

> As long as it is necessary to rule the vices, then, there is no full and complete peace. This is true both because our battle against the resisting vices is full of peril and because our triumph over defeated vices is still far from secure and effortless; it is only with an anxious and care-filled rule that we manage to hold them down. We live, then, in the midst of all these trials, which have been succinctly summarized in the divine discourse where it says, *Is not human life on earth a trial*? (Job 7:1). And who will presume that he is living in such a way that he has no need to say to God, *Forgive us our debts*? (Matt 6:12). Only an arrogant person would be so presumptuous, not someone who is truly great but someone puffed up and bloated with pride, who is justly resisted by the one who pours out his grace on the humble. That is why it is written, *God resists the proud but gives grace to the humble.*
>
> (Jas 4:6; cf. Prov 3:34; 1 Pet 5:5) (*ciu. Dei* 19.27; Babcock, 2.387; CCSL 48.697–98)

Therefore, in Book 19's argument, we find that "peace" is an analogical term, and its prime analogate is heaven's peace: the *summum bonum*.[23] In a twofold consideration for his two audiences, Augustine writes both that "in comparison to the peace of the just, the peace of the unjust ought not to be called peace at all" (*ciu. Dei* 19.12; Babcock, 2.367; CCSL 48.678), and that the heavenly peace beyond this mortal life "is so truly peace that, strictly speaking, it alone is to be called the peace of the rational creature" (*ciu. Dei* 19.17; Babcock, 2.375; CCSL 48.685).

[23] Cf. Billy 1994.

Calling peace the *summum bonum* has continuity with Augustine's early thought, as well as expresses the distinctiveness of the *ciu. Dei*. Augustine is famous for teaching that God and the *summum bonum* are equivalent; less well known is that in his early career he renamed God, among other titles, as the *summa pax* ("*ut deo quem diligit, id est summo bono, summae sapientiae, summae paci*"; *mor.* 1.24.44; CSEL 90.49). In Book 19, Augustine confirms that "the blessed life of human beings is God" (*ciu. Dei* 19.26; Babcock, 2.386; CCSL 48.696). This mutuality between peace and God as the *summum bonum* or ultimate end might assist debates that neglect this overlap in Augustine's terminology.[24] Moreover, several reasons could be ventured for our Book 19's distinctive emphasis on peace as the *summum bonum*. Pertaining to the *ciu. Dei*'s broad purpose, peace has a comprehensive application: the spiritual and the bodily, the intra-personal and the inter-personal, the philosophical and the theological, the earthly and the heavenly, the temporal and the eternal. This totality of application indicates how philosophical (explicitly in Book 19) and Pelagian (implicitly) searches for peace on earth are unfulfilled, and conveys Augustine's eschatological emphasis of heaven's reality. Perhaps most significantly for historical context, Augustine responds to the violence and unrest that occasioned the *ciu. Dei*, and so the focus on peace implies the relation between his teaching and the particular need in his first readers.

POSITION OF BOOK 19 WITHIN *CIU. DEI*

To appreciate the appeal for everlasting peace as the supreme good within the overarching argument of the *ciu. Dei*, we begin by returning to the work's theme announced in Book 1's preface. Augustine intends to treat the most glorious City of God under a twofold aspect: either through time, when it lives in pilgrimage among the impious, or in that stability of an eternal habitation with its ultimate victory and perfect peace. Some lines after establishing this intention, Augustine makes clear that he must also speak about the earthly city, which seeks to dominate but is itself dominated by the lust for dominating. Already, we know that perfect peace is found only in that City of God at rest in heaven, the principal thesis of Book 19, and the violence felt both within society and the heart. Moreover, the working of divine judgment and grace is announced in the preface through Augustine's employment of his

[24] For two contrasting studies, see Grisez 2008 and Sullivan 2010.

beloved Proverb, "God resists the proud, but he gives grace to the humble" (Prov 3:34; cf. Jas 4:6 and 1 Pet 5:5), used later, as we have already seen, near the end of Book 19. That divine intention, which Augustine understands to be the message of nearly every page of Sacred Scripture (*doc. Chr.* 3.23.33), calls all to find a peace of God's making reserved to those who in humility attain the final victory of the City of God's founder, Jesus Christ.

Now how does Book 19's argument about everlasting peace as the *summum bonum* for happiness fit within the *ciu. Dei*'s structure? In *ep.* 1A to Firmus (AD 426/7), Augustine divides up this massive and difficult work into Books 1–5 and 6–10 on the one hand, and Books 11–14, 15–18, and 19–22, on the other (cf. *ciu. Dei* 10.32 and 11.1). In the earlier double part, Augustine refutes those who consider the worship of the gods (i.e. demons) to contribute to the happiness of this life (Books 1–5), and those who, by that false worship, want life after death (Books 6–10). As a bridge between these two sets, Augustine uses Varro's *Antiquities* at the beginning of Book 6 to show how this most illustrious scholar put divine matters after human matters, because of Varro's understanding that human communities were first constituted and divine institutions are established by them (*ciu. Dei* 6.4). Thus, Book 19's argument about the end of happiness as God's establishment of peace in eternal life, and distinguishing that peace from experiences in this life, implicitly answers the two-pronged consideration of Books 1–10. Examples from Books 2 and 10 can illustrate how Book 19's argument relates to these first sets of books.

Of all connections to other books, Book 19 is most known for its tie to Book 2. In *ciu. Dei* 19.21, Augustine resumes the argument presented by Scipio in Cicero's *Republic*, discussed in *ciu. Dei* 2.21. Why does Augustine delay so long to show that there never was a Roman republic, according to the nearly tautological definition given by Scipio: *res publica res populi* – the republic is the matter or the common good of a people (*Republic* 1.25.39)? It is because he needs to establish what true justice is and how that is only "in the republic whose founder and ruler is Christ" (*ciu. Dei* 2.21; Babcock, I/6.59; CCSL 47.55). Robert Dodaro explains: "[Augustine's] argument for transforming Cicero's notion of right (*ius*) into true justice (*uera iustitia*) – a move that distinguishes their interpretations of *consensus iuris* and, thereby, disqualifies Rome as a commonwealth – becomes clear only in Book 19, by which point Augustine has contrasted Christ with Cicero's ideal statesman, as ruler of the City of God."[25]

[25] See Dodaro 2004, p. 11.

Book 10, as Book 19 later does, opens with a discussion on happiness and continues the engagement with philosophical traditions set out in the previous books. The concluding book to the two early sets regarding the earthly city's false worship offers an extended meditation on sacrifice, the perfect sacrifice of Christ which the faithful join, and how unlike that is to Porphyry's understanding of rituals. And so what sacrifices does God want from us? Augustine writes that there is only one: "a contrite heart, humbled by the sorrow of repentance" (*ciu. Dei* 10.5; Babcock, I/6.310; CCSL 47.277). That has great importance for understanding Book 19's argument, in which Augustine wants his audiences to be humbled.

According to *ciu. Dei* 11.1 (cf. Augustine's *ep.* 1A to Firmus and *ciu. Dei* 10.32), the other three sets of books look at the origins (Books 11–14), developments (Books 15–18), and ends (Books 19–22) of the two cities. Such an orderly tracing is appropriate for an encomium or an invective, and Augustine uses antitheses to praise one city and reproach the other in his comparison. Book 19 begins the final consideration, on ends, which in some sense mirrors the origins and shows the intelligibility of why the histories of the two cities occur as they do. By announcing both the *summum bonum* and the *summum malum*, Book 19 sets up the final judgment, reviewed in Book 20, as well as the eternal death in Book 21 and the eternal life in Book 22. Examples from Books 14, 18, and 22 can assist our consideration of how Book 19 fits within this second part of books, marked by its threefold division.

Out of the four books on the origins of the two cities, we turn to Book 14. In *ciu. Dei* 14.1, Augustine emphasizes that God's intention in creation, by creating one human being from whom all others would originate, is that all would be together in a harmonious unity in a bond of peace (*pacis uinculo* [CCSL 48.414]). But after sin, a duality has occurred in the human race. Taking a Pauline contrast to describe the two cities, Augustine writes that one city lives according to the flesh (*secundum carnem*), while the other lives according to the Spirit (*secundum spiritum* [CCSL 48.414]).[26] Augustine adds that *secundum carnem* means according to a lie (*secundum mendacium*), according to oneself (*secundum se ipsum*), and according to a human being (*secundum hominem*), while *secundum spiritum* means according to the Truth (*secundum veritatem*), not according to oneself (*non secundum se ipsum*), and according to God (*secundum Deum*) (*ciu. Dei* 14.4; CCSL

[26] See Rom 8:1–13.

48.418). Within Book 14, Augustine writes that each city "desires its own kind of peace, and, when it finds what it seeks, each lives in its own kind of peace" (*ciu. Dei* 14.1; Babcock, 2.99; CCSL 48.414). Although Augustine has here highly significant discussions on love and the emotions, in no chapters after its first does Book 14 explicitly treat peace, but that chapter of this final book of the treatment of the origins of the two cities points us to their ends in Book 19.

To represent the four books that trace the development of the two cities, we turn to Book 17 and how Augustine considers the peace associated with Solomon's reign. Considering the prophecy in 2 Samuel 7:10–11 that the people of Israel will be troubled no more, Augustine comments: "But anyone who hopes for such a great good as this here in this world, and here on this earth, is thinking like a fool" (*ciu. Dei* 17.13; Babcock, 2.264; CCSL 48.578). Augustine believes that it is simply impossible for any people to dwell untroubled on this earth. He concludes, "Therefore the place that is promised as such a peaceful and secure habitation is eternal, and it is due to those who live eternally in the free mother Jerusalem, where they will truly be the people of Israel" (*ciu. Dei* 17.13; Babcock, 2.264; CCSL 48.578). Foreshadowing the lengthy argument of Book 19, this points us to the end of an eternal peace, as no lasting peace can be found on this earth where the faithful long for a reward during their "wretched pilgrimage" (*ciu. Dei* 17.13; Babcock, 2.264; CCSL 48.578).

For our last point of comparison, we consider the final book, which concludes the argument about the end of the good started in Book 19. When Augustine begins his final two chapters in Book 22, he turns to Phil 4:7, "the peace of God that is beyond all understanding," to describe the saints, after the resurrection of the body, in their vision of God. In a letter to the widow Proba (c. AD 412), Augustine had used that verse for the present experience of prayer. In the search for "the one thing" (Psalm 27:4) of the happy life, we do not know what we ought to pray for (Rom 8:26).[27] Now, considering it from the perspective of the saints in heaven, Augustine gives yet another comparison for humility within the state of the City of God at rest in heaven: only God knows that peace. Not even the angels, and still less do the saints, understand God's own peace, when they become partakers of that peace in heaven. And yet there is a real peace for God's creatures in heaven. Augustine continues, "But, because we also are made partakers in his peace

[27] *Ep.* 130.14.27.

according to our capacity, we too know supreme peace in ourselves, among ourselves, and with him, insofar as what is possible for us" (*ciu. Dei* 22.29; Babcock, 2.546; CCSL 48.857). In heaven, the saints will experience the "true peace, for no one will suffer opposition either from himself or from others" (*ciu. Dei* 22.30; Babcock, 2.551; CCSL 48.862–63). There the divine intention, which had been warped by the seducer in the Garden of Eden, will be fulfilled: God "would have made us gods by participation in him, not by desertion of him" (*ciu. Dei* 22.30; Babcock, 2.553; CCSL 48.865).[28] Reaching the end of his work in the end of the heavenly city, Augustine writes, "For what else is our end but to reach the kingdom that has no end?" (*ciu. Dei* 22.30; Babcock, 2.554; CCSL 48.866).

This highly selective survey of how Book 19's argument fits within the *ciu. Dei* as a whole demonstrates how the book's appeal for peace encapsulates what Augustine intends in this magnificently structured work. Now we focus in detail on Book 19's major movements, tracing out the structure of this book with special attention to Augustine's principal message of peace.

MOVEMENTS OF BOOK 19

In response to Varro's treatment of all the possible ways of life, as we see summarized in the book's first three chapters, Augustine sets forth the City of God's response. How Augustine organizes Book 19's chapters can be debated, and the following outline offers one analysis:[29]

Chapters 1–3: Preface (1) and summary of Varro's *On Philosophy* (1–3)
Chapters 4–28: The City of God's reply regarding the *summum bonum* (4–27) and the *summum malum* (28) – first in response to Varro's *On Philosophy* (4–20), then to Cicero's *Republic* (21–25), before a general conclusion on the *summum bonum* (26–27) and brief consideration of the *summum malum* (28)
- Chapters 4–20: Response to Varro's *On Philosophy*
  - Chapters 4–17: Answering Varro's first three sets of characteristics: that naturally sought; that naturally sought in relation to virtue; that sought for one's own sake or for others

[28] For Augustine's understanding of deification, see Meconi 2013.

[29] The closest analysis to the one offered here is O'Donovan 2004, 50. O'Donovan contrasts his analysis with O'Daly 1999, p. 199; and Geerlings 1997, pp. 211–234. Fuchs 1926 has the following major sections of Book 19's chapters: 1–10; 11–17; and 18–28.

Chapter 4: Christian faith offering a happiness beyond this world (answering the first two sets of characteristics)
Chapters 5–16: Social considerations (answering the third set of characteristics)
Chapters 5–9: Social miseries
Chapters 10–13: Peace as the fulfillment of all goods
Chapters 14–16: The earthly city and the heavenly city in using temporal matters
Chapter 17: Summary of a heavenly city in pilgrimage on earth living by faith
Chapters 18–19: Answering Varro's final three sets of characteristics: certainty; dress/other living habits; and types of life
Chapter 18: matters of certainty (answering the fourth set of characteristics)
Chapter 19: dress/other living habit and types of life (answering the fifth and sixth sets of characteristics)
Chapter 20: Summary of the *summum bonum*: eternal and perfect peace
Chapters 21–25: In response to Cicero, a true republic must be in the true God by those with true virtue; comparison between the earthly and heavenly cities on what is true
Chapter 21: Never was there a Roman republic, properly speaking
Chapter 22: True God known in Christ
Chapter 23: Pagan errors (especially Porphyry's) about Christ and his city
Chapter 24: Alternative definition of a "people" based on being bonded together by objects of a common love
Chapter 25: Pagan virtues are really vices, because they are not ordered to the true God
Chapters 26–27: Conclusion regarding peace in its truest sense in the City of God at rest in heaven, compared to the earthly city's peace and the peace of the City of God on pilgrimage
Chapter 28: Answer concerning the *summum malum*: the second death's eternal war within a person.

Almost the entire book is dedicated to only one of the two ends: the intended end of the *summum bonum*. The destined end of the earthly city, *summum malum*, looks like an appendix in Chapter 28, when seen in comparison to the quest for the supreme good, and Augustine does not develop its social quality there. Yet, the *summum malum* of violence and unrest within both the heart and society was implied throughout in the search for the *summum bonum* of peace. Moreover, one should not neglect how the question of the true republic in Chapter 21, based on Cicero's *Republic*, launches into a prolonged discussion which in some ways mirrors the previous response to Varro's *On Philosophy* (Chapters 4–20). Because of the great social emphasis in Augustine's response to Varro, it is natural to return to the question of a true society or republic, as first announced in *ciu. Dei* 2.21. In both discussions of Book 19, Augustine responds to esteemed pre-Christian critical thinkers, useful to Augustine's distinctive argument to persuade readers after Christ – both Christian and non-Christian – to long for heaven's peace.

To begin his response to Varro, Augustine states that the *summum bonum* is eternal life, and the *summum malum* is eternal death (*ciu. Dei* 19.4). To attain the former and avoid the latter, we must live rightly. But we cannot do so without help from God, and during this life "we are saved in hope" (Rom 8:24). While Augustine wholeheartedly agrees with the philosophers that the wise have a social life, he shows how to understand the City of God in a way quite different from the earthly city. Augustine adduces examples from non-Christian authorities that demonstrate the fragility of this life in society, and even within one's family: Cicero's mourning over his daughter's death and the miseries of life (*ciu. Dei* 19.4); Terence's pain in marriage and children (*ciu. Dei* 19.5); Cicero's complaint of secret treachery within one's own household (*ciu. Dei* 19.5). Augustine proceeds to the next levels of society after the family as philosophically understood: the city (*ciu. Dei* 19.5–6), the world (*ciu. Dei* 19.7–8), and what the philosophers understood to be gods, but which Augustine underscores to have been demons (*ciu. Dei* 19.9).

Drawing on the pagan emphasis on heaven as the highest, after exposing that their gods are but demons, Augustine contrasts the two states of the heavenly city: the one on pilgrimage and the one having attained the highest end. Compared to the bliss of heaven, even what is known as peace on this earth is utter misery and is afflicted by the temptations from demons (*ciu. Dei* 19.10). A great lover of the psalms, which constantly pervade his thought, Augustine takes for inspiration the prayer: "Praise the Lord, O Jerusalem: praise your God, O Zion. For he has strengthened the bars of your gates: he has blessed your children within you: he has made your borders [*fines*] peace" (Ps 147:12–14; *ciu. Dei* 19.11; Babcock, 2.364; CCSL 48.674). The finality of the barred gates, meaning that there is at last no more entering or exiting, leads to the ends, or borders, being called "peace." Whereas Augustine seems to prefer the phrase "eternal life" to "peace" as the end of the city (cf. Rom 6:22), he points out that the wicked, too, have a sort of eternal life, i.e. an endless punishment. For that reason, he combines the two terms to describe the City of God's supreme good in the phrases *pax in uita aeterna* and *uita aeterna in pace* (*ciu. Dei* 19.11; CCSL 48.675). He therefore qualifies his early answer that the *summum bonum* is eternal life (*ciu. Dei* 19.4), and then gives the justification for his praise of peace.

> For peace is such a great good that, even in earthly and mortal affairs, nothing tends more gratefully to be heard, nothing is desired more intensely, and, in short, nothing better can possibly be found. And, if I choose to linger on the subject a little longer, I shall not, I think, be imposing any burden on my readers, both because peace is the end of the city we are discussing and because of the very sweetness of peace itself, which is dear to all.
>
> (*ciu. Dei* 19.11; Babcock, 2.365, altered; CCSL 48.675)

Augustine explains how basic the desire for peace in the human heart is. The desired end of those who go to war is peace, at least the kind of peace with glory that combatants want to win.[30] Robbers want to keep a kind of peace among themselves and want peace in their own homes with their families.[31] In these examples, people prefer a peace in which their own will dominates. To illustrate this basic desire, Augustine tells the story of Cacus, Vulcan's semi-human son whose name is taken from the Greek word for evil (*kakos*). One unfamiliar with the *Aeneid* may not realize that Augustine is telling a story of Rome before its founding (*Aen.* 8.184–279), as Cacus lived on Rome's Aventine Hill. Augustine relates that Cacus did not want anyone to disturb his peace, and that Cacus most wanted to be at peace with his own body. In order to achieve that peace, Cacus killed and devoured. After writing how this monster (who is evil personified) proves his point about the universal desire for peace, Augustine continues to see that even brute animals desire peace through the laws of nature. No animal can completely obliterate its nature, which seeks to be at peace, and even animal flesh, either in decaying or being eaten by other animals, follows the laws of

[30] Cf. Book 10 of Aristotle's *Nicomachean Ethics* 1177b. Cf. Broadie 1999, pp. 249–250. Elsewhere in the *ciu. Dei* for Augustine's discussion of peace as what is sought in war by the earthly city, see especially *ciu. Dei* 15.4.

[31] For Augustine's scathing likening of robbers with an unjust kingdom, see *ciu. Dei* 4.4.

peace in coming into a harmonious arrangement (*ciu. Dei* 19.12). All persons and all things, no matter how corrupt, want peace.

Augustine then lists ten different kinds of peace, each with a proper definition (*ciu. Dei* 19.13; Babcock, 2.368; CCSL 48.678–79).

1. Peace of the body: *properly ordered arrangement of its* parts
2. Peace of the irrational soul: *properly ordered satisfaction of the appetites*
3. Peace of the rational soul: *properly ordered accord of cognition and action*
4. Peace of the body and soul together: *properly ordered life and well-being of a living creature*
5. Peace of the mortal human with God: *properly ordered obedience, in faith, under eternal law*
6. Peace among humans: *properly ordered concord of mind with mind*
7. Peace of the household: *properly ordered concord, with respect to command and obedience, of those who are living together*
8. Peace of the city: *properly ordered concord, with respect to command and obedience, of its citizens*
9. Peace of the heavenly city: *perfectly ordered and wholly concordant fellowship in the enjoyment of God and of each other in God*
10. Peace of all things: *the tranquility of order, and order is the arrangement of things equal and unequal that assigns to each its due place*

Let us look closely at the expressions and ordering of these ten. Augustine places peace between one human and God only after he has laid out the building blocks of an anthropology of peace for the individual – taking into account body, lower soul, higher soul, and soul-body unity. Moreover, so cosmic is Augustine's understanding that "body" – in addition to being considered in anthropology – can describe any creature, and "irrational soul" can describe any living thing. The sixth statement, peace among people, is followed by two instantiations thereof: in the household and in the city. The ninth is identified as the peace of the "heavenly city." Notice that Augustine holds here that people are "enjoyed" in God, i.e. for God's sake, who is himself first listed as enjoyed (cf. *ciu. Dei* 19.17).[32] The tenth gives a highly

[32] This assertion can be compared to his early treatment of enjoyment of the Trinity alone, properly speaking, in *doc. Chr.* 1.3.3–5.5, 1.22.20–21, and 1.33.36–37. Augustine earlier held that "when you enjoy someone in God, you enjoy God

influential summation in describing peace as *tranquilitas ordinis*.[33] Rather than a virtue, peace is a state that exists following upon an order. That is why nature provides for peace even in inanimate creatures. Even the wicked can have a sort of peace, although theirs is not worthy of the name.[34]

Augustine affirms that God is the wise creator who has ordered all things justly, and so our peace depends on that order. Augustine employs his *uti-frui* doctrine to show the difference between the earthly city and the heavenly city in how they respectively see blessings of life on earth in temporal peace – such as peace within the human body, with various needs common to all met, or in fellowship with one another. One can either choose to use (*uti*) such temporal goods rightly in order to enjoy (*frui*) God and neighbor in God, or choose otherwise – and suffer unending loss. According to Augustine, all use of temporal things for the earthly city is for an earthly peace, but for the heavenly city all of that use is for the enjoyment of eternal peace (*ciu. Dei* 19.14). For right loving, Augustine gives not only the two chief precepts of love of God and love of neighbor as yourself, as he often does,[35] but he also adds two rules for concord among humans: "first, to harm no one and, second, to help anyone that one can" (*ciu. Dei* 19.14; Babcock, 2.371; CCSL 48.681). Moreover, Augustine explains that the "command-obedience" model of peace must not be for the pride of the one who commands, for the one who commands must do so out of compassion for the one who is meant to obey.

rather than that one" (*doc. Chr.* 1.33.37; my translation; CCSL 32.27). O'Donovan 1982 offers an argument for Augustine's development of the *uti-frui* distinction, and criticizes Augustine's pilgrimage motif in *doc. Chr.* 1 as detrimental to a proper love of neighbor. Many scholars have responded. Recently, Stewart-Kroeker defends the appropriateness of Augustine's pilgrimage motif in Stewart-Kroeker 2017, pp. 204–244. I am grateful to Irenaeus M. Dunlevy, O.P., for alerting me to Stewart-Kroeker's critique of O'Donovan. In *ciu. Dei* 19.17, Augustine combines the pilgrimage motif with a strong articulation of doing all for God *and neighbor*; cf. *ciu. Dei* 19.13.

33 To take one example of influence, Thomas Aquinas cites the definition and identifies Book 19 in the following texts: *In Sent.* 4, d. 49, q. 1, a. 2, qc. 4, co.; *STh* I, q. 103, a. 2, arg. 3; *STh* II-II, q. 29, a. 1 (mentioning Book 19 in arg. 1, and quoting Augustine's "tranquility of order" in the corpus and in the reply to the first objection); and *De div. nomin.*, cap. 11, lec. 1. He also names Augustine, without mentioning Book 19, and simply gives the definition, without mentioning Augustine, elsewhere.

34 Cf. *ciu. Dei* 19.12.

35 For an influential passage regarding biblical interpretation, see *doc. Chr.* 1.35.39–36.41.

Continuing the consideration of using temporal matters regarding command and obedience, Augustine addresses the questions of slavery and sin in Chapters 15 and 16. He comments on God's entrustment of animals to the human race (Gen 1:26): "He did not want a rational creature, made to his own image, to have dominion except over irrational creatures – not man over man but man over beasts" (*ciu. Dei* 19.15; Babcock, 2.372; CCSL 48.682). Alluding to Abel in Gen 4:2, Augustine underscores that this is why the righteous were shepherds of flocks, not kings over other human beings. He writes, "By nature, then, as God first created man, no one is a slave either to man or to sin" (*ciu. Dei* 19.15; Babcock, 2.373; CCSL 48.682). Although he denies slavery to be something of human nature, Augustine lamentably does not attempt to reverse the social order of slavery, and gives a theological reason for its continuance as being on account of sin.[36] Indeed, because of sin, there exists not only slavery, but also other kinds of dominion on earth – "until all unrighteousness passes away, all human rule and power are brought down, and God is all in all" (*ciu. Dei* 19.15; Babcock, 2:373; CCSL 48.682). Augustine propounds how those responsible must take care, especially spiritual care, of those beneath them on this side of heaven. "Until that home is reached, however," Augustine says, "fathers have a greater obligation to put up with being masters than slaves do to put up with being slaves" (*ciu. Dei* 19.16; Babcock, 2.373; CCSL 48.683).

Re-articulating principles in Chapters 4–16, Chapter 17 addresses peace on earth and the two cities by emphasizing that one city lives by faith and the other does not. Augustine subordinates everything of this world to the worship of the true God. The heavenly city "cares nothing about any differences in the manners, laws, and institutions by which earthly peace is achieved or maintained" (*ciu. Dei* 19.17; Babcock, 2.375; CCSL 48.685). The heavenly city can use the peace of the earthly city to its own end of heavenly peace. While still on pilgrimage, that heavenly city "lives justly when it directs toward the attainment of this peace every good act it performs for God and – since the life of a city is most certainly social – for neighbor" (*ciu. Dei* 19.17; Babcock, 2.375; CCSL 48.685).

Before the summary of Augustine's response to Varro in Chapter 20, Chapters 18 and 19 address the three final categories of Varro's classification: certainty, dress/manner of life, and the kinds of life. Regarding

[36] Garnsey 1996, pp. 206–219; and Ramelli 2016, pp. 152–159.

certainty, Augustine briefly defends the idea that we can be certain about various kinds of knowledge and sense experience, against the skeptics of the New Academy; but he still allows for doubt in matters not of the faith. For certainty in faith, Augustine stresses the canonical Scriptures, and he also shows the importance of trusting reliable witnesses. Augustine handles the question of dress/manner of life quickly, as such things do not really matter if they do not touch upon right doctrine. As for the contemplative and active lives, as well as a combination of the two, Augustine stresses that all three of them are appropriate in this life of faith – provided that all have charity. One living the contemplative life must still be concerned about the good of neighbor, and one living the active life must still be devoted to contemplating the truth. Before going on to his next topic, Augustine summarizes his response to Varro and affirms that the supreme good of the City of God is "eternal and perfect peace" (*ciu. Dei* 19.20; Babcock, 2.377; CCSL 48.687).

Chapters 21–25 fulfill Augustine's delayed promise, announced in *ciu. Dei* 2.21, to provide a definition of a republic – and concludes that there never was a Roman republic. Throughout this discussion, one must keep in mind his rhetorical strategy of *synkrisis/comparatio* in setting up an antithesis to show enormous difference between things that could be thought, by some, similar. Compared to the City of God, the Roman republic was not a republic. Compared to Christian justice, pagan justice is injustice. Compared to the Christian worship of the true God, pagan worship is demonic. Compared to Christian virtue, pagan virtue is vice. All of these comparisons are related in Augustine's response to Scipio's definition in Cicero's *Republic*: *res publica res populi*, i.e. the republic is "the common good of a people" (*Republic* 1.25.39.; cf. *ciu. Dei* 19.21; Babcock, 2.377; CCSL 48.687). Augustine denies that the earthly city has justice, divine worship, and any authentic virtue – because that city is not directed by the true God. True justice does not exist without true piety. Robert Dodaro writes, "Only the true philosophy (*uera philosophia*) of the Christian religion offers a pathway to God which promotes true virtue in the face of the soul's anxiety before death. In doing so, this true philosophy provides the pattern for the just society, demonstrating at the same time the structure of that society in relation to Christ."[37]

[37] Dodaro 2004, p. 31.

Augustine's account of Porphyry here continues a long-standing engagement with that Neoplatonist, perhaps most famously evidenced in Book 10.[38] In Book 19's discussion, Augustine emphasizes that the heavenly city on earth can make sacrifice to the true God in right worship through Christ whose unique mediatorial role is not recognized by Porphyry, who on one hand praises the God of the Hebrews but on the other hand attacks Christians. Reminiscent of *ciu. Dei* 10, Augustine says of God and his city: "And we ourselves – that is, his own city – are his best and most noble sacrifice" (*ciu. Dei* 19.23; Babcock, 2.387; CCSL 48.694–695).[39]

Yet Augustine does admit, echoing the end of Book 14, that a people can be formed together by a common object of love. The better their object of love, the better the society is. If we take this definition, Augustine concedes, "the Roman people is a people, and its common good is without doubt a republic" (*ciu. Dei* 19.24; Babcock, 2.385; CCSL 48.695). But a people without the true God is doomed, as their object of love is only of this world.

In Chapters 26 and 27, we have Augustine's concluding comments in his long discussion on peace – not surprisingly given in comparisons. In Chapter 26, Augustine looks at the earthly city's peace in relation to the heavenly city on pilgrimage. Far from deserving apathy, the earthly city's peace should be prayed for (cf. 1 Tim 2:2). The heavenly city makes good use of the earthly city's peace, in fulfillment of Jeremiah's prophecy about Babylon for the people of God: "because in its peace is your peace" (Jer 29:7). In Chapter 27, as we have seen above, the peace of the heavenly city on pilgrimage does not have the security and fullness of that city at rest. Every day here, Christians must pray this key line of the Lord's Prayer: "forgive us our trespasses" (Matt 6:12) – which Augustine quotes twice in this penultimate chapter. Only in heaven will we see the perfect order that Augustine repeatedly calls to mind in Book 19, where: "God will rule the person, the soul will rule the body, and the delight and ease with which we obey in that final peace will be as great as the happiness with which we live and reign in it" (*ciu. Dei* 19.27; Babcock, 2.387; CCSL 48.698; cf. *ciu. Dei* 19.4, 13, 14, 21, and 25 as well as *ciu. Dei* 9.5).

After such a lengthy and involved argument on eternal life's peace as the *summum bonum*, Augustine very briefly concludes Book 19 in its

[38] For an overview of Augustine on Porphyry, see Clemmons forthcoming.

[39] For Augustine's development in understanding the Church as sacrifice, see Lee 2017, pp. 95–122.

last chapter by considering the end of the other city (*ciu. Dei* 19.28). That supreme evil will be the never-ending second death. In mortal life various kinds of conflict and violence will cease due to death. One can reflect back on Augustine's cataloging of evils in this world, especially the evil of suicide. In the endless death after mortal life, suicide is not an option. Interminable life outside the City of God is an everlasting war within the heart.

CONCLUSION: BEING HUMBLED BY AUGUSTINE'S APPEAL FOR PEACE

As a master rhetorician, Augustine uses *synkrisis/comparatio* to a remarkable degree in the *ciu. Dei*, and especially in Book 19. Most obviously, he contrasts the end of the City of God with that of the earthly city, but one should not ignore how he also differentiates the two states of the City of God. In the latter comparison, one state is happy in a qualified sense in the status of being on pilgrimage, as that happiness is only *in spe* (in hope), not *in re* (in reality). Highly extolled in the *ciu. Dei* is the security of heaven, and praising it cannot alter its constancy – unlike that which is praised during this life on earth, due especially to human susceptibility to pride after praise is given. In the eternal state of the City of God, "the peace of this blessedness, or the blessedness of this peace, will be the supreme good" (*ciu. Dei* 19.27; Babcock, 2.387; CCSL 48.698). In comparison to that peace, Augustine humbles the peace of the pilgrim City of God, just as he humbles the peace of the earthly city in comparison to the peace of the City of God.

In having a double comparison, with two forms of humbling, Augustine addresses his two audiences. Each can recognize where they are humbled in terms of the peace, and its lack, that they now experience. The two cities on earth are so entangled that no heart on earth can experience perfect order in goodness as it longs for lasting peace, nor be so evil as to destroy the nature of its created goodness and not long for lasting peace. Will those finding themselves in the earthly city recognize their distance from the fullest and most certain peace, confess the violence and unrest within themselves, and so convert by faith to depend on God's help to use the world well for his glory? Will those claiming to be in the heavenly city on pilgrimage recognize their distance from the fullest and most certain peace, confess the violence and unrest within themselves, and so rely in faith on God's help to use the world well for his glory? Recall from Book 10 that the only sacrifice God wants is "a contrite heart, humbled by the sorrow of repentance" (*ciu. Dei* 10.5; Babcock, I/6.310; CCSL 47.277). In Book 19, Augustine has made his appeal for peace by humbling the peace of what each audience experiences. He wants his readers in humility to receive consolation now through hope in order for their lives to become an acceptable sacrifice: that they may be exalted by receiving the blessed life of sharing in the peace of the One who *resists the proud, but gives grace to the humble*. Sometime after that divine resistance to the proud and graciousness to the humble, God's final judgment will come, the subject of Book 20.[40]

FURTHER READING

Kent, B. (2012). Reinventing Augustine's Ethics: The Afterlife of City of God. In J. Wetzel, ed., *Augustine's City of God: A Critical Guide*. Cambridge: Cambridge University Press, pp. 225–244.

Meconi, D. V. (2013). *The One Christ: St. Augustine's Theology of Deification*. Washington, DC: Catholic University of America Press.

O'Donovan, O. (1982). *Usus et Fruitio in Augustine, De Doctrina Christiana* 1. *Journal of Theological Studies*, 33, 361–397.

Scully, E. (2016). Jerusalem's Lost Etymology: How Augustine Changed Latin Eschatology. *Vigiliae Christianae*, 70(1), 1–30.

40 For assistance on this chapter, I am grateful to Irenaeus M. Dunlevy O.P., Douglas Finn, John Baptist Ku O.P., Austin G. Murphy O.S.B., and Gabriel Torretta O.P.

13 Book 20: The Last Day: Judgment, Purification, and Transformation

ISABEL MOREIRA

"The whole Church of the true God holds, confesses and professes that Christ is going to come from heaven to judge the living and the dead" (*ciu. Dei* 20.1; Babcock 2.390), as Augustine shows throughout *ciu. Dei* 20. As simple as this affirmative statement may sound, its emphatic nature masks the complexity of thought about God's final judgment that had already come to challenge the Christian community by the early 5th century AD, and which Book 20 was designed, in part, to address. True enough, all known early creeds encapsulated the promise of a future judgment requiring Christians to affirm their belief that Christ, with the Father, would judge the living and the dead. But this still left many questions unanswered. When would this judgment occur? How would the events of the last day unfold? How would divine justice be done, and be seen to be done? How did the ordinary experience of human death relate to the events outlined in the Book of Revelation? And what kind of community would result?

Even beyond the spatter of pragmatic curiosities that accounts of the last days typically raised, there was by far the more difficult challenge of trying to imagine a day of divine judgment that must remain intractable and inscrutable at present because the human capacity for understanding it was lacking. Perhaps unsurprisingly, then, Augustine fixed his attention on a kind of judgment day of his own, surveying a multitude of scriptural texts, separating good interpretations from bad, and imposing order on chaos. Rather than trying to address the unknowable nature of God's justice head on, Augustine persuaded his readers that what they really needed to know, and what was central to providing answers to their questions, was how scriptural texts that appeared to be at variance should be understood and reconciled; how a prophecy of future events was in actuality a text that operated on two levels, the literal and the metaphorical, revealing some of the events of the end times, but perhaps more importantly, revealing information about the immediate fate of the human soul after death.

Augustine understood that he could not begin to address God's judgment and the events of the last days without first addressing the testimony given in the *Apocalypse of John*.[1] This book would have been familiar to his readers and so, too, would some of the expectations about the end times fueled by a literal reading of the text: that the end of the world was close, and after that Christ and his saints would reign for a thousand years. Even in Augustine's day, the Apocalypse was a problematic book that some communities accepted and others rejected. Furthermore, continuing traditions of prophetic writing in the form of visionary texts provided rival views of that lay beyond death.[2] The deep history of Jewish and Hellenistic apocalyptic eschatology that lay behind the Christian text, provided it with language, content, and a long history of interpretation that Augustine, like those before him, had absorbed.[3]

It also meant that the authority of this newest, Christian revelation, was important to affirm. In Book 20 Augustine affirmed the authority of Apocalypse, stripped of its literal millenarian interpretation, to answer questions about end times for Christians. In providing a key to its interpretation, Augustine solidified for the Western Church what the orthodox, spiritual interpretation of the book should be. But, at the same time, Augustine affirmed another profound truth about the text: while not denying entirely its authority as a prophecy of some of what the future held, Augustine made it a text about the spiritual life of the Christian, the fate of the individual, and the future of the Christian community. In short, the book of the Apocalypse with its description of the end times was to be understood also as a treatise *avant la lettre* on death and the afterlife. Augustine's exegetical method and some of his specific solutions to the text's interpretation were not entirely new, but as a much referenced authority on this issue in subsequent centuries, his well-considered exposition on the work carried enormous weight. As a result, God's judgment, the events of the last days, the fate of the

[1] Augustine prefers "Apocalypse" over the "Book of Revelation": "*in libro, qui dicitur apocalypsis*" (*ciu. Dei* 20.7). For the English translation, see Bettenson 1984.

[2] B. McGinn, "John's Apocalypse and the Apocalyptic Mentality" in Emmerson and McGinn 1992, pp. 3–19.

[3] The history of apocalyptic writing and interpretation in early Christianity and the Middle Ages is extensive. Some useful discussions: Hill 2001; Emmerson and McGinn 1992; and essays in Bynum and Freedman 2000; Landes 1988, pp. 137–211. See also the useful bibliography of commentaries on the Apocalypse to 1700 in Boxall and Tresley 2016.

dead, and the authority of the Apocalypse to inform on these matters, were intimately and indelibly connected for Western audiences.

At the same time as Book 20 of the *ciu. Dei* contributes to the history of the interpretation of the Apocalypse, and dominated that scripture's reception in the Middle Ages, Book 20 is also witness to an historical era of divergent opinions and contemporary debates about God, the last day, and the nature of justice. Augustine was grappling with his own intellectual stance vis á vis rejected theologies: The dualism and perfectionism of Manicheism, the purification and ascension narratives of the Platonic soul, the millenarian claims of Donatists, and the deeper challenge of Pelagianism that seemed to compromise the full autonomy of God's judgment.

The structure of Book 20 is complex. This is, in part, because Augustine needed to incorporate an extended spiritual interpretation of key passages of the Apocalypse within his account of the events of the last days. At the same time he streamlined his task by focusing on God's final judgment, rather than seeking to explain the ongoing nature of divine judgment in human affairs. The basic structure of the chapter is as follows: An introduction to some key terms and concepts that will inform the discussion; an analysis of a key passage in Apocalypse that exemplifies his method; the events of the last days culminating in the final judgment; the glory that follows for the Christian faithful; the ways in which other scriptural texts support this interpretation. And, interspersed throughout, there is discussion of some fundamental issues that concerned the Christian community, how it should consider its future, and the relationship between the living and the dead.

Because Augustine's explication of the Apocalypse was so profoundly important to later interpretations of that text, and to ideas about the last days in the West, the first part of this essay will give an overview of Augustine's approach to the text. The second part of the essay identifies some ideas that Augustine's analysis helped generate and disseminate to later ages. The list of these is not exhaustive, but includes the affirmation that God's justice is just, that the Christian community encompasses both the living and the dead, that the resurrection will be corporeal in nature, and that the blessed in heaven will know the punishment of the wicked. Other ideas were more entangled in contemporary debates so that, viewed from the long perspective of history, they were suggestive rather than definitive. Augustine's views on purification and purgation fits into the latter category.

THE APOCALYPSE AS EVIDENCE FOR THE LAST DAY

By Augustine's time, there was already a long tradition of interpreting the Apocalypse and a long history of disputing its authority. Even within Augustine's lifetime, on his own doorstep, the status of the Apocalypse, the main scriptural source for the events of the last day, had to be positively affirmed at the Council of Hippo in AD 393, and at the Councils of Carthage (AD 397 and AD 419). The canonicity of the book had still to be affirmed in Spain at the fourth Council of Toledo in AD 633.[4] Thus, when Augustine wrote on "the day of God's final judgment" (*die ultimi iudicii Dei*), he knew he was writing with an eye also to the sceptics, the *impios et incredulos* (*ciu. Dei* 20.1; Babcock 2.389; CCSL 48.699). This gives some context to the relentless documentation of scriptural proofs for God's judgment in Book 20.

Interpretations of the Apocalypse abounded, but at the most basic level there was a distinction between those who relied more heavily on a literal interpretation of the scriptural text for the events of the last days, and those who employed a spiritual interpretation in the Greek fashion, facilitated by the strong imagery of the text that lent itself to symbolic interpretation ('apocalypse' being a revelation of something hidden). A literal reading of the text, accessible to scholar and ordinary Christian alike, sketched dramatic and imminent future events. Some of these readings, which were once widely accepted, now appeared dangerous to the tranquility of the legal position of the Church. For example, in seeking to extract the date of the Second Coming from the many numbers supplied by the text, great injury was done to the reputation of the Church: Augustine called some of these views *ridiculas fabulas* (*ciu. Dei* 20.7; CCSL 48.708). Although he did not ignore the computational aspect of the text, and it did not disappear in later medieval works on the Apocalypse, Augustine appears to have taken to heart Tyconius' scepticism about "number mysticism" as it related to end times.[5] Thus Augustine set out to offer an account of the last days in which the Apocalypse was explicated in such a way as to

[4] Toledo IV, cap. 17. Denzinger 486, p.487. Isidore of Seville was a prime mover at this council. Canon 17 informs us that there were "many" who did not accept the authority of the apocalypse, and refused to preach it. Here it is affirmed, on the authority of many councils, that the apocalypse's author is the apostle John, and that refusal to accept the work will result in excommunication. Although not mentioned as an authority here, it can be imagined that Augustine's commentary will have added weight against those who refused its authority.

[5] "Lest the millennium be fulfilled" on the tradition of chronologies and its problematic association with eschatology, see Landes 1988, esp. p. 156 n.71.

maintain its central place in providing a prophecy on eschatology. This would be accomplished by carefully tiptoeing through the text, understanding it in places as literal, and others as metaphorical, for as Augustine explained, the prophetic style "loves to mingle figurative (*translata*) with literal expressions (*propriis uerbis*) and, in this way, to veil its meaning to some extent" (*ciu. Dei* 20.16; Babcock, 2.416; CCSL 48.727). The Apocalypse, for all its challenges, and the call in some quarters for it to be removed from the canon of biblical texts, was not to be discarded: it was to be explained. Fortunately, Augustine did not have to do this from scratch. It is widely accepted that Augustine's hermeneutic drew carefully but extensively on the work of earlier interpreters of the Apocalypse, in particular the work of Tyconius, a Donatist theologian who had reigned in some of the excessive millenarian hopes of the Donatist sect.[6] The loss of Tyconius's commentary on the Apocalypse, and the unreliable nature of second hand references to it by later authors, means that the full extent of Augustine's debt is unknown. But from what can be gleaned, it was considerable. From Jerome, too, Augustine accessed commentaries on apocalyptic prophesies of the bible.[7] Furthermore, Augustine had already rehearsed some of his thinking on the end of the world in correspondence with Hesychius, Bishop of Salona (*ep.* 197–199).

At the same time that Augustine worked with an eye to earlier models of exegesis, he was working with another eye to millenarian interpretations that grasped on to the image of the thousand years during which Christ and his saints would reign, a view Augustine resoundingly rejected. At the same time, Augustine may also have been prompted to respond to the contemporary popularity of the Vision of Paul, a work that claimed (erroneously) the apostle Paul as its author, and which did precisely what Augustine would strive to do in Book 20, that is, to provide a guide to the last days and to God's judgment by bringing together elements of the prophecy text with ideas about the immediate fate of the soul after death.[8] Although Augustine did not

[6] And behind Tyconius, an already long tradition of commentary on the millennium in the works of Papias (Irenaeus, Against the Heretics, 5.33), Irenaeus, Lactantius, and others. Irenaeus, *Proof of the Apostolic Teaching* 61. Trans, Joseph P. Smith, *St. Irenaeus: Proof of the Apostolic Preaching*, New York: Newman Press, 1952 [ACW 16]. See Hill 2001; Fredriksen 1991, pp. 151–183. For Tyconius, see R. Gryson, ed., *Tyconii Afri expositio Apocalypseos*, CCSL 107A.

[7] Jerome, *Commentary on Daniel*. Migne, PL 25; Ed. F. Glorie, *Commentariorum in Danielem III*, CCSL 75A.

[8] The Vision (Apocalypse) of Paul's debt to millenarian views such as those described by Ireneaus and others, resulted in a conflation of elements of the future times with an account of the fate of the dead. On this see the important study of Claude Carozzi

specifically reference the Vision of Paul in the *ciu. Dei*, he was familiar with a version of it, having dismissed it some years earlier as a text full of fables (*fabulis plenam*; *eu. Jo. tr.* 98.8.2).[9] Yet the Vision of Paul was a powerful text, and useful, in that it answered questions about the fate of the soul immediately after death while urging present penitence. Augustine, too, would look to the Apocalypse and his reconstruction of the end times, as a way to promote a pastoral message of repentance to his readers. His interpretation of the text, rejecting chronological literalism while foregrounding the pastoral, dominated the later tradition of commentary on the Apocalypse in the West. Nevertheless, his exegetical tour de force would not succeed either in curtailing enthusiasm for fabulous visions of the afterlife, or in curbing sporadic millenarian fervor in the future.

BREAKING THE CODE: SOME PRELIMINARY TERMS AND METHODS

How, and in what ways, did the Apocalypse inform Christians about the end of times? Augustine approached his task with the mindset of a code breaker. The Apocalypse was an enigma, and intended to be so, but it was not entirely inscrutable. As Augustine writes, "In this book called The Apocalypse many things are said obscurely in order to exercise the mind of the reader, but there are a few things in it that are put clearly so that, in their light, the rest can be searched out with hard work" (*ciu. Dei* 20.17; Babcock, 2.417). Anyone who has tackled the *New York Times* Sunday crossword puzzle is familiar with this tactic. Some clues are simple in order to facilitate uncovering those that are complicated. While some parts of the process of decoding was labor (*labore*), especially in cases where the author's repetitions obscured the fact that he is talking of the same thing, still there was evident excitement to be had in decoding its secrets, and Augustine approached this task with relish. Moreover, in sharing his ciphers with the reader, he took them along with him on his journey of exploration, anticipating that they worked intellectually alongside him. Once his interpretive method was understood, he explained, the reader may "simply [take] the trouble to make

(Carozzi 1994). In the Long Latin versions, it is made clear that this land of promise is where the souls of the just are sent for a while (interim). See Silverstein and Hilhorst 1997, p. 114.

9 Augustine shows that he was familiar with the Vision of Paul tradition in the *ench.* 112–113 where he references, without attribution, the refreshment of the damned.

use of the help provided by the passages we have already set forth" (*ciu. Dei* 20.20; Babcock, 2.424).

He relates that he will employ interpretative devices that are commonly understood when reading scripture. For example, when examining "the Last Day," he will take "day" to mean "time" and thereby allow that the last "day" may be more elastic than a human understanding of a 24-hour day. Whereas the judgment of the "last" or "final" day will be his subject, Augustine will argue that God is always judging and has done so from the beginning (*ciu. Dei* 20.1; Babcock 2.390). God is just; contrary to superficial appearances, God's justice is not capricious, just hidden (*ciu. Dei* 20.1). Augustine will prioritize the evidence of the New Testament over the Old, as it is revealed through Christ, and this dictates the order also in which the evidence will be presented (*ciu. Dei* 20.4). Christ will be aided in his judgment by twelve men, but the number twelve symbolizes a multitude of judges. Ambiguous passages will be left aside because their timeframe is unclear. "Judgment" means "condemnation," thereby explaining John the evangelist's otherwise problematic statement (Jn 5:23–24) that the faithful will not come to judgment (*ciu. Dei* 20.5–6). And early on Augustine introduces a major distinction (discussed below), the idea of a "first" and "second" death aligned to a "first" and "second" resurrection (*ciu. Dei* 20.6). Finally, the interpretation of some passages can be gleaned by comparing them with parallel passages in the synoptic gospels – a method he has used. In so doing, Augustine was using a classic mode of interpretation developed by ancient scholars – interpreting Homer from Homer, as the saying went.

Augustine was clear about the parameters he had set for his task. He would examine God's final judgment on the "Last Day," that is, the day when Christ would come to judge the living and the dead, not – he says – all the other days and ways that God has judged and judges still. (The latter lie in the future and will unroll according to the testimony of the Apocalypse). This was a concrete task. Yet it was also a tricky task that involved taking on a sub-set of other tasks. Augustine wanted to demonstrate that the Apocalypse was a prophetic text whose revelation dovetailed with evidence from other scriptural sources; that its wisdom could be unlocked by careful analysis of key terms and concepts. But also on a larger scale, Augustine wanted to extract a spiritual and pastoral lesson for his readers. In gaining a correct understanding of God's justice, and of the justice of God's justice, of the finality of the final judgment, he hoped to imprint on the minds of his readers the urgency that such knowledge must give to their examination of their lives.

UNLOCKING THE APOCALYPSE

In view of the length and complexity of the text, Augustine does not attempt a systematic commentary on the entire work. Rather, he starts by excerpting a critical passage that, as he explains, has been much misunderstood, but whose careful reading can unlock the way the entire text can be approached. It is worth quoting the passage here in full as this section of Book 20 arises from a close reading of this text. There are two paragraphs. The first is as follows:[10]

> And I saw an angel coming down from heaven, holding in his hand the key to the bottomless pit and a chain. And he took hold of the dragon, that ancient serpent, who is also named the devil and Satan, and bound him for a thousand years, and threw him into the pit, and shut and sealed it over him, so that he would no longer deceive the nations until the thousand years were ended. After that he must be released for a little while.
>
> (Rev 20:1–3, as at *ciu. Dei* 20.7; Babcock, 2.399)

Augustine's first task was to explain how the timeframe of this prophecy should be understood. He explains that there are time distinctions within the prophetic book so that instead of the work's entirety being understood as reflecting the future, some of the prophecy was already in the process of fulfillment; that is, some 'prophecies' reflected the present.

A linear, literal reading of the text would result in an interpretation that saw all these events as happening in the future. This was the error of the chiliasts (χιλιαστές), or millenarians (*miliarios*) according to Augustine. A fully futuristic, literal reading of this passage would result in a belief that at some point in the future, Christ would descend from heaven and there would be a frolicking good time for 1,000 years, with

[10] Taking a leaf from Augustine, the passage would read thus: "And I saw an angel coming down from heaven, holding in his hand the key to the bottomless pit (who represent the impious enemies of the Christians) and a chain. And he took hold of the dragon, that ancient serpent, who is also named the devil and Satan, and bound him (holding back his full power to destroy the faithful) for a thousand years (which is in the present time), and threw him into the pit (allowing him to work in the hearts of the impious), and shut (so that the Devil could not transgress against Christians) and sealed it (keeping it a secret who was evil and who was not) over him, so that he would no longer deceive the nations until the thousand years were ended (at some undetermined time in the future). After that he must be released for a little while (for three years and six months)."

fine feasts, plenty to drink, and general immoderation and excess. Augustine had once tried to interpret these feasts as being of the spiritual kind, but he now rejected even that solution. Rather, he argues, the events in this passage reflected not the future but the present. The 1,000 years refer to the last 1,000 years, or they may refer to the whole period of history, but they are ongoing and being lived in, having 'started' with the first coming of Christ. It is in these present times that the saints are reigning with Christ; the faithful members of the Church are already rejoicing in the knowledge of their salvation. Likewise, it is in the present 1,000 years that the Devil has been bound, that is to say, that the full force of the Devil's power to corrupt the faithful has been limited as the Church grows in strength (*ciu. Dei* 20.7). The angel threw the Devil into the "pit," which is interpreted here as a reference to the multitude of the impious – those living in his own time who have set their hearts against God and oppose the servants of the Church: "Other people who hate the Christians have been born to succeed them and will go on being born to succeed them until the world ends, and every day the devil is shut up in the blind depths of their hearts as in a bottomless pit" (*ciu. Dei* 20.8; Babcock, 2.403–404). The devil's power in such people has full rein, but it is not until a future time that the devil will be given a chance to destroy the faith of the faithful, but by that time, Augustine argues, Christians will be stronger in faith. The "sealing" of the pit means that a knowledge of who belongs to this impious group remains secret, for the present (*ciu. Dei* 20.7–8).

But in the future, the devil, or the 'strong man' will be loosed and for three years and six months he will be able to exercise his full powers of temptation. These will be difficult times for the faithful, but they will gain inner confidence and strength from having had the experience of resisting such evil.

> And I saw thrones and those seated on them, and judgment was given. And the souls of those who were slain for their testimony to Jesus and for the word of God, and any who had not worshiped the beast or its image and had not received its mark on their foreheads or their hands, reigned with Jesus a thousand years, but the rest of them did not come to life until the thousand years were ended. This is the first resurrection. Blessed and holy are those who have a part in this first resurrection. Over these the second death has no power, but they shall be priests of God and of Christ, and they shall reign with him a thousand years.
>
> (Rev 20:4–6 as at *ciu. Dei* 20.7; Babcock, 2.399)

Here Augustine explains that those who currently reign with Christ are the living faithful and the departed martyrs and saints who are still part of the Church. This present time, the time of the "first resurrection," is the 1,000 years when living souls can receive the Christian message and be made alive through the rejection of sin. They have not been corrupted by the "beast" which, Augustine reflects, could represent the godless "city" that is the inverse of the "City of God." Their participation in the "first resurrection" means that at the "second resurrection," the resurrection of the body on the Last Day, they will not be felled by the "second," eternal death. However, those who have not died to sin will be eternally condemned (*ciu. Dei* 20.9–10).

What Augustine has done here is to employ a two-pronged approach. The first is to shift the time parameters, so that events that are described as being in the future are now folded back so to speak, and transposed over the present, so that the events described in the text no longer seem remote and uncertain, but rather as a prophecy fulfilled.[11] This allowed Augustine to refute a strand of millenarian thinking that was increasingly untenable. In anticipating an imminent second coming, prophecies were going unfulfilled. The whole enterprise of calculating the end was inherently unspiritual. Furthermore, with the cessation of persecution and Christian emperors in power, a new age had dawned that did not conform to the signs of the last days. By pointing to the immediate and present relevance of the text to every Christian, and finding in it answers to the most intractable theological problems, Augustine exchanged one form of excitement for another. In a spectacular and radical reorientation of the text's subject, Augustine made the Apocalypse more relevant to the concerns of the contemporary Church. Instead of the future tense, the text was cast as present participle: God was judg*ing*, Christians were be*ing* resurrected, the faithful were reign*ing*, and Jerusalem was descend*ing*.

Augustine's second intervention was to explain the work's terminology and phraseology so that his explanation of the text's temporality could be seen to be supported by scripture. We have seen how metaphorical interpretation of "the pit" (the impious), the "binding" of the devil (the limits to the devil's power), and the "sealing" of the pit (the deliberate secrecy of divine knowledge), could open the passage to a

[11] Earlier apocalypses were interpreted in similar ways. "The idea of a two-storied universe which made apocalyptic eschatology possible was always present to some degree in the biblical tradition and indeed in the ancient Near East as a whole," see Collins 1974, p. 40.

more spiritual, and ultimately more immediately relevant, message for the faithful. Furthermore, by understanding "judgment" as "condemnation" Augustine was able to navigate some tricky passages. So, too, with the chronological indicators, the numbers were to be understood in a spiritual rather than a literal way.

Crucial, however, was Augustine's exposition of the two deaths and the two resurrections, neatly aligned. Augustine's interpretation of the Apocalypse's reference to the first and second death was not new, but was explained here in a simple and forceful way. The first death was a metaphorical death: the death of letting sin into the soul. The second death was the death of the body: it brought the whole individual, body and soul, to the judgment of the Last Day. The solution to the first death (of sin) was to be baptized as one of the faithful, leading to the (first) resurrection that brought life where previously there was death, and was a reflection of God's mercy. The second resurrection was the Last Day when the bodies would rise from the earth and the sea to come to judgment:

1st death: sin enters in.	*2nd death: dissolution of the mortal body.*
1st resurrection: rejection of sin (God's mercy).	*2nd resurrection: bodily resurrection (God's judgment).*

The first resurrection (of the soul- of mercy) is to be distinguished from the second resurrection (of the body- of judgment). The first happens in life, the second is on the Last Day, but as the idea of immediate postmortem judgment took hold, this latter was transposed to the moment of the individual's death.

In *ciu. Dei* 20.13 Augustine returned to the binding and loosing of the Devil. If the saints were to reign during the thousand years that the Devil was bound (i.e. the present life), what would happen to Christians during the three and a half years of persecution by the Antichrist? Would the saints be reigning with Christ then? Or were the three and a half years an additional time beyond the thousand years of the present age? After presenting arguments on both sides, Augustine argues that the reign of the saints will last longer than that of the binding of the devil, meaning that during the time of persecution (a time when Christians will have most need of support), the saints will still reign with Christ. This short time of persecution will be endured by the whole Church and heralds the coming final judgment. Satan will rile up the forces of destruction, the nations of Gog and Magog. Augustine roundly rejects the suggestion that Gog and Magog should be equated with the "barbarians" known to his readers, and whose penetration of the Roman territories was viewed in some quarters in apocalyptic terms. In this he was consistent with his argument in Book One – that the "barbarian" invasions were not a sign of the end of days: they were, in any case, often Christians (*Homoians*), even if viewed as heretical, and even pagans were possible future Christians. However, it became commonplace for later moralists and social commentators to look to military attack as a harbinger of the end times.[12]

THE RESURRECTION OF THE DEAD

It is perhaps surprising that Augustine's account of the resurrection, judgment, and attendant separation of the saved and the damned, covers scant two chapters. It is the crux of Book 20, and yet this truly most challenging component of the last days is given the briefest description. It is this moment of judgment that resolves the admixture of good and evil that characterizes the population of the earthly city, so that they separate, like oil from water. It is the most terrifying moment of the entire drama of the last days. There is no reversal of status, and no mercy for the wicked beyond it. This is the moment when the story of the two cities reaches the outer poles of their existence and when the division between the members of the two communities are no longer hidden, but revealed. The community of the City of God takes form as a recognizable entity. The dead will come out of their graves and will face a judgment that separates the saved from the damned in a radical and irreversible moment. This division of light and dark, of saved and damned, while not strictly dualist in theology since all exists under the one same God, nevertheless jars against the general tenor of the mature Augustine's habit of thinking about the nuances of human nature, and the importance of all parts of God's creation being integrated. If human nature is so complex an amalgam of thought, action, and motivation, how can a person be judged and separated out from others? Perhaps in consequence, Augustine's approach in these two chapters is largely an elucidation of procedure (for example, he explains that the devil, representing the ungodly city, was cast into eternal torment before the dead arose from their graves), and common sense

[12] Augustine's correspondent, Quodvultdeus, was one such: *Liber promissionum et praedictorum Dei.* Ed. René Braun, *Opera Quodvultdeo Carthaginiensi episcopo tributa*, CCSL 60 (Turnhout: Brepols, 1976). The connection of military invasion with the events of the last days proved resilient in the middle ages, as in the case of responses to the Vikings.

(God does not need a book to jog his memory). He also gave thought to those still alive on the Last Day, and sketched out distinctions between different regions of the underworld as described in scripture.

The interpretation of the "books" and the "book of life" described in the Apocalypse is given careful consideration at this point in the text. Books were important in the ancient world not only as a source for information, but in an age when it is estimated that only 10 percent of the population was literate, books were also symbols: of knowledge, of authority, of elite status, of power. For the learned, however, the crude interpretation of the "book of life" as a physical book recording every person's deeds opened the scripture to ridicule among the learned. Ridicule of Christian beliefs was a longstanding form of snobbish disparagement by non-Christian thinkers and provided an easy means of dismissing the Christian scriptures *in toto*. Augustine had indulged in such snobbery as a younger man. Having spent time outside the Christian community, looking in, Augustine was now sensitive to such appearances. Part of Augustine's solution was to distinguish between the literal "books" of the scriptures whose commandments would be the basis for judgment, from the metaphorical "book of life" that represented the individual's interior, moral life: "The book of the life of everyman; and the dead were judged according to their deeds, on the record in those books" (Rev 20:12). In this passage, Augustine envisaged the "book of life" as a kind of moral mirror reflecting on "the dead," that is, a means of judging both the good and the wicked (*ciu. Dei* 20:14–15). In the next chapter (*ciu. Dei* 20:16), however, he uses the "book of life" metaphor in a different way, as a record of those who are saved, for it is the damned who "are not written in the book of life" (*ciu. Dei* 20:16; Babcock, 2.415). Augustine is thus the author of two different interpretations of the "book of life" image (perhaps viewed sequentially as before and after judgment, although this is not made clear), and thereby providing divergent representations of this image for future readers. Both interpretations lived on, especially in visions of the afterlife where the image served multiple purposes. However, the idea that the "book of life" contained only the names of the blessed was especially popular in the middle ages and gave its name to prayer lists that were optimistically termed *libri uitae*, "Books of Life."[13]

To the modern reader, the care with which Augustine explains that the "book of life" is a symbol might seem excessive and redundant.

[13] See the study of these texts by Jan Gerchow (see Gerchow 1988).

However, his attention to this is testimony to the enormous appeal of the image of a book and the degree to which a literal understanding of the book had penetrated common understanding. The image was taken from the Book of Daniel 12:1–3 where a name in the book or scroll signified the deliverance of God's people. It was to be sealed until the end of time. And whereas the book does not appear as such in the Vision (or Apocalypse) of Paul, the process of recording good deeds and bad by angels is given in detail in that work. Through a process of conflation, the book of life in which good deeds and bad were recorded by angels, rendered in the imagination as a real book, made its way into medieval visionary literature in both East and West. So it was not redundant for Augustine to assert that there was no giant book in which every Christian's deeds were recorded, or that God resorted to such a book as a form of reference. Rather, each individual would be judged by their own conscience: "each man's knowledge will accuse or excuse his conscience." Augustine adds, "and thus each and all will be judged simultaneously," removing the idea of a tedious literal reading of the deeds of humanity.

Whereas the reading of the book of life remained a popular image in later visions of the afterlife, and in religious art, Augustine's explanation that the individual was judged by their own consciousness of sin also informed vision literature: We see the idea expressed in the Vision of Paul, and also in the seventh and eighth centuries AD where it appears as a means of judgment in the Vision of Fursey, and in the Vision of the Monk of Wenlock. But whereas visions of the afterlife dwelt on pageants of judgment, with demons acting as infernal lawyers upholding scripture as evidence for the soul's damnation, Augustine's instinct was to back away from the psychological trauma, and recrimination, of judgment. The dire consequences of sin for the wicked was plain enough. Ultimately, for Augustine, the "book of life" represented God's foreknowledge, that is, it was a symbol of the predestination of the elect.

Augustine's examination of the events of the last days, and of the fate of souls at judgment, may not have been as dramatic as depictions in visionary literature, but it was not without its cinematic qualities. Rather, in the manner of a continuity supervisor for a cinematic production, Augustine thought each sequence through, accounting for all categories of the saved. In an earlier chapter (cf. *ciu. Dei* 20.8) Augustine had addressed the likelihood that some would join the Church in the final three and a half years, and that others would fall away. Children would be born and baptized, and these, too would be added to the number of the Church. Here, now, was a slightly different problem: one consequence of the suddenness of the final events was that there would be people still alive on that day. How would they be accounted for? The answer Augustine provides is that in order to fulfill the prophecy that all will die, those living at the moment of rapture would have to die, instantaneously, and be made alive again instantaneously, in order to join the general resurrection of the dead. Furthermore, Augustine identified a prophecy that accounted for them: "And the sea gave up the dead that were in it, and death and hell gave back the dead which were in them" (Rev 20:13 as at *ciu. Dei* 20.14; Babcock, 2.414). Here, a literal understanding of the sea had to be rejected in order to reconcile the passage with Augustine's schema for where the dead resided between death and resurrection. If the dead were thought to be in the sea until judgment, then this presented a different place of the dead besides Hell, and furthermore, both good and wicked individuals would be found in the sea. The "sea" thus came to represent the current age for Augustine, so that the dead given up by the sea are the living "because they had not yet died" (*ciu. Dei* 20.15; Babcock, 2.414).

This reflection was followed by a short explanation of the location of the dead before Christ's resurrection. The righteous dead who had lived before Christ's crucifixion were in some netherworld, and it was from there, "places which, though in hell, were very far removed from the torments of the ungodly" that they were rescued at Christ's descent (*ciu. Dei* 20.15; Babcock, 2.415). It was important to Augustine that the righteous dead would never experience hell (or "Hades," here unusually understood as a place of torture, rather than more conventional designation of Gehenna).

CONFLAGRATION AND TRANSFORMATION

A key feature of the Apocalypse had been its triumphant affirmation of the glory that would be accorded the faithful. Here was the Christian's reward for fidelity to the faith, even in the face of persecution. The glory of the saints (all of the saved) would not be tarnished by anything of the old, sordid world. Their reward was complete transformation – a new, shining, gleaming, everything: new bodies, new heaven, new earth. The agent of this transformation was world-wide conflagration.

Drawing inspiration from the Second Letter of Peter (2 Pet 3:3–13) discussed in a later chapter (*ciu. Dei* 20.18), Augustine did not imagine that this fire was somehow flung down from on high (earlier at *ciu. Dei* 20.12 he had associated fire from heaven as the firmness of saints); he sought rather to understand it as a natural occurrence, such as the great flood had been, in which a natural element rose to superabundance, with fires joining fires, until a totality of fire was reached. This fire would remove all that was corruptible in the body so that what was left, the individual's substance, would be transformed – or transmuted – into an immortal body. The world "now renewed for the better" would be peopled by this new immortal population whose flesh was also renewed. Elsewhere Augustine explains to doubters that this transformation is not hard to believe. If God could transform Adam and Eve's immortal, spotless bodies into corruptible flesh as a result of the Fall, then he could certainly do it again in reverse (*ciu. Dei* 21.8)! But transformation would have a dark side, also: "It is not by its utter destruction, however, but rather by its transmutation that this world will pass away" (*ciu. Dei* 20.14; Babcock 2.413). If the bodies of the saints were to be transformed into immortal form, so too were the bodies of the wicked, and their torture would be compounded by immortal flesh that is imperishable and eternal. Annihilationalism, popular then as now, was not an option in Augustine's interpretation; such an option would violate the justice of God's justice.

The New Jerusalem is a real place on a transformed earth, populated by people with perfected bodies of flesh. The insistence on the fleshiness of this new world is continued in his comment that there will be no "traces of the old" (*ciu. Dei* 20.17; Babcock, 2.416), a subject to which he returns in *ciu. Dei* 22. At the same time as he depicts this as a real place, Augustine turns to a spiritual, pastoral interpretation: the city of Jerusalem has always been there. It is only that now that, through the transformative effects of the conflagration, the city's splendor "will shine out" (*ciu. Dei* 20.17; Babcock, 2.416). There is real elegance to this view of how one thing turns to another – not through the tedium of time, or space, or travel, but through transformation. It is an idea that requires no displacement of God's universe; it needs no astral voyaging or alternate universes: all that has been real on earth or under it, continues to exist and be real, only now it has been recalled into a single moment of transformation.

In the final chapter of *ciu. Dei* 20, Augustine wrapped up some loose ends. He had furnished his readers with his interpretation of the Apocalypse, sharing with them his analytical approach, and now he briefly addresses some key passages from the New Testament, and then the Old Testament, that address the events of the end times and the resurrection, judgment, and transformation of the dead. Some of these scriptural texts related information so obscure that Augustine frankly acceded to his ignorance of their meaning. Usefully, he relayed some of the ideas then current. Topics addressed briefly in these final chapters include: the advent of the Antichrist ("Christ will not come to judge the living and the dead without the prior coming of his adversary") and the Antichrist's use of true and false prophesies to deceive humankind (*ciu. Dei* 20.19); the fleeting death of those who were alive at the moment of Christ's return (*ciu. Dei* 20.20); Isaiah's words on the judgment are to be taken in a literal rather than a spiritual sense, prophesying about the future Church as the children of Israel (*ciu. Dei* 20.21); Daniel, whose prophesies undergird the Apocalypse, are well-explained by Jerome in his commentary in his refutation of Porphyry's attack on the prophecy (*ciu. Dei* 20.23); the psalms also reference the Last Judgment (*ciu. Dei* 20.24); Malachi on purifying punishments (*ciu. Dei* 20.25; see discussion below), sacrifices and judgment (*ciu. Dei* 20.26–7); the Law of Moses (*ciu. Dei* 20.28); references to Christ without naming him; concluding with the end of the wicked (*ciu. Dei* 20.28).

The work of aligning Old Testament texts to the story of the end times fit the Christian model that accorded greater importance to the New Testament to the Old. If those older works spoke more obscurely, that merely emphasized the importance of the new scriptures. We must remember that the place of the Old Testament, and its capacity to obscure, posed real problems for 4th century AD Christians. Was it to be taken literally, figuratively, or both? Augustine had encountered these problems during his time as an adherent to the Manichaean sect, but also in continuing encounters with Manichees in North Africa.[14] Incorporating Old Testament passages was thus important work for Augustine – it generated a holistic vision of the relationship of the scriptures, and the ages of the world, to the end of human history.

AUGUSTINE AND BEYOND

Augustine uses *ciu. Dei* 20 to transform the Apocalypse, a prophecy about the future of a persecuted community, into a roadmap for all Christians regarding their individual life, death, and afterlife. Millenarian interpretations of the Apocalypse had revealed a prophecy for the Christian elect about the end of time itself, but Augustine's metaphorical interpretation spoke to the end of each individual soul confronting death. As a result, a text that had had a specific niche in the

[14] van Oort 2010, pp. 505–546.

Christian library, now assumed an importance for every living being. Its enigmatic pronouncements and archaic images could now operate on a greatly expanded canvas of subjects that included the justice of God, the fate of community, and the fate of the individual soul. It was on some of these themes that later medieval communities dwelled.

GOD IS JUST: THE FORMATION OF A PURE COMMUNITY

A major thread of Christian thought centered on the idea that Christians formed their own community, and that they would live in community in heaven. Understandably, in a chapter dedicated to God's judgment, a judgment that would lead to the eternal condemnation of some members of the earthly community, and to the creation of a new community of the pure in heaven, it was important to establish that God's justice would, in fact, be just. Then, no less than today, the summary violence and wrath with which God seemed to operate in his dealings with mankind, especially in the Old Testament, prompted concern. This was especially the case because Romans, more in theory than in practice, expected justice to be visibly impartial, to be based on evidence, and for the magistrate to be a neutral arbiter. On the face of it, God's record of neutrality was not strong in the scriptures where he operated more in the manner of a tyrant-king than a magistrate – the former being an office disparaged by Romans as evidence of a lower order of civilization. For Augustine, it is God's perfect knowledge and cosmic control justified his judgment, and the lack of perfection that beset any human attempt to adjudicate fairly. The frailty of human law compared to God's justice had been raised already in Book 19, and the comparison was raised again in *ciu. Dei* 21.11 with respect to the justice of eternal punishment for crimes committed within a finite time-period. Here in Book 20, God's justice was affirmed, again on a cosmic level. Augustine explained that humanity's earthly, lapsed, existence (and that of demons, too) is a misery imposed by God's judgment. God judges the sinful actions of mankind that are a consequence of their condition, but "there is no injustice in God" and the faithful will enjoy full happiness in the future, and the impious complete unhappiness.

The image of the "book of life," discussed above, is another meditation on the nature of God's judgment. Can there be better proof of sound judgment than an official record? In the Book of Daniel and in the Apocalypse, the book represented divine knowledge. It was a secret, sealed, official record of the status of the soul. It was not mutable.

In the Vision of Paul, the angels who recorded good and bad deeds did so orally, but the conflation of the book image with the recording angels made its way into later visions. In the East, the *Apocalypse of Anastasia*, which drew heavily on the Vision of Paul, had angels both recording and erasing human sins as updates were necessary.[15] This would not have sat well with the Western notion of the "book of life" representing predestination. In the West, the book was a strictly cumulative document with a greater emphasis on displaying God's justice and its paper trail to the sinner, than in providing a reason for it.[16]

The saints' knowledge of the punishments of the wicked in the world to come (*ciu. Dei* 20.22) goes to the importance of justice but also to the nature of happiness. A great chasm divided these two regions, but each was visible to the other. The happiness of the saints was increased by knowledge of the wicked, and the misery of the wicked was intensified by knowledge of the joy of the elect. This stark comparison of heaven and hell was a feature of the literature of visions of the afterlife. It is reminiscent of the side-by-side aerial photographs of residential opulence and squalor in third world countries that provide visual social commentary today. Do the extremes of circumstance seem just? Augustine argued that once in possession of complete knowledge, good Christians will understand this portrait of justice. But it was a hard case to make on the face of it. Human compassion seemed violated by the saints' enjoyment of the torment of the wicked, and that this condition would be eternal. Augustine was not the only one trying to make this case. The Vision of Paul, known to Augustine and his contemporaries, has "God is Just" as an insistent refrain, while ending with a concession to compassion as Paul's tears for the wicked gain the damned a Sunday reprieve. The cause for compassion was a slippery slope, and potentially fatally so for the soul. It is one of the harder lines Augustine draws in the *ciu. Dei*: human compassion is an illusion that insults the full justice of God. Medieval visions of the afterlife often depicted the protagonist seeing both paradise and hell; or mansions set next to sewers as in Pope Gregory I's *Dialogues*. But it was never a very popular theme. Later Church pronouncements do not dwell on this aspect of the happiness of the saints, preferring rather to dwell on the saints' unmediated vision of God.[17]

[15] Ch. 40. See Baun 2007, pp. 409, 421.
[16] See Moreira 2010, pp. 109, 173.
[17] Benedict XII, *Constitution Benedictus Deus*, January 29, 1336. Denziger, 1000–1001, pp. 302–303.

TWO RESURRECTIONS AND AN AFTERLIFE

Christ was resurrected in the flesh; so, too, would be his followers. This was non-negotiable in the Catholic Western Latin tradition. That is not to say that ideas emanating from Greek philosophic schools did not occasionally surface in Western debates about the afterlife (a debate between Faustus of Riez on the corporeality of the soul, and Mammertus Claudianus's refutation of that position in the 5th century AD is an example), but in Western Catholic theology, history was on the side of the material reality of the resurrected body. After death, but before the general resurrection, the soul was sometimes 'seen' by visionaries as inhabiting a spiritual body of some kind that could both talk and feel. Augustine did not believe that it was actually the soul of a dead person that visionaries saw when they made such claims, although he grudgingly conceded the possibility that visions of the dead were effected by angels for the spiritual benefit of the viewer. However, he did believe in the incorporeal nature of the soul. Once bodies were joined to the soul after the resurrection, the soul would experience the afterlife in a transformed yet sensate body in which the torments of hell and the joys of heaven would be felt as real. Augustine's insistence on this helped affirm the Western, Latin, tradition that resurrection entailed transformed yet corporeal existence.

In explaining the two deaths and the two resurrections, Augustine had to negotiate between what was material and what was spiritual. The first death and the first resurrection were spiritually interpreted; sin (death) entered the individual, but in rejecting sin and accepting God's mercy, the individual was resurrected to spiritual life. Both these actions related to humanity's experience on earth; this gave the Apocalypse a pastoral importance. The second death was the death of the body resulting in its putrefaction; the second resurrection was on the Last Day when bodies would arise from their graves, and scattered or incinerated remains would reconstitute, so that the bodies of all mankind would join their souls in the afterlife in preparation for God's judgment.

In *ciu. Dei* 20, then, we find Augustine making clear divisions between things that were corporeal and material as opposed to those to be understood spiritually. These distinctions were still important to make at the turn of the 5th century AD, as the intersection of the Latin and Greek philosophic and religious traditions had led to misunderstandings and confusion in some cases. The idea of the two deaths, firmly entrenched in philosophic thought as well as in scripture, was probably fairly commonly known. Augustine's contemporary Macrobius, for example, collated a broad sampling of pagan beliefs on the soul and its relation to the universe, and attributed to the Pythagoreans and Platonists the idea that "there are two deaths, one of the soul, the other of the creature."[18] However, theological thinking may have been rudimentary or misunderstood in some communities. For example, even in Augustine's youth there may have been Christians who thought of God as a corporeal being, albeit perfected, or as a non-anthropomorphic material being.[19] Augustine attributed his own changed perception of God as incorporeal and immaterial to the influence of the Neoplatonic Christian bishop of Milan, Ambrose. Thereafter, Augustine navigated texts with a constant eye to how they should be interpreted. The Apocalypse spoke of the last days in very concrete yet also clearly symbolic terms. Augustine's contribution here was in codifying what Christians should interpret as literal or metaphorical. Augustine's success in transmitting these distinctions is evident in the many medieval interpretations of the Apocalypse text and of matters of the afterlife generally. It is notable that Augustine, a notable sceptic about things seen by contemporary Christians in dreams and visions, did not doubt the Apocalypse's veracity as a vision revealed to John, choosing rather to navigate the work's multiple meanings through the differential lens of literal and metaphorical.

JUDGMENT AND PURIFICATION

Although Augustine dealt with the idea of the purification of souls in other places in *ciu. Dei* (and in other writings such as the *ench.*), he briefly takes on purification and purgation in *ciu. Dei* 20.25 (on purifying punishments) and at 20.26 (on sacrifices). This brief discussion was relevant because purification was one of the unfolding events of the last day. As we have seen, Augustine asserted that all will come to judgment, good and wicked alike, but not all will be condemned. Drawing exclusively on the Old Testament prophets for his discussion of the purifying fire in this chapter, Augustine recalls the prophesy of Mal 3:1–6: "who will withstand the day of his coming, and who will be able to endure to look him in the face? For he comes like a refiner's fire and a fuller's herb; and he will sit, refining and purifying as it were gold and silver."

[18] Macrobius, *Commentary on the Dream of Scipio*, Book 1, ch. 11. (1990). Trans. William Harris Stahl, *Commentary on the Dream of Scipio by Macrobius*. New York: Columbia University Press, p. 130.

[19] There has been some disagreement as to whether some Christians adhered to anthropomorphic conceptions of God in the late 4th century AD. See Griffin and Paulsen 2000, pp. 97–118, which includes the background to the debate.

Thus a purification of souls will happen on the Last Day. Augustine explains that this purification will take place after the general resurrection, and after God's judgment has separated the souls of the elect from those of the wicked. This makes sense because purification was only available for the elect. However, the sequential placement of the purifying fire after judgment also allowed Augustine to promote a vision of communal purification alongside that of the individual. The individual must be cleansed, but the community will also be cleansed by the departure of the wicked, leaving the community of the elect pure; that, alongside individual purification, then, is the purpose of this purifying fire.

It seems, then, that the fire of purification was not to be equated with the fire of conflagration that was the transformative agent turning the old world into the new. Rather, the purging fire is part of the events of the Last Day, coming after the judgment that separates the good from the wicked. The fire is also linked, in Augustine's mind, with the issue of sacrifice. Sacrifices for sin would no longer be required after the purification. Once purified, the individual and the community will actually constitute a perfect sacrifice to God, becoming "righteous," and thereby requiring no further sacrifices. This point underscores the importance of the reverse situation: in the current life of stain and sin, sacrifices to God are needed. However, these sacrifices are to be spiritual sacrifices, not the animal sacrifices of the religions of the ancient world.

SOCIAL LIFE OF THE DEAD, AND PURGATION, TOGETHER

As we have seen, the formation of religious community is one of the major themes of Book 20. Augustine keeps the community of the elect in view at each stage of his discussion. So, when reflecting on the prophecy that the saints will reign for a thousand years (now interpreted as the current age), he emphasized that the dead are not separated from the living members of the Church. On the contrary, death can make no division within the Christian community. The saints in heaven (understood as the purified dead) are reigning alongside the living (*ciu. Dei* 20.9), maintaining their sense of community and helping each other. This idea is often termed the "communion of saints." It was immensely important to the way the Last Day unfolded, as we have seen, but it also had a direct impact on the way the living were taught to think of their dead; the aid that they could offer them in the afterlife, and the help they might seek in return. Eventually, as the idea of protracted purification after death (purgatory) became more firmly established in Western thought, the connection of these two communities – the living and the dead – became a crucial part of the way Christians thought about their work in the church.

Although this emphasis on the communion of the saints was crucial to the development of purgatory in Christian thought, Augustine was himself quite conflicted about promoting any such idea. That the soul needed to be purified of its contact with worldly matter to join the higher power was well-entrenched in Platonic philosophy, in Manichaeism, and in the theology of various pagan sects, as it was also in Christian scripture and in prayers for the dead. However, if there was one idea that Augustine was pushing throughout *ciu. Dei* 20.20 it was that there was no disruption between the living and the dead; that since the first resurrection had already taken place during the earthly life of the living, death was an inconsequential moment of transition. This reading of the Apocalypse did not allow space or time for an interim existence to occur after death. In Book 20, the entire discussion of purification by fire was confined to the events of the Last Day. Indeed, confronting the absence of the discussion at this point, in *ciu. Dei* 20.25, Augustine evaded the issue by stating: "But this question of purgatorial punishments must be postponed to another time for more detailed discussion" (*ciu. Dei* 20.25; Babcock, 2.436). In fact, he would briefly discuss purificatory punishment in *ciu. Dei* 21.13 where his concern was to distance Christian teaching from the pitfalls of Neoplatonic doctrines of purification. The strange purification practices and myths of the Manichees may also have shadowed his thoughts on this subject. By making sure that purification was situated in a specific moment of the Last Days' drama, he evaded tricky questions about purification brought about by God-willed earthly suffering. Nevertheless, and despite his calculated reticence, Book 20 contributed to Augustine's later reputation for being a pillar of purgatory precisely because of his discussion of the community of the living with the dead.

Would the damned likewise experience community? This not addressed by Augustine explicitly here, but if we consider the importance of opposites in crafting notions of heaven and hell, then the opposite of a community founded on notions of charity and virtue would not find its opposite in a nefarious community, but rather in a lack of community altogether among the selfish members of the damned. Indeed, visions of the afterlife underscored the isolation and lack of fellowship among the damned; it is an important feature of Dante's

Inferno. The metaphor of a city, peopled with the citizens of heaven, was a potent metaphor of community, far distant from the disruption, chaos, and pain of the dark topographies of the damned in hell.

CONCLUSION: DEALING WITH DISASTER

Almost two thousand years removed from the prophecies of the end that started the apocalyptic tradition in Western thought, it can be hard to comprehend or even know how to value the enormous energy and erudition expended in late antiquity and the middle ages by thoughts about the end of times. The sheer volume of careful reasoning and quest for exactitude sought in developing a better understanding of the future, can appear redundant and excessive. However, to understand Augustine's ideas on this matter, and their importance Western thought, requires us to take seriously the whole enterprise that he and his contemporaries engaged in. Augustine lived within four hundred years of the time of the apostles; counting the millennia of the world's history was in the single digits. The historical travails of the late Roman empire in Augustine's lifetime prompted many to speculate that the end of time was close at hand, and in the next few centuries, that urgency did not diminish. Augustine was agnostic about the timing of the end. But what he contributed was a pathway through the scriptures in which prophecies were tied to biblical texts, lines of orthodoxy were not crossed, categories not mistaken, and a pastoral message could emerge. His lead was followed, often verbatim, for centuries.[20]

Finally, when thinking about Augustine's views on God's judgment it is helpful to return to the human disaster that prompted the writing of the *ciu. Dei*: the sack of Rome. In *ciu. Dei* 1, Augustine tried to imagine the ways in which the horrors of slaughter, rape, theft, torture, and captivity into slavery, could have represented a kind of justice known

[20] On the medieval apocalyptic tradition, see essays in Emmerson and McGinn 1992, and essays in Bynum and Freedman 2000. Early medieval commentaries on the Apocalypse drew heavily on Augustine, as for example, Bede's. See Bede 2013; and Chazelle 2015, pp. 212–232. However, it has been noted that over the long medieval centuries, the commentary on the Apocalypse as a whole was sporadic, although it was mined to support more limited debates. (For example, Karl Morrison notes a 12th century "silence" in direct citations from the Apocalypse on matters apocalyptic while authors mined the text for discussion of other issues, such as violence, "The Exercise of Thoughtful Minds: The Apocalypse in some German Writings," in Emmerson and McGinn 1992). At the same time, Otto of Freising, for example, virtually plundered Augustine's *ciu. Dei* for his discussion of the afterlife in the Chronicon.

only to God, or in some cases known to God and to the sufferer. Looking for explanations for the disaster in an individual's sin (the secret pride in wealth, or vaunted pride in chastity), and in the moral lessons that were to be learned about excessive attachment to the things of the world, Augustine allowed that not all aspects of the disaster found a ready explanation, and he advised his readers to look to the last judgment for consolation because there, on the last day, all would be revealed and the perpetrators of wickedness would be punished. For those who held to their faith, the last judgment would be a consolation – a moment when the incomprehensible aspects of personal suffering would be understood. It was not a particularly strong argument placed in Book 1, but in the final books of the *ciu. Dei*, Augustine turned to eschatology and the nature of God's justice in way that far outlived the temporal stresses that had occasioned him to start his work. The sense of hopefulness expressed about the last days linked Augustine to an already long tradition of thought in the church, and to its future. As he commented to Hesychius, "We ought to long for and await the coming of the Lord, then, as you exhort us to in a holy fashion, when you say that his coming is great happiness for those who long for it" (*ep.* 199.5.14; Teske, II/3.334) and "He wanted them to await the coming of the Lord with loins girded and lamps lit" (*ep.* 199.1.2; Teske, II/3.330).

FURTHER READING

Baun, J. (2007). *Tales from another Byzantium: Celestial Journey and Local Community in the Medieval Greek Apocrypha*. Cambridge: Cambridge University Press.

Gerchow, J. (1988). Die Gedenkuberlieferung der Angelsachsen: Mit einem Katalog der libri vitae und Necrologien. In *Arbeiten zur Frühmittelalterforschung der Universität Münster*, vol. 20. Berlin: de Gruyter.

Moreira, I. (2010). *Heaven's Purge: Purgatory in Late Antiquity*. Oxford: Oxford University Press.

van Oort, J. (2010). Manichaean Christians in Augustine's life and work. *Church History and Religious Culture*, 90(4), 505–546.

14 Books 21 & 22: The End of the Body: Heaven and Hell in *The City of God*

DAVID G. HUNTER

As we arrive at *ciu. Dei* 21 and 22, we reach the final destination of the two cities after their long pilgrimage on earth. Book 21 deals with the final repudiation of the *ciuitas terrena*, the eternal punishment of the damned in Hell. Book 22 examines the ultimate fate of the *ciuitas Dei*, the eternal reward of the blessed in heaven. But, as I will argue in this chapter, one can also read the final books of the *City of God* as the endpoint of a specific intellectual journey on which Augustine had embarked decades earlier, one that led him to abandon much of the mental furniture of a late antique philosopher and to embrace – even to pioneer – a cosmology and a theological anthropology with specifically Christian contours.

At the center of these books is Augustine's claim that both eternal punishment and eternal blessedness require the existence of a body that is truly material, albeit one that has been dramatically transformed into a "spiritual body" at the final resurrection (cf. 1 Cor 15:44). Augustine's commitment to the notion of a resurrected body that was genuinely material would not have come easily to a late antique man, especially one with profound debts to Neoplatonic philosophy. Moreover, such a view would have surprised the young Augustine himself, for his embrace of bodily reality required him not only to reject a respectable philosophical tradition, but also to modify his own earlier writings as well.

The most compelling evidence of Augustine's development on the question of bodily existence is found in his own testimony in the *retr.*, written in AD 426/7, as he was completing the final books of *ciu. Dei*.[1] As he reviewed his own earlier writings, Augustine often noted that his views had changed on questions regarding the body. For example, when

[1] For a date of AD 426 for the final books of *ciu. Dei*, see O'Daly 1999, pp. 34–35. For a date of AD 426–AD 428 for the *retr.*, see Madec 1996, pp. 18–20. The most thorough discussion of the development of Augustine's thinking on the body is Miles 1979.

commenting on one of his earliest treatises, the two books of *Soliloquies*, Augustine pointed to the following passage as especially problematic:

> these things of the senses must be completely cast off. We must take great care, as long as we are in this body, that our wings do not become mired in the things of the senses, for we need complete and perfect wings to fly to that light from the darkness. That light does not deign to reveal itself to those trapped in this prison, unless they are able to break out of the prison and destroy it, and escape to their own higher places. So when have become such a person that no earthly thing at all gives you pleasure, believe me, at that moment, at that exact point in time, you will see what you desire.
>
> (*sol.* 1.14.24; Paffenroth, I/3.46)

Writing near the end of his life, Augustine regretted the extremely dualistic character of his language in this early philosophical dialogue. Commenting on this passage in his *retr.*, the elder Augustine observed: "And what I said there, 'You must entirely flee from things of sense,' should be treated with caution, lest we be thought to agree with the opinion of the false philosopher Porphyry, when he said that every body ought to be fled from" (*retr.* 1.4; Ramsey, I/2.34, slightly altered).[2] In hindsight, Augustine observed, he had meant to say these "corruptible things" instead of "sensible things," since in the new heavens and the new earth the sensible world would indeed exist, although no longer in a corruptible state.

It was especially his earlier statements on the resurrected body, Augustine informs us, that he now wished to retract or to modify. In the *retr.* he noted no less than five places in his earlier writings where he had erroneously implied that the resurrected body would be entirely spiritual. For example, in his later comment on the six books of *mus.* Augustine distanced himself from his earlier statement about the incompatibility of physical bodies and the soul that seeks wisdom:

> Bodies are better to the extent that they are more capable of being numbered by such numbers, but the soul becomes better by lacking those things that it receives through the body, when it turns itself away from the fleshly senses and is refashioned by the divine numbers of wisdom.
>
> (*mus.* 6.4.7; cf. *retr.* 11[10].2; Ramsey, I/2.55)

[2] In *ciu. Dei* Augustine devoted considerable attention to refuting this axiom of Porphyry; see *ciu. Dei* 10.29, 12.27, 13.17, and 22.26.

By the time he composed his *retr.* Augustine had determined that in the resurrection "incorruptible and spiritual bodies" would indeed contain physical members (and, therefore, embody number or proportion) and that these bodies would indeed be "much more beautiful and more shapely" (*speciosiora et decentiora*) because of their proportions.[3] While in this life the weakness of the soul makes it less capable of focusing on both fleshly and intelligible realities, in the next life the soul "will be so firm and perfect that it will not be turned away by bodily numbers from the contemplation of wisdom" (*retr.* 11[10].2; Ramsey, I/2.56). On the contrary, Augustine argued, in its resurrected state the soul will know the body and its proportions "in such a way as not to be seduced by them, and it will not become better by lacking them; but it will be so good and upright that they will be unable to be concealed from it or to take possession of it" (*retr.* 1.11 [10].2; Ramsey, I/2.55–56). In Book 22 of *ciu. Dei* Augustine will develop further the role of physical vision in the soul's experience of the vision of God.

Elsewhere in the *retr.* Augustine also showed that he had become especially concerned about his earlier interpretations of 1 Cor 15:50, where the apostle Paul had declared: "I tell you this, brethren: flesh and blood cannot inherit the kingdom of God, nor does corruption inherit incorruption." In several of his earlier writings Augustine had followed the lead of the Pauline text and tended to speak of the resurrected body as if it would not consist of "flesh and blood." In the *retr.* he repeatedly distanced himself from that earlier view. He "retracted" – or, better, qualified – his previous statements by noting that the "substance" of flesh and blood will remain in the resurrection, for the resurrected body will indeed be a *body*; what will change is its corruptible character.

Augustine stated this argument clearly in his *retractatio* on the early book *f. et symb.*, a treatise based on a sermon he had delivered as a presbyter to a plenary council in Hippo in 393 (Madec 1996, p. 40). Citing the words of Jesus from his post-resurrection appearance, "Touch and see that a spirit does not have bones and flesh as you see that I have" (Lk 24:39), the later Augustine argued that Paul did not deny that the substance of the flesh will exist in the kingdom of God. Rather, "by the term 'flesh and blood' he referred either to persons who live according to the flesh or to the actual corruption of the flesh (*in ipsam carnis corruptionem*), which will certainly not exist then" (*retr.* 1.17 [16];

[3] According to *Gn. litt.* 4.3.7, it is *numerus* that gives each thing its form or *species*. See the discussion in Harrison 1992, pp. 101–110. It might be best to think of "number" here as the "proportion" that gives a thing its unique form and beauty.

Ramsey, I/2.78). Augustine believed that the hermeneutical key to 1 Cor 15:50 lay in the second half of the verse, where Paul stated: "nor does corruption inherit incorruption." "Flesh and blood" must refer only to the corruptible character of the body, not to the substance of bodily "flesh and blood" itself.[4]

At this point in his comment on *f. et symb.*, Augustine observed: "Whoever reads the final book of *The City of God* will see that I discussed this difficult matter as carefully as I could with the intention of persuading unbelievers" (*retr.* 1.17 [16]; Ramsey, I/2.78). It is noteworthy that all of the writings Augustine regarded as deficient in their account of the bodily resurrection were relatively early works, the latest being *agon.* of 396/397. By contrast, the final book of *ciu. Dei*, in which he claimed finally to have dealt with the difficult matter of the Pauline "flesh and blood," dates from approximately thirty years later, as does the *retr.* In these mature writings Augustine showed himself to be acutely aware of the limitations of an excessively spiritualized notion of the resurrected body. Moreover, he set himself the explicit task of explaining to unbelievers, as well as to believers, how both eternal punishment and eternal beatitude were compatible with (and actually required) bodily existence.[5]

BOOK 21: THE PROBLEM OF ETERNAL PUNISHMENT

After spending the bulk of Book 20 arguing for a Christian doctrine of resurrection and final judgment, Augustine now turned to the specific issue of *how* a risen body might be capable of experiencing either eternal punishment in a genuinely material fire (Book 21) or eternal beatitude in a heavenly world (Book 22), depending on the outcome of the final judgment. Augustine's discussion of eternal punishment in Book 21 involved engaging three distinct questions, all of which revolved around the problem of eternal fire and its punitive effects. First, he examined the very possibility of a physical body suffering the pains of eternal fire; second, he discussed the justice of a person suffering eternally for sins that took only a limited time to commit; third, he explored various interpretations of 1 Cor 3:11–15, a mysterious passage in which

[4] Augustine stated similar sentiments in *retr.* 1.22 [21].3 regarding *c. Adim.*12.5; in *retr.*1.26 [25] regarding *quaestio* 47 of *diu. qu.*; and in *retr.* 2.3 regarding *agon.* 32.34.

[5] In addition to his misgivings about his early statements on the resurrection, in the *retr.* Augustine also distanced himself from earlier writings that might have implied a doctrine of *apokatastasis* (1.7 [6].6), the pre-existence of souls, and their *anamnesis* (1.8.2).

the apostle Paul stated that anyone who built upon the foundation of Christ would be tested or saved "through fire." Did this imply that the fires of hell would be merely temporary and purgatorial in nature? Each of these questions deserves further consideration.

CORPOREALITY AND ETERNAL PAIN

At the outset of Book 21 Augustine confronted a central problem with the notion of eternal physical punishment: in our bodily experience in this world, extreme pain ultimately leads to death, that is, to a separation of the body from the soul. How, then, is it possible for a physical body to experience the pain of eternal punishment without, in effect, dying again, that is, without separating from the soul and ceasing to exist? Augustine's response to this initial dilemma moved in several different directions, taking excursions through natural history, as well as philosophical anthropology and metaphysics. His initial argument was that even in this life certain natural phenomena display properties that seem to defy reason and to be inexplicable in human terms. Relying heavily on Varro and Pliny's *Natural History*,[6] Augustine cited many examples of phenomena such as worms that live in hot springs (*ciu. Dei* 21.2), cooked peacock flesh that does not rot (he himself had eaten peacock meat that was more than a year old), the ability of a bright substance, such as fire, to blacken what it burns, the marvelous power of magnetic stones (*ciu. Dei* 21.4), and so on. Augustine's point was that if God could create physical entities with such wondrous power in this life, it was not unreasonable to assume that God could do so with bodies in the next life as well.

But appeal to the wonders of the natural world was only part of Augustine's argument. He acknowledged that the characteristics of the resurrected body would be significantly different from those of the earthly body. Therefore, it was not enough simply to point to the fact that God could produce wondrous phenomena in this life; he also had to explain precisely what constituted the difference between the earthly bodies that we know here and now and the spiritual bodies that would be present in the resurrection. For Augustine, the key to this enigma was the intimate relation between the body and soul. It is well known that Augustine himself never resolved the vexed question of the origin

[6] O'Daly 1999, pp. 218–220.

of the soul.[7] But in the course of his reflections on the body, especially during the early decades of the 5th century AD, he had evolved a robust sense of the original compatibility of body and soul.[8]

The years AD 410–AD 412 seem to have been a decisive turning point in Augustine's thought on the matter.[9] Already in Book 7 of *Gn. litt.* Augustine had affirmed that the soul was created with a natural desire to be present in a body, "just as it is natural for us to wish to live" (*Gn. litt.* 7.27.38). But by the final book of that commentary, he had determined that a disembodied soul was incapable of enjoying the vision of God as long as it remained separate from its body:

> this may be due to some more hidden cause, or the reason may be that there is ingrained in the soul a kind of natural appetite for administering the body, and that as long as it does not have a body at its disposal, it is somehow or other held back by this unsatisfied appetite from pressing on with undivided attention to that highest heaven.
>
> (*Gn. litt.* 12.35.68; Hill, I/13.504–505)

I will return below to the implications of this teaching for Augustine's sense of the embodied beatific vision in Book 22. But for now one should note that in Book 21 he mobilized the union of body and soul to explain the possibility of a body suffering eternal pain.

The issue of body-soul relations had previously emerged in *ciu. Dei* 13 and 14 and was closely connected to the notion of original sin. Augustine had clearly articulated the character of the first sin as revolt against God that was experienced immediately in the revolt of the bodies of Adam and Eve against themselves. All of the weaknesses and pains associated with human embodiment, including the unruly character of sexual desire, could be attributed to the lack of integration caused by the alienation of the body from the soul that had resulted from the soul's alienation from God (*ciu. Dei* 14.15). The ultimate symptom of this disintegration was to be found in death, which sundered the original and natural unity of body and soul: "For the very force that tears apart the two that were conjoined and intertwined in the living person produces an anguished feeling that is contrary to nature

[7] A good overview of Augustine's discussion of the origin of the soul and its fall can be found in Rombs 2006.

[8] For Augustine's development on the question of bodily existence, see van Bavel 1995; Miles 1979, pp. 99–125; and Hunter 2012.

[9] Rist 1994, pp. 108–112

and that lasts until all feeling is gone, which was present precisely due to the joining of soul and flesh" (*ciu. Dei* 13.6; Babcock, 2.73).

Here in Book 21 Augustine applied this insight to the prospect of the re-union of body and soul in the resurrection. Unlike life in this world, which is characterized by a rather tenuous connection between soul and body, owing to sin, the next life will be marked by a new and unbreakable union of body and soul:

> The reason why some pain causes death is that the soul is connected to this body in such a way that, in the face of extreme pain, it withdraws and departs ... But in the life to come the soul will be connected to such a body and will be connected to it in such a way that, just as no length of time will dissolve the connection, neither will any form of pain break the connection.
>
> (*ciu. Dei* 21.3; Babcock, 2.449)

Not only will the risen body experience a new kind of life, but this new existence will also make possible a new kind of death: eternal death. Unlike the first death, which expels the soul from the body, the second death will compel the soul to remain in the body. Eternal death will entail the loss of God (and, therefore, of life), but also the soul's inability to escape bodily pain by dying, that is, by separating from the body.

THE JUSTICE OF ETERNAL PUNISHMENT

Augustine's forceful account of the horror of eternal death raised the question of whether or not it was just for human beings to receive eternal punishment for sins that were merely temporal in nature, that is, for sins which, however grave, took only a moment to commit. Once again Augustine's answer to this question was multifaceted. On the one hand, he drew analogies with the punishments present in human laws, which are apportioned without regard to the length of time it took to perform the crime: for example, a slave may be shackled for years in punishment for momentarily striking his master; a man may be flogged and suffer at length for kissing another man's wife, an act which took only a moment. But such an answer, as Augustine realized, begged the fundamental question: why an *eternity* of punishment for an act that was merely finite in character? Would it not be more just for the guilty to suffer some temporary purgatorial punishment, but ultimately to experience divine mercy?

Augustine's discussion of the justice of eternal punishment had a variety of opponents in view. He explicitly mentioned "Platonists" (*Platonici*), who believed that "all punishments are meant to serve remedial purposes, whether they are imposed by human or divine laws, and whether they are imposed in this life or after death" (*ciu. Dei* 21.13; Babcock, 2.467–68). He cited as evidence a passage from Virgil that spoke of purgation by wind, water, and fire.[10] Augustine believed that in this matter, as in others, Virgil derived his notions from Plato, a view that Augustine may have derived from a Neoplatonic commentary on Virgil.[11] Augustine did not dispute that purgatorial punishments exist, both in this life and the next, but he felt bound by scripture to hold that after the final judgment the fires of hell will burn for all eternity (cf. Mt 25:41), even if there will be some variation in the degree of pain that reprobates will actually feel, depending on the gravity of their sins (*ciu. Dei* 21.16).

But non-Christians were not Augustine's only target. He devoted even more attention to the views of "the merciful persons among us" (*misericordibus nostris*), that is, those Christians who believed that ultimately there would be no eternal damnation: "they hold that the damned are to be set free from hell at the end of a fixed period of time, which will be longer or shorter depending on the extent of each person's sin" (*ciu. Dei* 21.17; Babcock, 2.472). The only specific author Augustine mentioned in this regard was Origen, who was widely thought to have held that even the devil could be saved.[12] The main problem with Origen's position, Augustine argued, was that it implied "a ceaseless alternation between blessedness and misery." If the misery of the devil and his angels was merely temporary and they were capable of a turn for the better, then the blessedness of the saints in heaven might also be merely temporary; in other words, if the saints were capable of a turn for the worse, they would lack "true and secure joy in eternal good untouched by any fear of loss" (*ciu. Dei* 21.17; Babcock, 2.473).

At this point Augustine began to discuss a wide array of views that did not go to the Origenist extreme of claiming salvation for the devil, but nevertheless offered a view of mercy that he considered erroneous. Without naming specific persons, he noted that some Christians held that even the wicked would ultimately be saved through the prayers of the saints (*ciu. Dei* 21.18); others claimed that at least all who were

[10] Virgil, *Aen.* 6.733–42.

[11] See *ciu. Dei* 10.30, 14.3, 14.5, and 22.26, with the comments of O'Daly 1999, p. 247.

[12] See Origen, *Prin.* 1.6. There is serious doubt about whether or not Origen actually held that the devil would ultimately be saved. Augustine also discussed Origen's views in *Ad Orosium contra Priscillianistas et Origenistas* 5.5; see also *De haeresibus* 43, where refers to his more extensive discussion in *De civitate dei* 21.17.

baptized and participated in the sacraments would be saved (*ciu. Dei* 21.19); some extended this privilege only to those who persevered in the communion of the Catholic church (*ciu. Dei* 21.20); still others believed that only those who failed to show mercy would be condemned forever (*ciu. Dei* 21.22).

Augustine responded in detail to the specific scriptural and theological arguments of these "merciful" Christians, but he constantly returned to the same basic principles: on the one hand, he pointed to certain biblical texts that spoke explicitly about the "eternal fire prepared for the devil and his angels" (Mt 24:41) and about "eternal punishment" and "eternal life" (Mt 25:46); on the other hand, he argued that human sensibilities failed to grasp the magnitude of the first sin (*ciu. Dei* 21.12). It was "just" that all should be condemned because of Adam's transgression. The "whole mass of mankind is condemned (*massa damnata*)," Augustine believed, because his offspring were present "in him as in a root" (*ciu. Dei* 21.12; Babcock, 2.467).[13] The justice of God is demonstrated in the eternal punishment of some, which all deserve; the mercy of God is demonstrated in the free gift of God's salvation bestowed on some, which none deserve.

Excursus: Interpreting 1 Cor 3:11–15

In the midst of his discussion of the various "erroneous" opinions on the ultimate mercy to be shown to sinners, Augustine devoted an extended excursus to interpreting 1 Cor 3:11–15, a passage that had been cited by Christians who believed in a purgatorial fire that was merely temporary and in the ultimate salvation of those who had their "foundation" in Christ. The passage reads as follows:

> For no one can lay any foundation other than the one that has been laid, which is Jesus Christ. Now if anyone builds on the foundation with gold, silver, precious stones, wood, hay, straw – each one's work will become manifest, for the Day will disclose it, because it will be revealed with fire, and the fire will test what sort of work each has done. If what has been built on the foundation survives, the builder will receive a reward. If the work is burned up, the builder will suffer loss, though he will be saved, but only as through fire.

[13] On the history and sources of Augustine's use of the phrase *massa damnata* to describe fallen humanity, see Folliet 1992.

The Pauline text raised several dilemmas. What did it mean to build on the foundation of Jesus Christ? How was a person's work to be tested by fire? Most importantly, what did it mean for a person to be saved, "but only as through fire"? What was this "fire"?

For Augustine's opponents the passage signified that, if a person had faith in Christ as a foundation, that person would be saved, whether or not their works were good (gold, silver, precious stones) or bad (wood, hay, straw). In response, Augustine developed a set of differentiated reflections on the role of faith, works, and the "foundation" of Christ. He argued that to build on the foundation of Jesus Christ meant to put nothing before Christ, that is, to place the love of Christ before all else. Such a stance did not require an absolute renunciation of all earthly loves, he insisted. As an illustration Augustine offered the example of marital and family life. The apostle Paul allowed that married people might engage in sex, even apart from the desire to procreate; to love one's wife carnally ("in the disease of lust") was the "concession" granted to married persons, according to Augustine's reading of 1 Cor 7:6.[14] Works such as these should be considered wood, hay, and straw; they were imperfect, even "sinful," yet permitted within marriage. Complete sexual abstinence, by contrast, was considered equivalent to silver, gold, and precious stones. The "carnal" love of one's wife and family was allowed, Augustine maintained, as long as one loved Christ more and put Christ first.

As for the testing by fire, Augustine argued that a person's earthly loves would be "burned up" in the sense that people would experience pain at the loss of these pleasures, a pain that eventually would come either in this life (through bereavements or other calamities) or in the next life. However, as long as their primary attachment was to Christ – that is, as long as they had Christ as their foundation – those with lesser or carnal loves would be saved. By contrast, those persons who built on the foundation with gold, silver, or precious stones – that is, those who abstained from the earthly attachments of marriage and family life and who lived with undivided love for God (cf. 1 Cor 7:32) – such persons would not experience the pain of loss; their good works (i.e. their buildings of gold, silver, and precious stones) would endure for all eternity. Both sets of works would be "tested" by fire: the earthly loves would be burned away and cause the pain of loss; the heavenly loves would persist and bring joy to those who have them.

[14] Augustine developed this theme most extensively in his treatise *b. conjug.*; he also discussed it frequently in his preaching. See Hunter 2002.

Finally, regarding the precise nature of the "fire" that would ultimately burn away earthly loves and reveal the character of one's building, Augustine was reluctant to offer a fixed interpretation. It could refer to the inevitable losses of earthly pleasures that come about in this life; it could refer to the "fires" of persecution that the martyrs endured and that all Christians suffer in one form or another; it could also refer to the tribulation at the end of the world when Antichrist appears: "How many buildings there will be then to be proved by that fire!" Perhaps most intriguing is the way that Augustine tentatively acknowledged the possibility of an interval of time between death and the final judgment, when the souls of those who have built with wood, hay, and straw would endure some kind of bodily pain that would chastise them and consume their earthly loves. But Augustine's acceptance of this temporary phase of "purgatory" remained very tentative.[15] He retained an admirable reticence to commit to any specific interpretation of this "fire," whether it was experienced after death, before death, or both before and after death. He even speculated that the very death of the flesh itself might be part of this fiery tribulation (*ciu. Dei* 21.26).

BOOK 22: THE PROSPECT OF ETERNAL BEATITUDE

As Augustine turned to the final book of *ciu. Dei*, his preoccupation with the bodily nature of the resurrection – and specifically the body-soul relation – became even more prominent. Here, again, a multitude of questions presented themselves: how is it possible for an earthly body to exist in heaven (*ciu. Dei* 22.4)? In what state will infants or aborted fetuses be raised (*ciu. Dei* 22.12)? What will happen to the bodies of those lost at sea or consumed by cannibals (*ciu. Dei* 22.12)? Will men and women retain their respective sexual characteristics (*ciu. Dei* 22.17)? Will the blessed in heaven actually see God and will they do so with the eyes of the body (*ciu. Dei* 22.29)? In the course of his response to these and other questions Augustine developed a series of reflections that infused the body with a transcendent significance that stretched the human imagination to its very limits.[16] Once again Augustine's focus on the soul-body unity provided a consistent

[15] For the transformation of Augustine's hesitations on "purgatory" into the certainties of Gregory the Great, see Atwell 1987.

[16] Burrus 2009. Further reflections in Burrus and MacKendrick 2010, a study that has strongly influenced my own understanding of Augustine's emphasis on beauty in the risen body.

foundation to his discussion of a variety of topics: (1) the reasonableness of belief in the resurrected body; (2) the priority of beauty in the resurrected body; (3) the prospect of beatific vision in the resurrected body. Each of these will be considered further here.

REASONABLENESS OF THE RESURRECTED BODY

Augustine's initial question at the start of Book 22 derived from a classic philosophical conundrum: how was it possible for a corporeal body to exist in a spiritual or ethereal environment? Augustine illustrated the philosophical view with a quotation from the now-lost third book of Cicero's *De re publica*. Explaining how Hercules and Romulus were human beings who became gods, Cicero maintained: "Their bodies were not taken up into heaven, for nature would not allow what comes from earth to remain anywhere but on earth."[17] Later in Book 22 Augustine pointed to the Platonic doctrine of the four elements as the basis of the philosophical opposition to the resurrected body. Following Plato's *Timaeus*, according to Augustine, some Platonists said that there was a fixed hierarchy of elements – earth, water, air, heaven (or fire) – and that each element was held in place by its own weight, so that the proper order was maintained.[18]

Augustine had little difficulty dispensing with these objections. He first pointed to notable exceptions to the alleged order: corporeal animals in the air (birds), water above the air (rain clouds), fire on the earth and even in the earth (volcanoes), et cetera (*ciu. Dei* 22.11). But Augustine also had a more profound response to the philosophical concern, and it pertained directly to the nature of bodily existence itself. He argued that the very joining of incorporeal souls to physical bodies called into question the philosophical rejection of bodily resurrection. If humans were pure souls and knew only the heavenly world, the notion that a spiritual entity might be joined to a corporeal entity would be totally incomprehensible to them, even absurd. But the joining of souls to bodies is precisely the reality that people experience every day and know with certainty to be true:

> And yet the earth is full of souls giving life to their earthly members, which are joined and entwined with them in wondrous

[17] Cicero, *De re publica*, fragment 40.

[18] Plato, *Timaeus* 31c–32d and 53c–55c, with the commentary of O'Daly 1999, pp. 228–229.

> fashion ... Because we see it all the time, the joining of soul to body does not astonish us, but in fact it is far more wondrous than what these people refuse to believe.
>
> (*ciu. Dei* 22.4; Babcock, 2.499)

People should be more astonished at the fact that incorporeal souls are joined to earthly bodies, Augustine argued, than that the earthly body should be elevated to heavenly abodes, which are still in some sense corporeal. As he saw it, anyone instructed by "sober reason" (*sobria ratione*) would acknowledge that "it is a more wondrous divine work to interweave corporeal and incorporeal things in some way than it is to link heavenly and earthly things which, although different, are nevertheless both corporeal" (*ciu. Dei* 22.4; Babcock, 2.500).

At this point in Book 22 Augustine began another line of argument to defend the bodily resurrection. Rather than focus on the resurrected body itself, he turned his attention to the phenomenon of belief in the resurrection, that is, to the fact that belief in the resurrection of Christ had already spread widely throughout the world. The fact that something so incredible as the resurrection of Christ had come to be widely accepted was taken as evidence of its truth. Augustine had in mind partly the classic Christian apologetic claim that the truth of Christianity is demonstrated in the fact that it has been so widely accepted despite its origin in the preaching of "a tiny number of obscure, unimportant, unlearned men" (*ciu. Dei* 22.5; Babcock, 2.501).[19] But Augustine went on to underscore the presence of a divine power in the first apostles that was able to effect conversion not by eloquence, but by miraculous signs and wonders:

> The world has believed a tiny number of obscure, unimportant, unlearned men precisely because divinity has made itself even more miraculously convincing by using such contemptible witnesses. For the eloquence that made them persuasive in what they said was the eloquence not of words but rather of miraculous works.
>
> (*ciu. Dei* 22.5; Babcock, 2.501)

With numerous allusions to the stories of miraculous healings and even resurrections performed by the apostles, Augustine concluded that it was the presence of such miraculous power that persuaded so many to believe: "Those who had not seen Christ rise in the flesh and ascend with his flesh into heaven believe the men who told of seeing it because

[19] The argument was made as early as Origen's *Contra Celsum* 1.62.

they not only spoke of it but also performed miraculous signs" (*ciu. Dei* 22.5; Babcock, 2.501).

Augustine's book now took an unexpected turn, at least one that would have surprised the younger Augustine. In what appears, at first glance, to be a lengthy *divertissement*, he offered an extended and detailed account of miraculous healings that had been accomplished in his own day, most of them in North Africa. Here again we encounter a matter in which Augustine's thought had developed considerably. In *uera rel.* (composed early in 390), he had suggested that miracles such as those performed by the apostles no longer took place: "Those miracles have not been permitted to continue until our own times, lest the soul always be seeking visible realities and the human race grow cold through being accustomed to things whose novelty attracted it."[20] By the time he composed his *retr.* Augustine had moved beyond this view. Citing the famous healing of the blind man at Milan, which occurred after the discovery of the bodies of Gervasius and Protasius, Augustine "retracted" his earlier comment: "I knew of some other miracles as well; so many of them occur even in these times that we would be unable either to be aware of all of them or to number those of which we are aware" (*retr.* 1.13[12].7; Ramsey, I/2.62).

A similar enthusiasm for the miraculous, especially for healings associated with the shrines and relics of martyrs, has surfaced in Book 22. Indeed, as one scholar has put it, Augustine's concern to document and publicize miraculous events – even to have them proclaimed in church – "reads much more like the Bede of two centuries later than the Augustine of twenty years before."[21] How can we explain this rather dramatic change in Augustine's perspective? Several factors must be taken into account. First, the cult of martyrs and their relics had attained a prominence in North Africa in the early decades of the 5th century AD that it did not have previously. As historian Robert Wiśniewski has put it in his recent study of the cult of relics, "something actually began to happen at the tombs of the saints":

> The reason for the evolution of Augustine's opinion was not his readings, reflections, or pastoral considerations; it was rather the observation of what was happening in Africa in the early fifth

[20] Cited in *retr.*1.13[12].7; Ramsey, I/2.62. Cf. *retr.* 1.14[13].5, where Augustine expressed similar reservations about his earlier teaching in *util. cred.* 16.34.

[21] Miles 1979, p. 36.

century, especially in Hippo and Uzalis, after the arrival of the relics of Gervasius and Protasius and those of Stephen.[22]

Another consideration may have been the fact that the Donatist communities in North Africa, with their long tradition of reverence for the martyrs, were being increasingly assimilated into Catholic Christianity, especially after the Conference of Carthage in 411. These new adherents would have brought with them some of their customary religious practices.[23]

But it is difficult to deny that another significant factor in Augustine's development was his enhanced appreciation of the importance and persistence of bodily reality, which, as we have noted, accelerated markedly in the early decades of the 5th century AD. As Margaret Miles has observed, Augustine introduced the catalogue of miraculous healings in *ciu. Dei* 22.8 to "prove the bond between Christ's resurrection and the value of the body and the objects of sense."[24] Citing Augustine's claim that all of the contemporary miracles attest to the "faith which proclaims that Christ rose in the flesh and ascended into heaven in the flesh," Miles has argued that the elder Augustine valued miracles as "a paradigm and earnest of the eventual redemption of the whole human being in the resurrection of the body."[25] The intense physicality of the healing stories that Augustine tells are signs of the possibility of broken bodies being transformed by divine power. In this sense Augustine's catalogue of contemporary miracles in *ciu. Dei* 22.8 is less a diversion than an introduction to the final chapters of Book 22.[26]

PRIORITY OF BEAUTY IN THE RESURRECTED BODY

In *ciu. Dei* 22.12 Augustine turned from the issue of miracles to deal with a series of questions about the resurrected body. Some of these questions, he tells us, were raised by skeptics only in order to mock the notion of bodily resurrection. Were aborted fetuses to be raised? If all bodily parts are to be restored, what is to become of cut hair and clipped toenails? What will become of bodies eaten by cannibals and thus become parts of other bodies? Augustine's responses to these conundrums, whether uttered mockingly or not, follow consistent scriptural

[22] Wiśniewski 2018, p. 28.
[23] For this argument, see Brown 2000, pp. 416–418.
[24] Miles 1979, p. 37.
[25] Miles 1979, p. 38.
[26] My argument here follows Miles 1979, pp. 35–39. Cf. Brown 2000, pp. 416–422.

and theological principles. His primary scriptural resources were Eph 4:13, where the apostle stated that all would come "to the measure of the age of the fullness of Christ" (*in mensuram aetatis plenitudinis*) and Rom 8:29, where Paul referred to those "whom he predestined to be conformed to the image of God's Son." For Augustine the former text meant that both aborted fetuses (*ciu. Dei* 22.13) and infants (*ciu. Dei* 22.14) would rise as adults; they would be restored to the state they would have reached if they had lived to the age of Christ, that is, about thirty years old. Even if such a restoration required God to add to the bodily substance of these resurrected bodies, Augustine avers, we should not doubt that the creator who made all things is capable of producing the missing matter.[27]

Augustine thought it likely that the same principle obtained in the case of young persons and old: all would be restored to the size of body that they had (or would have had) at the peak of their youth. Here Augustine followed a traditional schema that saw "youth" (*iuuentus*) beginning around the age of thirty, the stage of life that succeeded *adulescentia*.[28] He refused, however, to assert any dogmatic opinions about these biblical texts. Commenting on Rom 8:29, for example, Augustine acknowledged that "to be conformed to the image of God's Son" could refer to conformation to Christ in the "inner man," or it could mean conformation to Christ in his immortality, just as he shared human mortality. If it did refer to the resurrected body, he maintained, it would refer to conformity to the age of the risen Christ. But Augustine did not think the matter was worthy of "a tiresome round of arguments and counter-arguments," and he was willing to concede that a person might rise in the same size and age of body in which they died, that is, either old or young (*ciu. Dei* 22.16; Babcock, 2.525–526).

Other, more consequential arguments follow, as Augustine explored further questions about the risen body, applying the principle that perfect proportion and beauty ought to characterize the body in its risen state. Returning to Eph 4:13 and Rom 8:29, Augustine noted that on the basis of these texts "some people believe that women will not rise again with their female sex; instead, they claim, all will rise as males, because God made only the man from clay but the woman from the man" (*ciu. Dei* 22.17; Babcock, 2.526). At the heart of this issue, Augustine realized, was the question of whether or not sexual

[27] It should be noted that in *ciu. Dei* 22.13 Augustine expressed some uncertainty about whether aborted fetuses would be raised.

[28] O'Daly 1999, p. 229.

differences were "natural" or essential to human identity. Many Christian writers, following a pattern set by previous Greek and Hellenized Jewish thinkers, preferred to think of the original creation of humanity as an androgynous being that was later divided into male and female.[29] Similarly, Origenist-inspired authors, such as Gregory of Nyssa, tended to think of the sexual differentiation as part of a secondary creation, produced by God as a response to the first sin, which entailed both corporeality and consequent mortality.[30]

By contrast, although Augustine considered sexual differences to be inherently linked to procreation, he did not relegate them to a secondary creation. From the early decades of the 5th century AD, that is, during the years in which he composed his *Gn. litt.*, Augustine had gradually accepted the idea that God had originally created the first human beings to "increase and multiply" in genuine physical intercourse; their bodies, therefore, were both genuinely corporeal and inherently gendered (Clark 1986). One result of this development is that Augustine came to see sexual difference as a "natural" and permanent aspect of human identity. Therefore he believed that both sexes would rise in their original gendered state: "All faults will be removed from those bodies, but their nature will be preserved. And female sex is not a fault but rather a matter of nature, and it will then be exempt from intercourse and childbirth" (*ciu. Dei* 22.17; Babcock, 2.526).

This move led Augustine to examine the question from another perspective: why should the sexual characteristics of women be preserved in the resurrected body, if they would no longer serve their original procreative function? At this point, considerations of beauty – and ultimately praise of God – became germane to Augustine's discussion. While female genitalia would no longer function to produce children, in the resurrection they would serve a more elevated purpose: to elicit praise of God for their beauty:

> The female organs will still be present. Now, however, they will be accommodated not to their former use but to a new beauty which will not excite the lust of the beholder, for there will be no lust. Instead, they will evoke praise for the wisdom and compassion of God, who both created what was not and freed what he created from corruption.
>
> (*ciu. Dei* 22. 17; Babcock, 2.526)

[29] See the classic discussion of this issue in Meeks 1974.
[30] Miles 2012.

Augustine here assumes that bodily parts can have both a practical purpose (*usus*) and a purely ornamental purpose (*decus*); the distinction is analogous to his famous distinction between "to use" (*uti*) and "to enjoy" (*frui*).[31] Augustine was firmly convinced that all bodily parts – indeed, all aspects of the physical world – were capable of eliciting praise of God for their beauty (*ciu. Dei* 22.24), even if, in this life, people often lack the technical knowledge to appreciate certain forms of beauty (e.g. the intricacy of the system of veins in the human body).

Augustine found a helpful parallel in the male body to illustrate his point. While some bodily parts serve a practical purpose as well as an ornamental purpose (the sexual characteristics of women), other bodily parts serve no practical purpose at all, but only an ornamental one. His example of the latter are male nipples or male beards, features that have no discernible use, but serve only to make the male body more beautiful. As he remarked in a sermon preached in the octave after Easter: "Take away the nipples from the manly breast, and see how much beauty you have spoiled, how much ugliness you have introduced" (*s.* 243.6; Hill, III/7.92). The same logic applied to the bodies of women. Although the genital organs will no longer serve the practical and necessary function of procreation, in the resurrection they will serve an even more elevated purpose: "After all, these necessities are going to pass away, and the time is going to come when we shall enjoy each other's beauty for itself alone, utterly without lust. And this in particular should lead us to praise the creator, to whom it is said in the Psalm: *You are clothed with praise and with beauty* (Ps 104:1)" (*ciu. Dei* 22.24; Babcock, 2.541). For Augustine, beauty transcended utility, because utility (*usus*) served only a temporary purpose, whereas beauty (*decus*) played a role in the divine-human relationship that would endure for all eternity.

But what constituted "beauty"? This, too, was a question to which Augustine devoted some attention. Adopting a standard Stoic definition of beauty,[32] Augustine argued that "all bodily beauty is a matter of the symmetry of the parts, together with a certain attractiveness of color" (*ciu. Dei* 22.19; Babcock, 2.529). According to this principle, God would reshape the resurrected human body using the available material and supplementing it where necessary in order to produce a body that was

[31] The former refers to things to be sought for the sake of something else (i.e. an instrumental good); the latter refers to things to be sought for their own sake (i.e. a good in itself). See further discussion in O'Connor 1983.

[32] O'Daly 1999, p. 230.

properly proportioned. Fat people and thin people would be restored to their desired weight. The short and the tall would be similarly raised or reduced to ideal proportions. Like that of the risen Christ, Augustine believed that the bodies of the redeemed will have an overwhelmingly attractive color, as the biblical text proclaims: "The righteous will shine like the sun in the kingdom of their Father" (Mt 13:43).

There was, however, one class of bodies that seemed to defy this restoration to perfection of beauty, that of the martyrs. People so loved the martyrs, Augustine declared, that they wanted to see on their bodies, "even in the kingdom of heaven," the very marks of the wounds that they suffered for Christ's sake. Perhaps it would be so, Augustine speculated. In this case, their wounds would not be a deformity or lack of proportion, but rather marks of honor: "a kind of beauty will shine in them which, although in the body, will be a beauty not of the body but of virtue" (*ciu. Dei* 22.19; Babcock, 2.530). While their severed limbs would be reattached, Augustine claimed, "it is fitting for the marks of their glorious wounds to be visible in their immortal flesh in that new age" (*ciu. Dei* 22.19; Babcock, 2.530). Although their limbs would be restored, the martyrs would continue to bear their bodily scars as visible testament to their glory in the flesh.

Corporeality and the Vision of God

The issue of beauty and the materiality of the resurrected body come together again in the final major topic that Augustine discussed in Book 21: the vision of God. Having once again confronted and repudiated Porphyry's claim that "one must flee from every kind of body" in order to enjoy eternal beatitude (*ciu. Dei* 22.26–28), Augustine now began to explore the character of the eternal vision of God that would sustain the saints (*ciu. Dei* 22.29). Once again, we see Augustine distancing himself from positions taken earlier in his life. In several earlier writings Augustine had raised, but dismissed, the possibility of seeing God through the eyes of the risen body.[33] For example, in *ep.* 147, a letter-treatise also known as *De uidendo deo*, which was written at least a decade prior to *ciu. Dei* 22, Augustine mentioned that some Christians believed that the substance of God might be seen with the eyes of the body, at least after the body had been transformed into a spiritual body. But he preferred to maintain that the vision of God was a matter of the heart, not the eyes (*ep.* 147.48).[34]

[33] Madec 1996, p. 70.
[34] Cf. Augustine's comments on this work in *retr.* 2.67.

By the time he composed the final book of *ciu. Dei* Augustine showed a new willingness at least to speculate on the possibility that the eyes of the resurrected body might see God.[35] Augustine's discussion of the matter was tantalizingly tentative. On the one hand, he stated clearly that the scriptures contained no explicit teaching on the matter. The biblical texts that might suggest a vision of God through bodily eyes – passages such as 1 Cor 13:12 ("Now we see in a mirror dimly, but then face to face") and Luke 3: ("All flesh shall see God's salvation") – could be interpreted in a variety of ways and, therefore, were not a secure basis on which to assert a vision of God through bodily eyes. On the other hand, Augustine cannot quite let go of the thought that the eyes of the body, and not merely the mind, will play a critical role in the beatific vision. Was it not possible, he reasoned, that in the life to come the eyes would have some special power or excellence similar to that of the mind and thus be able to see the incorporeal nature of God?

Although Augustine did not reject the possibility of such direct vision of God through the eyes of the body, he also proposed another interpretation that was "easier to understand" (*ad intellegendum facilius*). Perhaps in the next life the saints will see God in the same way in which we now perceive life within people by seeing their living bodies with our bodies:

> Alternatively ... God will be known to us in such a conspicuous way that we shall each see him by the spirit in ourselves, in each other, in himself, in the new heaven and the new earth, and in every created thing that will then exist; and, at the same time, by the body we shall each see him in every body, wherever the eyes of the spiritual body are directed with their penetrating gaze.
>
> (*ciu. Dei* 22.29; Babcock, 2.550–551)

Why was Augustine so intent on pursuing this question about which Scripture gave no definitive answer and which surpassed any human knowledge or experience?[36] Would it not have been simpler to maintain a strict agnosticism on the question or even to continue his previous denials?

Augustine's desire to push to the limit the role of the bodily eyes in the beatific vision served several purposes. It reinforced his polemical arguments against the philosopher Porphyry's claim that "one must flee every kind of body" (*omne corpus fugiendum*). It provided a way to

[35] Boersma 2018, pp. 27–32.

[36] Cf. *ciu. Dei* 22.29; Babcock, 2.550: "It is difficult, however, or even impossible to support this view with any examples or testimonies from Divine Scripture."

underscore the social character of salvation by linking the vision of God to the vision of other saved human beings, as well as the vision of a transfigured creation. Perhaps most importantly Augustine's insistence on the role of the body in heavenly vision also offered a way to engage the entire person – body and soul – in the eschatological activity of eternal praise:

> All the members and organs of the incorruptible body, which we now see assigned to the various functions that the necessities of life require of them, will contribute to praising God; for then there will be no such necessities but only full, certain, secure, and eternal felicity. All the proportions of bodily harmony, of which I have already spoken and which are hidden from us, will no longer be hidden. Distributed through all the parts of the body, within and without, they – along with all the other great and wondrous things that will then be seen – will set rational minds on fire with praise for such a great artist from sheer delight in their rational beauty.
>
> (*ciu. Dei* 22.30; Babcock, 2.551)

As I suggested at the outset of this chapter, Augustine's emphasis on the truly corporeal character of the afterlife, whether experienced by the saved or by the damned, was the end product of a long development in which he discarded many of the philosophical perspectives that had informed his earlier thought. By the time he composed *ciu. Dei* 21 and 22, Bishop Augustine had concluded that the final end of the body was precisely to have no end.

FURTHER READING

Burrus, V. (2009). Carnal Excess: Flesh at the Limits of Imagination. *Journal of Early Christian Studies*, 17, 247–265.

Burrus, V. and MacKendrick, K. (2010). Bodies without Wholes: Apophatic Excess and Fragmentation in Augustine's *City of God*. In C. Boesel and C. Keller, eds., *Apophatic Bodies: Negative Theology, Incarnation, and Relationality*. New York: Fordham University Press, pp. 79–93.

Hunter, D. G. (2002). Augustine, Sermon 354A: Its Place in His Thought on Marriage and Sexuality. *Augustinian Studies*, 33(1), 39–60.

(2012). Augustine on the Body. In M. Vessey, ed., *The Blackwell Companion to Augustine*. Oxford: Blackwell, pp. 353–364.

Miles, M. (1979). *Augustine on the Body. AAR Dissertation Series*, vol. 31. Missoula, MT: Scholars Press.

Rombs, R. J. (2006). *Saint Augustine and the Fall of the Soul*. Washington, DC: Catholic University of America Press.

van Bavel, T. J. (1995). "No One Ever Hated His Own Flesh": Eph. 5:29 in Augustine. *Augustinianum*, 45, 45–93.

15 Epilogue: The Architectonic Plan of *The City of God*

JOHN C. CAVADINI

Nothing is more evident, seemingly, about Augustine's *ciu. Dei* than its structure. Any reasonably serious relevant website reveals that it is divided into two "halves," comprising Books 1–10 and 11–22, each further subdivided into halves and thirds, respectively. Augustine himself accounts for the structure in just this way. In *retr.* he distinguishes the first ten books and the last twelve as the main textual units. The first ten respond to "two groundless opinions that are opposed to the Christian religion." The first five reply to "those who would have it that human success depends on what they regard as the essential observance of the many gods whom they customarily worship"; the next five books rebut those who argue that the observance they make to the multitude of gods by sacrificing brings profit to life after death." Augustine adds, lest it be objected that he would then have done nothing but refute the opinions of others without asserting any of his own, the last twelve books accomplish this goal: "in the twelve books that come later, the first four contain an account of the rise of the two cities, the City of God and the city of this world, the second four expound their growth or progress, and the third and final four their appointed ends." Thus the first "half" leads with response and refutation, and the second half with constructive theology. As Augustine also observes, however, this distinction is not absolute: "Nonetheless, where necessary I both maintain our own standpoint in the first ten books, and reject the opposing views in the later twelve" (*retr.* 2.69; see also, *ep.* 1A*.1).

At the outset, Augustine tells Marcellinus, "I have taken up the task of defending the most glorious City of God … against those who prefer their own gods to its founder" (*ciu. Dei* 1.*praef*; Babcock, 1.1).[1] Augustine thus situates *ciu. Dei* into the genre of apologetics. He continues by specifying that he will treat the City of God "whether in

[1] All translations come from William Babcock, and adjusted where necessary.

the course of these present times when it is on pilgrimage among the ungodly, living by faith, or in the stability of its eternal home which it now awaits impatience" (*ciu. Dei* 1.*praef*; Babcock, 1.1). In other words, the apologetics will be accomplished through a constructive exposition. At this early stage, there are not two "halves" in view yet. The ultimate defense is offense, the presentation of an alternative view, a perspective which response and refutation reflects. Understanding this should keep us from interpreting the structure that eventually develops as indicating two fundamentally different aims, apologetics and constructive exposition. There is one aim throughout, "the task of defending the most glorious City of God," and one way of accomplishing that aim, an exposition that presents the character and destiny of the City of God.

The combination of refutation with constructive theology without which the refutation makes no sense is a longstanding feature of Christian apologetics. One has only to think of Justin Martyr's articulation of his *Logos* theology and his disclosure of the meaning and practice of authentic Christian worship to realize how intertwined rebuttal can be with erecting an edifice of positive theology. O'Daly, who comments that "[t]he *City of God* is arguably the culmination of the Latin Christian apologetic tradition in antiquity," notes that "[a]pologetic did not merely attack paganism and defend Christianity; it also provided elements of positive Christian teaching." He adds that in "this dual aspect it anticipates both the polemical and the doctrinal aspects of the *City of God*."[2] O'Daly notes this feature of the work as his commentary moves from Book 10 to Book 11: "The end of Book 10 marks the conclusion of what Augustine often refers to as the part of the work devoted to refutation" ('In the previous ten books, with the help of our Lord and king, we have responded to the enemies of this holy city as best we could.'; *ciu. Dei* 11.1; Babcock, 2.2)." Nevertheless, O'Daly notes that "the continuity between this new section of the work and what went before is greater than Augustine's scheme suggests," and that "[b]eneath the structural edifice, more subtle connections are discernible."[3]

Not only are "more subtle connections" discernible, but not-so-subtle disruptions of the distinction between the two halves jump out. They demand that we seek a unity deeper than the formal scheme indicates, one corresponding to Augustine's initial statement of

[2] O'Daly 1999, pp. 39, 47. O'Daly provides an excellent overview of the literature on the structure of *ciu. Dei* at pp. 67–73.

[3] O'Daly 1999, p. 135.

purpose, which, in fact, the later scheme is intended to enable, not to occlude. We actually do find that rebuttal is subordinated to construction, as Augustine's opening words imply. One of the biggest disruptions of the formal scheme is the treatment of the Incarnation in Book 10, instead of at its expected place in the exposition of the progress of the two, specifically, in Book 18. There we get only the laconic announcement, "During the reign of Herod in Judea ... Christ was born in Bethlehem of Judah in accord with the earlier prophecy." This is accompanied by the scantiest crumb of constructive Christology: "Outwardly he was human, a man born from a human virgin; hiddenly he was God from God the Father" (*ciu. Dei* 18.46; Babcock. 2.332). As a climax to the exposition of salvation history, this is underwhelming. The Incarnation is almost an afterthought. But no exposition is needed here because the heavy constructive lifting on the Incarnation has occurred already, in Book 10, where the exposition of the person of the Mediator and his "universal way" of salvation served as the climax of the first "half." In other words, the subordination of refutation to construction is performed even in the half formally dedicated to refutation, mirroring the subordination of the "first half" as propaedeutic to the second. Meanwhile, some of the most sustained refutation of pagan views in the second "half," for example, the critique of cyclical theories of the world history at *ciu. Dei* 12.10–21, and the critique of pagan mythology and divination in the section dealing with the progress of the earthly city from *ciu. Dei* 18.2–26.

One clue as to the underlying architectonic unity of *ciu. Dei* might be found by examining the seam between the two "halves," the opening of Book 11. After Augustine summarizes the first ten books as response to opponents, he announces that he will now "begin to discuss, to the best of my ability, the origin, the course, and the merited ends of the two cities," starting with "how these two cities took their origins in a prior division among the angels" (*ciu. Dei* 11.1; Babcock 2.2). Picking up his discussion of Christ the Son of God who as a human being became our Mediator and Way, he mentions that it was he who established the canonical Scriptures, having spoken first through the prophets, then through himself, and then through the apostles. We find this speaking in the Scriptures, and it is to their authority that we must turn if we are to learn about the origin, the progress, and the merited ends of the two cities, starting with their origin in a division among the angels. Since the angels have their origin in creation, ultimately the origin of the two cities is in creation itself, and so, after having stated the source of the authority of Scripture in the words of the Mediator, Book 11 begins the discussion of the origin, progress and ends of the two cities starting with Gen 1:1, *In the beginning God made heaven and earth* (*ciu. Dei* 11.4). The second "half" is thus identified formally as Scriptural commentary. It is true that after quoting Gen 1:1, Augustine immediately turns to respond to a critique about "why did the eternal God decide to make heaven and earth just then, when he had not made them before?" (*ciu. Dei* 11.4; Babcock, 2.4). But the response is in the service of the exposition of Scripture (just as it is to a similar question at *conf.* 11.10.12–11.13.15), subordinated, as it has been all along, to the primary intention of constructive exposition. Perhaps we could say there is a formal genre change at Book 11 such that we have, beginning there, an extended continuous commentary on Scripture that occupies the rest of the work.

Book 19 may seem to be an exception since it conforms more to the style of engagement of opposing positions characteristic of the first half. But here it is used to recapitulate the work of all of the earlier books, especially the work of Book 10 on true worship, of Books 13 and 14 on death and passion, and of 15–17 on the pilgrim character of the City of God in this world, all in order to answer the question first raised in Book 2 about the nature of a true commonwealth. This in turn has implications for the discussion of the supreme good or the supreme evil (the opening subject of Book 19) that turn out to be the destiny of the "cities," respectively. But the destinies of these cities are discovered through Scriptural commentary in Books 20–22. As propaedeutic to those books, Book 19 is the exception that proves the rule, namely, that critical response is ordered toward Scriptural exegesis, even if the current relevance of that exegesis arises because one needs to answer opponents. In fact, the way in which Book 19 returns, by structural design, to the question raised back at *ciu. Dei* 2.21, one of the most polemical of all the Books, has the effect of showing that from the perspective of Scripture the critiques posed by the pagans can actually be resolved to the more fundamental question of what true human community is. Only when you have an answer to that question can you see, by contrast, what is not.

In a sense, the fact that we have scriptural commentary starting at Book 11 – the beginning of the discussion of the "origin, progress and ends" of the two cities – means that this second half of the work stakes a claim on what scripture is *about*. It is about this very thing, for the main subject of scripture is nothing other than the City of God. Commenting on the narrative of Noah's ark, for example, Augustine observes that the ark is a "figure of the City of God on pilgrimage in this world, that is, a figure of the Church which is saved through the wood on which hung *the mediator between God and man, the man Christ Jesus"* (1 Tim 2:5; *ciu. Dei* 15.26; Babcock, 2.178). What Augustine says about this passage applies to Scripture as a whole, as everything which is spoken of therein "must refer in one way or another to the City of God of which we are speaking, which is on pilgrimage in the midst of this wicked world as though in the midst of a flood" (*ciu. Dei* 15.26; Babcock, 2.179). The books of the Old Testament would not have been so carefully preserved if they were simply a repository of "*res gestas*," mere historical facts (*ciu. Dei* 15.27). They were preserved because they present figures of the great mystery of Christ and the Church:

> We search out these hidden meanings of Divine Scripture as best we can, sometimes more aptly and sometimes less so, but always holding faithfully to the certainty that these things were not done and recorded without some prefiguration of things to come and that they are to be referred to nothing other than Christ and his Church, which is the City of God. From the very beginning of the human race there have been prophetic anticipations of that City, and we now see those prophecies being fulfilled in every respect.
>
> (*ciu. Dei* 16.2; Babcock, 2.187)

In order to be able to interpret scripture prophetically, to recognize the figures in scripture and their meaning, you have to know *of what* they are figures. One must know the reality which one is looking for, understanding the prophetic perspective, the light as it were, in which the figures can be seen as such and interpreted as foreshadowings. This is the accomplishment of the first half of the treatise. It culminates in an exposition of the Incarnation, of Christ and the Church both, as the fulfillment of all prophecy. The work of the first half has the effect of shining the great light of the Incarnation on the interpretive project of the second half, as the truth from which prophecy originates and to which it ultimately refers.

Nor does Scripture lose its prophetic character in the New Testament, for the appointed ends of the two cities are there foretold more openly than in the Old. Exegesis of the Gospels, the letters of Paul and the Book of Revelation, constitute the matter of the last three books to which the nineteenth is subordinated. The Book "called The Apocalypse" (*ciu. Dei* 20.17) in particular has a style of "prophetic speech" (*ciu. Dei* 20.16). It speaks figuratively as well as literally, just like the Old Testament: Rev 20:2–5 describes the "great City, the new Jerusalem, coming down out of heaven from God." Augustine comments that this is a figure for the Church as it exists in the present age. He says it is described as coming down from heaven "because the grace by which God made it is heavenly" (*ciu. Dei* 20.17; Babcock, 2.416). In that sense, Augustine adds, this City "has been coming down out of heaven from its very beginning" (*ciu. Dei* 20.17; Babcock, 2.416), increasing in numbers by the grace of God given in Baptism. This image of the Church as a City coming down from heaven is revealed in the context of proclamation of the Last Judgment, when God will wipe away every tear from the eyes of the elect. It is then that the splendor of the City which has since its origin been coming down from Heaven "will shine out by God's gift with a clarity so bright and so new that no traces of the old will remain" (*ciu. Dei* 20.17; Babcock, 2.416). Still, the Church, despite the "tares" that have yet to be purified, is already the presence of that final splendor, or at least of the same reality whose splendor will be disclosed.

The Church is "even now ... the kingdom of Christ." The souls of the pious dead are still joined to the Church as Christ's members, and as the Apocalypse shows, "so even now the saints reign with [Christ], although not in the same sense in which they will ultimately reign" (*ciu. Dei* 20.9; Babcock, 2.406). The Church is thus a kind of heavenly space in this world, its communion transcending the boundary of death. It is the presence of the Apocalypse now, the presence in the world of a communion or solidarity among human beings that, though present in the world, cannot be derived from the world, but comes from the heavenly grace of Baptism. In other words, we need prophetic figures to be able to identify and properly know *present* reality, not only past and future reality. We have to know what is true community, what community therefore has a future, and what does not. By contrast, the world, which can only be seen as the "city of this earth" by its contrast with the heavenly City, is a city that is no city, a mirage of community destined to have its essential fragmentation revealed as the "second death" of the Apocalypse. The Church is thus the refraction *in* the world of the apocalyptic vision *of* the world.[4]

This vision, formally speaking, is prophecy. The architectonic plan of *City of God* is thus the most traditional of all Christian apologetic plans, namely, that of prophecy and fulfillment. The first half of *ciu. Dei*

[4] Lest it seem too shocking to associate the word "apocalyptic" with Augustine, see Hughes 2005, pp. 94–105; O'Regan 2009, p. 20; and Paula Fredrickson, "Tyconius and Augustine on the Apocalypse" in Emmerson and McGinn 1992, pp. 20–37.

culminates in the discussion of the Incarnation because the Incarnation is the fulfillment of prophecy. In turn, faith in the Incarnation is what allows one to read the Scriptures prophetically. The second half of *ciu. Dei* is the figurative or prophetic reading of Scripture it makes possible. Since prophecy, inspired by the Spirit, arises from the Father's eternal plan for creation as expressed in his Word, Jesus Christ, the architectonic plan of *ciu. Dei* is nothing more and nothing less than the economy of salvation as it existed in the plan of God from all eternity and as it has been executed in history, and as it will be consummated eschatologically. God's plan is the underlying architectonic plan. There is only one plan, corresponding to one unified structure that defends the City of God through the exposition of God's plan from all eternity as the prophetic Scriptures have revealed it. The first half of the treatise progressively invokes and explains this plan in its contrast with pagan views. Simultaneously it progressively invokes and explains the economy of prophecy and miracle that revealed this plan, distinguishing prophecy from pagan oracles and divination, and miracles from prodigies of power and force engineered by demons.

Each of the two halves that Augustine identifies as comprising the first part of the treatise, Books 1–5, followed by Books 6–10, culminates in a constructive exposition, the second one building on the first. Book 4 opens with a review of the first three books. Then, Augustine says, he will fulfill the promise made at the end of Book 1, namely, "to show what the morals of the Romans were, and why the true God, who holds all kingdoms in his power, deigned to help them increase their empire – and to show, as well, how little help they got from those whom they count as gods, and how much harm these gods actually did by their trickery and deceit" (*ciu. Dei* 4.2; Babcock, 1.110). This is an explicitly "constructive" agenda. It is nothing less than the first introduction, in *City of God*, of God's eternal plan, including the fact that God *has* a plan. The demonstration of the uselessness of the gods is carried over from Books 1–3 into Book 4, while the constructive task of saying why God willed that the Roman empire be spread so widely and last so long (*ciu. Dei* 5. *praef.*), is left to Book 5. But the way is prepared for this exposition in the demonstration of the gods' uselessness. They did nothing to improve the moral character of the Romans, but instead contributed to its degradation (Book 2) while they could not save Rome from the relentless savagery that characterized its history from the beginning (Book 3). How useful were the gods, actually, in the enterprise of empire building? Book 4 shows that most of them were hopelessly bureaucratized into their own departments.[5] In each case a gift the true God gives was mistaken for a god, even Felicitas, who strictly speaking should have made all the other gods redundant. The God who gives even this gift cannot be Jupiter; Jupiter is morally unfit to be the giver of true happiness, as the mythic accounts of his adulteries prove. While Cicero blames the poets for connecting Jupiter with these stories, he does not go on to critique the obscene cults that dramatize the myths (*ciu. Dei* 4.25). The Empire grew despite the bad moral influence of the cult and its endorsement by the learned establishment. Cicero mocked augury, yet was himself an augur and held that the Roman polytheist religious institutions "should be treated with reverence." In fact, the endorsement of the cult by the intelligentsia was part of a strategy of political control, of consolidation of Roman political power (*ciu. Dei* 4.32). Augustine contrasts this politically interested confusion of the gifts of God with mythic divinities with the Bible's view, which enables us to see this confusion apocalyptically, by contrast to the positive vision. The reader is introduced to the two Testaments, and to prophecy in particular (*ciu. Dei* 4.33) which, distinguished from augury, is accompanied by "miraculous signs," and these, without any assistance from the gods of Rome, fostered the development of the kingdom of the Jews (*ciu. Dei* 4.33–34).

But in asking why was the blessing of empire given by God to the Romans (*ciu. Dei* 5. *praef.*), Augustine opens a frankly "constructive" agenda. He accordingly constructs a vision of God's Providence by distinguishing it from "fate" or "destiny" against astrologers and Stoics alike. Astrological 'prophecy' and other augury is based on a deterministic view of the world. Cicero, in order to advocate for human freedom, denies the efficacy of augury and with it the foreknowledge even of God (*ciu. Dei* 5.9). But, as Creator, God is sovereignly free. He establishes and guarantees the freedom of the wills he has created as true causes, the effects of which, precisely as free, he can foresee. He works through the freedom of a creature without compromising its freedom: "To some he grants empowerment, to some he does not" (*ciu. Dei* 5.9; Babcock, 1.155). Thus are we first introduced, in *City of God*, to the *Creator*, who is the Trinity: "The supreme and true God, therefore, with his Word and his Spirit, which three are one, is the almighty God, the creator and maker of every soul and every body. It is by participation in him that all are happy (*felices*) who are happy in

[5] See Cavadini 2012, pp. 93–110, esp. pp. 107–108.

truth and not in empty illusion" (*ciu. Dei* 5.11; Babcock, 1.158). As *Creator*, God's almighty power is such that it underwrites freedom rather than restricts it. To say that, the "the kingdoms of men, their dominions and their enslavements" fall "outside the laws of his providence" (*ciu. Dei* 5.11; Babcock, 1.159) is, paradoxically, to provide a vantage point for appreciating more fully the work of human agency, in its decadence and grandeur alike. We see the greatness of the imperial Roman spirit, which quested for excellence (*uirtus*) with truly "miraculous" feats of bravery, fidelity, loyalty, and self-sacrifice to the point of preferring country over kin and poverty over wealth, in order to create a truly glorious empire, one known not only for its justice, but for its mercy when it "spares the conquered, but beats down the proud" – a majestic reprise of the verse from Virgil first found in the Preface to Book 1. The work of prophecy, ever to expose and confront idolatry and to demythologize the idols, allows a view of free human agency in God's sovereign freedom. We can see that the disintegration of the Roman pagan imperial culture has nothing mysterious about it, for the seeds of its demise were present in the very engine for its greatness, the lust for glory.

After this magnificent exposition of the Creator and his divine plan with its concomitant bird's eye "apocalyptic" view of the Roman empire, Augustine now has a vantage point to be able to discuss whether the cult of the gods is useful, if not for Empire building, then for eternal benefits after death. If we turn the apocalyptic vision of prophecy on the cults of the gods with this question in view, what do we see? In Books 6 and 7 Augustine trains his sights on the civic cult, on what Varro called "civil theology." Augustine allows the skepticism of Varro, who heaps scorn on the poets and their "mythic theology," to help establish the gods' worthlessness for any kind of salvation, while noting that Varro and other scholars did not have the courage to challenge the cultic establishment (*ciu. Dei* 6.9). Their skepticism generated allegories of the myths – "natural theology" – but did not challenge the cult based on the myths. In Varro's version of this "natural theology" we find, not a true theology, but an ideology, the scholarly way of underwriting the cult. Augustine does not so much deconstruct the myths, as natural theology already does that for him, but rather shows that the natural theologies all represent ways, in effect, of justifying the cult even at its cruelest and most irrational.

This is especially clear in the obscene and cruel rites associated with the Great Mother. Everything in the ritual is allegorized, even the meaning of the *Galli* who gash and castrate themselves:

> These, then, are the celebrated mysteries (*praeclara mysteria*) of Tellus and the Great Mother, in which everything is referred back to perishable seeds and the practice of agriculture. The timbrel, the towers, the Galii, the frenzied flinging about of the limbs, the noise of the cymbals, the images of the lions – all are related to seeds and referred to an agricultural purpose. But do any of these hold the promise of eternal life? The castrated Galli serve this great goddess in order to signify (*ut significent*) that those who lack seed should seek the earth. But is it not rather their very service to her that caused them to be without seed? Do they acquire the seed they lack by following the goddess? Or is it rather that they lose the seed that they have by following the goddess? (*ciu. Dei* 7.24; Babcock, 1.230)

The natural theology exhibited here has rationalized not only the myths, but the castrated men enacting the myths in the cult, reducing both myth and men to the status of mere signifiers, bearers of a signification supplied, after the fact, by "natural theology." Even the philosopher Porphyry (d. AD 305), here first mentioned in *ciu. Dei*, justifies the cult by an allegory in which the castrated Attis, whom the cultic eunuchs signify, is allegorized. Augustine remarks, pointedly, "And what about the rest of him, whatever was left after the mutilation? What is that said to signify (*significari dicitur*)? To what does it refer? What interpretation is provided for it? (*qua refertur? quae interpretatio inde profertur?*; *ciu. Dei* 7.25; Babcock, 1.231; CCSL 47.207). The human being is left over as the byproduct of signification, as wreckage and trash, sacrificed by the natural theology to justify the cults by making them appear rational, rather than political:

> That these episodes were sung or written may be due to the audacity and impudence of the poets. But that they were added to the divine rites and honors at the express command and demand of the divinities themselves can only count as a crime on the part of the gods, or rather as a confession on the part of the demons and a deception of miserable human beings. As for the notion that the mother of the gods is rightly worshipped by the consecration of mutilated men, the poets did not make that up. Far from reciting it in verse, they recoiled from it in horror.
>
> (*ciu. Dei* 7.26; Babcock, 1.232)

In other words, not the poets, but the civil cults, are primary, for the poets did not invent, but rather shrank from, the idea that the Mother of the Gods was to be worshiped by such cruel rites. It is the political authorities who established and promoted the public cult. It is "civil theology" which is ultimately the target of Augustine's demythologization. Far from any promise of life eternal, we have the sacrifice of human value to political interests. The scholarly establishment manages to displace the scorn occasioned by the myths onto the poets, away from where judgment should ultimately be lodged.

Contrasted to the World Soul, which Varro's natural theology claimed to be what the various images and statues used in the cult represented (*ciu. Dei* 7.6), is the transcendent Creator (*Creator*) who made every soul and all matter (*ciu. Dei* 7.29) and created and rules (*et creauit et regit*) everything he has made, the earth and all its seeds, including the procreative union of man and woman, utterly free, guaranteeing the freedom of his creation even as he directs it. From *this* God we hope for eternal life (*ciu. Dei* 7.30). He gave us the intellect that enables us to search for him in everything he has created, and he sent his Son when we were overwhelmed by the burden of our sins, as a revelation of his great love (*magnae dilectionis indicium*) for us. By his sacrifice we are purified from our sins, and the love of the Holy Spirit poured into our hearts so that we may come to eternal contemplation. No one can adequately thank him for these gifts, added to creation (*ciu. Dei* 7.31). The mystery of eternal life has been proclaimed through the ministry of angels from the very beginning of the human race, with signs and sacraments appropriate to given times and places, and the Hebrew people were raised up, among whom Christ was prophesied, in words and in all the ceremonies consecrated to the worship (*latreia*) due to God. We see these now fulfilled and expect their final perfection (*ciu. Dei* 7.32). This economy of prophecy and fulfillment affords the perspective from heaven, the apocalyptic vision, on the gods of the nations which are seen in this perspective to be unclean demons aiming not at human freedom but domination, something they achieved partly by oracles and partly by deceptive miracles in partnership with political leaders who use the cult to maintain their domination.

In Book 8 Augustine builds on this expanded statement of God's plan and purpose as revealed by prophesy to examine the claims of the philosophers. He chooses the Platonists because they have a conception of the God who made (*fecit*) the visible world and every soul, who gives happiness to rational souls by giving them a share in his unchangeable and immaterial light. Yet they do not consider that worshipping this one God is enough to gain eternal life, but endorse the worship of many gods, admittedly made and established by God (*conditos atque institutos*). On this Christians and Platonists agree (*ciu. Dei* 8.1). But

Augustine rarely uses the word *creare* or *Creator* to describe the agreement between Christians and Platonists on God as the source of the world. We've already seen this word used: it is used in strict association with the God who has an eternal *plan*. Nor does Augustine name the Trinity in stating Platonist agreement with Christian teaching, despite Plato's threefold division of philosophy (*ciu. Dei* 8.5). Platonists and Christians agree that God is the *principium* of the world (*ciu. Dei* 8.6, 9), the light of the mind (*ciu. Dei* 8.7) and the *Summum Bonum* (*ciu. Dei* 8.8), but they do not agree that God is "Creator" or "Trinity," something not explicitly stated but observable in Augustine's word choice (often obscured by translations which use the word "create" as though it were simply a synonym for other words of making and derivation).[6] Thus even as Augustine is stating the agreement between Platonist and Christian, he is constructing the contrast in perspective which results in the anomaly that though the Platonists know the one transcendent God, and know that happiness means participation in the light and enjoyment of the Good which is the *principium* of all things, they nevertheless do not worship this God.

Augustine's diagnosis of this anomaly is expressed using Rom 1:19–22, quoted in *ciu. Dei* for the first time here (Rom. 1:19–20 first at *ciu. Dei* 8.6, and Rom. 1:19–22 first at *ciu. Dei* 8.10). Though God's invisible realities have been revealed to them through his works, they did not glorify God nor give him thanks. In other words, they failed to worship him properly – because they gloried in their fame as possessing wisdom – and so they descended into the folly of idolatry (*ciu. Dei* 8.10). Augustine never wavers from this diagnosis of what we might call the philosophers' bad faith. Despite the continuity of Platonic teaching about God up to the time of Porphyry (in Greek) and Apuleius (in Latin), all of them, including Plato himself, "thought that worship should be given to many gods" (*ciu. Dei* 8.12; Babcock, 1.257).

This brings up the *reason* they thought the many gods ought to be worshipped, namely, to get to the One God through the good gods – the only true "gods" according to Plato. The problem is the gods are themselves sufficiently transcendent, sufficiently participatory in the One God, that, even according to Plato, "no god has dealings with human

[6] Though he uses it when summarizing a Scriptural verse, e.g. when stating in his own words the teaching of Rom 1:19–20, as at *ciu. Dei* 8.6). Even when discussing the *Timaeus*, which references the Demiurge, Augustine says that Plato there talks not of the "creation" but of the "establishment" (*de constitutione*) of the world (*ciu. Dei* 8.11).

beings" (*ciu. Dei* 8.18; Babcock, 1.263, citing *On the God of Socrates* §6–8.12; see also *ciu. Dei* 8.20). We humans need some kind of mediation that can bridge the gap between the transcendence of the divine, and our corporeal, mortal misery. Thus the long discussion in Book 8 of the "demons," beings intermediate between gods and humans, and their cultivation as part of the process of trying to reach the gods, and ultimately, God. Cultivation of the demons through religious ceremonies is intended to invoke their *mediation* between the gods and humans, since they are halfway in between (*medios daemones inter deos et homines*; *ciu. Dei* 8.22; CCSL 47.239). But why would the gods have contact with unclean demons, just because they are physically closer, and not with humans who are reverent and of good spirit (*ciu. Dei* 8.21)?

The demons persuade the multitude, through deceitful signs, including miracles of prediction ("prophesy"), that they are gods, and they treat the multitude as subjugated captives (*ciu. Dei* 8.22). In an important passage, Augustine explains the prophecy of Ps 96:1:

> *Sing to the Lord a new song; sing to the Lord all the earth.* In fact, the title of this Psalm is *When the house was being built, after the captivity.* And, in truth, a house is now being built (*aedificatur*) for the Lord in all the earth – namely, the City of God, which is the holy Church – following the captivity in which demonic forces held captive the people, now believers in God, from whom the house is being built from living stones.
>
> (cf. 1 Pet 2:5; *ciu. Dei* 8.24; Babcock, 1.272)

Human worship of man-made gods inevitably draws us into fellowship with demons: "Uncleans spirits, however, bound to these images by that nefarious art, had miserably enslaved the souls of their worshippers by gathering them into company (*societatem*) with themselves" (*ciu. Dei* 7.24; CCSL 47.244). False worship binds people into a *societas* with each other and the demons. True worship frees them by binding them into fellowship in the City of God, the Church. In the Church, we are bound by true worship also to the good "gods," actually the holy angels, with whom in true worship we are incorporated into the one City of God. Our closeness to the "gods" is not a matter of who is lower or higher or more or less physical, but of a communion formed by sharing of true worship.

Augustine has considerably advanced his constructive vision here. It is further developed in Book 9, in the course of furthering his critique of the bad faith of the Platonists. This brings Augustine, once again, even more insistently, to the Incarnate Word, under his aspect as the true Mediator, the *Mediator between God and man* who is the uncreated

Word. It is as Man – *the man Christ Jesus* (1 Tim 2:5) – that he is the Mediator (*ciu. Dei* 9.15, though 1 Tim 2:5 is not cited until *ciu. Dei* 9.17):

> As for man, then, who is mortal and miserable, far removed from the immortal and blessed, what intermediary should he choose to unite him with immortality and blessedness? The source of delight he might find in the immortality of the demons is nothing but misery; the source of offence he might find in the mortality of Christ no longer exists. On the one side, there is eternal misery to be aware of; on the other, death is not to be feared, since it could not last eternally, and there is eternal blessedness to be loved.
>
> (*ciu. Dei* 9.15; Babcock, 1.294)

In the Crucified One, what we might have feared in Christ, his mortality, has been removed as something to fear because in Christ, "death is not to be feared, since it could not last eternally, and there is eternal blessedness to love." The demons, being immortal but wretched, could at best mediate an unhappy immortality. But the mortal and blessed (*mortalis et beatus*) mediator intervenes precisely so that, having enacted his mortality, he might make the dead immortal, as he showed by his own resurrection, and might give the miserable blessedness, from which he never departed" (*ciu. Dei* 9.15; Babcock, 1.294).

This development of Augustine's positive theology of mediation shows by contrast that the very terms in which the issue of mediation is posed by the Platonists, the very 'structure' of mediation as they conceived it, is what is being challenged. We see immediately that the true Mediator is not in an "intermediate state," somewhere between human and divine, but rather he *is* human, he is in *our* state and place, not somewhere in between. "It is God who is blessed in himself and also makes us blessed, and, because he became a participant in our humanity (*factus particeps humanitatis nostrae*; CCSL 47.263), he provided a shortcut (*compendium*) to participation in his divinity." In Christ, we do not come to participate in the nature of the immortally happy angels (the "good gods"), but in the Trinity itself (*ad illam Trinitatem*), participation in which makes us happy as well. In fact, God himself, the happy and happy-making (*beatus et beatificus*) eternal God, "willed (*uoluit*) to be lower than the angels (Heb 2:7, 2:9), in the form of a servant (Phil 2:7), in order to be the mediator, he still remained higher than the angels in the form of God" (*ciu. Dei* 9.15; Babcock, 1.294–95).

Augustine critiques the whole Platonist 'structure' of mediation by challenging the kind of transcendence it assumes, one that, in a way, is so transcendent that it "fears contamination" by contact with humans.

The true Mediator evidently did not have this fear: "For the God who is utterly beyond contamination would never fear contamination from the man with whom he clothed himself or from the men among whom he lived as a man" (*ciu. Dei* 9.17; Babcock, 1.297). It is the Platonist assumption that divine transcendence is such that God can't "empty himself" or bend down, that his transcendence is such that it imprisons him, that creates the "space" for the structure of mediation Augustine is rejecting. This is the space filled by the cults and the self-centered political establishment, with its academic avatars, that has an interest in keeping God distant, holding God off, keeping him properly "transcendent." Knowing about this transcendence is a mark of those fixated on *claiming to be wise* instead of *glorifying God and giving thanks to him* (Rom 1:21). They therefore justify the worship of gods who are not gods so their own cultural achievement and status – as wise – is left intact. God is reduced to a credential on their *Curriculum Vitae.*

Augustine approvingly echoes Plotinus (*ciu. Dei* 9.17): it is "unlikeness to God" which is the only separation from him. But what is the purification that will make us similar to God, and what is this similarity in the first place? It cannot be purification from contamination by the flesh. "And meanwhile there are two matters of no small importance that he showed us, for our salvation, by his incarnation – that true divinity cannot be contaminated by the flesh, and that we should not think that the demons are superior to us just because they do not have flesh" (*ciu. Dei* 9.17). This is, in effect, the revelation of a new kind of transcendence, one in which the absolutely unchangeable God nevertheless can "will" to "become" something. God is free, even, ironically, of his own transcendence. We become like God, then, purified of unlikeness, when we participate in the free self-gift of the One whose transcendence did not cause him to "fear" us and, to protect his transcendence, refuse to come among us (*ciu. Dei* 9.20).

The demons predict the future because they are more alert to the causes operative in temporal affairs and can make reasonable inferences based on the evidence. But the good angels cling to God with charity and so they see "the eternal and immutable laws of God, which dwell in his Wisdom." And this Wisdom is not knowledge of Platonic forms. Rather it is "to know the will of God, which is the most certain and most powerful of all causes, by participation in his Spirit" (*ciu. Dei* 9.22; Babcock, 1.300). True prophecy originates from giving oneself over to the eternal plan of God's love. The good angels are inflamed with the beauty of the love of God and therefore they have a surer knowledge of the future through their loving adherence to the eternal plan they see in that love. Humans have access to that plan through faith in the Mediator whose Incarnation fulfilled the prophetic economy. By this faith they are purified to contemplate the spiritual knowledge of God's loving plan (*ciu. Dei* 9.21).

This programmatic moment prepares for its own fulfillment in the dramatic resolution of Book 10, perhaps the most "constructive" Book in *ciu. Dei*. Having dispensed with those who believe that divine honors are to be offered to demons, Augustine proposes to take up in Book 10 the question as to whether those beings non-Christian philosophers call "gods" are "worthy of worship and of veneration" (*ciu. Dei* 10.4; Babcock, 1.309) and thus ones to whom religious sacrifice should be offered.[7] But what does it mean to offer sacrifice truly? While God did order animal sacrifice early on, "those sacrifices had to be changed at the opportune and pre-established moment ... to keep people from believing that such sacrifices in themselves, rather than the things they signified, were desirable to God" (*ciu. Dei* 10.5; Babcock, 1.310). And what is desirable to God? The contrite heart, the *act* intended by the one sacrificing, in particular, an act or work of mercy (or compassion): "To him we offer, on the altar of our heart, the sacrifice of humility and praise, kindled by the fire of love" (*ciu. Dei* 10.3; Babcock, 1.308). Such acts fulfill the divine commands to love God and neighbor (*ciu. Dei* 10.5) and are thereby intended to unite us to God in a *sancta societas*, a holy fellowship in clinging to God (*ciu. Dei* 10.6), provided such an act is performed or offered for the sake of God, an act of offering oneself wholly, body and soul, to God. The essential structure of true sacrifice is that of an act of self-giving.

The true Mediator is the one who can perfectly mediate a perfect act of self-giving to us, so that we can participate in it and thus in true sacrificial worship:

> In the form of God, then, the true mediator – since, by taking the form of a servant (Phil 2:6), he became the mediator between God and man, the man Christ Jesus (1 Tim 2:5) – receives sacrifice together with the Father, with whom he is the one God. In the form a servant, however, he chose to be a sacrifice rather than to receive sacrifice, and he did so in order to keep anyone from thinking that this sacrifice should be offered, even in this case, to

[7] See further Klein 2018, esp. pp. 57–110.

> any creature (*creaturae*) at all. At the same time, he is also the priest, himself making the offering as well as himself being the offering.
>
> (*ciu. Dei* 10.20; Babcock, 1.328)

This may well be the central passage in the whole *ciu. Dei*: Jesus Christ, God the Word, is the sacrifice, since his humanity is as much himself as his divinity. He did not fear contamination in compassionately stretching out his own hand to us, who lay fallen (*ciu. Dei* 10.26). His transcendence did not preclude his acting. Augustine's exposition of the Incarnation is at the same time the deconstruction of the Platonist construal of mediation, invested as it is in a transcendence that limits God's freedom and so occludes his humility and his love:

> it obviously follows that the whole redeemed city (*ciuitas*), that is, the congregation and fellowship (*congregatio et societas*) of the saints, is offered to God as a universal sacrifice through the great priest who, in his passion, offered himself for us in the form of a servant, to the end that [*ut*] we might be the body of such a great head. For it was this servant form that he offered, and it was in this form that he was offered, because it is according to this form that he is the mediator, in this form that he is the priest, and in this form that he is the sacrifice.
>
> (*ciu. Dei* 10.6; Babcock, 1.311)

There is no "space" in this mediation. It is one magnificent act of self-gift, undertaken, in fact, so that there might be no longer be "space" between us humans. The great Priest, the divine Word made flesh, offered himself in his suffering as a man *in order that*, as man, he might be the "head" – the principle holding together a new way of saying and being "we," a new *societas* – of a new "body," the "body of such a great head." Augustine says *we* are offered by *his* sacrifice because the *intention* of this sacrifice was to unite us into a new "we" constituted by his mercy, perfectly and unsurpassably expressed in his sacrifice on the Cross. The visible communion, the *societas*, held together by no achievement, no "excellence" of its own, but by Christ's mercy, is thereby the objective, visible representation of his sacrifice, its presence in the world. In this way, it *is* his sacrifice. Its presence *in* the world is the locus of the apocalyptic perspective *on* the world, casting perspective on all other claims to communion, all other *societates*.

Thus the Eucharist is not a stage show or a spectacle, a representation of the myths that we watch; rather *we* become the representation;

we become a new "we," constituted as an objective representation of his sacrifice. Our very identity is a re-formation as we are made members of each other in his memory and love. The "sacrifice of Christians" is their identity as a body where the mutual relations are not configured to the lust of domination, to the "world," but to Christ's self-gift: "This is the sacrifice of Christians: although many, one body in Christ" (*"Hoc est sacrificium Christianorum: multi unum corpus in Christo"*; ciu. Dei 10.6; Babcock, 1.312; CCSL 47.279). Instead of the "space" which the lust for domination creates between each of us, we are "individually members of one other" (ciu. Dei 10.6; Babcock, 1.312; CCSL 47.279; see also *singuli autem alter alterius membra*; Rom 12:5). It is in this new unity with *each other*, this new *societas* in the shell of the old, that we have the participation in God that makes us happy. The true Mediator mediates us to each other. This is why Augustine associates the Eucharist so emphatically, here and elsewhere, with Rom 12:1–8 (and not, e.g. John 6). As his sacrifice, bound to each other in his love, the Eucharistic communion is a sacrifice of all other claims on the neighbor, claims based on the will to power. We are configured to his sacrifice as to a dynamic of reform, *"re-formed in the newness of [our] mind"* (Rom 12:2), de-conformed to the city of this world in soul and thus offering our bodies as living victims. As members of each other in his sacrificial love, *we* are *one whole sacrifice* (*totum sacrificium nos ipsi sumus; ciu. Dei* 10.6; CCSL 47.279). The good angels are all already bound together in a communion of self-giving, and they in their compassion do everything they can not to seek worship from us but to ensure that we are welcomed into this communion, "for they know that, together with us, they are themselves his sacrifice. For, along with them, we are the one City of God, tow which it is said in the Psalm, *Glorious things are spoken of you, O City of God* (*ciu. Dei* 10.7, quoting Ps 87:3; Babcock, 1.312).

This reprise of Ps 87:3, cited in the Prologue to Book 1 and not again until here, shows that we have reached a point of recapitulation. We begin to see the whole of God's economy of self-giving love laid out in its fulfillment. It is the angels who have mediated the economy of prophecy and miraculous works which themselves bear prophetic import (*ciu. Dei* 10.7). The mighty miracles recorded in Scripture were worked by God through the ministry of angels, the Lord appearing in visible and audible signs as someone's intention appears in speech. Miracle and prophecy aren't part of the "structure of mediation" as laid out by the Platonists, which used God's transcendence as a way of holding him distant, but they are acts of self-expression, stemming from

God's self-giving, true acts of the nevertheless unchanging God. The greatest miracle is Creation itself (*ciu. Dei* 10.12). Miracle and prophecy bear witness to an all-encompassing Providential plan (*ciu. Dei* 10.15), eternally intended by God, begun with Creation and culminating in the Incarnation in the last days of the fulfillment of the plan. Miracle and prophecy are persuasive not because they "prove" to "reason" the existence of God and the truth of revelation, but because they are consistent markers of a loving plan with its own consistency, not derivable from reason on it own. It is by seeing, in faith, this consistency, that the prophecies and miracles are persuasive. The difference between the prodigies and prophecies (oracles) given by demons is the intention behind the signs expressing the intention (*ciu. Dei* 10.16). The demonic prodigies, worked by demons because God is too transcendent to bend down, support the cults of civil theology and the imperial power they underwrite. The divine prodigies are signs of God's eternal intention to form a true and satisfying human communion in fellowship with angels. They render visible the lust for domination that clothes itself in simulacra of true human communion.

From this point of view, Augustine mounts his criticism of Porphyry, pointing him out as the supreme instance of the "bad faith" of the Platonists. He knows that the sacrificial rites intended to cultivate the gods' help purify us for a vision of the transcendent God, can't actually help us, but this doesn't stop him from endorsing them for the masses who cannot win their way to vision by their own strength. He endorses the oracles received in such rites as divine prodigies (*ciu. Dei* 10.26), the best the unphilosophical masses must settle for. Like the allegorists of the cults which create of human beings debris of the gods, reduced to ciphers of the myths no matter how much this reduction enables the cult to destroy them, Porphyry hands over the mass of humanity to the tender mercies of demons, thus making these people signifiers, by contrast, of the strength of philosophers who can purify themselves. That self-made purification is the ultimate myth.

These human beings are not the only casualties of philosophical pride. The Trinity is, too. Support for theurgical rites of purification reflect a commitment to the structure of mediation that we have seen Augustine critique throughout the first half of *ciu. Dei* where God's transcendence is so far "above" the depths of human flesh that God, and even the good gods, must avoid contaminating contact. This commitment so "clouds" (*ciu. Dei* 10.29) the vision of the Trinity that the Trinity, debased and disfigured into three *principia* in descending emanation (*ciu. Dei* 10.23–24), is forced to conform to the structure of mediation which holds God conveniently "distant." The Trinity, just like the human scrap left behind as the byproduct of scholarly allegory justifying the civil cult, is also trashed, turned into a signifier for the prestigious wisdom of the Platonists, imaging the distance they had to climb and their achievement in climbing it. So much for the hope that the philosophers could actually afford some true perspective on the imperial project, instead of acquiescing to the project of prestige and glory mongering that keeps it going.

True language about the Trinity does not speak of *principia* in the plural since there is only one "principle" of Creation and purgation alike (*ciu. Dei* 10.27). Porphyry despised Christ because of his body and the shame of the Cross (*ciu. Dei* 10.28), located in the contaminating depths of the structure of mediation, and therefore did not recognize Christ as the one and only *principium*, "the mind or intellect of the Father, which, with the Father, knows the Father's will," revealing it as wisdom in the folly of the Cross (*ciu. Dei* 10.28, citing 1 Cor 20:25; Babcock, 1.338). Because Porphyry was "so puffed up with pride in empty knowledge" (ciu. Dei 10.28; Babcock, 1.337), he failed to give thanks for the grace of the Incarnation, just as Rom 1:21 scripts it. In fact, Porphyry recognizes grace but only as that which enabled the philosophers to attain vision by the power of their intelligence (*ciu. Dei* 10.29), with no need for a mediator. In despising Christ's body, including his Eucharistic body, Porphyry despised not merely a sign of the *principium*, but the *principium* himself, and in despising Christ, he simultaneously despised the masses on whom Christ had compassion. He was too proud and thus "ashamed of the medicine by which [he] could be healed" by joining the masses in the Church (*ciu. Dei* 10.29; Babcock, 1.341; note here the allusion to Marius Victorinus as first recalled in *conf.* 8.2).

We end Book 10 with the grand vision of prophecy, tendered to Abraham and continuously forming the Jews as a *res publica* wholly consecrated in the prophetic vocation of prefiguring the one true sacrifice which fully revealed the divine compassion, "as it pleased God in his wisdom to ordain them" (*ciu. Dei* 10.32; Babcock, 1.346). This is the preparation we need to read the bible prophetically in the upcoming second "half." True love of wisdom, we can see now, is love of this divine compassion, attested by so many miracles and figures, "the tabernacle and the temple and the priesthood and the sacrifices." But "[f]inally, the mediator himself, present in the flesh, and his blessed apostles, now revealing the grace of the New Testament, disclosed more openly what had, in earlier times, been signified more obscurely" (*ciu. Dei* 10.32; Babcock, 1.346). True love of wisdom is therefore love of Christ, above whom there is no wisdom. It doesn't mean love of the eternal Word pre-Incarnation or cleansed of the Incarnation. The "pre-Incarnate Word" or better "dis-Incarnate Word" (since "pre-Incarnate" is a way of evoking the self-emptying of the Word-made-flesh) is a construct of the imperial imagination, no matter how scholarly, trying to imagine its way to a God who has not expressed himself and does not care to. Such a God leaves human beings without any basis for communion except their own attempts at mutual domination. There *is* true knowledge of God in some of the philosophers, but it can only be recognized as such in retrospect from the Incarnation, which reveals at the same time its disfigurements and its political investments.

Augustine comes to the end of Book 10 with a magnificent evocation of "daughter Zion" (*ciu. Dei* 10.18), the most glorious City of God. He thus comes to the end of Book 10 with, ironically, all of the major "constructive" work done, at least in principle – for the *principium* of it all has been disclosed and discussed, Jesus Christ the Word Incarnate. This is why the Incarnation is only barely discussed in its assigned chronological place in Books 11–22. It is because it is the formal structural *principium* from which it all unfolds, fully presented as such by the end of Book 10. Now the reference of the prophecies and figures in Scripture may be recognized. One thing is clear – they won't be obvious to "reason" alone. What has seemed obvious to "reason" as Augustine has presented the academic and philosophic establishment, is the support of the imperially backed cult, because "reason" is impressed by power and prestige and sees force, human *uirtus*, as the only true historical agency. If it were the rational force of the prophecy or miracle that leveraged a kind of respectable reasonableness for Christianity, it could easily be co-opted by an imperial narrative toward a triumphalist Christian empire. One doesn't have to *believe* in power. The oracles of the pagan gods, which also come true, and the prodigies arranged by demons, can be impressive in themselves. But Augustine says they all have explanations in the temporal sequence of observable physical and psychological causality, discovered by the demons, who can see historical actors better than we can, and so make predictions on a prudential basis better than we can. They also have aerial bodies whose powers seem wonderful to mortal flesh. These oracles and prodigies afford no perspective on power structure from which they emerge.

Prophecy and true miracle, by contrast, arise from the foolishness of God's loving gift of himself, to which the angels, who see in the Wisdom of God the plan of God's self-gift in Christ, cling. The demons can't see it, because it is not "reasonable." Prophecy and miracle invite one to a perspective that can't be reduced to what "reason," be it scholarly or philosophical, sees. Prophecy is not a proof that obviates faith, but one that invites faith in God's Wisdom as a plan for his self-expression in Creation and history. The consistency of prophecy and miracle is unsettling of established wisdom, which is a function of the logic of power and prestige. True prophecy and miracle signify instead the sacrificial self-gift of the Word made flesh and the final consummation it allows us to glimpse. It requires a sacrifice to see something with so little power and prestige as the center of history, instead of an empire. Christ's sacrifice remains present in history not as an empire or nation or any other human group constituted by human reason or virtue, but as the Church, the visible representation of Christ's sacrifice in the world.[8] It generates apocalyptic perspective by pointing always to the sacrifice of Christ as a revelation of what *truly* constitutes historical agency: not force, but God's love. Its eternal purposes will be fulfilled in the eschatological communion of angels and saints in the one City of God. In fact, that there *is* any history at all, properly speaking, and not just unending and directionless power struggle, is due to God's plan. Because the Church is the visible presence of that plan in history, the Church, it can be said, is the sacrament of history.

There is no need to consider in detail the material in the latter half more than we already have, to make our structural point. Books 1–10 of *ciu. Dei* function something like Book 1 of *doc. Chr.* providing an account, in this case for a specific audience of pagan critics and Christian waverers, of the "things" that are to be found in Scripture. Books 11–22 find them, always tailored for this same audience. Books 11–14 comment on Genesis 1–3. Having been introduced already to the Trinitarian Creator, we know the creation account is the first part of the triune God's economy of self-revelation. By contrast, we can see that cyclical views of the world (analyzed in Books 11–12) stem from a false sense of God's transcendence, preserving it at the expense of perpetual human misery.[9] Included is an account of the body as an integral part of the human, including gender, with its prophetic signification of God's self-emptying love as revealed in Christ and the Church. Against Manichean and Platonist alike, neither death (Book 13) nor lust (Book 14) warrant displacing the body from its status as integral to the human, since the very Word of God had a body. Book 22 (skipping to the third section of the last half) displays the consummation of God's plan as

[8] See further Lee 2017, pp. 95–107, "The Church as Sacrifice."
[9] See further Cavadini 2014.

embodied communion, the glorified City of God. It argues against scientific and philosophical foreclosure of the terms of final vision to exclude bodies. In fact, vision as a category is itself modified because communion, not vision, is the primary category. Vision is the vision, not in the first instance of an incorporeal substance as such, but of God's Sabbath rest, his purposes accomplished in our embodied communion in Christ's sacrifice. The city of this world, by contrast, the communion that is no communion, is handed over to the incoherence it was always seen to be in the prophetic perspective.

We find the most poignant section of *City of God* in the middle books of the last half, as we follow, through figure, the City of God on pilgrimage. Hannah's prophecy is representative: in this "devout mother," the Church herself speaks on behalf of the weak, the humiliated, and the barren. The work of God in history is through such as these, not in the works of power and strength (*quia non in uirtute potens est uir*; *ciu. Dei* 17.4; CCSL 47.559–60). Hannah, a mere woman, unseen and unrecognized by the learned historians looking for the stories of empires, prophesies. "God is, she says, *a God who makes his own plans* (1 Sam 2:3 LXX). What plans should we think these are, except that the proud should fall and the humble rise?" In a magnificent reprise of the scriptural motto *of ciu. Dei*, aptly found in the opening preface: "For in another passage we read, *God resists the proud but gives grace to the humble* (Jas 4:6), and this is the import of the whole declaration of this woman whose name means 'his grace'" (*ciu. Dei* 17.4; Babcock, 2.245).

Augustine expects his learned readers to scoff at his exegesis as unlearned. The words of this prophetic woman are wiser than the minds of the philosophers who are blind to the light of truth. "Blind to the truth" means blind to true prophecy, and that means blind to the Trinity whose "word is not bounded" (2 Tim 2:9; *ciu. Dei* 17.4) by any false transcendence. But the learned establishment was never really open, Augustine has shown, to the truth, for that requires a renunciation of status. "Blind to the truth" means able to see only power as an historical force and what it generates as historical reality. But the Church was not formed by an act of power. To "see" her in history means to be divested of the ideological commitments which direct "reason" only to status, even when it is disguised as "sparing the conquered and beating down the proud," a simulacrum of the work of God. It takes a sacrifice to see the meaning of the prophetic words.[10]

[10] See further Cavadini 2019, pp. 210–238, esp. at 228.

It takes eyes formed by the vision of the Word made flesh, Eucharistic vision, as of the Church coming down from Heaven from God.

FURTHER READING

Cavadini, J. C. (2012). Ideology and Solidarity in Augustine's *City of God*. In J. Wetzel, ed., Augustine's *City of God:* A Critical Guide. Cambridge: Cambridge University Press, pp. 93–110.

Fredriksen, P. (1992). Tyconius and Augustine on the Apocalypse. In R. K. Emmerson and B. McGinn, eds., *The Apocalypse in the Middle Ages*. Ithaca, NY: Cornell University Press, pp. 20–37.

Hughes, K. (2005). *Constructing Anti-Christ*. Washington, DC: Catholic University of America Press.

Lee, J. K. (2017). *Augustine and the Mystery of the Church*. Minneapolis, MN: Fortress Press.

O'Regan, C. (2009). *Theology and the Spaces of Apocalyptic*. Milwaukee, WI: Marquette University Press.

References

AUGUSTINE

- Babcock, W. (2012). *Augustine: The City of God. Introduction and translation (The Works of Saint Augustine Part I. Vol 6: Books I–X)*. New York: New City Press.
- *agon.*
- *b. conjug.*
- *c. Acad.*
- *c. Adim.*
- *c. adu. leg.*
- *c. Faust.*
- *c. Jul. imp.*
- *c. Prisc.*
- *cat. rud.*
- *conf.*
- *de patientia*
- *diu. Qu.*
- *doc. Chr.*
- *en. Ps.*; Boulding, III/15; CCSL 40
- *ench.*
- *epp.*
  - *ep.* 102
  - *ep.* 130
  - *ep.* 135–136
  - *ep.* 147
  - *ep.* 157
  - *ep.* 1A
  - *ep.* 1A*
  - *ep.* 2*.3; Teske, II/4; CSEL 88
  - *ep. Jo. tr.*
  - *epp.* 128, 129, 133, and 134
  - *epp.* 135–138
  - *epp.* 138 and 155
  - *epp.* 197–199
  - *epp.* 22, 29, and 36
- *eu. Jo. tr.*

- *Gn. adu. Man.*
- *Gn. litt.*
- *gr. et pecc. or.*
- *haer.*
- *lib. Arb.*
- *loc. in Hept. (Locutiones in Heptateuchum)*
- *mor.*
- *mus.*
- *nat. et gr.*
- *nupt. et conc.*
- *pecc. mer.*
- *qu.*
- *retr.*, Hill, I/2
- *retr.*; Ramsey, I/2; CCSL 57.
- *s. Dom. mon.*
- *sermones*
  - *s.* 17.2
  - *s.* 25A.1; CCSL 41
  - *s.* 296.9
  - *s.* 299a
  - *s.* 34.6; PL 38
  - *s.* 81.9; Hill (III/3) 365.
  - *s. 83*
- *sol.*
- *spir et let.*
- *Trin.*; CCSL 50A
- *uera rel.* 27.50; Hill, I/8
- *util. cred.*

SECONDARY LITERATURE

Agaësse, P. and Solignac, A. (2001). Note complémentaire 46, La chute du diable. In *La Genèse au sens littéral.* BA 49, Paris: Institut d'Études Augustiniennes, pp. 545–553.

Al-Farabi, A. N. (1961). *Fuṣūl al-Madanī: Aphorisms of the Statesman.* Translated by D. Dunlop. Cambridge: Cambridge University Press.

Al-Farabi, A. N. (1962). Attainment of Happiness. In *Al-Farabi's Philosophy of Plato and Aristotle.* Translated by Muhsin Mahdi. Ithaca, NY: Cornell University Press, pp. 13–50.

Al-Farabi, A. N. (1985). *Al-Farabi on the Perfect State.* Translated by Richard Walzer. Oxford: Oxford University Press.

Al-Farabi, A. N. (1993). The Political Regime. In *Medieval Political Philosophy.* Translated by Charles Butterworth. Ithaca, NY: Cornell University Press, pp. 36–55.

Al-Farabi, A. N. (2001). Selected Aphorisms. In *Al-Farabi: The Political Writings.* Translated by Charles Butterworth. Ithaca, NY: Cornell University Press, pp. 1–67.

Al-Farabi, A. N. (2002). *Al-Farabi's Philosophy of Plato and Aristotle*. Translated by Muhsin Mahdi. Ithaca, NY: Cornell University Press.
Alfeche, M. (1995). Augustine's Discussions with Philosophers on the Resurrection of the Body. *Augustiniana*, 45, pp. 95–140.
Ando, C. (2010). The Ontology of Religious Institutions. *History of Religions*, 50(1), 54–79.
Angus, S. (1906). The Sources of the First Ten Books of Augustine's De civitate Dei. Unpublished Ph.D. thesis, Princeton University.
Arendt, H. (1996). *Love and Saint Augustine*. J. V. Scott and J. C. Stark, eds. Chicago: University of Chicago Press.
Aristotle. (1999). *Nicomachean Ethics*. Translated by Martin Ostwald. Upper Saddle River, NJ: Prentice Hall.
Aristotle. (2002). *Nicomachean Ethics: Translation, Introduction and Commentary*. S. Broadie, ed. Translated by Christopher Rowe. New York: Oxford University Press.
Arnold, B. T. (2009). *Genesis: New Cambridge Bible Commentary*. Cambridge: Cambridge University Press.
Atwell, R. R. (1987). From Augustine to Gregory the Great: An Evaluation of the Emergence of the Doctrine of Purgatory. *The Journal of Ecclesiastical History*, 38(2), 173–186.
Audano, S. (2009). Agostino tra Bruto, Livio e Virgilio (civ. 3.16; 5,18): Un Possibile Tirannicidio Cristiano? In F. Gasti and M. Neri, eds., *Agostino a scuola: letteratura e didattica. Atti della Giornata di studio di Pavia (13 Nobembre 2008)*. Pisa: ETS, pp. 103–153.
Babcock, W. (1988). Augustine on Sin and Moral Agency. *Journal of Religious Ethics*, 16, 28–55.
Bardy, G. (1959). Notes complémentaires 32: Saint Augustin et le grammaire. In *La Cité de Dieu: Livres XI–XIV*. BA 35. Paris: Desclée de Brouwer.
Barnes, T. D. (1995). Statistics and the Conversion of the Roman Aristocracy. *The Journal of Roman Studies*, 85, 135–147.
Barr, R. (1962). The Two Cities in Saint Augustine. *Laval Théologique et Philosophique*, 182, 211–229.
Baun, J. (2007). *Tales from another Byzantium: Celestial Journey and Local Community in the Medieval Greek Apocrypha*. Cambridge: Cambridge University Press.
Beard, M., North, J. and Price, S. (1998). *Religions of Rome*, 2 vols. Cambridge: Cambridge University Press.
Beatrice, P. F. (1989). Quosdam libros Platonicos. *Vigiliae Christianae*, 43, 248–281.
Becker, M. (2015). *Porphyrios: Gegen die Christen*. New York: De Gruyter.
Bede (2013). *Commentary on Revelation. Translated Texts for Historians*, vol. 58. Translated by Faith Wallis. Liverpool: Liverpool University Press.
Bettenson, H. (1984). *St. Augustine Concerning the City of God Against the Pagans*. Translated by H. Bettenson. London: Penguin Classics.
Bidez, J. (1913). *Vie de Porphyre*. Ghent: E. Van Goethem.
Billy, D. (1994). The Analogy of "Peace" in Augustine's City of God. *Studia Moralia*, 32, 317–339.
Bittner, R. (1999). Augustine's Philosophy of History. In G. B. Matthews, ed., *The Augustinian Tradition*. Berkeley: University of California Press, pp. 345–360.

Bloch, H. (1945). A New Document of the Last Pagan Revival in the West, 393–394 AD. *The Harvard Theological Review*, 38(4), 199–244.
Bobb, D. J. (2010). The Humility of True Religion: Augustine's Critique of Civil Religion. In R. Weed and J. von Heyking, eds., *Civil Religion in Political Thought: Its Perennial and Enduring Relevance in North America*. Washington, DC: Catholic University of America Press, pp. 66–92.
Bochet, I. (2004). *"Le Firmament de l'Écriture": L'Herméneutique Augustinienne*. Paris: Institut d'Études Augustiniennes.
Bochet, I. (2009). Résurrection et réincarnation. La plémique d'Augustin contre les platoniciens et contre Porphyre dans les Sermons 240–242. In G. Partoens, A. Dupont, and M. Lamberigts, eds., *Ministerium sermonis. Philological, Historical and Theological Studies on Augustine's Sermones ad populum*. Turnhout: Brepols, pp. 267–298.
Bochet, I. (2010). The Role of Scripture in Augustine's Controversy with Porphyry. *Augustinian Studies*, 41, 7–52.
Bochet, I. (2016). Le corps: un poids pour l'âme. *Revues des Sciences Philosophiques et Théologiques*, 100, 27–43.
Boersma, H. (2018). *Seeing God: The Beatific Vision in Christian Tradition*. Grand Rapids, MI: Eerdmans.
Bonner, S. F. (1949). *Roman Declamation in the Late Republic and Early Empire*. Liverpool: University Press of Liverpool.
Bouton-Touboulic, A.-I. (2013). Virgile au prisme d'Augustin (*Cité de Dieu*, livre 3). In O. Devillers and G. Flamerie de Lachapelle, eds., *Poésie augustéenne et mémoires du passé de Rome: En hommage au Professeur Lucienne Deschamps*. Bordeaux: Ausonius éditions, pp. 163–175.
Bowlin, J. (2012). Hell and the Dilemmas of Intactable Alienation. In J. Wetzel, ed., *Augustine's City of God: A Critical Guide*. Cambridge: Cambridge University Press, pp. 186–204.
Boxall, I. and Tresley, R. M., eds. (2016). *The Book of Revelation and Its Interpreters: Short Studies and an Annotated Bibliography*. London: Rowman and Littlefield.
Brittain, C. (2001). *Philo of Larissa*. New York: Oxford University Press.
Brocca, N. (2011). *Lattanzio, Agostino e la Sibylla Maga: Ricerche sulla fortuna degli "Oracula Sibyllina" nell' Occidente latino*. Rome: Herder.
Brown, P. (2000). *Augustine of Hippo: A Biography*, Rev. ed. Berkeley: University of California Press.
Brown, P. (2012). *Through the Eye of a Needle: Wealth, the Fall of Rome, and the Making of Christianity in the West, 350–550 AD*. Princeton: Princeton University Press.
Bruggisser, P. (2009). Numa Pompilius et la Rome sacrée. Regards croisés d'Augustin et de Thémistios. *Revue d'études augustiniennes et patristiques*, 55, 3–21.
Burleigh, J. H. S. (1949). *The City of God: A Study of St. Augustine's Philosophy*, Croall Lectures, 1944. London: Nisbett & Co.
Burnell, P. (2010). Justice in War in and before Augustine. In J. Baun, A. Cameron, M. Edwards, and M. Vinzent, eds., *Studia Patristica* 49. Leuven: Peeters, pp. 107–110.

Burns, P. C. (2001). Augustine's Use of Varro's *Antiquitates Rerum Divinarum* in his *De Civitate Dei. Augustinian Studies*, 32(1), 37–64.

Burrus, V. (2009). Carnal Excess: Flesh at the Limits of Imagination. *Journal of Early Christian Studies*, 17, 247–265.

Burrus, V. and MacKendrick, K. (2010). Bodies without Wholes: Apophatic Excess and Fragmentation in Augustine's *City of God*. In C. Boesel and C. Keller, eds., *Apophatic Bodies: Negative Theology, Incarnation, and Relationality*. New York: Fordham University Press, pp. 79–93.

Burt, D. (1999). *Friendship and Society: An Introduction to Augustine's Practical Philosophy*. Grand Rapids, MI: Eerdmans.

Butler, A. J. (1902). *The Arab Conquest of Egypt and the Last Thirty Years of Roman Dominion*. Oxford: Clarendon Press.

Byers, S. (2012). The Psychology of Compassion: Stoicism in City of God 9.5. In J. Wetzel, ed., *Augustine's City of God. A Critical Guide*. Cambridge: Cambridge University Press, pp. 130–148.

Bynum, C. W. and Freedman, P., eds. (2000). *Last Things: Death and the Apocalypse in the Middle Ages*. Philadelphia: University of Pennsylvania Press.

Cameron, A. (2011). *The Last Pagans of Rome*. New York: Oxford University Press.

Cardauns, B. (1978). Varro und die Religion: Zur Theologie, Wirkungsgeschichte und Leistung der "Antiquitates Rerum Divinatum." *ANRW* II, 16(1), 80–103.

Carozzi, C. (1994). *Eschatologie et l'au-delà: Recherches sur l'Apocalypse de Paul*. Aix-en-Provence: Publications de l'Université de Provence.

Carruthers, M. (2013). *The Experience of Beauty in the Middle Ages*. Oxford: Oxford University Press.

Cavadini, J. C. (1999). Ambrose and Augustine *De Bono Mortis*. In W. E. Klinshirn and M. Vessey, eds., *The Limits of Ancient Christianity: Essays on Late Antique Thought and Culture in Honor of R. A. Markus*. Ann Arbor: University of Michigan Press, pp. 232–249.

Cavadini, J. C. (2012). Ideology and Solidarity in Augustine's *City of God*. In J. Wetzel, ed., *Augustine's* City of God: *A Critical Guide*. Cambridge: Cambridge University Press, pp. 93–110.

Cavadini, J. C. (2014). God's Eternal Knowledge According to Augustine. In D. Meconi, S.J. and E. Stump, eds., *The Cambridge Companion to Augustine*, 2nd ed. Cambridge: Cambridge University Press, pp. 37–59.

Cavadini, J. C. (2019). Spousal Vision: A Study of Text and History in the Theology of Saint Augustine. In *Visioning Augustine*. Hoboken, NJ and West Sussex, UK: Wiley-Blackwell, pp. 210–238.

Chan, J. and Dupont, A. (2016). *Restauratio* in *De ciuitate Dei*: The Role of the Restoration Motif in Understanding Augustine's Theology of History. *La Ciudad de Dios*, 229(1), 55–78.

Chazelle, C. (2015). Debating the End Times with Bede. *Irish Theological Quarterly*, 80(3), 212–232.

Chesterton, G. K. (1908). *Orthodoxy*. New York: Greenwood Press, Inc.

Clark, G. (2010). Augustine's Varro and Pagan Monotheism. In S. Mitchell and P. van Nuffelen, eds., *Monotheism between Pagans and Christians in Late Antiquity*. Leuven: Peeters, pp. 181–201.

Clark, G. (2016). Caritas: Augustine on Love and Fellow Feeling. In R. R. Caston and R. A. Kaster, eds., *Hope, Joy, and Affection in the Classical World*. New York: Oxford University Press, pp. 209–225.

Clarke, E. C., Dillon, J. M., and Hershbell J., eds. (2003). *Iamblichus, On the Mysteries*. Atlanta: SBL.

Classen, C. J. (1991). The Speeches in the Courts of Law: A Three-cornered Dialogue. *Rhetorica*, 3, 195–207.

Collins, J. J. (1974). Apocalyptic Eschatology as the Transcendence of Death. *The Catholic Biblical Quarterly*, 36(1), 21–43.

Copenhaver, B. (1992). *Hermetica*. Cambridge: Cambridge University Press.

Counet, J. M. (2013). Speech Act in the Demiurge's Address to the Young Gods in Timaeus 41 A–B: Interpretations of Greek Philosophers and Patristic Receptions. In M. Vinzent, ed., *Studia Patristica 58.6: Neoplatonism and Patristics*. Leuven-Paris-Walpole, MA: Peeters, pp. 73–82.

Courcelle, P. (1953). Les sages de Porphyre et les viri novi d'Arnobe. *Revue des Etude Latines*, 31, 157–171.

Courcelle, P. (1964). *Histoire littéraire des grandes invasions germaniques*, 3rd ed, augmentée et illustrée. Paris: Éd. Augustiniennes.

Crosson, F. J. (2005). Esoteric versus Latent Teaching. *Review of Metaphysics*, 59 (1), 73–93.

Deane, H. A. (1963). *The Political and Social Ideas of St. Augustine*. New York: Columbia University Press.

Denecker, T. (2017). *Ideas on Language in Early Latin Christianity From Tertullian to Isidore of Seville*. Leiden: Brill.

Dihle, A. (1982). *The Theory of Will in Classical Antiquity*. Berkeley: University of California Press.

Dillon, J. M. (1983). "Metriopatheia and Apatheia": Some Reflections on a Controversy in Later Greek Ethics. In J. Anton and A. Preus, eds., *Essays in Ancient Greek Philosophy*, vol. 2. New York: State University of New York Press, pp. 508–517.

Dillon, J. M. (1989). Tampering with the Timaeus: Ideological Emendations in Plato. *American Journal of Philology*, 110, 50–72.

Dillon, J. M. (2007). What Price the Father of the Noetic Triad? Some Reflections on Porphyry's Doctrine of the First Principle. In G. Karamanolis and A. Sheppard, eds., *Studies on Porphyry*. London: British Institute of Classical Studies, pp. 51–59.

Dodaro, R. (2004). *Christ and the Just Society in the Thought of Augustine*. Cambridge: Cambridge University Press.

Dodaro, R. (2012). Augustine on the Statesman and the Two Cities. In M. Vessey and S. Reid, eds., *A Companion to Augustine*. Chichester: Wiley, pp. 386–397.

Dombart, B. and Kalb, A., eds. (1954). *Augustine: De civitate Dei*. Turnhout: Brepols.

Dougherty, J. (1979). The Sacred City and *The City of God*. *Augustinian Studies*, 10(1), 81–90.

Drecoll, V. H. (2010). Is Porphyry the Source Used by Victorinus? In J. Turner and K. Corrigan, eds., *Plato's Parmenides and Its Heritage*, vol. 1. Atlanta: Society of Biblical Literature, pp. 65–81.

Drecoll, V. H. (2015). Augustin und Pelagius. Vergleich zweier Mentalitäten. Ciu. 11–14 auf dem Hintergrund des Pelagianischen Streits. In C. Müller, R. Dodaro, and A. Fitzgerald, eds., *Kampf oder Dialog? Begegnung von Kulturen im Horizont von Augustins* De ciuitate dei. Würzburg: Augustinus bei Echter, pp. 367–386.

Dupont, A. (2010). John 3,5 and the Topic of Infant Baptism in Augustine. A Case Study to Evaluate the Continuity of His Thinking on Grace. *Vetera Christianorum*, 47, 41–62.

Dupont, A. et al., eds. (2018). *Preaching in the Patristic Era: Sermons, Preachers, and Audiences in the Latin West*. Vol. 6 of *A New History of the Sermon Series*. Leiden: Brill.

Edwards, M. J. (1990). Porphyry and the Intelligibile Triad. *Journal of Hellenic Studies*, 110, 14–25.

Emmerson, R. K. and McGinn, B., eds. (1992). *The Apocalypse in the Middle Ages*. Ithaca: Cornell University Press.

Erler, M. (1996–2002). Epicurei, Epicurus. In *Augustinus-Lexikon* 2. Basel/Berlin: Schwabe Verlag, pp. 858–861.

Fakhry, M. (2002). *Al-Farabi: Founder of Islamic Neo-Platonism: His Life, Works and Influence*. Oxford: Oxford University Press.

Fazlur, R. (2011). *Prophecy in Islam: Philosophy and Orthodoxy*. Chicago: University of Chicago Press.

Folliet, G. (1992). "Massa damnata" – "massa sanctorum" chez saint Augustin. *Revista Agustiniana*, 33, 95–109.

Fortin, E. L. (1996a). Augustine and Roman Civil Religion: Some Critical Reflections. In J. B. Benestad, ed., *Classical Christianity and the Political Order: Reflections on the Theologico-Political Problem*. Lanham, MD: Rowman & Littlefield, pp. 85–106.

Fortin, E. L. (1996b). The Political Thought of St. Augustine. In J. B. Benestad, ed., *Classical Christianity and the Political Order: Reflections on the Theologico-Political Problem*. Lanham, MD: Rowman & Littlefield, pp. 1–30.

Fowden, G. (1993). *The Egyptian Hermes*. Princeton: Princeton University Press.

Franchi, R. (2012). Lucrezia, Agostino e i retori. *Latomus*, 71, 1088–1101.

Fredriksen, P. (1991). Apocalypse and Redemption in Early Christianity from John of Patmos to Augustine of Hippo. *Vigiliae Christianae*, 45, 151–183.

Fredriksen, P. (1992). Tyconius and Augustine on the Apocalypse. In R. K. Emmerson and B. McGinn, eds., *The Apocalypse in the Middle Ages*. Ithaca, NY: Cornell University Press, pp. 20–37.

Freeman, C. (2009). *A New History of Early Christianity*. New Haven, CT: Yale University Press.

Fuchs, H. (1926 [reprint 1965]). *Augustin und der antike Friedensgedanke: Untersuchungen zum neunzehnten Buch der Civitas Dei*. Berlin: Weidmann.

Fuhrer, T. (2011). Krieg und (Un-)Gerechtigkeit. Augustin zu Ursache und Sinn von Kriegen. In M. Formisano and H. Böhme, eds., *War in Words: Transformations of War from Antiquity to Clausewitz*. Berlin: de Gruyter, pp. 23–36.

Fürst, A. (2008). Paganer und christlicher "Monotheismus": Zur Hermeneutik eines antiken Diskurses. *Jahrbuch für Antike und Christentum*, 51, 5–24.

Garnsey, P. (1996 [reprint 1999]). *Ideas of slavery from Aristotle to Augustine.* Cambridge: Cambridge University Press.

Geerlings, W. (1997). De civitate dei XIX als Buch der Augustinischen Friedenslehre. In C. Horn, ed., *Augustinus, De civitate Dei.* Berlin: Akademie Verlag.

Gerchow, J. (1988). Die Gedenkuberlieferung der Angelsachsen: Mit einem Katalog der libri vitae und Necrologien. In *Arbeiten zur Frühmittelalterforschung der Universität Münster*, vol. 20. Berlin: de Gruyter.

Green, W. W. (1949). Initium omnis peccati superbia: Augustine on Pride as the First Sin. *University of California Publications in Classical Philology*, 13, 407–432.

Gregory, E. (2008). *Politics and the Order of Love: An Augustinian Ethic of Democratic Citizenship.* Chicago: University of Chicago Press.

Griffin, C. W. and Paulsen, D. L. (2000). Augustine and the Corporeality of God. *The Harvard Theological Review*, 95(1), 97–118.

Griffiths, P. J. (2012). Secularity and the saeculum. In J. Wetzel, ed., *Augustine's City of God: A Critical Guide.* Cambridge: Cambridge University Press, pp. 33–54.

Griffiths, P. J. (2014). *Decreation: The Last Things of All Creatures.* Waco, TX: Baylor University Press.

Grisez, G. (2008). The True Ultimate End of Human Beings: The Kingdom, Not God Alone. *Theological Studies*, 69, 38–61.

Grossi, V. (2009). Il libro XIV del *De civitate Dei.* In *Lettura del De civitate Dei. Libri XI–XVI: Studia Ephemeridis Augustinianum 115.* Rome: Institutum Patristicum Augustinianum, pp. 105–126.

Grossi, V. (2015). L'antropologia delle 'passiones' nella costruzione delle 'civitates' (ciu.14). Per nuovi rapporti tra cristiani, romani e barbari. In C. Müller, R. Dodaro, and A. Fitzgerald, eds., *Kampf oder Dialog? Begegnung von Kulturen im Horizont von Augustins* De ciuitate dei. Würzburg: Augustinus bei Echter, pp. 333–366.

Hadot, P. (1968). *Porphyre et Victorinus*, vol. 2. Paris: Études Augustiniennes, pp. 213–344.

Haehling, R. (1978). *Die Religionszugehörigkeit der hohen Amtsträger des Römischen Reiches seit Constantins I. Alleinherrschaft bis zum Ende der Theodosianischen Dynastie: (324–450 bzw. 455 n. Chr.).* Bonn: Habelt.

Hagendahl, H. (1967). *Augustine and the Latin Classics*, 2 vols. Göteborg: Elander.

Hammer, D. (2014). *Roman Political Thought: From Cicero to Augustine.* Cambridge: Cambridge University Press.

Hanson, R. P. (1985). *Studies in Christian Antiquity.* London: T. and T. Clark.

Harding, B. (2008). *Augustine and Roman Virtue: Continuum Studies in Philosophy.* London: Continuum.

Harrison, C. (1992). *Beauty and Revelation in the Thought of Saint Augustine.* Oxford: Clarendon Press.

Harrison, S. (2000). *Apuleius. A Latin Sophist.* Oxford: Oxford University Press.

Harrison, S. (2006). *Augustine's Way into the Will: The Theological and Philosophical Significance of De libero arbitrio.* Oxford: Oxford University Press.

Helleman, W. (2013). Augustine and Philo of Alexandria's "Sarah" as a Wisdom Figure (*De Civitate Dei* XV 2F.; XVI 25–32). In M. Vinzent, ed., *Studia Patristica* LXX. Leuven: Peeters, pp. 105–116.

Herdt, J. A. (2008). *Putting on Virtue: The Legacy of the Splendid Vices*. Chicago: University of Chicago Press.

Herdt, J. A. (2012). The Theater of the Virtues: Augustine's Critique of Pagan Mimesis. In J. Wetzel, ed., *Augustine's* City of God: *A Critical Guide*. Cambridge: Cambridge University Press, pp. 111–129.

Silverstein, T. and Hilhorst, A., eds. (1997). *Apocalypse of Paul: A New Critical Edition of the Three Long Latin Versions*. Geneva: Patrick Cramer.

Hill, C. E. (2001). *Regnum Caelorum. Patterns of Millennial Thought in Early Christianity*. Grand Rapids, MI: Eerdmans.

Hollerich, M. J. (1993). Augustine as a Civil Theologian? In J. T. Lienhard, E. C. Muller, and R. J. Teske, eds., *Augustine-Presbyter Factus Sum*. New York: Peter Lang, pp. 57–69.

Holmes, R. L. (1999). St. Augustine and the Just War Theory. In G. B. Matthews, ed., *The Augustinian Tradition*. Berkeley: University of California Press, pp. 323–344.

Holt, L. (2009). De Divinatione Daemonum. In A. Fitzgerald, ed., *Augustine through the Ages*. Grand Rapids, MI: Eerdmans, pp. 277–278.

Hooker, M. (2008). The Use of Sibyls and Sibylline Oracles in Early Christian Writers. Unpublished Ph.D. diss. University of Cincinnati. OhioLINK (ucin1210693456).

Horsfall, N. (2008). *Virgil,* Aeneid 2: *A Commentary*. Leiden: Brill.

Hose, M. (1994). Erneuerung der Vergangenheit. Die Historiker im Imperium Romanum von Florus bis Cassius Dio. In *Beiträge zur Altertumskunde*, vol. 45. Stuttgart-Leipzig: de Gruyter.

Hose, M. (2015). Intertextualität als hermeneutisches Instrument in spätantiker Literatur. Das Beispiel Ammianus Marcellinus. In J. Stenger, ed., *Spätantike Konzeptionen von Literatur*. Heidelberg: Universitätsverlag Winter, pp. 81–96.

Hughes, K. (2005). *Constructing Anti-Christ*. Washington, DC: Catholic University of America Press.

Hunter, D. G. (2002a). Augustine, Sermon 354A: Its Place in His Thought on Marriage and Sexuality. *Augustinian Studies*, 33(1), 39–60.

Hunter, D. G. (2002b). Reclaiming Biblical Morality: Sex and Salvation History in Augustine's Treatment of the Hebrew Saints. In P. Blowers et al., eds., *In Dominico Eloquio/In Lordly Eloquence. Studies in Patristic Biblical Interpretation in Honor of Robert L. Wilken*. Grand Rapids, MI: Eerdmans, pp. 317–335.

Hunter, D. G. (2012). Augustine on the Body. In M. Vessey, ed., *The Blackwell Companion to Augustine*. Oxford: Blackwell, pp. 353–364.

Inglebert, H. (1996). *Les Romains chrétiens face à l'histoire de Rome. Histoire, christianisme et romanités en Occident dans l'Antiquité tardive (3e-Ve siècles)*. Paris.

Inglebert, H. (2014). Orosius. In *Augustinus-Lexikon 4* (fasc. 3/4). Basel/Berlin: Schwabe Verlag, pp. 398–403.

Ingremeau, C., ed. (1982). *Lactance: La Colère de Dieu*. Paris: Cerf.

Inwood, B. (1985). *Ethics and Human Action in Early Stoicism*. Oxford: Oxford University Press, pp. 173–175.
Kahlos, M. (2007). *Debate and Dialogue: Christian and Pagan Cultures c. 360–430*. Aldershot: Ashgate.
Kaster, R. A. (2001). Controlling Reason: Declamation in Rhetorical Education at Rome. In Y. L. Too, ed., *Education in Greek and Roman Antiquity*. Leiden: Brill, pp. 317–337.
Kaufman, P. I. (2010). Christian Realism and Augustinian (?) Liberalism. *Journal of Religious Ethics*, 38(4), 699–724.
Kennedy, G. A. (2003). *Progymnasmata: Greek Textbooks of Prose Composition and Rhetoric. Writings from the Greco-Roman World*. Atlanta, GA: Society of Biblical Literature.
Kent, B. (2012). Reinventing Augustine's Ethics: The Afterlife of City of God. In J. Wetzel, ed., *Augustine's City of God: A Critical Guide*. Cambridge: Cambridge University Press, pp. 225–244.
Keys, M. M. (2013). Augustinian Humility as Natural Right. In A. Ward and L. Ward, eds., *Natural Right and Political Philosophy: Essays in Honor of Catherine Zuckert and Michael Zuckert*. Notre Dame: University of Notre Dame Press, pp. 97–113.
Klauck, H. (2007). Nature, Art, and Thought: Dio Chrysostom and the *Theologia Tripertita*. *The Journal of Religion*, 87(3), 333–354.
Klein, E. (2018). *Augustine's Theology of Angels*. Cambridge: Cambridge University Press.
Kohl, R. (1915). *De scholasticorum declamationum argumentis ex historia petitis*. Paderborn.
Kries, D. (2010). Reason in Context: Augustine as Defender and Critic of Leo Strauss's Esotericism Thesis. American Catholic Philosophical Society, *Proceedings of the ACPA*, 83, 241–252.
Labhardt, A. (1996–2002). Curiositas. In *Augustinus-Lexikon* 2. Basel/Berlin: Schwabe Verlag, pp. 188–196.
Lamberigts, M. (1988). De polemiek tussen Julianus van Aeclanum en Augustinus van Hippo. Een bijdrage tot de theologiegeschiedenis van de tweede pelagiaanse controverse. Unpublished Doctoral Disseration, Katholieke Universiteit Leuven.
Lamberigts, M. (1990). Julien d'Éclane et Augustin d'Hippone: deux conceptions d'Adam. In B. Bruning, M. Lamberigts, and J. Van Houtem, eds., *Collectanea Augustiniana. Mélanges T.J. van Bavel* (BETL, 92). Leuven: Peeters, pp. 373–410.
Lamberigts, M. (2000). *A Critical Evaluation of Critiques of Augustine's View of Sexuality*. In R. Dodaro and G. Lawless, eds., *Augustine and his Critics: Essays in Honour of Gerald Bonner*. London/New York: Routledge, pp. 176–197.
Landes, R. (1988). Lest the Millennium be Fulfilled: Apocalyptic Expectations and the Pattern of Western Chronography 100–800 CE. In W. Verbeke, D. Verhelst, and A. Welkenhuysen, eds., *The Use and Abuse of Eschatology in the Middle Ages*. Leuven: Leuven University Press, pp. 137–211.

Lee, J. K. (2016). Babylon becomes Jerusalem: The Transformation of the Two Cities in Augustine's Enarrationes in Psalmos. *Augustinian Studies*, 47(2), 157–180.

Lee, J. K. (2017). *Augustine and the Mystery of the Church*. Minneapolis, MN: Fortress Press.

Lefèvre, E. (1992). Die Bedeutung des Paradoxen in der römischen Literatur. In P. Geyer and R. Hagenbüchle, eds., *Das Paradox. Eine Herausforderung des abendländischen Denkens*. Tübingen: Stauffenburg Verlag, pp. 209–246.

Lenski, N. E. (2016). *Constantine and the Cities: Imperial Authority and Civic Politics*. Philadelphia: University of Pennsylvania Press.

Leyser, C. (2000). *Authority and Asceticism from Augustine to Gregory the Great*. Oxford: Clarendon Press.

Lieberg, G. (1984). The Theologia Tripertita as an Intellectual Model in Antiquity. Translated by E. C. Polomé. In E. C. Polomé, ed., *Essays in Memory of Karl Kerényi*. Washington, DC: Institute for the Study of Man, pp. 91–115.

Liebeschuetz, W. (1999). The Significance of the Speech of Praetextatus. In P. Athanassiadi and M. Frede, eds., *Pagan Monotheism in Late Antiquity*. Oxford: Oxford University Press, pp. 185–205.

Lienhard, J. (1999). Paulinus of Nola. In A. Fitzgerald, ed., *Augustine Through the Ages*. Grand Rapids, MI: Eerdmans, pp. 628–629.

Long, A. A. (1996). *Stoic Studies*. Berkeley: University of California Press, pp. 227–230.

Longman III, T. and Walton, J. (2019). *The Lost World of the Flood: Mythology, Theology, and the Deluge Debate*. Downers Grove, IL: IVP Academic.

MacCormack, S. (1998). *The Shadows of Poetry: Vergil in the Mind of Augustine*. Berkeley: University of California Press.

MacDonald, S. (1999). Primal Sin. In G. B. Matthews, ed., *The Augustinian Tradition*. Berkeley: University of California Press, pp. 110–139.

Madec, G. (1996). *Introduction aux "Revisions" et à lecture des Oeuvres de Saint Augustin*. Paris: Institut d'Études Augustiniennes.

Magny, A. (2014). *Porphyry in Fragments*. Fanham: Ashgate, pp. 99–147.

Maier, F. G. (1955). *Augustin und das antike Rom*. Stuttgart: Kohlhammer.

Majercik, R., ed. (1989). *The Chaldaean Oracles: Text, Translation and Commentary*. Leiden: Brill.

Malamud, M., ed. (2018). *Rutilius Namatianus' Going Home*. London: Routledge Later Latin Poetry.

Manchester, P. (1992). The Noetic Triad in Plotinus, Marius Victorinus and Augustine. In R. T. Wallis and J. Bregman, eds., *Neoplatonism and Gnosticism*. New York: State University of New York Press, pp. 207–222.

Mankin, D., ed. (1995). *Horace: Epodes*. Cambridge: Cambridge University Press.

Mann, W. E. (1999). Inner-Life Ethics. In G. B. Matthews, ed., *The Augustinian Tradition*. Berkeley: University of California Press, pp. 140–165.

Marincola, J. (2009). Ancient Audiences and Expectations. In A. Feldherr, ed., *The Cambridge Companion to the Roman Historians*. Cambridge: Cambridge University Press, pp. 11–23.

Markus, R. A. (1988). *Saeculum: History and Society in the Theology of St. Augustine*. Rev. ed. Cambridge: Cambridge University Press.

Markus, R. A. (1990). De civitate Dei: Pride and the Common Good. In J. C. Schnaubelt and E. Van Fleteren, eds., *Collectanea Augustiniana: Augustine, Second Founder of the Faith*. New York: Peter Lang, pp. 245–259.

Markus, R. A. (1994). Response. In A. H. Sommerstein, ed., *Religion and Superstition in Latin Literature*. Bari: Levante Editori, pp. 77–80.

Marrou, H.-I. (1958). *Saint Augustin et la fin de la culture antique*. Paris.

Martin, J. P. (1991). Philo and Augustine, De civitate Dei XIV,28 and XV. *Studia Philonica Annual*, 3, 283–294.

Mastandrea, P. (1979). *Cornelio Labeone: Un Neoplatonico Latino*. Leiden: Brill.

Matthews, G. B., ed. (1999). *The Augustinian Tradition*. Berkeley: University of California Press.

Matthews, J. (1970). Olympiodorus of Thebes and the History of the West (AD 407–425). *The Journal of Roman Studies*, 60, 79–97.

Matthews, J. (1975). *Western Aristocracies and Imperial Court, AD 364–425*. Oxford: Clarendon Press.

Mayer, C. et al., eds., (1986). Aaron–Conuersio. In *Augustinus-Lexikon 1*. Basel/ Berlin: Schwabe Verlag.

McCarthy, M. C. (2007). "We Are Your Books": Augustine, the Bible, and the Practice of Authority. *Journal of the American Academy of Religion*, 75(2), 324–352.

Meconi, D. V. (2013). *The One Christ: St. Augustine's Theology of Deification*. Washington, DC: Catholic University of America Press.

Meeks, W. (1974). The Image of the Androgyne: Some Uses of a Symbol in Earliest Christianity. *History of Religions*, 13, 165–208.

Menchaca-Bagnulo, A. (2019). Deeds and Words: *Latreia*, Justice and Mercy in Augustine's Political Thought. In R. Dougherty, ed., *Augustine's Political Thought*. Rochester: University of Rochester Press, pp. 74–104.

Milbank, J. (1991). *Theology and Social Theory: Beyond Secular Reason*. Cambridge: Blackwell.

Miles, M. (1979). *Augustine on the Body. AAR Dissertation Series*, vol. 31. Missoula, MT: Scholars Press.

Miles, M. (1986–1994). Corpus. In *Augustinus-Lexikon I*. Basel/Berlin: Schwabe Verlag, pp. 6–19.

Miles, M. (2012). From Rape to Resurrection: Sin, Sexual Difference, and Politics. In J. Wetzel, ed., *Augustine's City of God: A Critical Guide*. Cambridge: Cambridge University Press, pp. 75–92.

Moreira, I. (2010). *Heaven's Purge: Purgatory in Late Antiquity*. Oxford: Oxford University Press.

Muehlberger, E. (2013). *Angels in Late Ancient Christianity*. Oxford: Oxford University Press.

Müller, C. (2004–2010). Historia. In *Augustinus-Lexikon 3*. Basel/Berlin: Schwabe Verlag, pp. 366–377.

Nauck, A. (1986). *Porphyrii Opuscula*. Leipzig: Teubner.

Nesselrath, H.-G., ed. (2010). *Plutarch on the Daimonion of Socrates*. Tübingen: Mohr Siebeck.

Norris, J. (2006). Augustine's Interpretation of Genesis in the *City of God* XI–XV. In F. Young, ed., *Studia Patristica* XLIII. Leuven: Peeters.
O'Daly, G. J. P. (1986–1994). Civitate dei (De -). In *Augustinus-Lexikon I*. Basel/ Berlin: Schwabe Verlag, pp. 970–1010.
O'Daly, G. J. P. (1994). Augustine's Critique of Varro on Roman Religion. In A. H. Sommerstein, ed., *Religion and Superstition in Latin Literature*. Bari: Levante Editori, pp. 65–76.
O'Daly, G. J. P. (1999). *Augustine's City of God: A Reader's Guide*. Oxford: Clarendon Press.
O'Donnell, J. J. (1992 [2012 reprint]). *Augustine: Confessions, Text and Commentary*. Clarendon: Oxford University Press.
O'Donovan, O. (1980). *The Problem of Self-love in St. Augustine*. New Haven, CT and London: Yale University Press.
O'Donovan, O. (1982). *Usus et Fruitio in Augustine, De Doctrina Christiana* 1. *Journal of Theological Studies*, 33, 361–397.
O'Donovan, O. (2004). The Political Thought of City of God 19. In O. O'Donovan and J. L. O'Donovan, *Bonds of Imperfection: Christian Politics, Past and Present*. Grand Rapids, MI: Eerdmans, pp. 48–72.
O'Meara, J. (1959). *Porphyry's Philosophy from Oracles and Augustine*. Paris: Études Augustiniennes.
O'Meara, J. (1961). *Charter of Christendom: The Significance of the City of God*. New York: Macmillan.
O'Regan, C. (2009). *Theology and the Spaces of Apocalyptic*. Milwaukee, WI: Marquette University Press.
O'Donnell, J. J. (1979). The Demise of Paganism. *Traditio*, 35, 45–88.
Ogilvie, R. M. (1978). *The Library of Lactantius*. Oxford: Clarendon Press, pp. 50–57.
Ogle, V. R. (2019). Therapeutic Deception: Cicero and Augustine on the Myth of Philosophic Happiness. *Augustinian Studies*, 50(1), 13–42.
Patterson, L. (1967). *God and History in Early Christian Thought*. New York: Seabury Press.
Pelland, G. (1972). *Cinq études d'Augustin sur le début de la Genèse*. Tournai: Desclée; Montreal: Bellarmin.
Pépin, J. (1956). La "théologie tripartite" de Varron. Essai de reconstitution et recherche des sources. *Revue d' Etudes Augustiniennes Et Patristiques*, 2(3–4), 265–294.
Perkams, M. (2008). Augustinus' Auseinandersetzung mit der stoischen Schicksalslehre in *De civitate Dei* 5. *Gymnasium*, 115, 347–359.
Pernot, L. (2005). *Rhetoric in Antiquity*. Translated by W. E. Higgins. Washington, DC: Catholic University of America Press.
Piccolomini, R. (2012). Trans. with introduction and notes. *La Pace: il libro XIX de La città di Dio*. Torino: Città Nuova Editrice.
Piret, P. (1991). *La destinée de l'homme: La cité de Dieu. Un commentaire du "De Civitate Dei" d'Augustin, Collection Institut d'Etudes Théologiques 12*. Bruxelles: Institut d'Etudes Théologiques.
Plato. (1984). Apology of Socrates. In T. G. West and G. S. West, eds., *Four Texts on Socrates*. New York: Cornell University Press, pp. 63–97.

Plato. (1991). *Republic*, 2nd ed. Translated by Allan Bloom. New York: Basic Books.

Pollmann, K. (2009). *Nullus quippe credit aliquid, nisi prius cogitauerit esse credendum*: Augustine as Apologist. In A.-C. Jacobsen, J. Ulrich, and D. Brakke, eds., *Critique and Apologetics: Jews, Christians and Pagans in Antiquity (Early Christianity in the Context of Antiquity vol. 4)*, Frankfurt am Mainz: Peter Lang, pp. 303–327.

Pouderon, B. et al., eds., (2003). *Aristide: Apologie*. Paris: Cerf.

Pranger, M. B. (2006). Politics and Finitude: The Temporal Status of Augustine's *Civitas Permixta*. In H. de Vries and L. E. Sullivan, eds., *Political Theologies: Public Religions in a Post-Secular Word*. New York: Fordham University Press.

Proclus. (1904). *Commentary on the Timaeus 1.77.21–23 Diehl*. Leipzig: Teubner.

Pulsiano, P. (1995). Language Theory and Narrative Patterning in *De Ciuitate Dei*, Books XV–XVIII. In D. Donnelly, ed., *The City of God: A Collection of Critical Essays*. New York: P. Lang, pp. 241–352.

Ramelli, I. (2015). Mysterium and Sacramentum in the Vetus Africa. In R. Dupont, M. A. Gaumer, and M. Lamberigts, eds., *The Uniquely African Controversy: Studies on Donatist Christianity*. Leuven: Peeters, pp. 349–375.

Ramelli, I. (2016). *Social Justice and the Legitimacy of Slavery: The Role of Philosophical Asceticism from Ancient Judaism to Late Antiquity*. Oxford: Oxford University Press.

Rebillard, É. (2012). *Christians and Their Many Identities in Late Antiquity: North Africa, 200–450 CE*. Ithaca, NY: Cornell University Press.

Ribreau, M. (2015). Quand un déclamateur devient évêque: l'influence des déclamations sur les œuvres polémiques et les sermons d'Augustin. In R. Poignault and C. Schneider, eds., *Présence de la declamation*. Clermont-Ferrand: Université Blaise Pascal, pp. 283–311.

Riedl, M. (2010). Truth versus Utility: The Debate on Civil Religion in the Roman Empire of the Third and Fourth Centuries. In R. Weed and J. von Heyking, eds., *Civil Religion in Political Thought: Its Perennial and Enduring Relevance in North America*. Washington, DC: Catholic University of America Press, pp. 47–65.

Rist, J. M. (1994). *Augustine: Ancient Thought Baptized*. Cambridge: Cambridge University Press.

Rives, J. B. (1995). *Religion and Authority in Roman Carthage: From Augustus to Constantine*. Oxford: Clarendon Press.

Roberts, V. (2016). Augustine's Ciceronian Response to the Ciceronian Patriot. *Perspectives on Political Science*, 45(2), 113–24.

Roller, M. (2009). The Exemplary Past in Roman Historiography and Culture. In A. Feldherr, ed., *The Cambridge Companion to the Roman Historians*. Cambridge: Cambridge University Press, pp. 214–230.

Rombs, R. J. (2006). *Saint Augustine and the Fall of the Soul*. Washington, DC: Catholic University of America Press.

Rotelle, J. E. (1990). *The Works of Saint Augustine: A Translation for the 21st Century*. New York: New City Press.

Rousseau, P. (2009). Language, Morality, and Cult: Augustine and Varro. In P. Rousseau and M. Papoutsakis, eds., *Transformations of Late Antiquity: Essays for Peter Brown*. Burlington, VT: Ashgate, pp. 159–175.

Rüpke, J. (2012). Varro's *tria genera theologiae*: Crossing Antiquarianism and Philosophy. In *Religion in Republican Rome: Rationalization and Ritual Change*. Philadelphia: University of Pennsylvania Press, pp. 172–185.

Schindler, A. (1989). Augustine and the History of the Roman Empire. Studia Patristica 22. Papers presented at the Xth International Conference on Patristic Studies held in Oxford 1987. Leuven, pp. 179–201.

Schindler, D. (2005). Freedom Beyond Our Choosing: Augustine on the Will and Its Objects. In J. Doody, K. L. Hughes, and K. Paffenroth, eds., *Augustine and Politics*. Lanham, MD: Lexington Books, pp. 67–96.

Schlabach, G. (2001). *For the Joy Set Before Us: Augustine and Self-denying Love*. Notre Dame: University of Notre Dame Press.

Scott, W. B. (1936). *Hermetica IV*. Oxford: Clarendon Press, pp. 9–27.

Scully, E. (2016). Jerusalem's Lost Etymology: How Augustine Changed Latin Eschatology. *Vigiliae Christianae*, 70(1), 1–30.

Shanzer, D. (2012). Augustine and the Latin Classics. In M. Vessey and S. Reid, eds., *A Companion to Augustine*. Chichester: Wiley, pp. 161–174.

Sheerin, D. (1998). Rhetoric and Hermeneutic Synkrisis in Patristic Typology. In J. Petruccione, ed., *Nova & Vetera: Patristic Studies in Honor of Thomas Patrick Halton*. Washington, DC: Catholic University of America, pp. 22–39.

Shields, C. (2015). The Summum Bonum in Aristotle's Ethics: Fractured Goodness. In J. Aufderheide and R. M. Bader, eds., *The Highest Good in Aristotle and Kant*. Oxford: Oxford University Press, pp. 83–111.

Seyyed, H. N. (2006). *Islamic Philosophy from Its Origin to the Present: Philosophy in the Land of Prophecy*. New York: State University of New York Press.

Silk, M. (2004). Numa Pompilius and the Idea of Civil Religion in the West. *Journal of the American Academy of Religion*, 72(4), 863–896.

Simmons, M. B. (2015). *Universal Salvation in Late Antiquity*. New York: Oxford University Press.

Smith, A. (1984). Did Porphyry Reject the Transmigration of Human Souls into Animal Bodies? *Rheinisches Museum* 127, 276–284.

Smith, A. (1987). Porphyrian Studies since 1913. In H. Temporini and W. Haase, eds., *Aufstieg und Niedergang des Römischen Welt II.36.2*. Berlin: De Gruyter, pp. 766–768.

Sodano, A. (1958). *Porfirio: Lettera ad Anebo*. Naples: L'Arte Typografica.

Solignac, A. (1956). La condition de l'homme pécheur d'après Saint Augustin. *Nouvelle Revue Théologique*, 88, 359–385.

Sorabji, R. (2000). *Emotion and Peace of Mind*. Oxford: Oxford University Press, pp. 372–385.

Steel, C. (2014). Rethinking Sulla: The Case of the Roman Senate. *Classical Quarterly*, 64, 657–668.

Stewart-Kroeker, S. (2017). *Pilgrimage as Moral and Aesthetic Formation in Augustine's Thought*. Oxford: Oxford University Press.

Straw, C. (1999). Martyrdom. In A. Fitzgerald, ed., *Augustine through the Ages*. Grand Rapids, MI: Eerdmans, pp. 538–542.

Strohm, M. (1955). Der Begriff der "natura vitiate" bei Augustin. *Theologische Quartalschrift*, 135, 184–203.

Sullivan, E. (2010). Seek First the Kingdom: A Reply to Germain Grisez's Account of Man's Ultimate End. *Nova et Vetera (Eng)*, 8(4), 959–995.

Sweeney, M. J. (March 2007). Al-Farabi on Compulsion to Happiness. *The Review of Metaphysics*, 60, 543–572.

Sweeney, M. J. (June 2009). Aquinas on the Limits to Political Responsibility for Virtue: A Comparison to Al-Farabi. *The Review of Metaphysics*, 62, 819–847.

Sweeney, M. J. (September 2011). Greek Essence and Islamic Tolerance: Al-Farabi, Avicenna and Al-Ghazali. *The Review of Metaphysics*, 65, 41–62.

Szidat, J. (2004–2010). Imperium Romanum. In *Augustinus-Lexikon 3*, pp. 546–560.

Testard, M. (1958). *Saint Augustin et Cicéron. I. Cicéron dans la formation et dans l'oeuvre de saint Augustin*. Paris, p. 281.

Thaniel, G. (1973). Lemures and Larvae. *American Journal of Philology*, 94, 182–187.

Theiler, W. (1933). *Porphyryius und Augustin*. Halle: Niemeyer.

Theiler, W. (1970). Die Seele als Mitte bei Augustin und Origenes. In *Untersuchungen zur Antiken Literatur*. Berlin, pp. 554–563.

Thomas, P., ed. (1970). *Apulei De Philosophia Libri*. Leipzig: Teubner, pp. 6–35.

Tornau, C. (2006a). *Zwischen Rhetorik und Philosophie: Augustins Argumentationstechnik in De civitate Dei und ihr bildungsgeschichtlicher Hintergrund*. Berlin/New York: de Gruyter.

Tornau, C. (2006b). Does Augustine Accept Pagan Virtue? The Place of Book 5 in the Argument of the *City of God*. Papers presented at the XIVth International Conference on Patristic Studies held in Oxford 2003. *Studia Patristica*, 43, 263–275.

Tornau, C. (2015). Happiness in This Life? Augustine on the Principle That Virtue Is Self-sufficient for Happiness. In Ø. Rabbås et al., eds., *The Quest for the Good Life: Ancient Philosophers on Happiness*. Oxford: Oxford University Press, pp. 265–280.

Tzamalikos, P. (2007). *Origen: Philosophy of History & Eschatology*. Leiden: Brill.

van Bavel, T. J. (1995). "No One Ever Hated His Own Flesh": Eph. 5:29 in Augustine. *Augustinianum*, 45, 45–93.

van der Horst, P. W. (1984). *Chaeremon: Egyptian Priest and Stoic Philosopher*. Leiden: Brill.

van Fleteren, F. (1999). Plato, Platonism. In A. Fitzgerald, ed., *Augustine through the Ages*. Grand Rapids, MI: Eerdmans, pp. 651–654.

Van Horne, W. A. (1981). St. Augustine: Death and Political Resistance. *Journal of Religious Thought*, 38, 34–50.
Van Nuffelen, P. (2010). Varro's Divine Antiquities: Roman Religion as an Image of Truth. *Classical Philology*, 105(2), 162–188.
van Oort, J. (1991). *Jerusalem and Babylon: A Study into Augustine's* City of God *and the Sources of His Doctrine of the Two Cities*. Leiden: Brill.
van Oort, J. (2010). Manichaean Christians in Augustine's Life and Work. *Church History and Religious Culture*, 90(4), 505–546.
van Oort, J. (2012). The End Is Now: Augustine on History and Eschatology. *HTS Teologiese Studies/Theological Studies*, 68(1), 1–7.
Vessey, M. (2012). *The History of the Book: Augustine's* City of God *and post-Roman Cultural Memory*. In J. Wetzel, ed., *Augustine's* City of God: *A Critical Guide*. Cambridge: Cambridge University Press, pp. 14–32.
Vessey, M. (2014). Fashions for Varro in Late Antiquity and Christian Ways with Books. In C. Harrison, C. Humfress, and I. Sandwell, eds., *Being Christian in Late Antiquity: A Festschrift for Gillian Clark*. Oxford: Oxford University Press, pp. 253–277.
Vessey M. and Reid S., eds., (2012). *A Companion to Augustine*, Chichester: Wiley.
von Heyking, J. (2001). *Augustine and Politics as Longing in the World*. Columbia, MO: University of Missouri Press.
Walsh, P. G. (2007). *Augustine: De civitate dei (The City of God). Books 3 & IV*. Oxford: Oxford University Press.
Webb, M. (2015). Samson, Abraham, and "Certain Holy Women": Augustine on Suicide and Rape in City of God 1.26. In D. Meconi, ed., *Sacred Scripture and Secular Struggle*. Leiden: Brill, pp. 201–234.
Weissenberg, T. J. (2005). Die Friedenslehre des Augustinus. In *Theologische Grundlagen und ethische Entfaltung*. Stuttgart.
Weithman, P. (2014). Augustine's Political Philosophy. In D. V. Meconi and E. Stump, eds., *The Cambridge Companion to Augustine*. Cambridge: Cambridge University Press, pp. 234–252.
Wetzel, J. (1992). *Augustine and the Limits of Virtue*. Cambridge: Cambridge University Press.
Wetzel, J., ed., (2012). *Augustine's City of God: A Critical Guide*. Cambridge: Cambridge University Press.
Wetzel, J. (2012a). A Tangle of Two Cities. *Augustinian Studies*, 43(1), 5–23.
Wetzel, J. (2012b). Augustine on the Origin of Evil: Myth and Metaphysics. In *Augustine's City of God: A Critical Guide*. Cambridge: Cambridge University Press, pp. 167–185.
Wetzel, J. (2012c). Introduction. In J. Wetzel, ed., *Augustine's City of God: A Critical Guide*. Cambridge: Cambridge University Press, pp. 1–13.
Winiarczyk, M. (2013). *The Sacred History of Euhemerus of Messene*. Berlin: De Gruyter.

Wolterstorff, N. (2012). Augustine's Rejection of Eudaimonsim. In J. Wetzel, ed., *Augustine's City of God: A Critical Guide*. Cambridge: Cambridge University Press, pp. 149–166.

Yates, J. (November 2018). Salvation through Water?: 1 Peter 3:20–21 in the Ancient Latin Tradition. *Worship*, 92, 492–510.

Index

Milton Keynes UK
Ingram Content Group UK Ltd.
UKHW022307161024
449521UK00023B/273

9 781108 435444